I0532194

SigmaXL®
and
Lean Six Sigma

A Guide to Improve Business Performance Metrics

Forrest W. Breyfogle III and Liviu Ibanescu

Copyright © 2023 by Forrest W. Breyfogle III and Liviu Ibanescu

Published by Citius Publishing, Inc., Austin, Texas: www.citiuspublishing.com

All rights reserved. No part of this book may be reproduced by any mechanical, photographic, or electronic process or in the form of audio recording; nor may it be stored in a retrieval system, transmitted, or otherwise be copied for public or private use – other than for "fair use" as brief quotations embodied in articles and reviews – without prior written permission of the publisher.

Limit of Liability/Disclaimer of Warranty: While the publisher and author have used their best efforts in preparing this book, they make no representations or warranties with respect to the accuracy or completeness of the contents of this book and specifically disclaim any implied warranties of merchantability or fitness for a particular purpose. No warranty may be created or extended by sales representatives or written sales materials. The advice and strategies contained herein may not be suitable for your situation. You should consult with a professional where appropriate. Neither the publisher nor authors shall be liable for any loss of profit or any other commercial damages, including but not limited to special, incidental, consequential, or other damages.

For general information about our other products and services, contact us at www.SmarterSolutions.com.

Paperback ISBN: 979-8-9873697-2-2
E-book ISBN: 979-8-9873697-3-9

To receive a copy of the datasets referenced in this book, send your datasets request to info@smartersolutions.com

A free app for creating 30,000-foot-level reports from Excel-formatted datasets throughout this book is available through the link https://smartersolutions.com/free-business-process-management-software/ (Smarter Solutions 2020).

OTHER BOOKS BY FORREST W. BREYFOGLE III

Statistical Methods for Testing, Development, and Manufacturing

Implementing Six Sigma, Second Edition: Smarter Solutions Using Statistical Methods

Solutions Manual, Implementing Six Sigma: Smarter Solutions Using Statistical Methods

Managing Six Sigma: A Practical Guide to Understanding, Assessing, and Implementing the Strategy That Yields Bottom-Line Success

Wisdom on the Green: Smarter Six Sigma Business Solutions

Lean Six Sigma in Sickness and in Health: An Integrated Enterprise Excellence Novel

The Integrated Enterprise Excellence System: An Enhanced, Unified Approach to Balanced Scorecards, Strategic Planning, and Business Improvement

Integrated Enterprise Excellence, Vol. I: The Basics: Golfing Buddies Go Beyond Lean Six Sigma and the Balanced Scorecard

Integrated Enterprise Excellence, Vol. II: Business Deployment: A Leaders' Guide for Going Beyond Lean Six Sigma and the Balanced Scorecard

Integrated Enterprise Excellence, Vol. III: Improvement Project Execution: A Management and Black Belt Guide for Going Beyond Lean Six Sigma and the Balanced Scorecard

Solutions Manual: Integrated Enterprise Excellence Volume III: Improvement Project Execution

Lean Six Sigma Project Execution Guide: The Integrated Enterprise Excellence (IEE) Process Improvement Project Roadmap

The Business Process Management Guidebook: An Integrated Enterprise Excellence BPM System

Management 2.0: Discovery of Integrated Enterprise Excellence

Leadership System 2.0: Implementing Integrated Enterprise Excellence

Minitab and Lean Six Sigma: A Guide to Improve Business Performance Metrics

Contents

PREFACE

This book describes how to use SigmaXL® to execute process improvement projects using an Integrated Enterprise Excellence (IEE) Define-Measure-Analyze-Improve-Control (IEE-DMAIC) roadmap. The IEE-DMAIC project execution roadmap offers many benefits over a traditional Lean Six Sigma (LSS) DMAIC roadmap.

The following books provide more details about the concepts described in this book:

- *Management 2.0: Discovery of Integrated Enterprise Excellence* [Breyfogle, F. W. 2020a)]
- *Leadership System 2.0: Implementing Integrated Enterprise Excellence* [Breyfogle, F. W. 2020b)]
- *Integrated Enterprise Excellence (IEE), Volume II – Business Deployment: A Leaders' Guide for Going Beyond Lean Six Sigma and the Balanced Scorecard* [Breyfogle, F. W. (2008b)]. **Referenced as IEE Volume II in this book.**
- *Integrated Enterprise Excellence (IEE), Volume III – Improvement Project Execution: A Management and Black Belt Guide for Going Beyond Lean Six Sigma and the Balanced Scorecard* [Breyfogle, F. W. (2008c)]. **Referenced as *IEE Volume III* in this book.**
- *Lean Six Sigma Project Execution Guide: The Integrated Enterprise Excellence (IEE) Process Improvement Project Roadmap* [Breyfogle, F. W. (2010), **Referenced as *Lean Six Sigma Project Execution Guide* in this book.**

This book references many *IEE Volume III* examples with an emphasis on how to use SigmaXL to create the outputs shown in the book. For more information about the presented example and appropriate statistics, readers should reference the section of *IEE Volume III* included with the illustration.

Nomenclature and Service Marks

SigmaXL® Inc. is a registered trademark. Portions of the inputs and outputs contained in this book are printed with permission of SigmaXL Inc. This material remains the exclusive property and copyright of SigmaXL Inc. All rights reserved.

Integrated Enterprise Excellence, IEE, satellite-level, 30,000-foot-level, and 50-foot-level are Smarter Solutions, Inc registered service marks. When implementing the programs or methods identified in this text, one can refer to these marks in a manner that is consistent with the standards set forth herein by Smarter Solutions, Inc. Still, all use of the marks shall inure to the sole benefit of Smarter Solutions, Inc. Smarter Solutions is a registered service mark of Smarter Solutions, Inc.

Workshop Material, Datasets, and Software App

We at Smarter Solutions, Inc. take pride in creating an excellent learning environment for the wise application of tools that will improve organizational business systems.

Licensing inquiries for training material can be directed through www.smartersolutions.com. Articles, newsletters, and the latest information on how Smarter Solutions, Inc. works with various organizations and universities are also described on this website.

To receive a copy of the datasets referenced in this book, send your datasets request to info@smartersolutions.com

The free app for creating 30,000-foot-level reports from Excel-formatted datasets throughout this book is available through https://smartersolutions.com/free-business-process-management-software/

Contacting the Authors:

<u>Forrest Breyfogle</u>

For more information about business measurements and improvement strategies, sign up for Smarter Solutions' newsletter, webinars, or email us for a free initial business consultation:

FORREST W. BREYFOGLE III
Smarter Solutions, Inc.
P.O. Box 202644
Austin, Texas, 78720 USA
Forrest@SmarterSolutions.com
www.SmarterSolutions.com
512-918-0280

<u>Liviu Ibanescu</u>

For more information about Lean and Lean Six Sigma implementation and deployment, training, coaching and certification please contact us:

LIVIU IBANESCU
Lean Six Sigma Canada
48 Burnhamthorpe Crescent
Toronto, ON M9A 1G7
liviu.ibanescu@leansixsigmacanada.com
www.leansixsigmacanada.com
416-575-5754

PART 1:

Lean Six Sigma Background,
Business System Integration, and
Improvement Project Selection

1

Six Sigma and Lean Six Sigma

1.1   Six Sigma and Lean Tools

Traditionally, Six Sigma is considered a quality improvement methodology that focuses on creating/completing projects that reduce errors and waste. These projects utilize statistical and non-statistical tools to improve processes, where there is an emphasis on executing financial-cost-savings projects.

In the name "Six Sigma," the term sigma (σ) is a letter in the Greek alphabet used to describe variability, i.e., standard deviation. The classical Six Sigma unit of measure is defects per opportunity.

Lean often is associated with manufacturing, but the techniques apply to all business areas. In Lean, there is a focus on process speed and efficiency and reducing waste. The seven types of waste frequently referenced with Lean are overproduction, waiting, transportation, inventory, over-processing, motion, and defects. More recently, some have added people utilization to this list; however, we can expand the list even further to include wasted space, wasted effort, wasted energy, and so forth.

Both Lean and Six Sigma have practical tools; however, deployments that don't equally consider using Lean and Six Sigma tools for process improvement are missing out on the benefits of having a complete toolset at their disposal.

This situation is analogous to someone using a wrench instead of a hammer to drive a nail into a board. Yes, one could complete the nailing task with a wrench tool; however, the job would be more complicated than if one used a hammer. Similarly, a Lean improvement effort to reduce machine defects might not consider the power of design of experiments (DOE) techniques as a viable tool for defect reduction if this tool is not part of the practitioner's tool set.

1

1.2   Organizational Deployments of Six Sigma and Lean

A consensus should be that all organizations need to improve to survive. Organizations attempting to fulfill this need structurally often initiate a Lean, Six Sigma, or Lean Six Sigma program. However, these programs frequently end because leadership does not see the financial benefits of these efforts.

One reason for the leadership's termination of a program is process improvement efforts often occur in organizational silos and do not benefit the whole-business financials.

Lean and Six Sigma efforts traditionally have no structural linkage with the corporate business management system. Also, traditional Lean and Six Sigma improvement efforts do not show how process improvement efforts positively impacted a performance metric important to the business reported from a process output perspective.

Integrated Enterprise Excellence (IEE) is a business management system that overcomes these shortcomings by integrating Lean and Six Sigma process improvement tools within its methodology and providing a robust 30,000-foot-level reporting methodology for process output responses.

1.3   Integrated Enterprise Excellence (IEE)

The Integrated Enterprise Excellence (IEE) business management system consists of the nine steps shown in Figure 1.1.

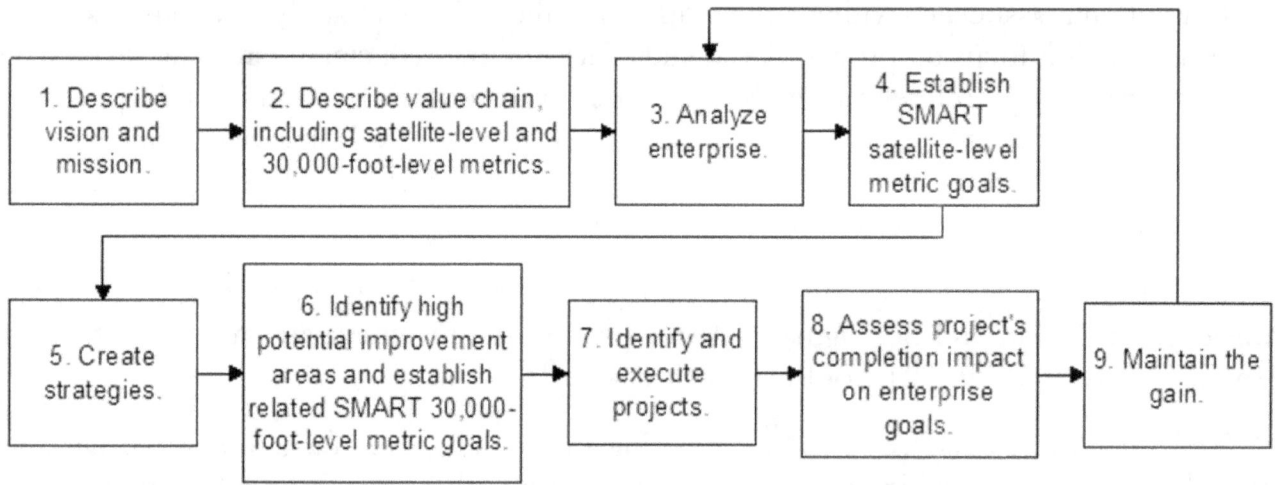

Figure 1.1: Integrated Enterprise Excellence (IEE) 9-step Business Management System

A summary of the aspects of the IEE 9-step system with considerations for each step is:

- Step 1: Includes the company's vision, mission, values, and responses to Jim Collins' three-circle questions about a business: What can you be the best in the world at? What drives your economic engine? What are you deeply passionate about? (Collins 2001). High-level statements created in a traditional executive retreat could be considered an aspect of this first step of the IEE system, which provides direction for the subsequent eight steps.

- Step 2: The organization creates an IEE value chain, which includes its satellite-level (financial) and 30,000-foot-level (operational) performance metrics. An IEE value chain describes what an organization does and how it measures what is done. For an organization, an IEE value chain should maintain fundamental consistency over time, independent of leadership, competition, and environmental changes. However, the specifics of what is done in an organization's IEE value chain should be enhanced continuously to make the enterprise, as a whole, better over time. The identification and execution of enterprise-as-a-whole enhancement activities are what the next steps of the IEE 9-step system provide.

- Step 3: In 'Analyze enterprise,' the current state of high-level value-chain metrics are evaluated collectively with other information such as voice of the customer (VOC), theory of constraints (TOC) information, and competitive analyses. This analysis should use statistical techniques, when appropriate, to determine the strengths and shortcomings of an organization for providing direction in the execution of Steps 4 through Step 7.

- Step 4: This step of the 9-step system states, 'Establish SMART (specific, measurable, actionable, relevant, time-based) satellite-level metric goals.' In IEE, satellite-level measures are to be financial. As the response to underlying processes, this step's objective is to have a numerical quantity consistent with fulfilling step 1's organizational vision and mission statements and satisfying customer needs. An appropriate financial satellite-level goal for a for-profit organization might be a mean monthly EBITDA (earnings before interest, taxes, depreciation and amortization) objective. A step 4 goal does not need to be an enhancement to the satellite-level metric's current response level but could be the continuance of the organization's current response level. For government, schools, non-profits, and other similar organizations, EBITDA, or any measure of profit or revenue, may not be an appropriate measurement to address in this step. For these situations, there is a need for an alternative high-level organizational performance measurement for this step. Non-profits and government agencies might state that money is not relevant to them. However, managing expenses in non-profits, government agencies, and schools are still necessary, which can address step 4's monetary goal objective. For non-profit organizational situations, a step 4 satellite-level metric goal might be 'mean monthly operating expenses of 33.4 million dollars.' For this situation, the intention would be to enhance organizational processes so that there is an enrichment in the organization's deliverables consistent with this step's stated satellite-level metric goal.

- Step 5: The results from Steps 1 – 4 provide input to targeted strategy creation.

- Step 6: Identify high potential improvement areas and establish 30,000-foot-level performance metric goals. An enterprise improvement plan (EIP) graphic presents the results of this work.

- Step 7: Identify and execute process improvement projects that improve operational 30,000-foot-level metrics and benefit the whole enterprise.
- Step 8: Assess how the completion of projects impacts the achievement of step 4's enterprise goal. An EIP is to show the alignment of undertaken projects to the needs of the enterprise and step 4's fulfillment. Staging a project's IEE 30,000-foot-level report to an enhanced level of performance shows the amount of statistical benefit achieved to a metric through a project's execution.
- Step 9: Error-proofing a process is the best means of process control; however, that is not possible for all situations. A high-level metric-tracking control methodology is available by periodically monitoring organizational 30,000-foot-level process-output responses to ensure nothing has degraded. The Enterprise Performance Reporting System (EPRS) system software provides automatic updates for a project's 30,000-foot-level metric in the organization's IEE value chain, which can be monitored periodically for degradation to ensure timely corrective action when appropriate.

There is more information about the IEE business management system and its implementation in the novel-written books:

- *Management 2.0: Discovery of Integrated Enterprise Excellence* (Breyfogle, F. W. 2020a)
- *Leadership System 2.0: Implementing Integrated Enterprise Excellence* (Breyfogle, F. W. 2020b)

1.4   Strategic Process Improvement in the 9-step IEE System

This book focuses on executing step 7 in the IEE system using an enhanced Define-Measure-Analyze-Improve-Control (IEE-DMAIC) improvement project roadmap shown in Figure 1.2.

A tabbed reference book for this IEE DMAIC roadmap with its drill downs is *Lean Six Sigma Project Execution Guide* (Breyfogle, F. W. 2010).

A book that provides executing details for the steps in this roadmap is *Integrated Enterprise Excellence (IEE) Volume III* (Breyfogle, F. W. 2008c).

NOTE: In *Implementing Six Sigma* [1st edition published in 1999 and 2nd edition published in 2003] (Breyfogle, F. W. 2003), the traditional DMAIC roadmap was enhanced so that there was a more detailed drill-down tools-description in the Measure phase that was consistent with a GE implementation (i.e., first large company in the 1990s to implement Six Sigma following a DMAIC roadmap). This book references this enhanced IEE DMAIC roadmap, which is shown in Figure 1.2.

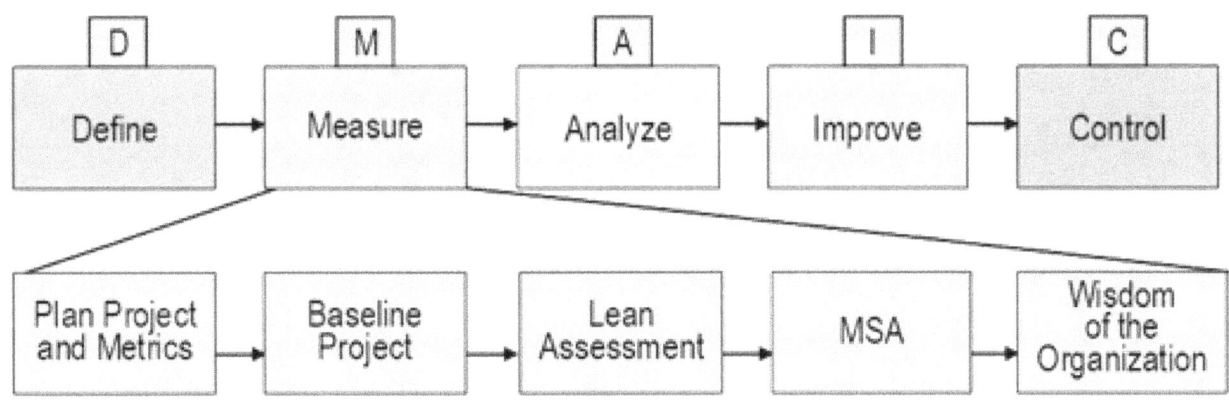

Figure 1.2: IEE DMAIC Project Execution Roadmap

Clickable drill-downs of this IEE-DMAIC roadmap are available through www.smartersolutions.com/roadmap. Reference to this clickable version of the IEE-DMAIC roadmap, as shown in Figure 1.3, is made throughout this book.

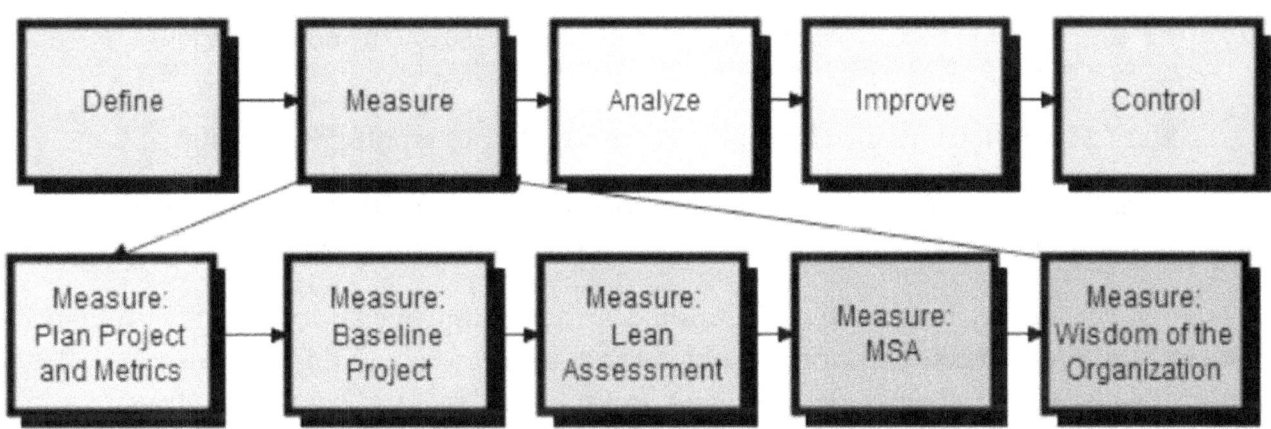

Figure 1.3: IEE DMAIC Clickable Project Execution Roadmap
(www.smartersolutions.com/roadmap.)

1.5 IEE Performance Metric Reporting and Process Improvement

The IEE 30,000-foot-level reporting methodology for tracking the output of processes to monitor the effectiveness of improvement efforts has many beneficial additional applications throughout an organization.

Organizations use performance metrics at various levels in their organizations. Tracking these metrics only as a table of numbers or a red-yellow-green scorecard has many shortcomings and can lead to unhealthy, if not destructive, organizational behaviors.

This book provides the means to track these metrics from an IEE 30,000-foot-level (operational) or satellite-level (financial) process-output point of view (See Figure 1.4). This high-level form of response tracking has many advantages over traditional reporting practices.

With IEE metrics reporting, data used to create the charts can extend over a long-time period, e.g., years.

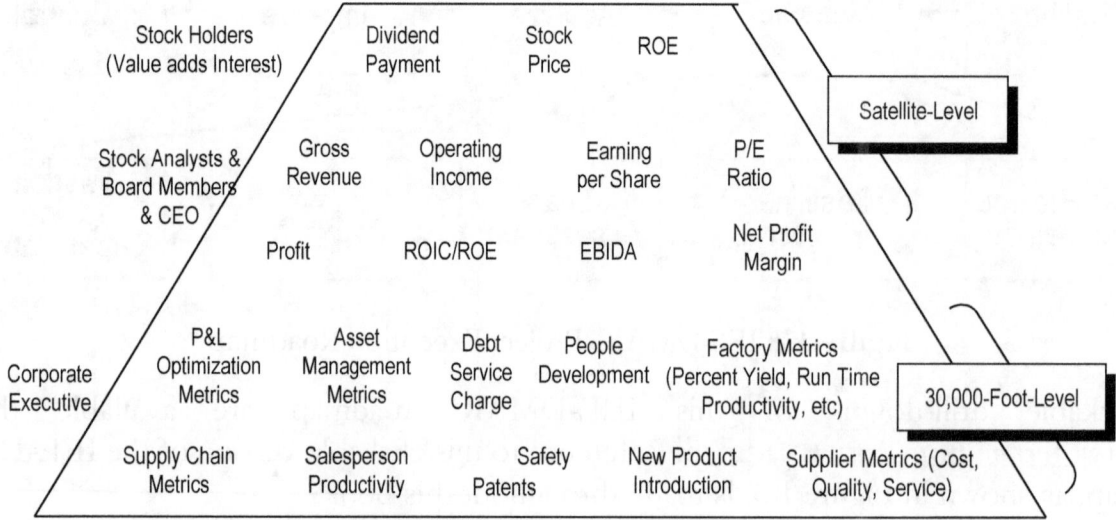

ROE = Return on Equity; OI = Operating Income; P/E = Price to Earnings; ROIC = Return on Invested Capital
P&L = Profit & Loss; EBIDA = Earnings Before Interest Depreciation, and Amortization; VOC = Voice of the Customer

Figure 1.4: Organizational Performance Metrics and IEE Reporting

This book focuses on improving 30,000-foot-level metrics that will benefit the whole-enterprise financials by executing IEE-DMAIC improvement projects.

Figures 1.5 and 1.6 illustrate the execution of process improvement projects by enhancing a project's output responses reported at a high level. IEE references this response as a 30,000-foot-level response for operational processes and satellite-level for financial metrics.

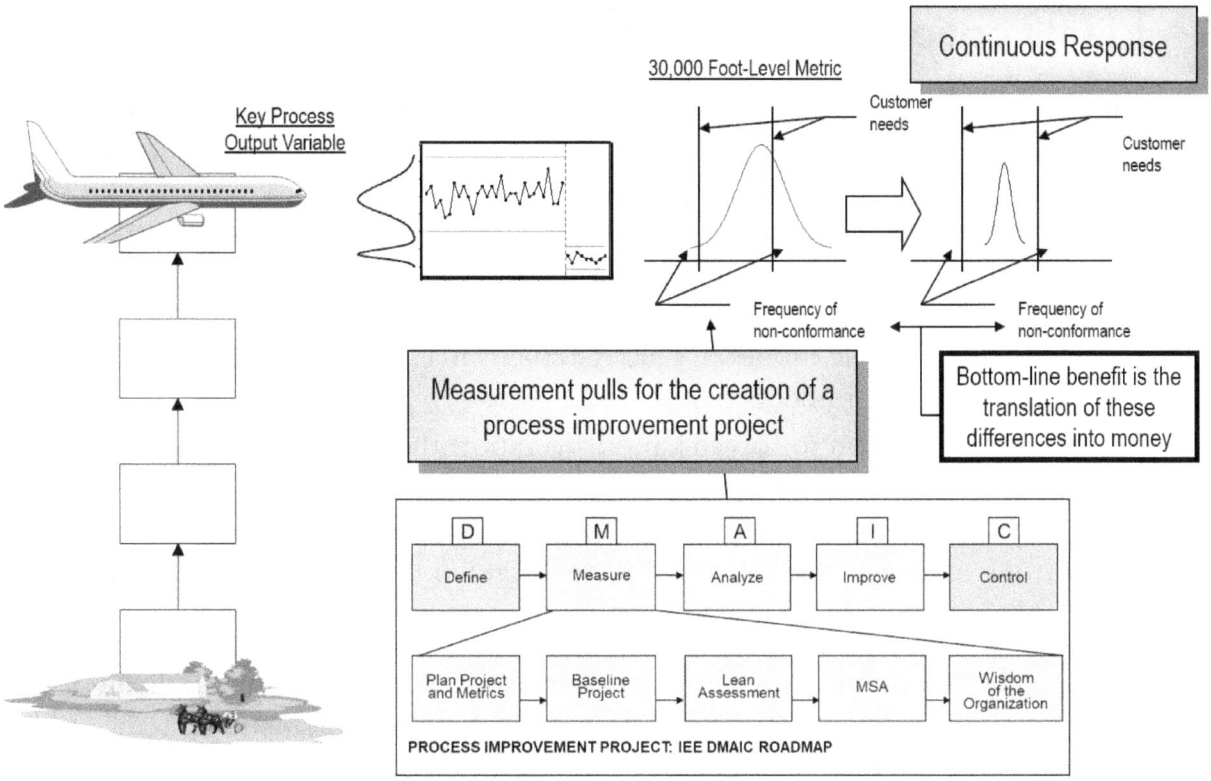

Figure 1.5: IEE Project creation, execution, and the benefits for a continuous response

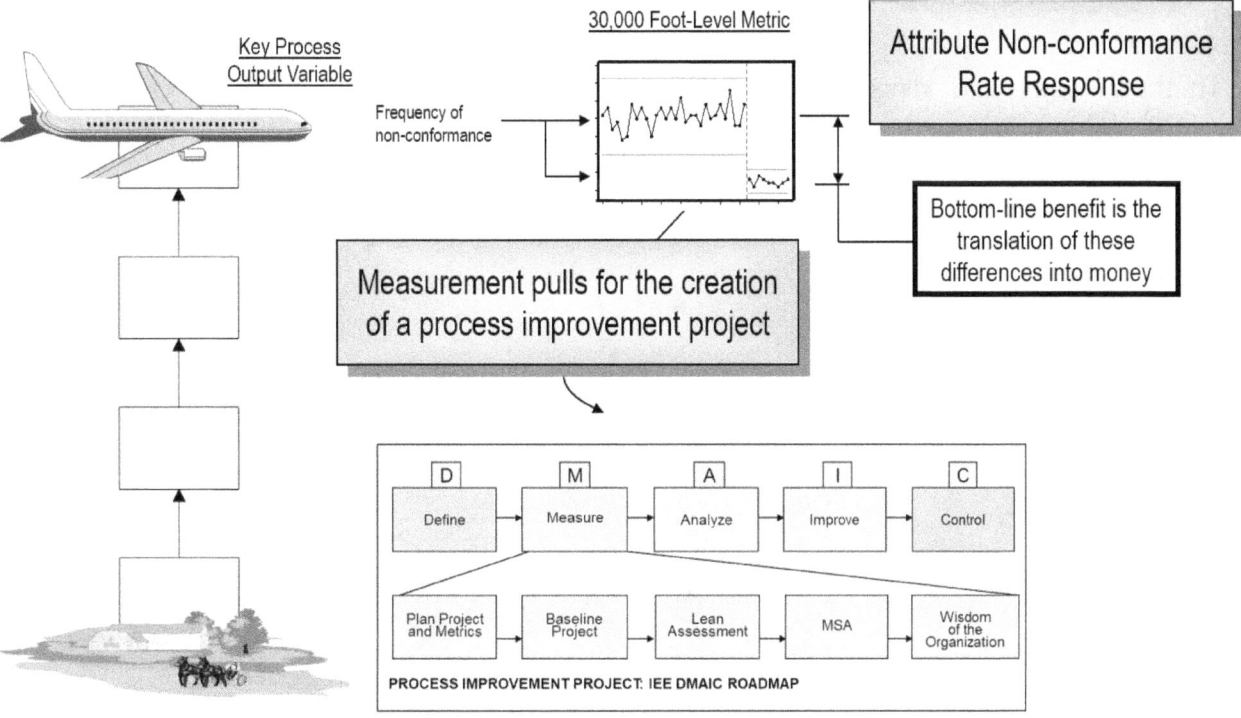

Figure 1.6: IEE Project Creation, Execution, and Benefits for an Attribute Defective Rate Response

1.6   Identification of Improvement Project Opportunities

Traditional Six Sigma and Lean Six Sigma organizational implementations often have a "push for project creation" system. To illustrate this "push" statement, consider the following:

- The measurement success of a Six Sigma or Lean Six Sigma deployment is often total project-reported savings. However, an honest assessment of this approach can often yield a statement like, "We have a reported savings of 100 million dollars, but no one can find the money." This statement may sound absurd, but I have heard this and similar comments many times.

- It is not uncommon for organizations to report the number of people trained (e.g., over 500 Lean Six Sigma green belts), where perhaps only 10% of those trained have completed even one project. From this, one might infer that this type of reporting conveys that planned projects are not essential to management, and perhaps Lean Six Sigma is only a training exercise in the company.

This book and other publications by Forrest Breyfogle suggest integrating Lean Six Sigma into an Integrated Enterprise Excellence (IEE) business management system. With this approach, one focuses on measures and goals so that there is a pull for a project created to meet these goals systematically. In this system, there is an emphasis on creating financial benefits that the entire company feels, not just at the individual local sub-process measurement level.

In the IEE system, risks versus benefits assessments are made to create organizational strategies and specific, actionable improvement items. Figure 1.7 illustrates the management and orchestration of this effort through an Enterprise Process Management (EPM) function.

Figure 1.7: IEE Business Management Orchestration

An output example from an overall business assessment to determine process improvement opportunities that will benefit the organization's overall finances is the Enterprise Improvement Plan (EIP), shown in Figure 1.8 (Steps from the 9-step IEE system [Figure 1.1] are show at the top of this figure). This EIP shows the direct alignment of potential project opportunities (right column) with business goals and the voice of the customer inputs (left column).

These identified improvement projects are significant to meet the business' specific measurement goals via completing identified projects that impact these metrics.

In the IEE system, EIP results orchestrate improvement project selection.

Business Goal	Strategies	High Potential Areas	Projects
Step 4	Step 5	Step 6	Step 7

Return reported monthly profit margin median to 11.9% in 14 months.	Increase monthly revenue	Marketing	Return market share to a monthly mean of 56% in 14 months.
	Improve customer view of services satisfaction. Return level of customer dis-satisfaction to no higher than a proportion of 0.10 in 14 months	Housekeeping	Return level of house keeping quality to a monthly mean of 8.1 in 14 months.
		Patient transportation	Reduce diagnosis to bed time compliance rate of 30 minutes from 93% to 50% in 14 months.
	Reduce costs	Delivery of clinical services	Reduce wastage by 10% in 10 months.

Figure 1.8: EIP Example for a Hospital

1.7 Reporting Process Response Outputs: 30,000-foot-level Reports

Traditional metrics reporting at the business and process-improvement project levels have elephant-in-the-room issues (Figure 1.9). Conventional metrics reporting and goal-setting approaches have fundamental problems and can lead to unhealthy, if not destructive, behaviors. Problems that can occur with many traditional methodologies and what to do differently to avoid these commonplace issues is provided in a webpage (Smarter Solutions 2015a).

Organizations need a metric reporting approach that leads to the best actions or non-actions for various situations. A 30,000-foot-level reporting approach fulfills this need.

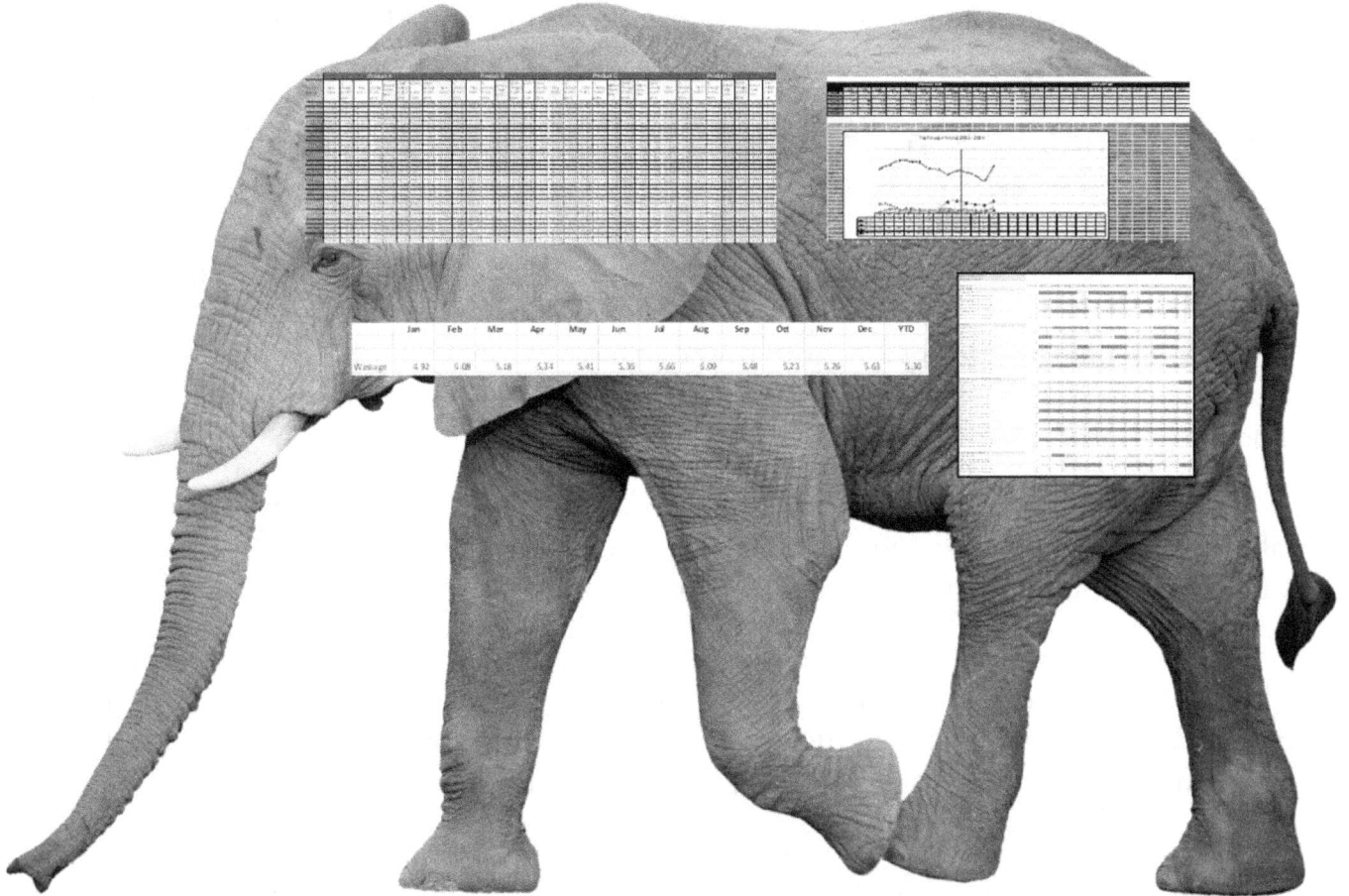

Figure 1.9: Conventional Metric Reports – An Elephant in the Room

The output of a process is Y in the relationship Y=f(X), where Xs are the inputs and steps within the related process.

It is essential to report Y so that the most appropriate action or non-action occurs. This statement applies to Key Performance Indices (KPI), business functional performance (e.g., non-conformance rates, lead times, work in progress [WIP]), and product quality metric reporting).

In IEE, the approach to accomplish this objective is 30,000-foot-level reports, which provide a predictive statement (i.e., the expectation for future responses if nothing were to change) for stable-response processes. There is a need for process improvement whenever a predictive bottom-of-the-chart 30,000-foot-level reporting is undesirable.

A free R-coded app with over ten instructional videos is available at https://smartersolutions.com/free-business-process-management-software/(Smarter Solutions 2020). This app created the 30,000-foot-level reports shown in this book.

The following three sections provide more details, benefits, and example outputs from this 30,000-foot-level report-creation app. Section 1.11 of this book displays a webpage that provides additional examples and instructions on creating 30,000-foot-level reports for most process-output-response situations.

1.8　Metrics Reports that Lead to the Best Behaviors: Goal Setting and Benefits of 30,000-Level Reports

Consider the time it takes someone to commute from home to work by car. The time to travel would not be precisely the same every day because commute time is a function of the amount of traffic encountered and delays from traffic signals, among other things. Mathematically this relationship is $Y=f(X)$, where Y is commute time and Xs are the inputs to the process, e.g., amount of traffic and traffic signals delays.

A commuter tracked her commute time for several weeks and observed that it typically takes 25-35 minutes to commute. One can consider this commute-time variation "noise" within her commute from home-to-work process time.

When collecting daily commute times, she noticed two unusually long commute times. These two commute times took over an hour, much longer than her typical 25-35 minutes commute time. A significant traffic accident caused one commuting delay, and in the other situation, the travel delay occurred because of a snow storm.

From a data analysis point of view, we can "talk about" the specifics of exceptionally long commute times, e.g., a major traffic accident and inclement weather. One should not "talk about" the specifics of what occurred on a particular day within the 25-35 typical commute-time response. Discussing the particulars of any "noise" datum point in a process response can lead to an erroneous conclusion and inappropriate actions relative to improving the magnitude of a process output response.

This commuter wanted to reduce her commute time; hence, she set a goal for her time to commute, similar to the red-yellow-green measured goal-setting approach used in the company where she is employed. Her goal was for commute time to be no longer than 33 minutes. If a commute time exceeded 33 minutes, she would try to determine what happened during that commute and decide what to do so this problem commute time would not happen again.

However, as previously stated, one should not focus on attempting to understand the specifics of what occurred for specific process response "noise" datum points. This commute from home to work goal-setting scenario is similar to organizations using red-yellow-green scorecards to monitor the output response from processes. A red color triggers action for this scorecard approach because a specific datum point did not meet a goal. Red-yellow-green scorecards and similar goal-tracking methods for data points can lead to firefighting "noise" variation as though it were abnormal occurrences, resulting in much organizational waste and even destructive behaviors.

In the 1980s, Edwards Deming (Deming 1986) highlighted problems with the commonplace meet-the-numbers goals management approach in his workshops' using his red bead experiment exercise. The issues described by Deming in this workshop exercise are no different than those of red-yellow-green scorecards (Breyfogle 2018).

If this home-to-work commuter wants to reduce her typical commute time of 25-35 minutes, she must do something differently within her overall commute from the home-to-work process. When reconsidering the Xs in her commute time process, she thought of another process input X in addition to variation in delays from the amount of traffic and traffic signals on her commute. This additional input that could affect her commute time was when she left home. She theorized that she might encounter less traffic if she left a half-hour earlier, reducing her commute time significantly.

She was happy to see that data supported her theory. Data indicated that her commute time when leaving one half-hour earlier was 18-22 minutes. This commute-from-home-to-work process change significantly reduced her average and variation in commute times.

The primary message from this commute from home to work illustration is that if a typical process-output response is undesirable, one needs to improve the overall process inputs, not attempting to uncover the reasons for specific measurement occurrences within the usual "noise" of a process response.

In organizations, it is vital to create metric reports that lead to the best actions or non-actions. The following sections use data from this commute-from-home-to-work process to describe, in general, the tracking of a process response, goal setting, and process improvement from both a traditional metric reporting approach and a better 30,000-foot-level reporting alternative.

Traditional Metrics Reports

Figure 1.10 shows a time series tracking of commute times for our commuter over 30 days for her described commute from home to the work situation.

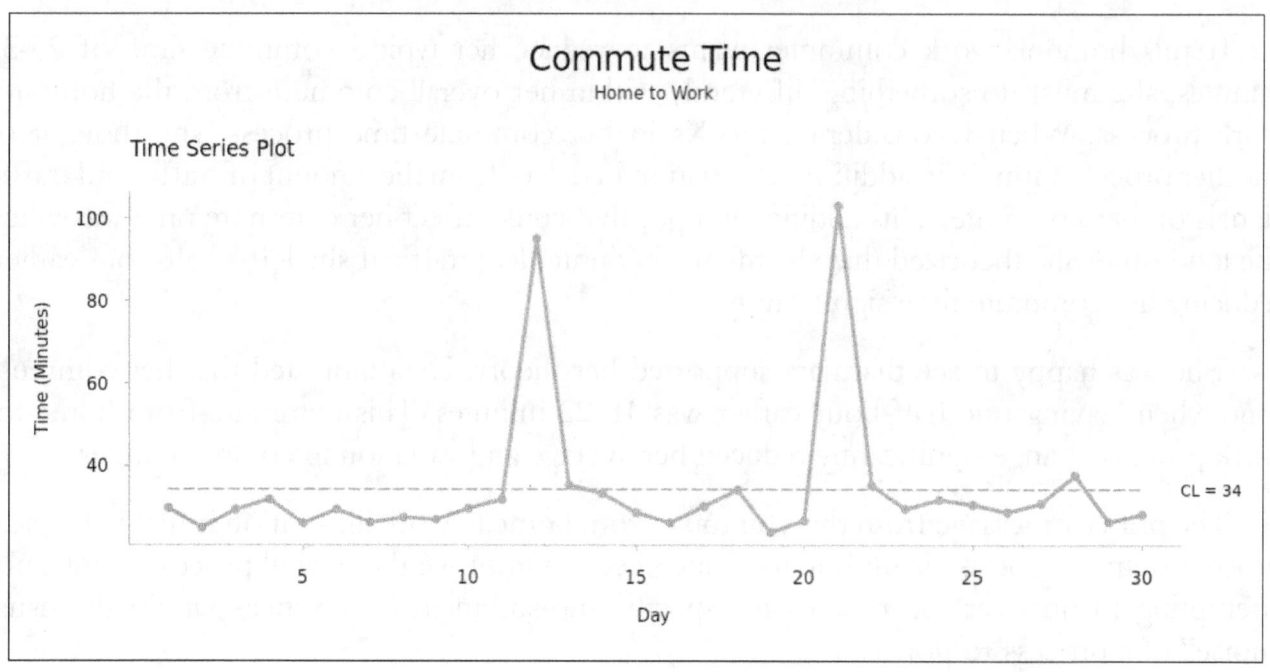

Figure 1.10: Commute Time Home-to-Work: Time-Series Tracking

To examine typical commute times, one could eliminate, in this metric tracking, the two atypical occurrences that occurred because of a major traffic accident and inclement weather, as shown in Figure 1.11.

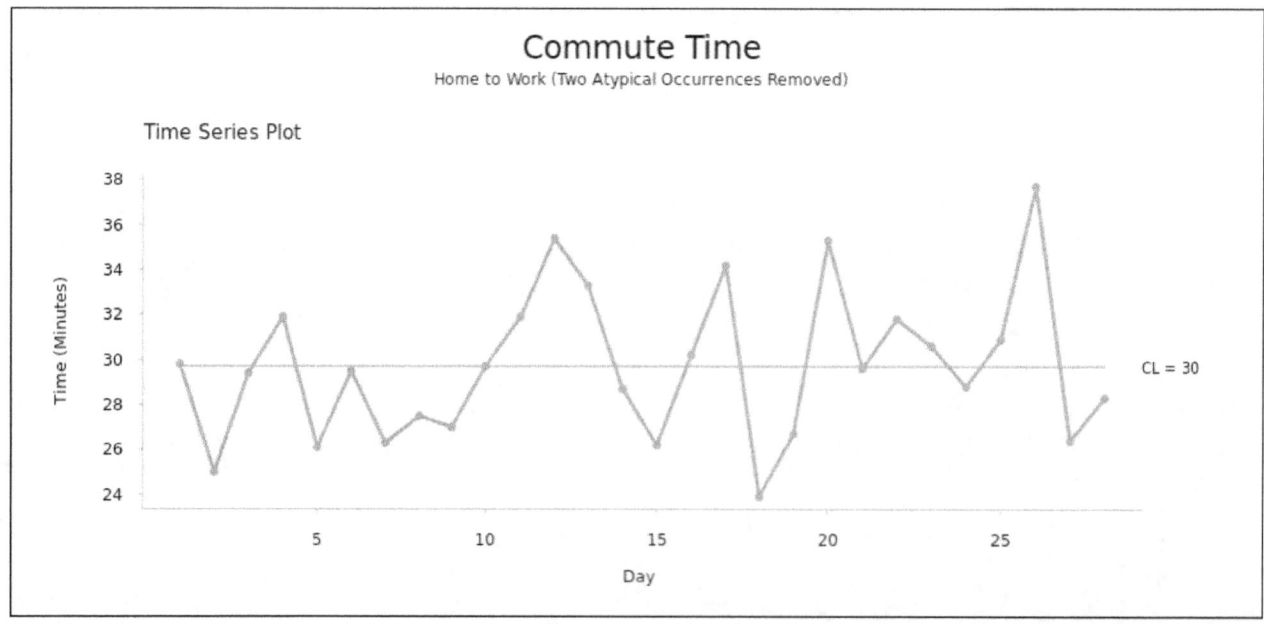

Figure 1.11: Commute Time Home-to-Work: Time-Series Tracking (Two Atypical Commutes Removed)

With this form of reporting, one often sets a specific-day response goal if there is a desire to improve typical commute times. Figure 1.12 includes the commuter's 33-minute goal as a horizontal line. With this form of reporting, one attempts to understand why a goal was not met and then takes action so future events will not have the same problem that occurred on a specific day. In Figure 1.12, there are five occurrences beyond the not-to-exceed goal of 33 minutes in this report. These data points can stimulate investigations for causal understanding that will provide little if any value.

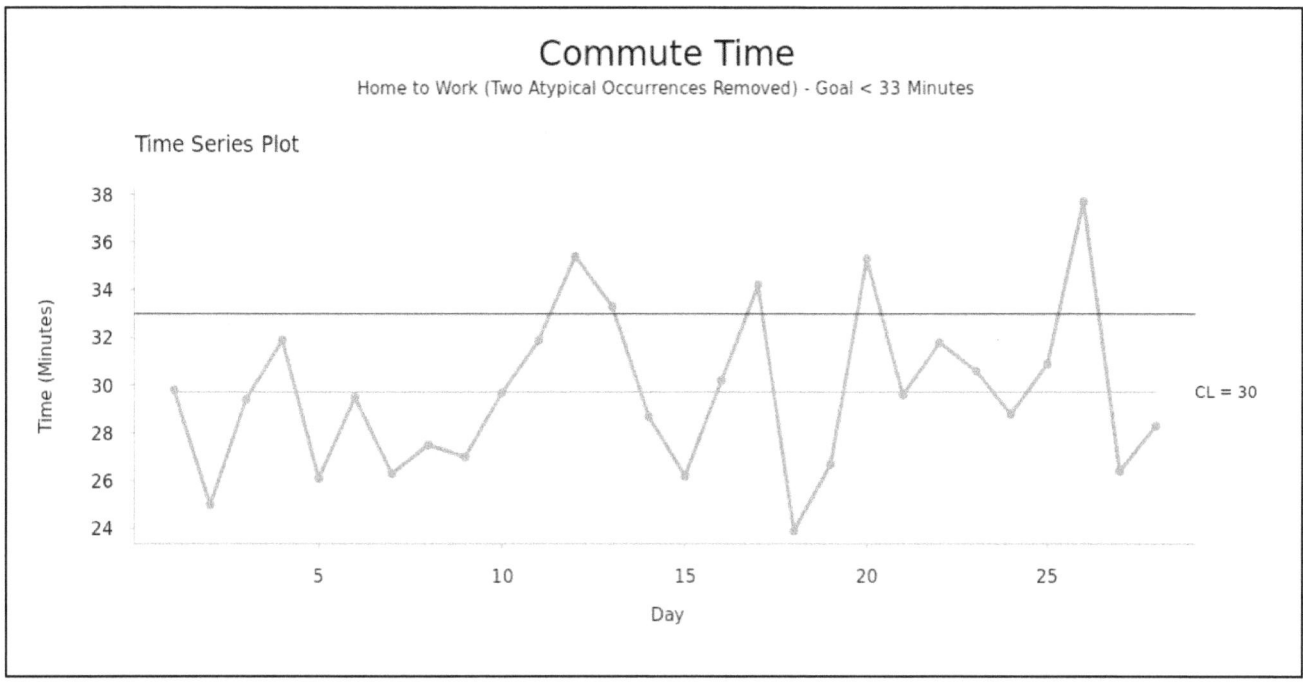

Figure 1.12: Commute Time Home-to-Work: Time-Series Tracking (Two Atypical Commutes Removed); Includes a line for the not-to-exceed goal of 33 minutes

Time-series charts do not separate typical process-output responses from atypical events (e.g., a significant accident or inclement weather in our illustration) and quantify the expectation of a process output if there were no atypical events. *If a process output expectation (with no atypical events) is unsatisfactory, there is a need for process improvement that enhances the <u>overall</u> metric's response. Metric reporting giving focus to an understanding with an attempt to resolve the occurrence of individual unsatisfactory outputs over time does not provide this comprehensive process improvement insight.*

30,000-foot-level reporting overcomes this shortcoming (Breyfogle 2014).

30,000-foot-level reporting

The 30,000-foot-level reports (Breyfogle 2014) shown in this section were created using a free app (Breyfogle 2021 and Smarter Solutions 2020).

Figure 1.13 shows a 30,000-foot-level report of commute times before implementing our commuter's process improvement.

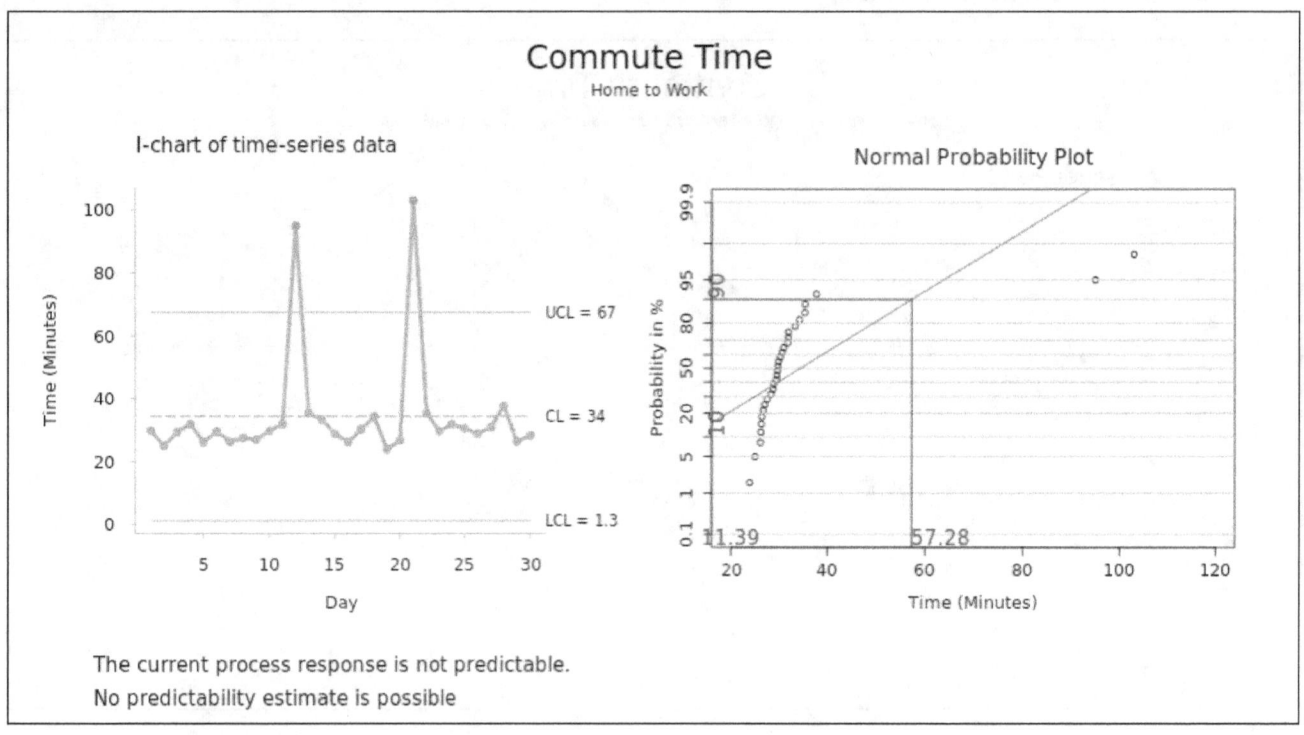

Figure 1.13: Commute Time Home-to-Work: 30,000-foot-level Reporting

The 30,000-foot-level report shown in Figure 1.13 has three components:

1. The individuals chart (left graph) is for assessing a measured response for "stability" from a high-level point of viewpoint, i.e., a 30,000-foot-level point of view (not unlike a window's view perspective from an airplane in a flight of the terrain below). The mathematics for creating this chart is the same as that of a Statistical Process Control (SPC) individuals control chart; however, the primary use of the individuals chart is entirely different in a 30,000-foot-level report application. With 30,000-foot-level reporting, one is not attempting to "control" a process and identify special-cause signals for resolution. With 30,000-foot-level reporting, the individuals chart only assesses whether a process is stable or not from a high-level vantage point. Suppose there are no points beyond the data-calculated UCL (upper control limit) and LCL (lower control limit) lines. In this case, the process is considered stable and predictable from this high-level perspective.

2. The probability plot (right graph) is a plot of data from an individuals chart. If a recent region of a process' output measurements is stable/predictable, the data for creating this plot is considered a random sample of future responses. This

prediction statement assumes that future process inputs will be similar to those in the past.

3. The statement at the bottom of the chart addresses process predictability. A prediction statement is determined from the probability plot and provided if the process is considered stable.

Figure 1.13 shows a commute time that is not stable because of the two abnormal commute times caused by a major traffic accident and a snowstorm. Since we want to reduce commute time under normal conditions and have identified the cause for these atypical responses, we can remove these two data points from our chart to create Figure 1.14.

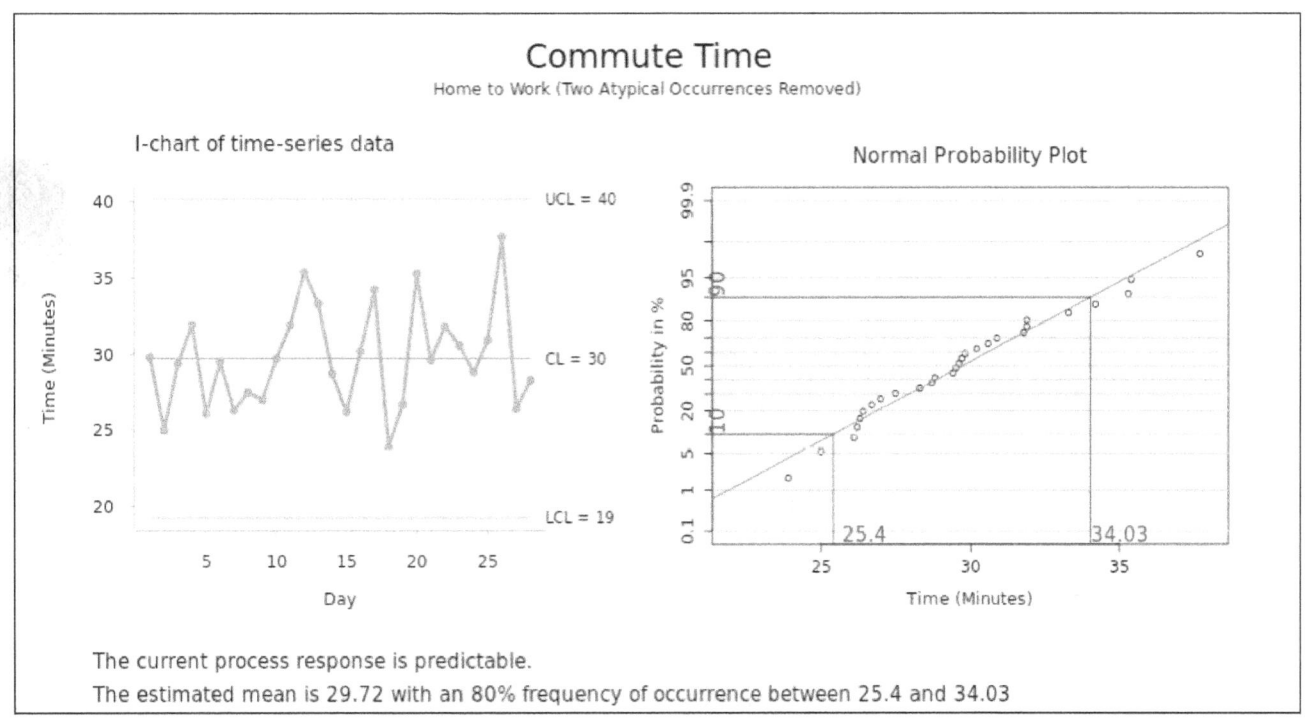

Figure 1.14: Commute Time Home-to-Work: 30,000-foot-level Report (Two Atypical Commutes Removed)

From the individuals chart in Figure 1.14, one observes that the process output response indicates stability; hence, the process is predictable. At the bottom of the 30,000-foot-level report is the statement that the current commuting process time has an estimated mean response of about 30 minutes, with 80% (or four out of five) commute times between 25 and 34 minutes.

In this illustration, our commuter selected a process improvement to her commute process where she departed home one half-hour earlier than what she did previously. The resulting 30,000-foot-level report for her compute time is shown in Figure 1.15. This figure includes the times before and after her change in home departure times.

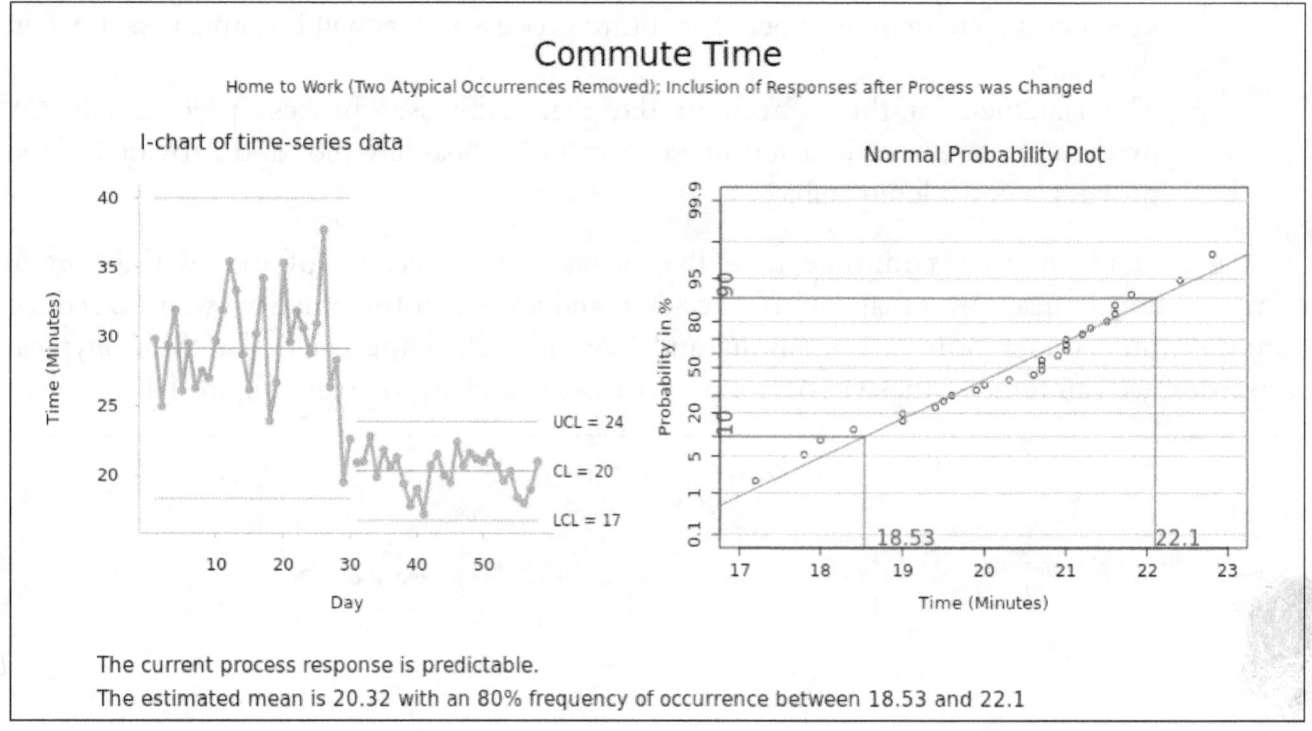

Figure 1.15: Commute Time Home-to-Work: 30,000-foot-level Report (Two Atypical Commutes Removed); Includes responses after changing the process

There is a staging of the individuals chart in Figure 1.15, where the commuter's new process began. The probability plot uses only data from the recent stability region to create the graph and provide the predictive statement details at the bottom of the report.

Our commuter's new process (departing ½ hour earlier) estimated mean commute time is about 20 minutes, with four out of five commute times (80%) between about 19 and 22 minutes. This mean-commute-duration time is much less (and with a lesser amount of variation) than her past process (not departing earlier) estimated mean of 30 minutes, with four out of five commute times (80%) between 25 and 34 minutes.

30,000-foot-level Reporting Summary

Traditional metrics reporting often encourages reacting to the ups and downs of commonplace "noise" responses, leading to much organizational wasted efforts and even destructive behaviors. 30,000-foot-level reporting provides a high-level process output response point of view that encourages process improvement thinking to improve overall metric responses.

1.9 Example: 30,000-foot-level Report Creation: One Continuous Process Y Response Reported over Time

This illustration uses the data in Figure 1.16 for creating Figure 9.7 in the book *Management 2.0* (similar to Figure 1.17 shown below).

Month	Expense
1/1/2018	93775
2/1/2018	110227
3/1/2018	103807
4/1/2018	101687
5/1/2018	104395
6/1/2018	96925
7/1/2018	91662
8/1/2018	107527
9/1/2018	92272
10/1/2018	106026
11/1/2018	100058
12/1/2018	103634
1/1/2019	94531
2/1/2019	110784
3/1/2019	115965
4/1/2019	87983
5/1/2019	100520
6/1/2019	88103
7/1/2019	92422
8/1/2019	98831
9/1/2019	96741
10/1/2019	111167

Figure 1.16: Expense Data (Monthly)

Applications of this type of Y process output response data tracked over time are lead time, costs, cycle time, and WIP.

Figure 1.17 shows a 30,000-foot-level report for this process-output response dataset.

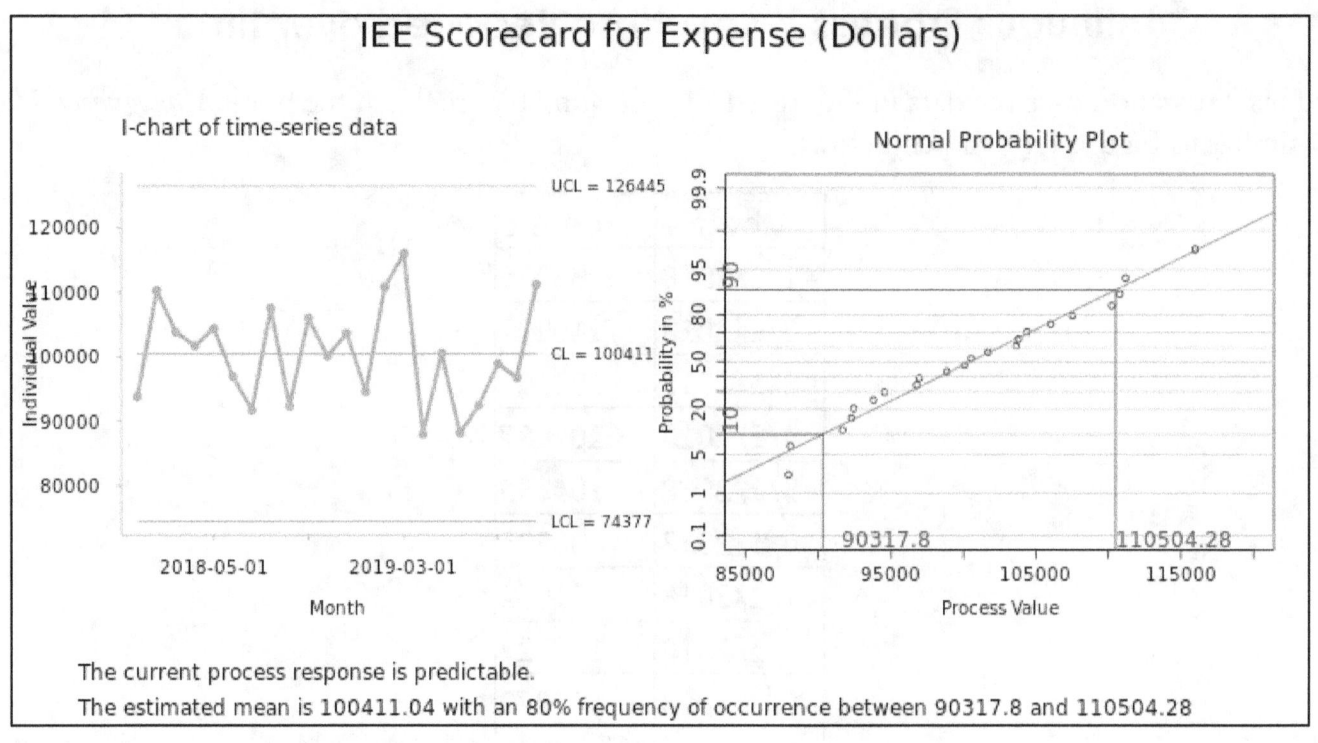

Figure 1.17: Expense 30,000-foot-level Report

30,000-foot-level reports for a single continuous Y-output response contain three components:

1. An individuals chart (report-outs left chart) determines if the process response is stable. The purpose of this individuals chart report is very different from a traditional control chart in that the primary objective is not to identify special-cause signals to take timely action on (monthly reported data). This chart is not attempting to control anything in a timely fashion. This chart's purpose is to determine if the process is stable, i.e., the default is that no datum points beyond the statistically calculated upper control limit (UCL) and lower control limit (LCL).

2. For this illustration, the process is considered stable; hence, the accompanying probability plot (report-out right chart) is used to determine a best-estimate prediction statement. In 30,000-foot-level reports, whenever there is no specification (the situation in this illustration), there is a determination and reporting of an estimated process output median or mean response with an 80% frequency of occurrence (four out of five values) range for the future. If this futuristic expectation is undesirable, there is a need for process improvement.

3. A statement at the bottom of the report provides a prediction statement if the process is stable. If this futuristic statement is undesirable, there is a need for process improvement.

1.10 Example: 30,000-foot-level Report Creation: Non-conformance Rate Process Y Response Reported over Time

This illustration uses the attribute non-conformance rate response data in Figure 1.18 for creating Figure 9.9 in the book *Management 2.0* (similar to Figure 9.19 shown below).

Month	Non-conformance Rate
01/2018	0.0607
02/2018	0.0440
03/2018	0.0295
04/2018	0.0456
05/2018	0.0467
06/2018	0.0484
07/2018	0.0499
08/2018	0.0353
09/2018	0.0519
10/2018	0.0547
11/2018	0.0456
12/2018	0.0433
01/2019	0.0558
02/2019	0.0414
03/2019	0.0379
04/2019	0.0525
05/2019	0.0347
06/2019	0.0516
07/2019	0.0501
08/2019	0.0315
09/2019	0.0380
10/2019	0.0415

Figure 1.18: Non-conformance Rate Monthly Data

Figure 1.19 shows a 30,000-foot-level report for this process-output response dataset.

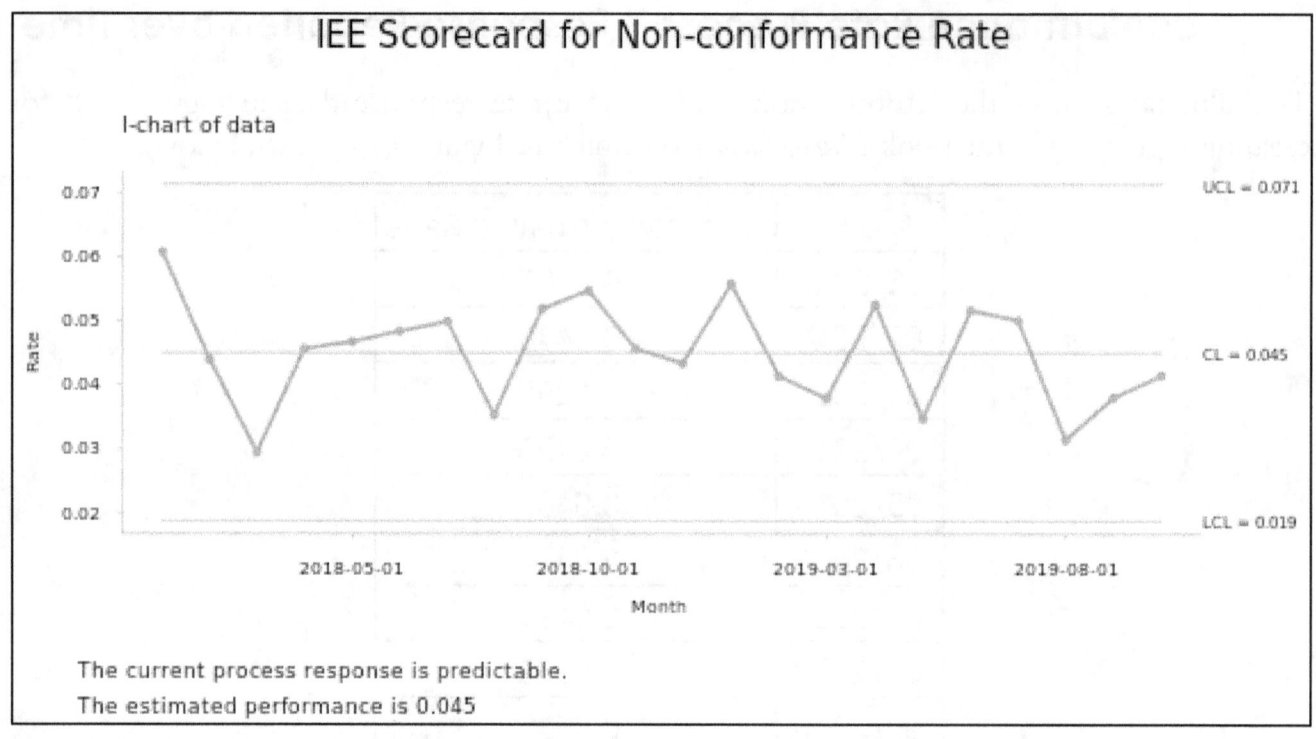

Figure 1.19: 30,000-foot-level Report of a Non-conformance Rate

30,000-foot-level reports for a non-conformance rate attribute Y-output response contain two components:

1. An individual chart to assess process stability. A traditional p-chart is not appropriate for 30,000-foot-level reporting for many reasons. Many articles and books by Forrest describe the problems with p-chart reporting and the benefits of a 30,000-foot-level reporting alternative, e.g., "Issues and Resolution to p-chart Control Limits Formula False Signals" (Smarter Solutions 2015b)
2. A statement at the bottom of the report relative to process stability provides a prediction statement if the process is stable. If this futuristic statement is undesirable, there is a need for process improvement.

1.11 Additional 30,000-foot-level Reporting Formats

The "Free Business Process Management Software" link (Smarter Solutions 2020) provides instructions and videos to create 30,000-foot-level reports for the following situations:

- Continuous Data, No Subgroups
- Continuous Data, No Subgroups, Process Improvement
- Continuous Data, No Subgroups, Non-normal Data
- Continuous Data, With Subgroups
- Continuous Data, With Subgroups, Process Improvement

- Attribute Data, Failure Rate
- Attribute Data, Infrequent Failures
- Pareto Chart to Target Improvements

1.12 IEE Value Chain and Enterprise Performance Reporting System (EPRS) software

Step 2 in the 9-step IEE business management system (Figure 1.1) states, "Describe value chain, including satellite-level and 30,000-foot-level charts." An IEE value chain describes what an organization does and how it measures what is done. Behind an organization's firewall, Enterprise Performance Reporting System (EPRS) software provides a means to view an organization's IEE value chain.

Enterprise Performance Reporting System (EPRS) software provides a vehicle for:

- Viewing an organization's IEE value chain by all authorized 24x7
- Providing automatic updates for 30,000-foot-level and satellite-level organizational metrics, e.g., daily
- Linking process-output metrics with the processes that created them
- Showing an updated organization's Enterprise Improvement Plan (EIP) 24x7
- Displaying the status of Lean Six Sigma process improvement projects, including PowerPoint report-outs 24x7 to all authorized
- A no-cost means to provide "control" in the DMAIC Lean Six Sigma process improvement roadmap

"Integrated Enterprise Excellence (IEE) Business Management System Software" (Smarter Solutions 2019) provides a description and video demonstration of the EPRS enterprise software and its benefits.

PART 2:

SigmaXL and IEE-DMAIC Process Improvement Roadmap

2

IEE-DMAIC Roadmap and SigmaXL Introduction

2.1   Applying IEE-DMAIC Roadmap

This book focuses on using SigmaXL's statistical functions to gain insight into improving business processes for the organization's big-picture benefit. One can conduct these analyses at the business and the Lean Six Sigma improvement project levels. This book focuses on utilizing SigmaXL tools at the Lean Six Sigma improvement project level.

The book *Integrated Enterprise Excellence Volume III* (Breyfogle, F. W. [2008c]) {referenced in this book as *IEE Volume III*} provides the details for implementing the IEE Lean Six Sigma Define-Measure-Analyze-Improve-Control (DMAIC) roadmap shown in Figure 2.1.

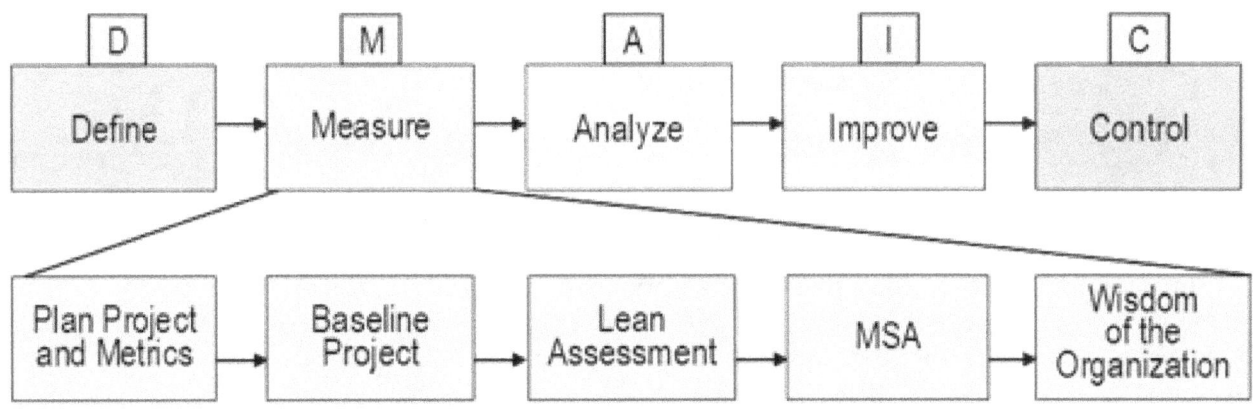

Figure 2.1: IEE DMAIC Roadmap

The book *Lean Six Sigma Project Execution Guide* (Breyfogle, F. W. [2010]) provides the drill-down details for executing each step in this roadmap. www.Smartersolutions.com/roadmap also provides drill-downs for this IEE DMAIC roadmap.

IEE Volume III provides many output figures and tables; however, *IEE Volume III* does not include the stats software syntax to create these figures and tables.

This book will describe how to use SigmaXL to create the figures and analyses outputs shown in *IEE Volume III*. After some initial topics, the flow of the books will progress through the thought process of applying this Lean Six Sigma IEE-DMAIC process improvement roadmap and show the use of SigmaXL within this project execution process.

This book will show how SigmaXL can provide insight into statistically significant $Y=f(X)$ relationships. Understanding how an X response impacts a Y response can provide valuable awareness of what an organization might do to improve an IEE 30,000-foot-level process-output response.

2.2   SigmaXL Introduction

Figure 2.2 shows a SigmaXL spreadsheet and some aspects of data within this spreadsheet.

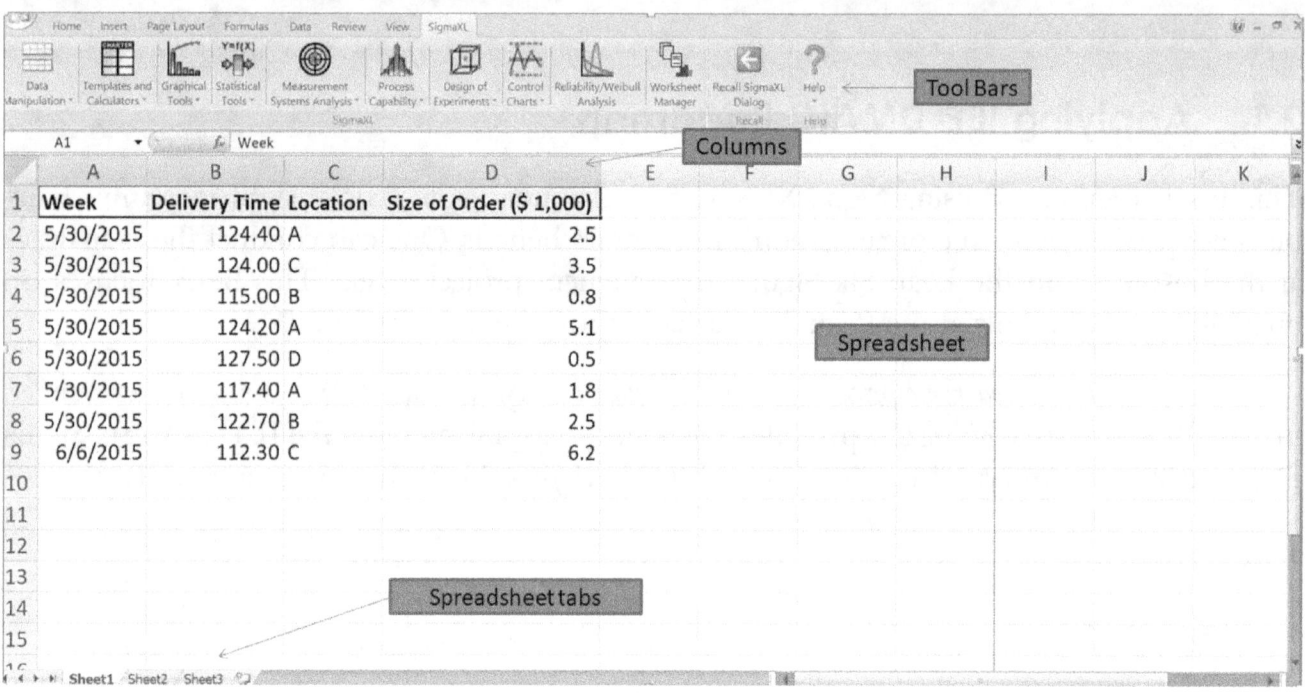

Figure 2.2: SigmaXL Worksheet

Graphs and statistical analysis outputs appear in subsequent tabs.

Figures 2.3 and 2.4 illustrate an example of SigmaXL dialog box.

SigmaXL Chart Function:

-Choose: Statistical Tools>One-Way ANOVA and Means Matrix

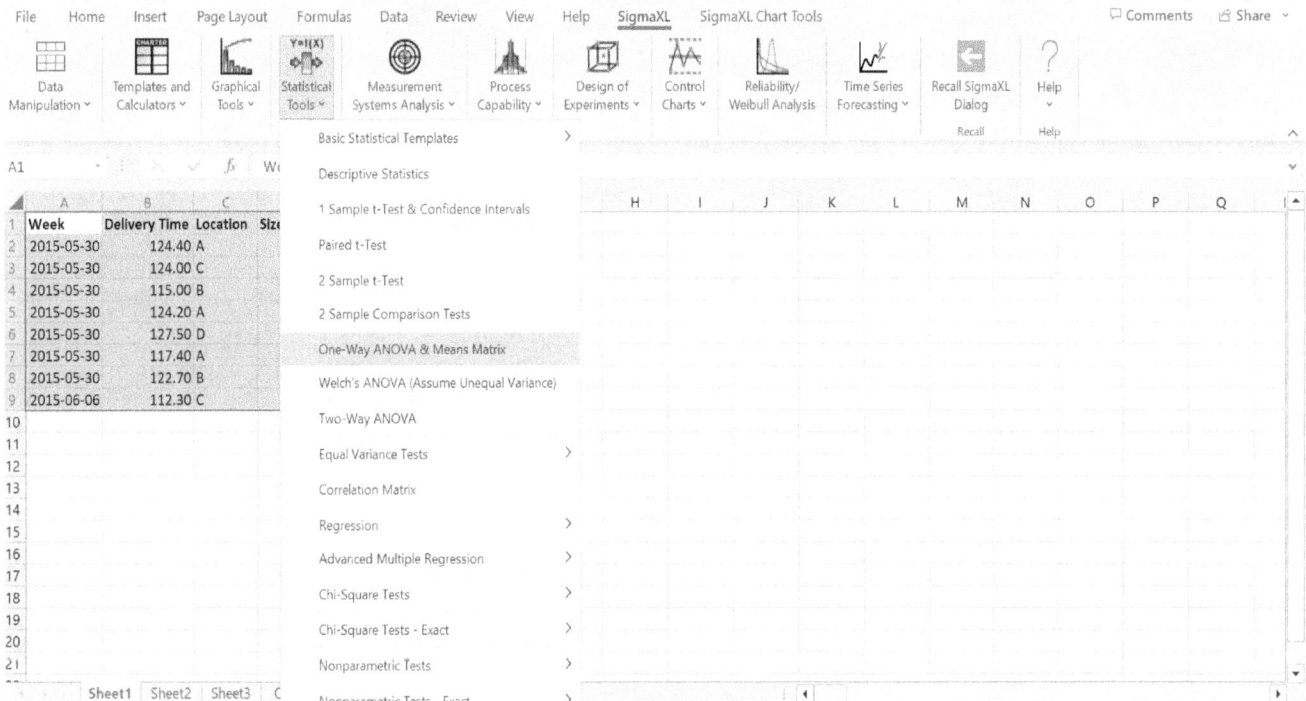

Figure 2.3: SigmaXL Dialog Box

The primary entries to make in a SigmaXL dialog box, as illustrated in Figure 2.3, are:

1. Select "Use Data Labels" and **always ensure that "Use Entire Data Table" is checked**
2. Select the data presentation format next to "Stacked Column Format (1 Numeric Data Column & 1 Group Category Column)"
3. Enter a value in the box next to "Numeric Data Variable (Y)" by selecting one of the values on the left side of the SigmaXL dialog box. For example: select "Delivery Time" and then click the "Numeric Data Variable (Y)>>" button. This will populate the "white entry box" on the right side of the dialog box.

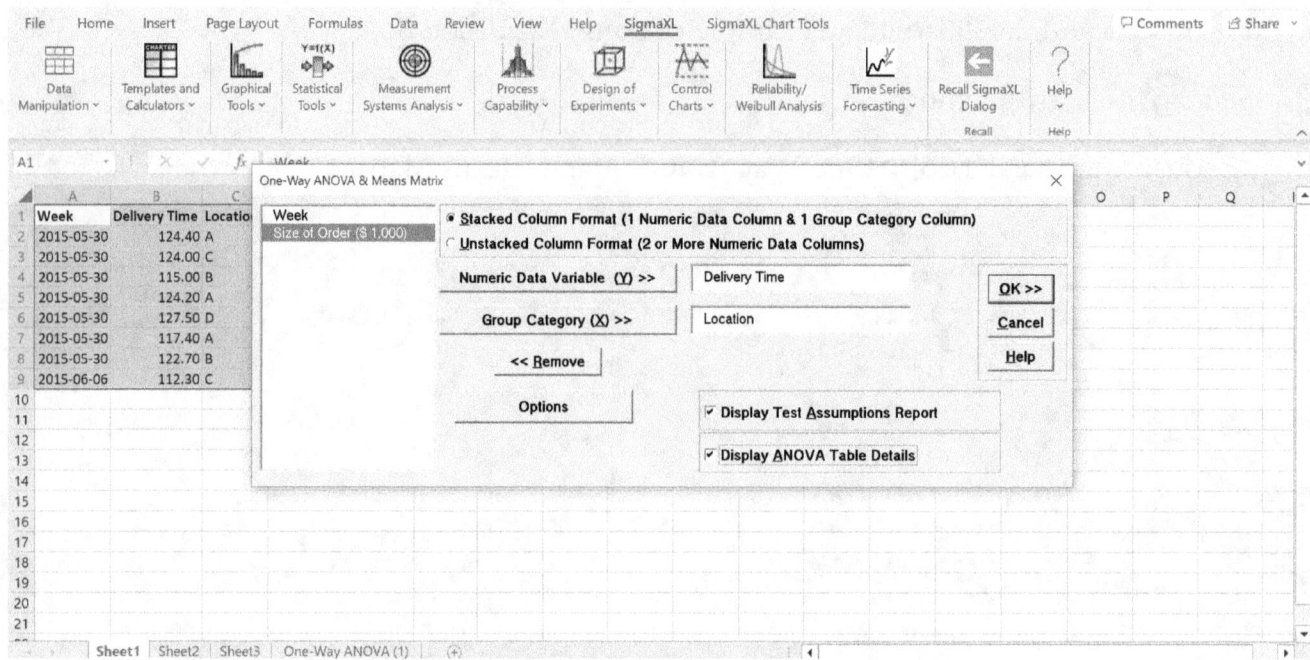

Figure 2.4: SigmaXL Dialog Box

Later sections of this book will show the use of SigmaXL dialog boxes for various situations.

PART 3:

IEE-DMAIC Roadmap

3

IEE-DMAIC — Define Phase

3.1 IEE-DMAIC Roadmap Component

Book 1 Reference: *IEE Volume III* – Chapter 4

Book 2 Reference: *Lean Six Sigma Project Execution Guide* – Section 1

Internet: www.smartersolutions.com/roadmap (clicking on highlighted area provides the flowchart below)

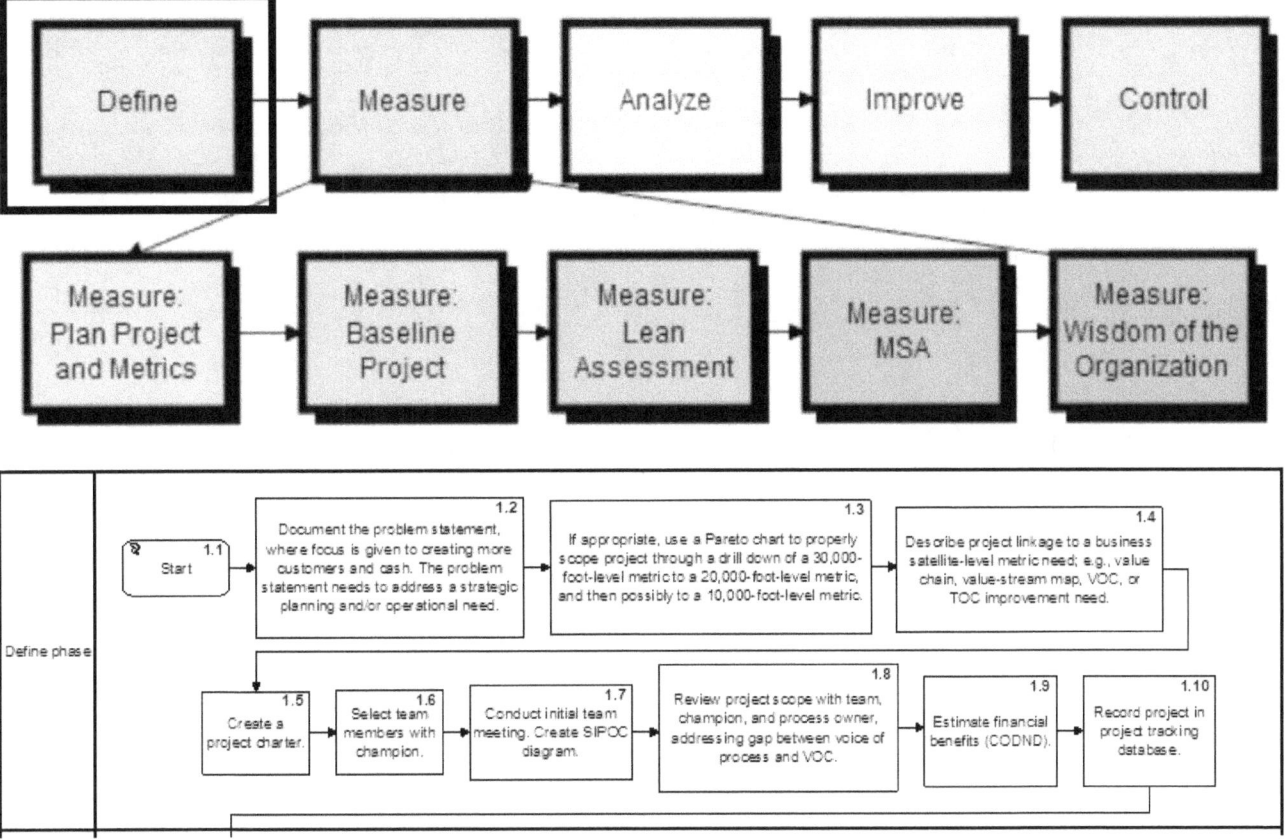

3.2   Primary Project Metric

In Six Sigma, each process improvement project has a problem statement. *In IEE, an essential aspect of the problem statement is the project's metric selection, which has a 30,000-foot-level reporting format.*

Project charters should have a single primary metric with an improvement goal for the metric—a single primary metric leads to upcoming straightforward numerical analyses and decision-making steps. In the IEE system, the reporting of this metric is at the 30,000-foot-level.

To illustrate the creation of project metrics that have interdependencies, the performance of a process is a function of three primary aspects: cost, quality, and time. Fix one of the three performance aspects, and one should see improvements in the other two. We can track these other two measurement aspects in projects as secondary metrics. Secondary project metrics can ensure that a Lean Six Sigma Belt in their process improvement effort does not improve a primary metric to the detriment of secondary metrics.

4

Response Statistics, Graphical Representations, and Data Analyses

Reference: *IEE Volume III*, Chapter 8

4.1 Example: Time-series Plot

A run chart or time-series plot permits the study of data over time, where the x-axis is time, and the y-axis is the measured variable. Generally, 20-25 points are needed to establish patterns and baselines. Note that run charts should be used only on data in its original chronological sequence.

IEE Volume III Example and Dataset

- *IEE Volume III* Example 8.1: Time Series Plot of Gross Revenue
- Dataset (Smarter Solutions (2022): V3 C08, Exam 08-01, Time Series Plot Gross Revenue.xlsx

SigmaXL Input/Output

- Figure 4.1: SigmaXL Input (Time-series Plot)
- Figure 4.2: SigmaXL Output (Time-series Plot)

SigmaXL Chart Function

-You can either click SigmaXL > Templates and Calculators > Basic Graphical Templates > Run Chart or

- Choose Graphical Tools>Basic Graphical Templates>Run Chart

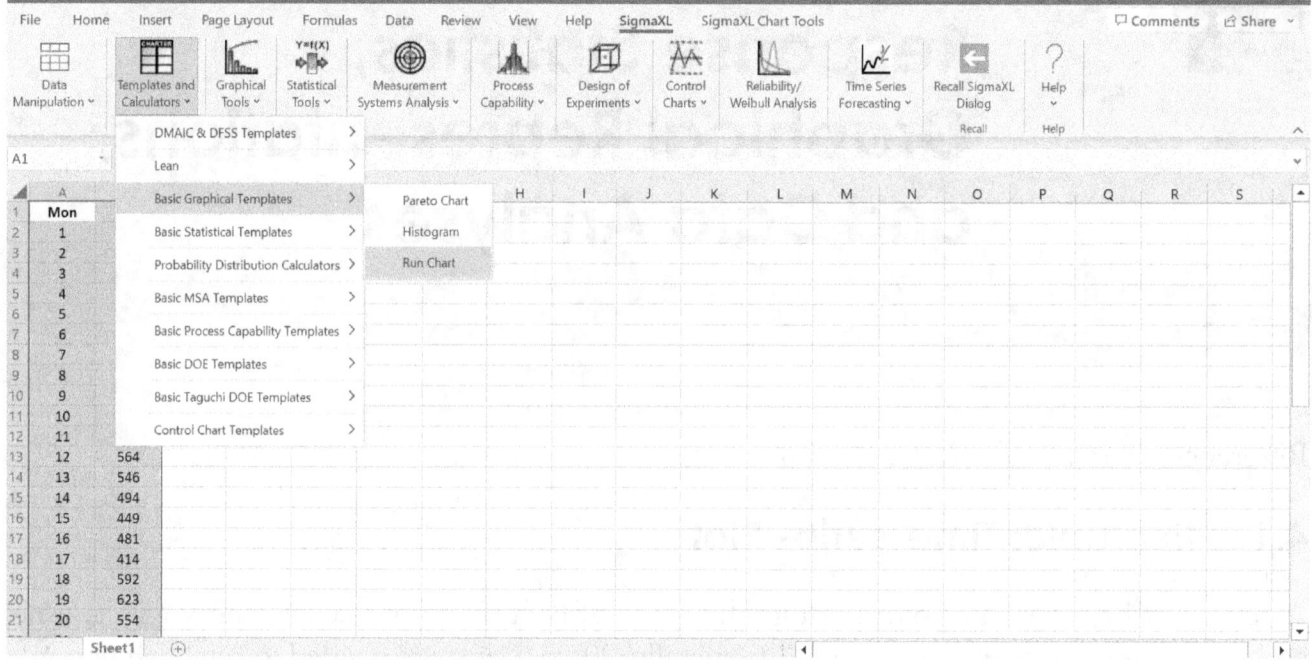

Figure 4.1: SigmaXL Input (Run Chart)

- Copy the data from sheet 1, paste it into the new 2nd tab and click on Run Chart:

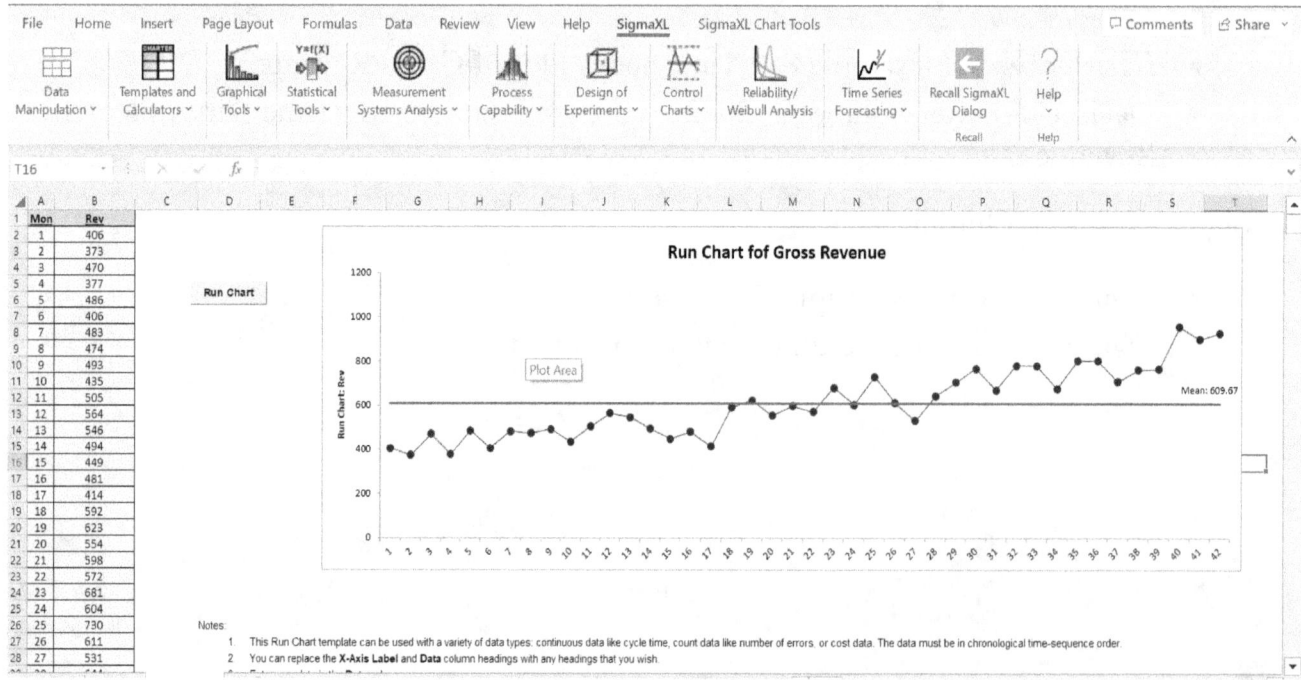

Figure 4.2.1: SigmaXL Output (Run Chart)

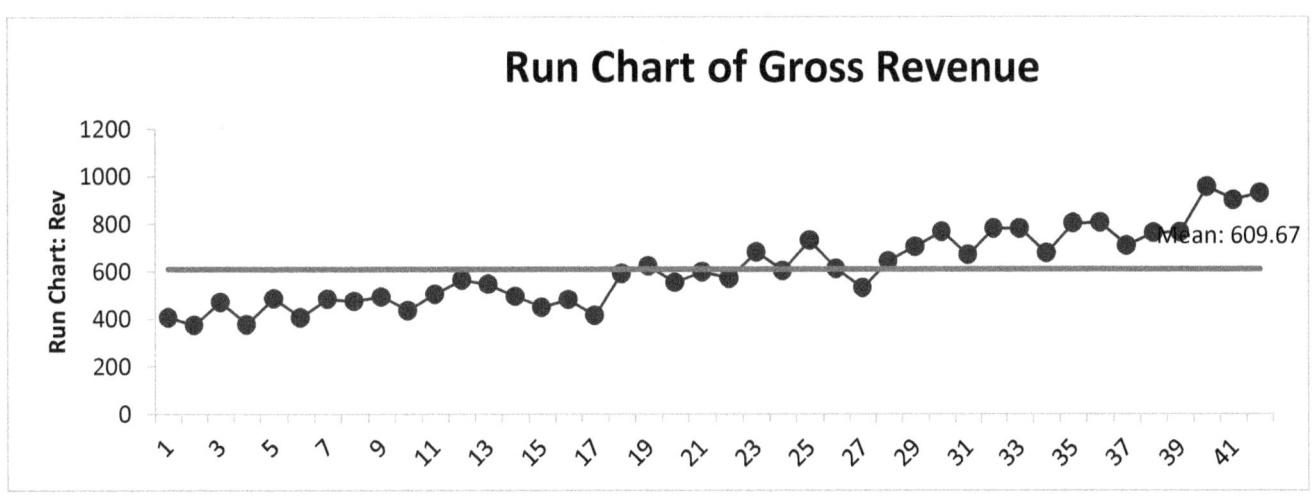

Figure 4.2.2: SigmaXL Chart Output (Run Chart)

Comment

- You can add, remove or change chart elements such as title, labels, gridlines and data labels by clicking on the chart and selecting "+".

4.2 Example: Histogram and Dot Plot

It can be meaningful to present data in a form that visually illustrates the frequency of occurrence of values. A histogram and a dot plot are means to achieve this objective.

The histogram divides your sample data into intervals called bins. The bars represent the frequency, or the number of observations falling within each bin. A histogram works best when the sample size is at least 20. When just a few variable data points are available, dot plots are also useful to assess the distribution.

IEE Volume III Example and Dataset

- *IEE Volume III* Example 8.3: Histogram and Dot Plot
- Dataset (Smarter Solutions (2022): V3 C08, Exam 08-03, histogram.xlsx

SigmaXL Input/Output

- Figure 4.3: SigmaXL Input (Histogram)
- Figure 4.4: SigmaXL Output (Histogram)
- Figure 4.5: SigmaXL Input (Dot Plot)
- Figure 4.6: SigmaXL Output (Dot Plot)

SigmaXL Chart Function: Graphical Tools>Basic Histogram

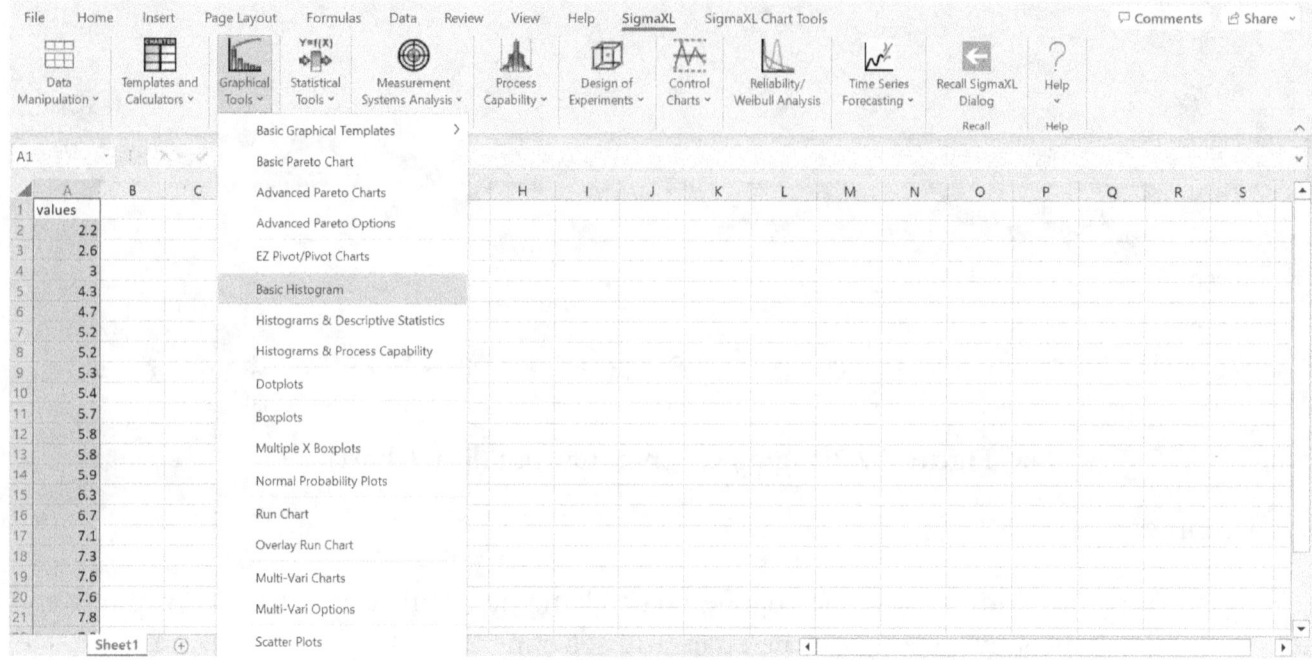

Figure 4.3: SigmaXL Input (Histogram)

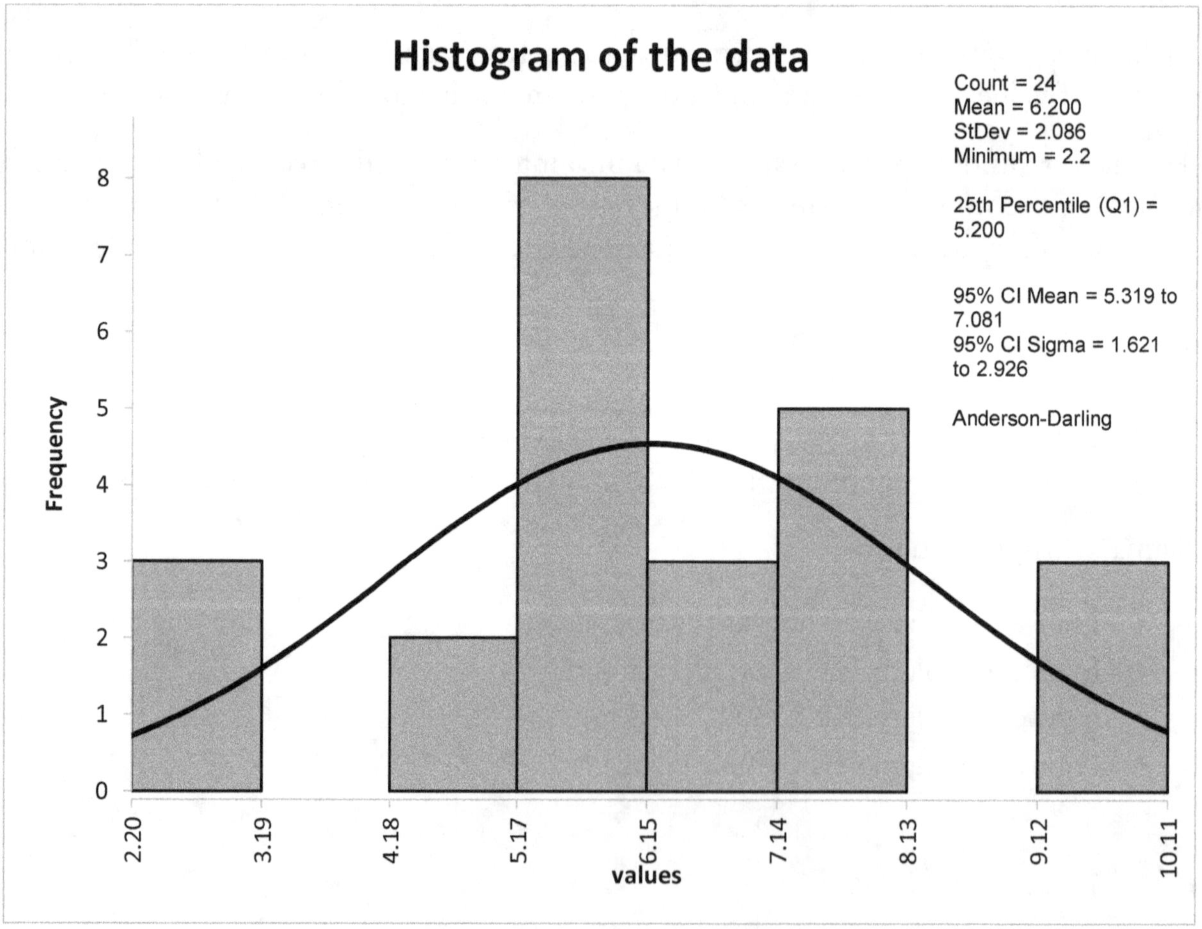

Figure 4.4: SigmaXL Output (Histogram)

Comment

- By default, the histogram output will also show the descriptive statistics. The histogram starting point, bin width and number of bins can be changed in the dialog box. You can add, remove or change chart elements such as title, labels, gridlines and data labels by clicking on the chart and selecting "+".

SigmaXL Chart Function: Graphical Tools>Dotplots

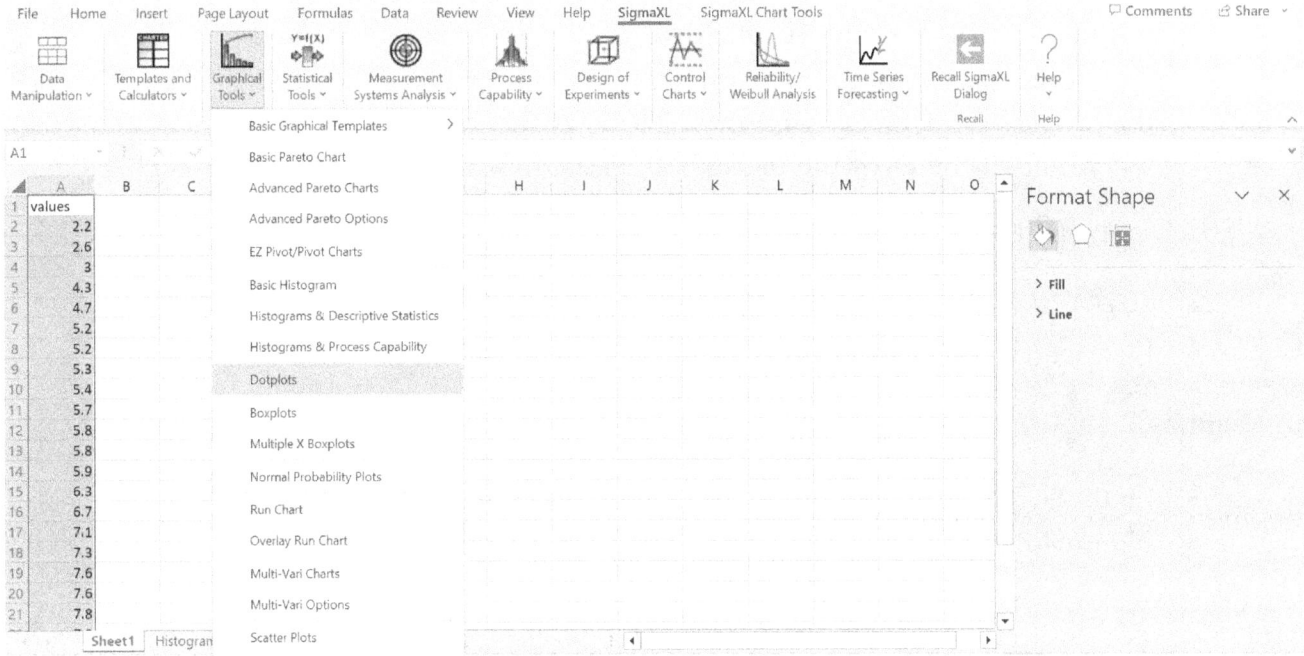

Figure 4.5: SigmaXL Input (Dot Plot)

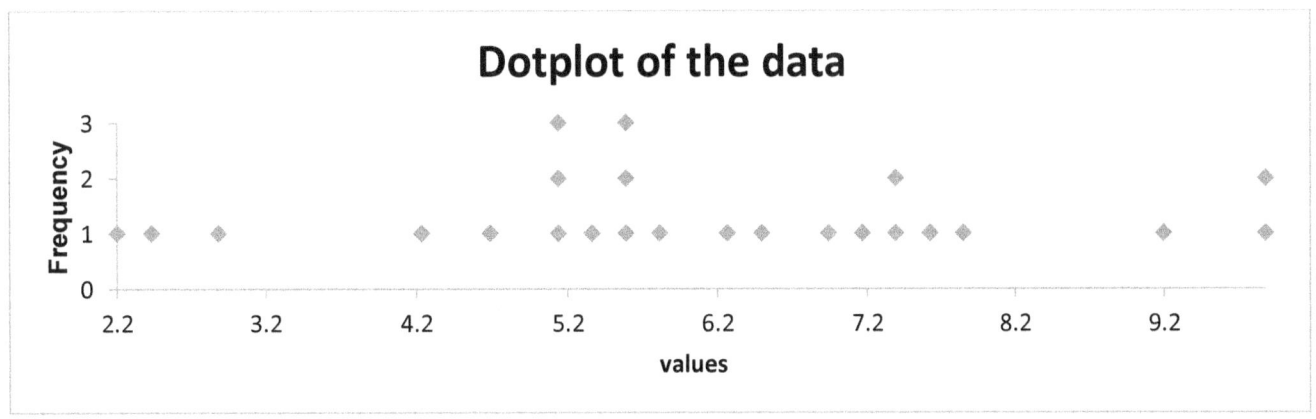

Figure 4.6: SigmaXL Output (Dot Plot)

Comment

- You can add, remove or change chart elements such as title, labels, gridlines and data labels by clicking on the chart and selecting "+".

4.3   Example: Descriptive Statistics

It can be meaningful to present data in a tabular form that shows various statistical calculations.

IEE Application Examples

- A random sample of invoices from the last 17-month region of process stability from a 30,000-foot-level report, i.e., days sales outstanding (DSO), where the number of days beyond the due date was measured and reported
- A random sample of parts manufactured over the last five months (the time when the process changed to an improved level as shown in the 30,000-foot-level report), where the diameter of the pieces was measured and reported

IEE Volume III Example and Dataset

- *IEE Volume III* Section 8.11: Descriptive Statistics
- Dataset (Smarter Solutions (2022): V3 C22, Exam 22-01, Two Samples.xlsx

SigmaXL Input/Output

- Figure 4.7: SigmaXL Input (Descriptive Statistics)
- Figure 4.8: SigmaXL Output (Descriptive Statistics)

SigmaXL Chart Function: Statistical Tools>Descriptive Statistics

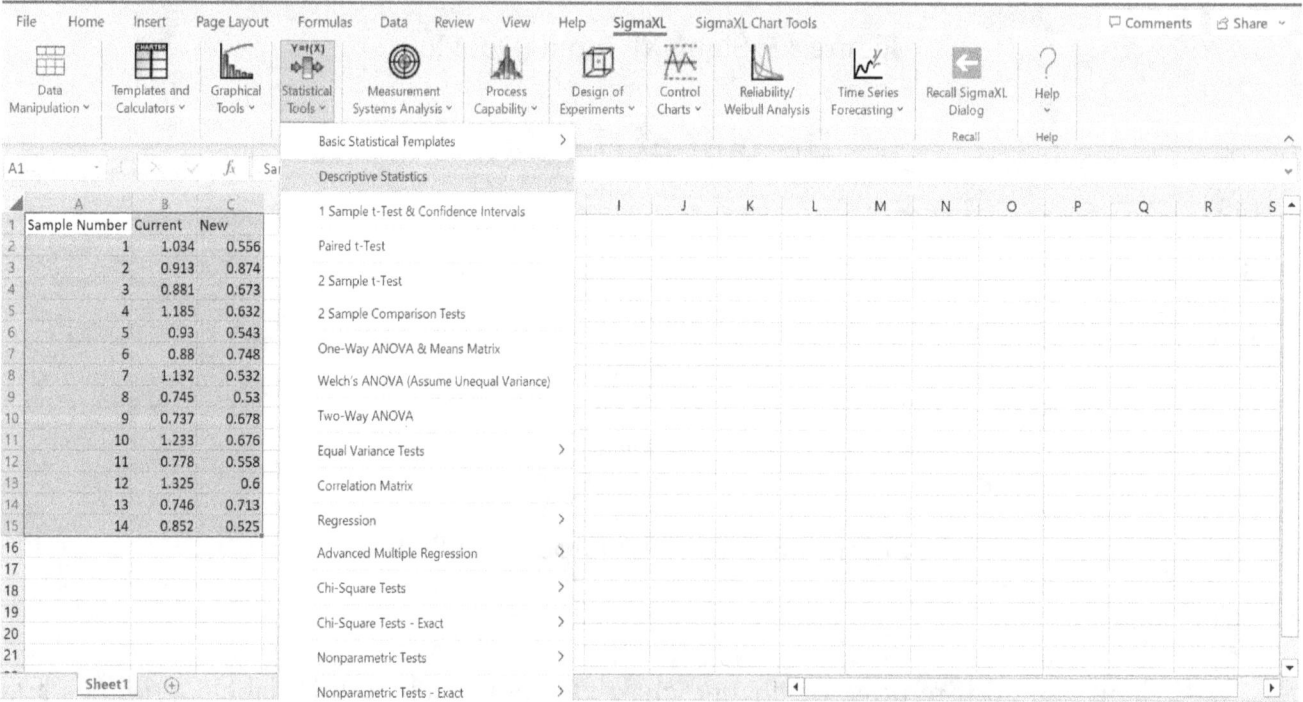

Figure 4.7: SigmaXL Input (Descriptive Statistics)

Descriptive Statistics	Current	New
Count	14	14
Mean	0.955071	0.631286
StDev	0.195209	0.102415765
Range	0.588000	0.349000
Minimum	0.737000	0.525000
25th Percentile (Q1)	0.770000	0.540250
50th Percentile (Median)	0.897000	0.616000
75th Percentile (Q3)	1.145	0.686750
Maximum	1.325	0.874000
95.0% CI Mean	0.84236 to 1.0678	0.57215 to 0.69042
95.0% CI Sigma	0.14152 to 0.31449	0.074247 to 0.165
Anderson-Darling Normality Test	0.512700	0.533691
P-Value (A-D Test)	0.1604	0.1408
Skewness	0.650648	0.997510
P-Value (Skewness)	0.2609	0.0934
Kurtosis	-0.824833	0.792028
P-Value (Kurtosis)	0.4760	0.3881

Figure 4.8: SigmaXL Output (Descriptive Statistics)

4.4   Example: Pareto Charts

The Pareto principle states that 80 percent of the trouble comes from twenty percent of the problems, i.e., the vital few problems. A Pareto chart is a graphical technique used to quantify problems so that efforts focus on fixing the "vital few" causes instead of working on the "trivial many." By ordering the bars from largest to smallest, the Pareto chart is useful to identify the main contributors to the issue on hand. A cumulative percentage line helps you judge the added contributions of each category.

An organization was experiencing a situation where a 30,000-foot-level reported process-output attribute failure rate was stable but was unacceptably high. A team created a Pareto chart to determine where to focus improvement efforts.

IEE Volume III Example and Dataset

- *IEE Volume III* Example 8.4: Improving a Process that has Defects
- Dataset (Smarter Solutions (2022): V3 C08, Exam 08-04, process that has defects

Creating the chart in SigmaXL:

- Figure 4.9A: SigmaXL Input (Pareto Chart)
- Figure 4.9B: SigmaXL Basic Pareto "Chart Options"
- Figure 4.9C: SigmaXL Basic Pareto "Other Options"

- Figure 4.10: SigmaXL Output (Pareto Chart)

SigmaXL Chart Function: Graphical Tools>Basic Pareto Chart

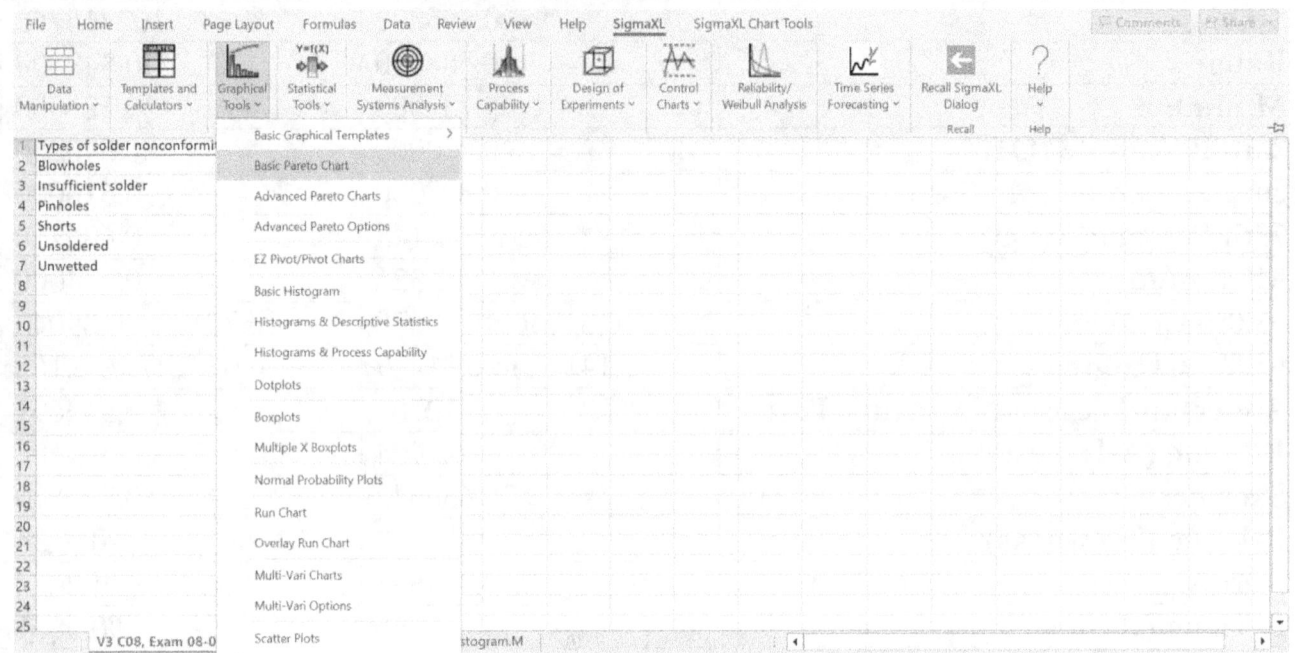

Figure 4.9A: SigmaXL Input (Pareto Chart)

When using the Pareto chart for the first time, you need to set the Basic Pareto chart options. Once you have saved your defaults, you can bypass the below options, by clicking Finish instead of Next in the Basic Pareto Chart dialog box, as the saved defaults will automatically be applied.

-Tab "Other" Bar/Cum Sum: check the "After Cumulative %" and "On Top of First Bar"

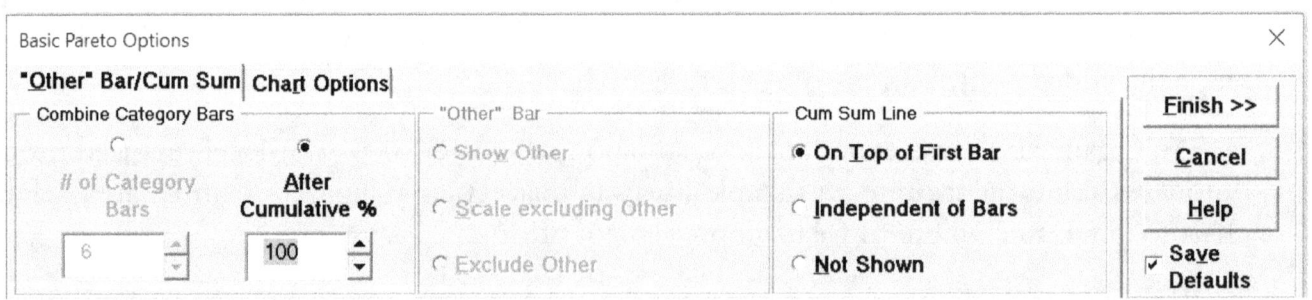

Figure 4.9B: SigmaXL Input Basic Pareto options "Other"

-Tab Chart Options: Category (X) Font: check Slanted; Data Labels: check Bars and Cum Sum; Secondary Y Axis: check Percent. Check Save Defaults and Finish.

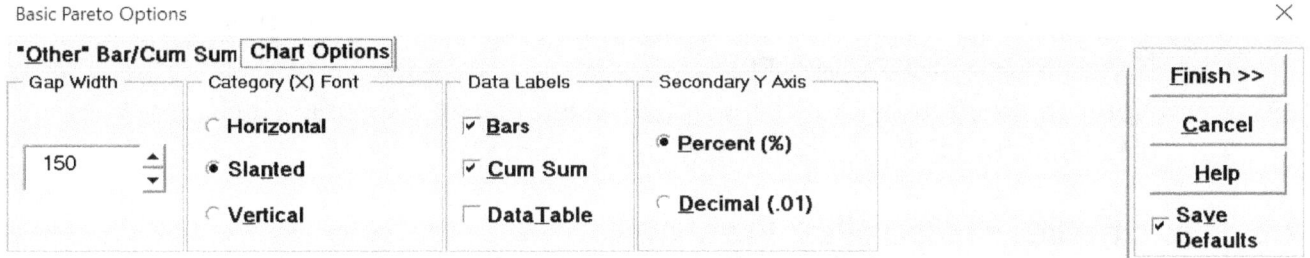

Figure 4.9C: SigmaXL Input Basic Pareto "Other Options"

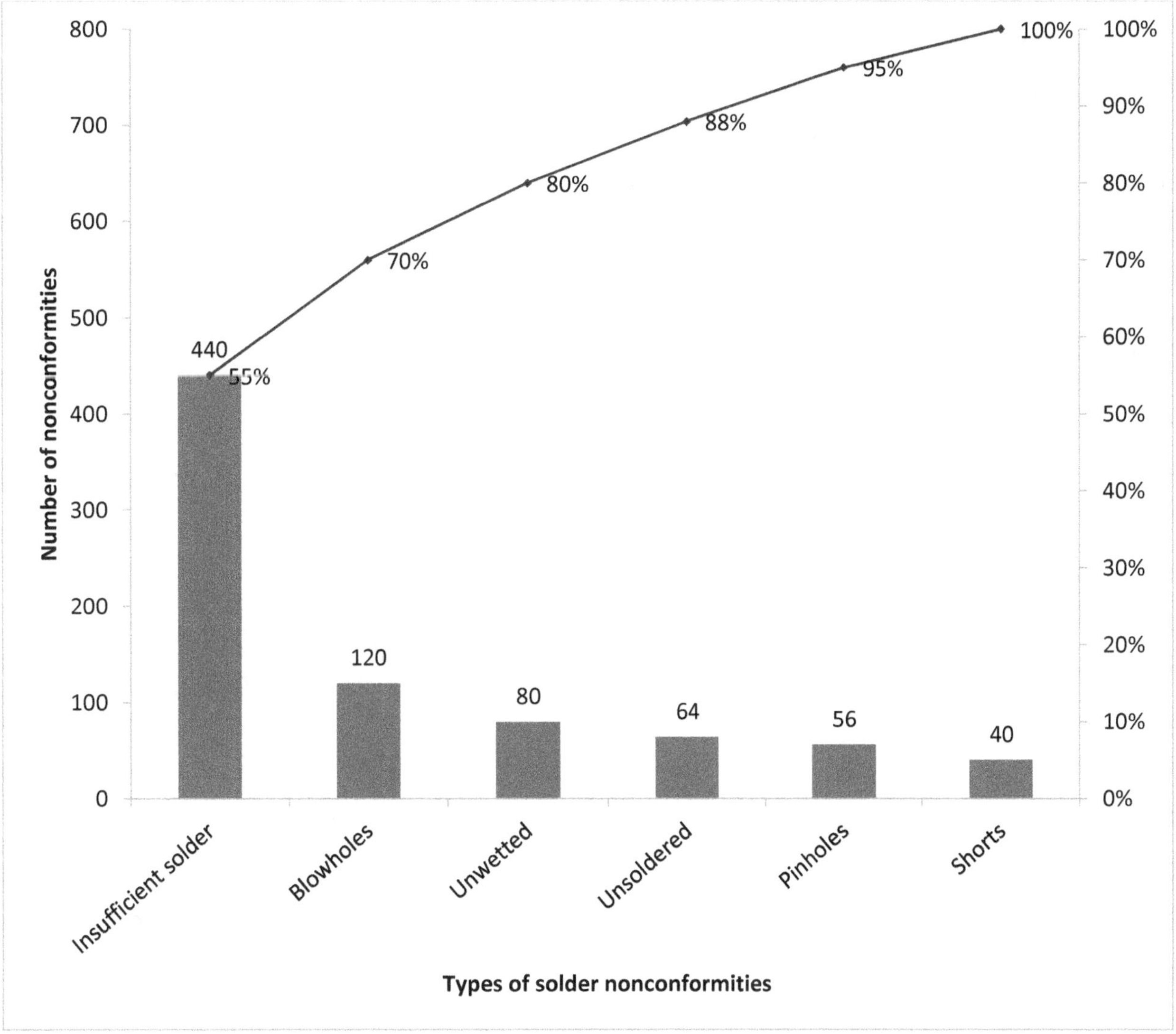

Figure 4.10: SigmaXL Output (Pareto Chart)

Comment

- From Figure 4.10, one observes that focusing on the reduction of insufficient solder can provide the most benefit to improving an overall non-conformance rate 30,000-foot-level report process-output response
- You can add, remove or change chart elements such as title, labels, gridlines and data labels by clicking on the chart and selecting "+".

4.5 Example: Probability Plotting

Probability plots are helpful in visually assessing how well data follow distributions and estimating from data the unknown parameters of a probability density function (PDF) and Cumulative Distribution Function (CDF).

The normal distribution is the most common type of distribution used in a variety of statistical analysis. You should use normality test to determine whether your data does not follow a normal distribution, typically by comparing the p-value to the significance level. Usually, a significance level (α) of 0.05 works well.

Application: Probability Plot when there is a no specification

IEE Volume III Example and Dataset

- *IEE Volume III* Example 8.6: PDF, CDF, then a Probability Plot
- Dataset (Smarter Solutions (2022): V3 C08, Exam 08-06, pdf, cdf, and then prob plot.xlsx

SigmaXL Input/Output

- Figure 4.11: SigmaXL Input (Probability Plot with no Specification)
- Figure 4.12: SigmaXL Output (Probability Plot with no Specification)

SigmaXL Chart Function: Graphical Tools>Normal Probability Plots

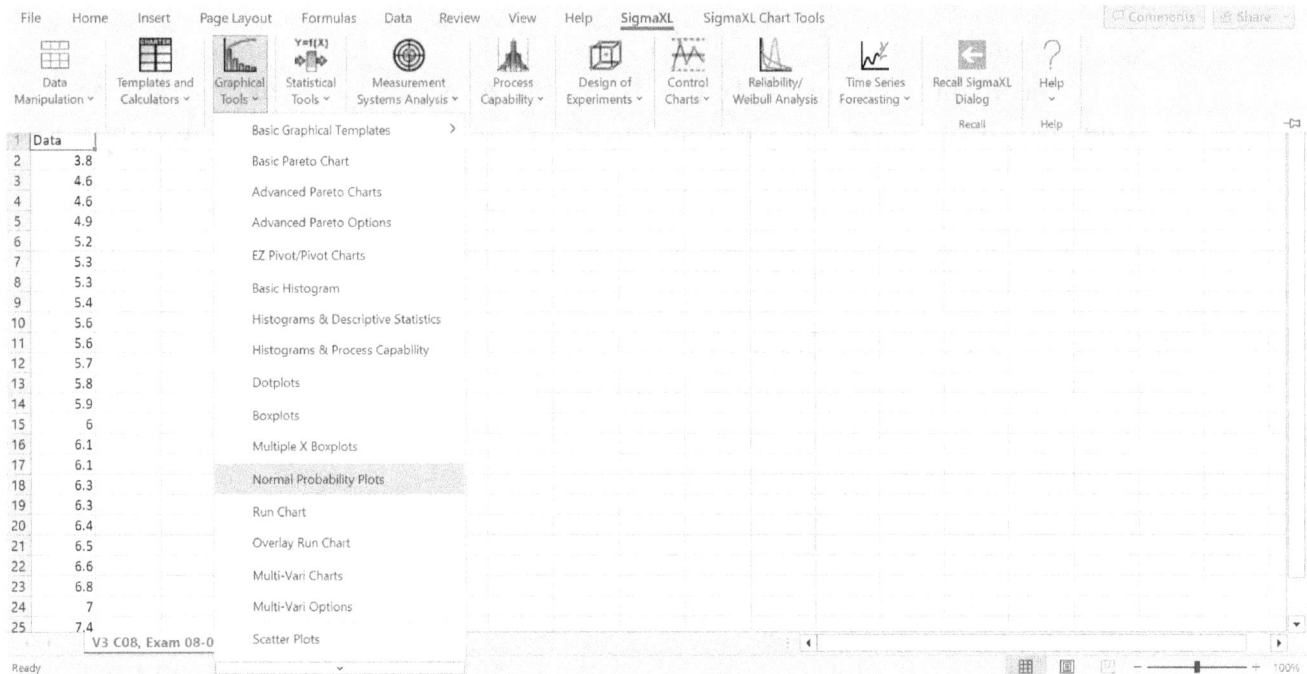

Figure 4.11: SigmaXL Input (Probability Plot with no Specification)

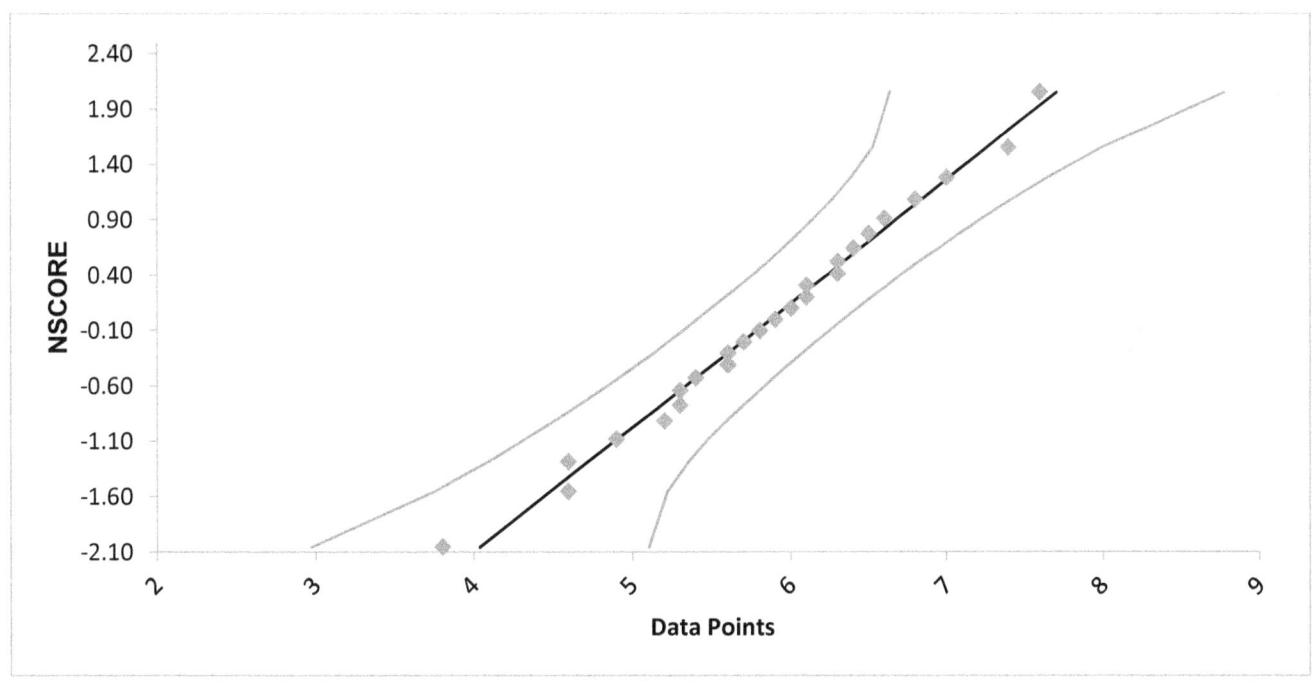

Figure 4.12: SigmaXL Output (Probability Plot)

Comments from Figure 4.12 normal-probability plot

- An informal approximation of a normality test, called "the fat pencil test", is often applied to a probability plot. Imagine a "fat pencil" lying on top of the fitted line. If it covers all the data points on the plot, the data are probably normal. However, if points are far enough from the fitted line that they are visible beyond the edges of the fat pencil, the data are probably nonnormal.

- Keep in mind that the "fat pencil test" is not a substitute for the statistical inference of the normality test itself, but it is useful as a quick visual assessment. For Anderson-Darling normality test and for comparing the p-value to the significance level, you can use the Histogram and Descriptive Statistics SigmaXL chart function
- You can add, remove or change chart elements such as title, labels, gridlines and data labels by clicking on the chart and selecting "+".

4.6 Example: Process Capability/Performance with a Specification, Probability Plotting

Process Capability and Probability plot

IEE Volume III Example and Dataset

- *IEE Volume III* Example 8.6: PDF, CDF, then a Probability Plot
- Dataset (Smarter Solutions (2022): V3 C08, Exam 08-06, pdf, CDF, and then prob plot.xlsx

SigmaXL Input/Output

- Figure 4.13: SigmaXL Input (Process Capability Combination Report)
- Figure 4.14: SigmaXL Output (Process Capability Report and Probability Plot)

SigmaXL Chart Function: Process Capability>Capability Combination Report (Individuals)

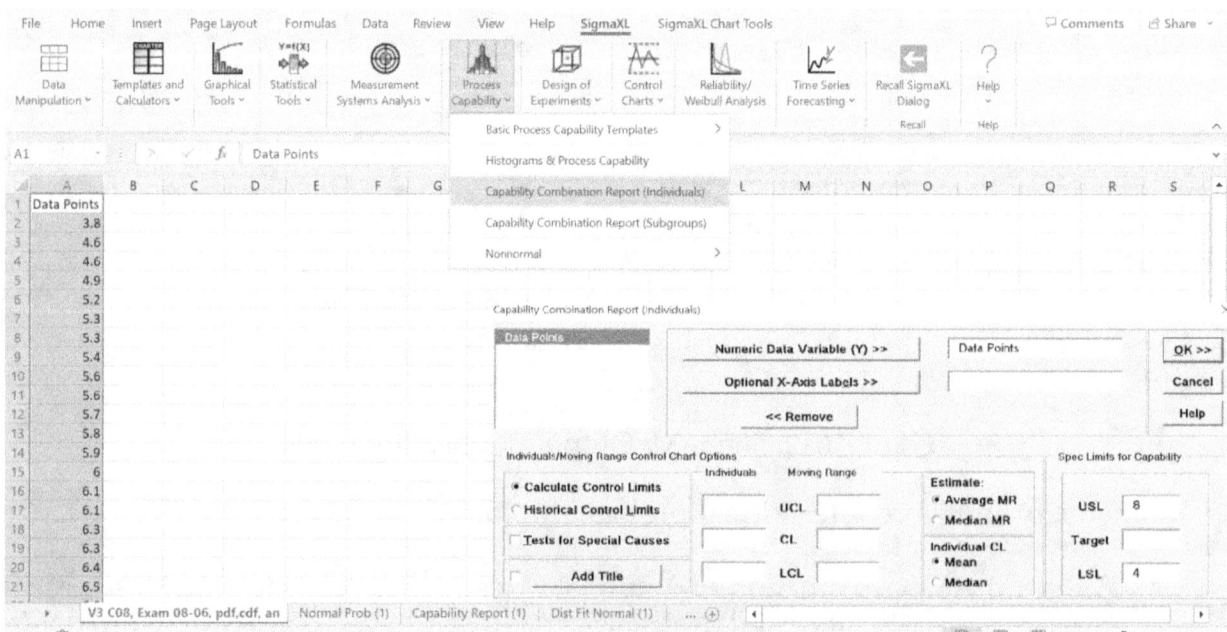

Figure 4.13: SigmaXL Input (Process Capability Combination)

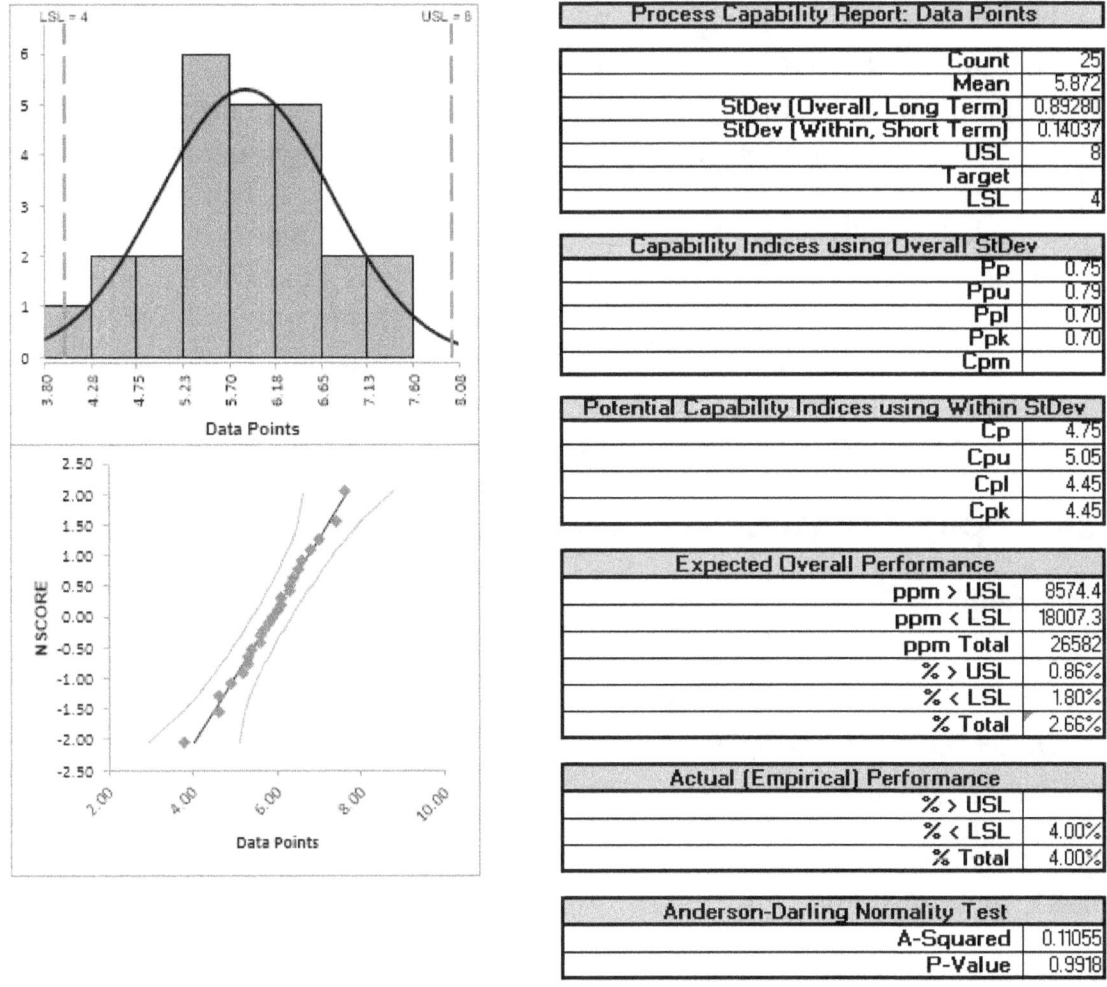

Figure 4.14: SigmaXL Output (Process Capability Report and Probability Plot)

Comments

- We have no reason not to believe data follow a normal distribution, i.e., the data follow a straight line on the probability plot, and the hypothesis of the normality P-value of 0.992 is a higher value than an agreed-to hypothesis-test risk level of 0.05

- The calculated mean is 5.872

- Approximately 0.86% of the population occurrences are above the upper specification limit of 8.0

- About 1.80% of the population occurrences are below the lower specification limit of 4.0

- You can add, remove or change chart elements such as title, labels, gridlines and data labels by clicking on the chart and selecting "+".

Comments

- Often, the output of a process or processes does not have a specification (e.g., work-in-process [WIP]). Using a traditional reporting approach, one cannot make a process capability/performance statement for these no-specification situations.

However, understanding the variation in the magnitude of process-output responses is essential when undertaking process improvement efforts.

- Table-of-numbers reporting and red-yellow-green scorecards do not structurally provide insight into the variability of a process-output reaction. A probability plot can provide this insight. With IEE, a probability plot (which can be lognormal) is included in 30,000-foot-level continuous-response report-outs and can give a process capability/performance statement. For this situation, a report contains the best-estimated mean or median value with an 80% frequency of occurrence (i.e., 4 out of 5 future events expected range). A process capability/performance statement from a probability plot is much easier to interpret than a process capability statement that provides Cp, Cpk, Pp, and Ppk values, as illustrated in Figure 5.8.

4.7   Example: Distribution Fitting with Estimate Percentiles

Estimate Percentile

IEE Volume III Example and Dataset

- *IEE Volume III* Example 8.6: PDF, CDF, then a Probability Plot
- Dataset (Smarter Solutions (2022): V3 C08, Exam 08-06, pdf, CDF, and then prob plot.xlsx

SigmaXL Input/Output

- Figure 4.13: SigmaXL Input (Process Capability Distribution Fitting)
- Figure 4.14: SigmaXL Input (Process Capability Normal Distribution Fitting and Estimate Percentiles)
- Figure 4.15: SigmaXL Output (Process Capability Normal Distribution Fitting and Estimate Percentiles)

Note: Percentiles for a Normal Distribution may be obtained adjacent to a Probability Plot by using SigmaXL>Process Capability>Nonnormal>Distribution Fitting

SigmaXL Chart Function: Choose Process Capability>Non-normal>Distribution Fitting

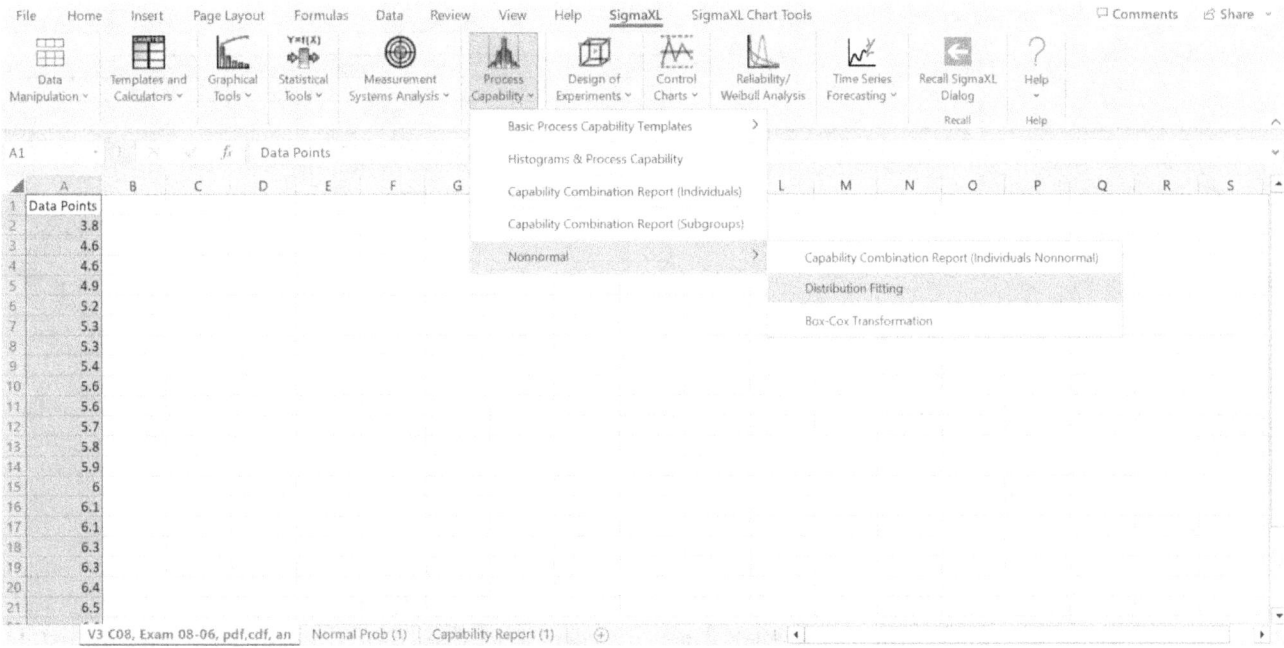

Figure 4.13: SigmaXL Input (Process Capability Distribution Fitting)

Select Specify Distribution>Normal and Estimate Percentiles for 10% and 90%

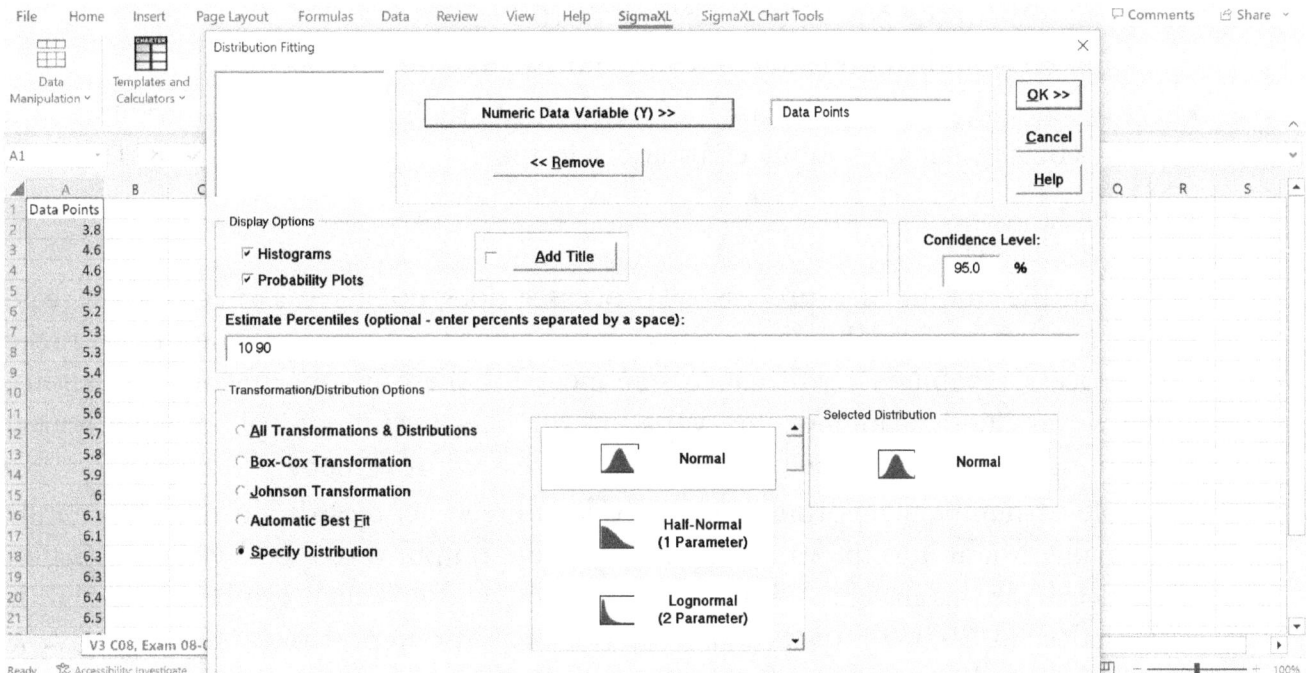

Figure 4.14: SigmaXL Input (Process Capability Normal Distribution Fitting and Estimate Percentiles)

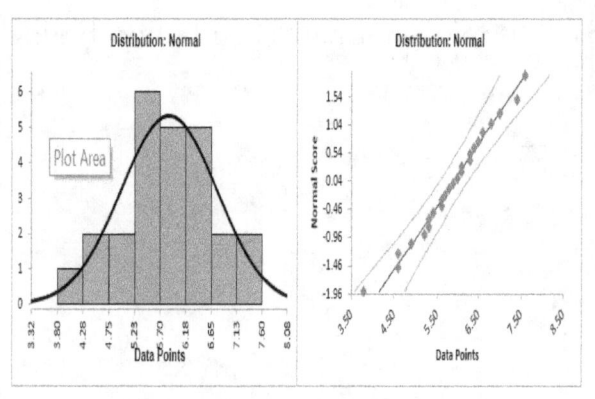

Distribution Fitting Report: Data Points			Model Summary and Goodness-of-Fit	
Distribution: Normal			Log-Likelihood	-32.128
Sample Count	25		Normal	0.110548
Sample Mean	5.872		Normal P-Value	0.9918

Parameter Estimates				
Parameter	Estimate	SE Estimate	Lower 95.0 CI	Upper 95.0 CI
Mean	5.872	0.174953269	5.529097894	6.214902106
StDev	0.892805	0.126270166	0.676695514	1.177992748

Percentile Report				
Percentage	Data Points	SE Percentile	Lower 95.0 CI	Upper 95.0 CI
0.135	3.194	0.417254092	2.375803839	4.011409823
10	4.728	0.238314283	4.260737494	5.194912317
50	5.872	0.174953269	5.529097894	6.214902106
90	7.016175094	0.238319418	6.549077618	7.48327257
99.865	8.550393169	0.41726095	7.732576735	9.368209602

Figure 4.15: SigmaXL Output (Process Capability Normal Distribution Fitting and Estimate Percentiles)

Comments

- We have no reason not to believe data follow a normal distribution, i.e., the data follow a straight line on the probability plot, and the hypothesis of the normality P-value of 0.992 is a higher value than an agreed-to hypothesis-test risk level of 0.05
- The calculated mean is 5.872
- Approximately 10% of the population is below 4.728
- About 90% of the population is below 7.016
- About 80% of the population is 4.728 and 7.016
- You can add, remove or change chart elements such as title, labels, gridlines and data labels by clicking on the chart and selecting "+".

Additional Comments

- Often, the output of a process or processes does not have a specification (e.g., work-in-process [WIP]). Using a traditional reporting approach, one cannot make a process capability/performance statement for these no-specification situations. However, understanding the variation in the magnitude of process-output responses is essential when undertaking process improvement efforts.
- Table-of-numbers reporting and red-yellow-green scorecards do not structurally provide insight into the variability of a process-output reaction. A probability plot can provide this insight. With IEE, a probability plot (which can be lognormal) is included in 30,000-foot-level continuous-response report-outs and can give a process capability/performance statement. For this situation, a report contains the best-estimated mean or median value with an 80% frequency of occurrence (i.e., 4 out of 5 future events expected range). A process capability/performance statement from a probability plot is much easier to interpret than a process capability statement that provides Cp, Cpk, Pp, and Ppk values, as illustrated in Figure 5.8.

5 Traditional Control Charting and Process Capability Indices

Reference: *IEE Volume III*, Chapters 10 and 11

Background: Shewhart control charts track processes by plotting data over time. *The only purpose of control charts is to identify special cause conditions, as determined through the chart's mathematical equations, to stimulate timely actions for these special-identified-cause issues. Control charts can track either variables (continuous response) or attribute (e.g., failure rate) process output parameters. Control charts do not quantify process capability/performance.*

5.1   Example: $\bar{x}$ and R Control Chart

The $\bar{x}$ and R chart displays a control chart for subgroup means and a control chart for subgroup ranges in the same graph window. By seeing both charts together, allows you to track both the process level and process variation at the same time and detect the presence of special causes.

Use $\bar{x}$ and R chart to track the process level and process variation for samples size 8 or less. For samples larger than 8 use $\bar{x}$ and S chart.

Control chart of variables subgroup data

IEE Volume III Example and Dataset

- *IEE Volume III* Example 10.1: $\bar{x}$ and R Control Chart
- Dataset (Smarter Solutions (2022): V3 C10, Exam 10-01, x-bar and R.xlsx

SigmaXL Input/Output

- Figure 5.1: SigmaXL Input ($\bar{x}$ and R Control Chart)
- Figure 5.2: SigmaXL Output ($\bar{x}$ and R Control Chart)

SigmaXL Chart Function: Control Charts>Xbar & R

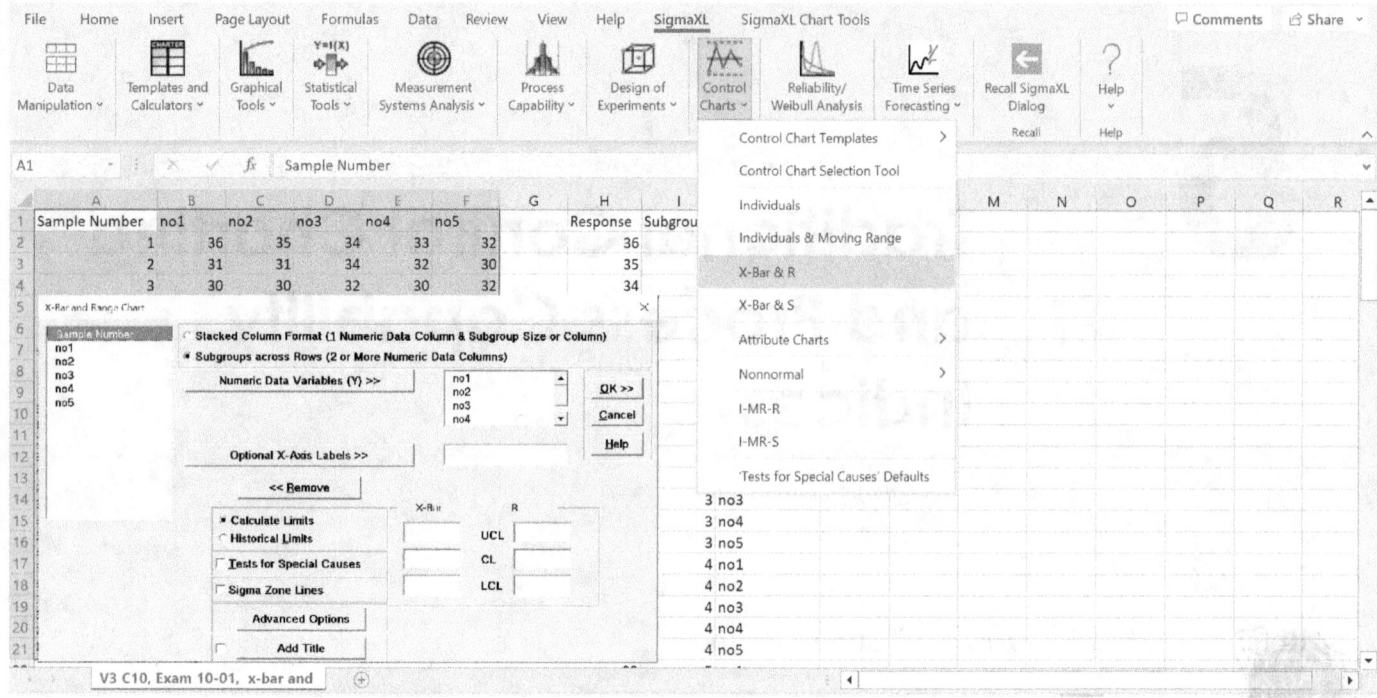

Figure 5.1: SigmaXL Input ($\bar{x}$ and R Control Chart)

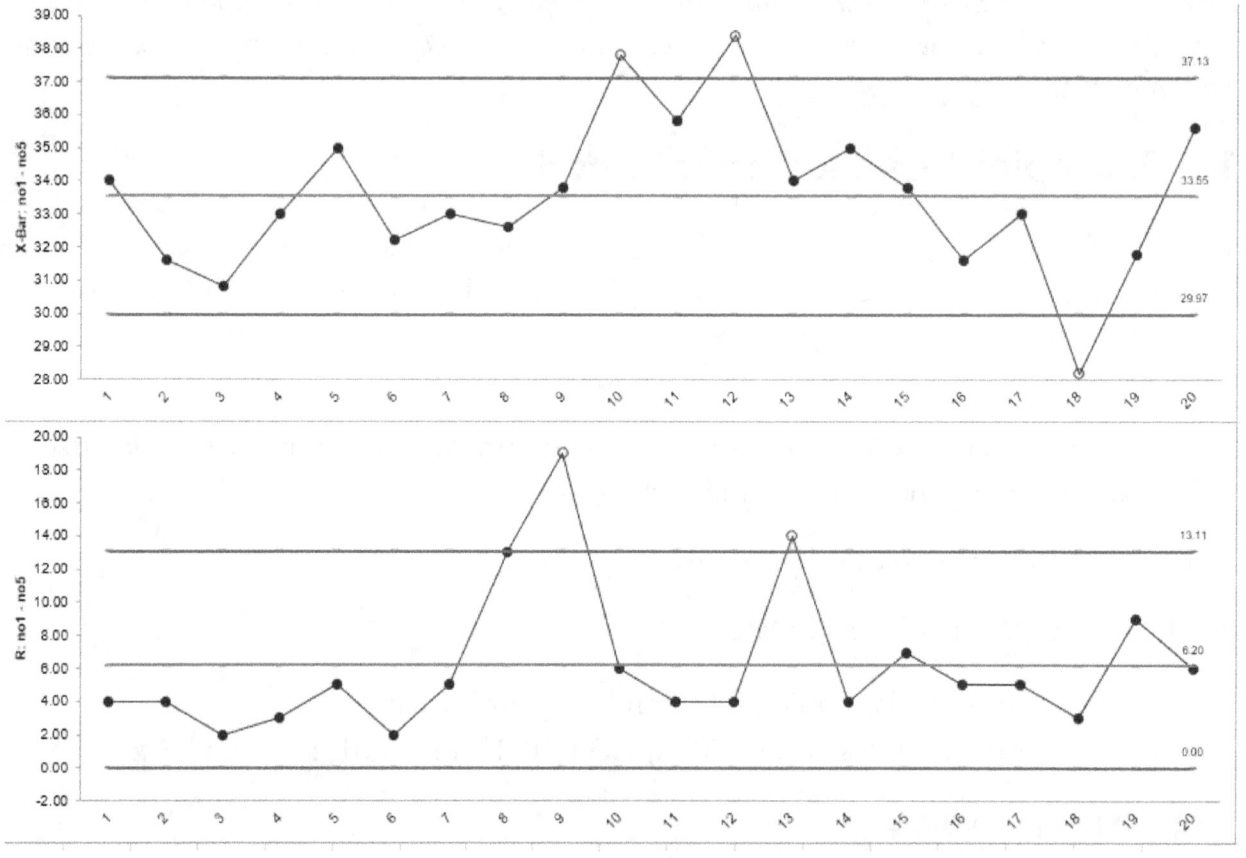

Figure 5.2: SigmaXL Output SigmaXL Input ($\bar{x}$ and R Control Chart)

Comment

- The control chart has out-of-control signals
- You can add, remove or change chart elements such as title, labels, gridlines and data labels by clicking on the chart and selecting "+".

5.2   Example: XmR Chart

The XmR is an Individuals chart and Moving Range chart in the same graph window. By seeing both charts together allows you to track both the process level and process variation at the same time and detect special cause variation.

Control chart of variables (continuous response), no subgroup data

- *IEE Volume III* Example and Dataset
- *IEE Volume III* Example 10.2: XmR Charts

Dataset (Smarter Solutions (2022): V3 C10, Exam 10-02, xmr chart.xlsx

SigmaXL Input/Output

- Figure 5.3: SigmaXL Input (XmR Chart)
- Figure 5.4: SigmaXL Output (XmR Chart)

SigmaXL Chart Function: Control Charts> Individuals & Moving Range

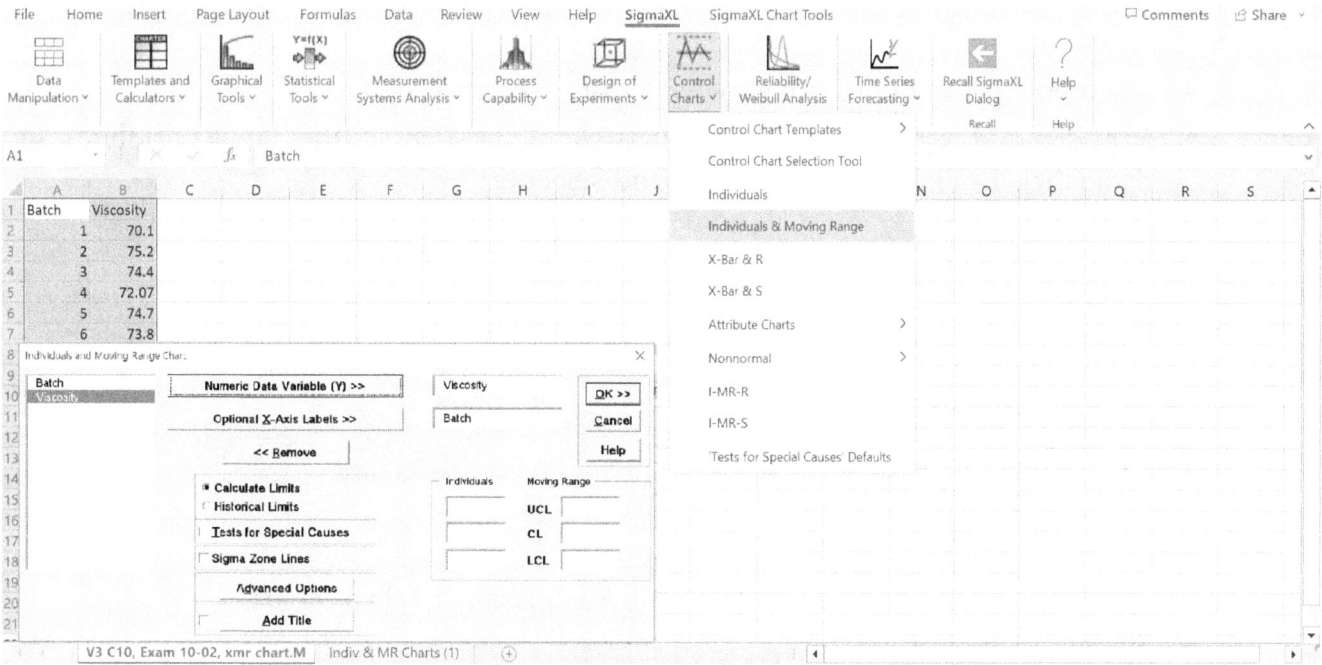

Figure 5.3: SigmaXL Input (XmR Chart)

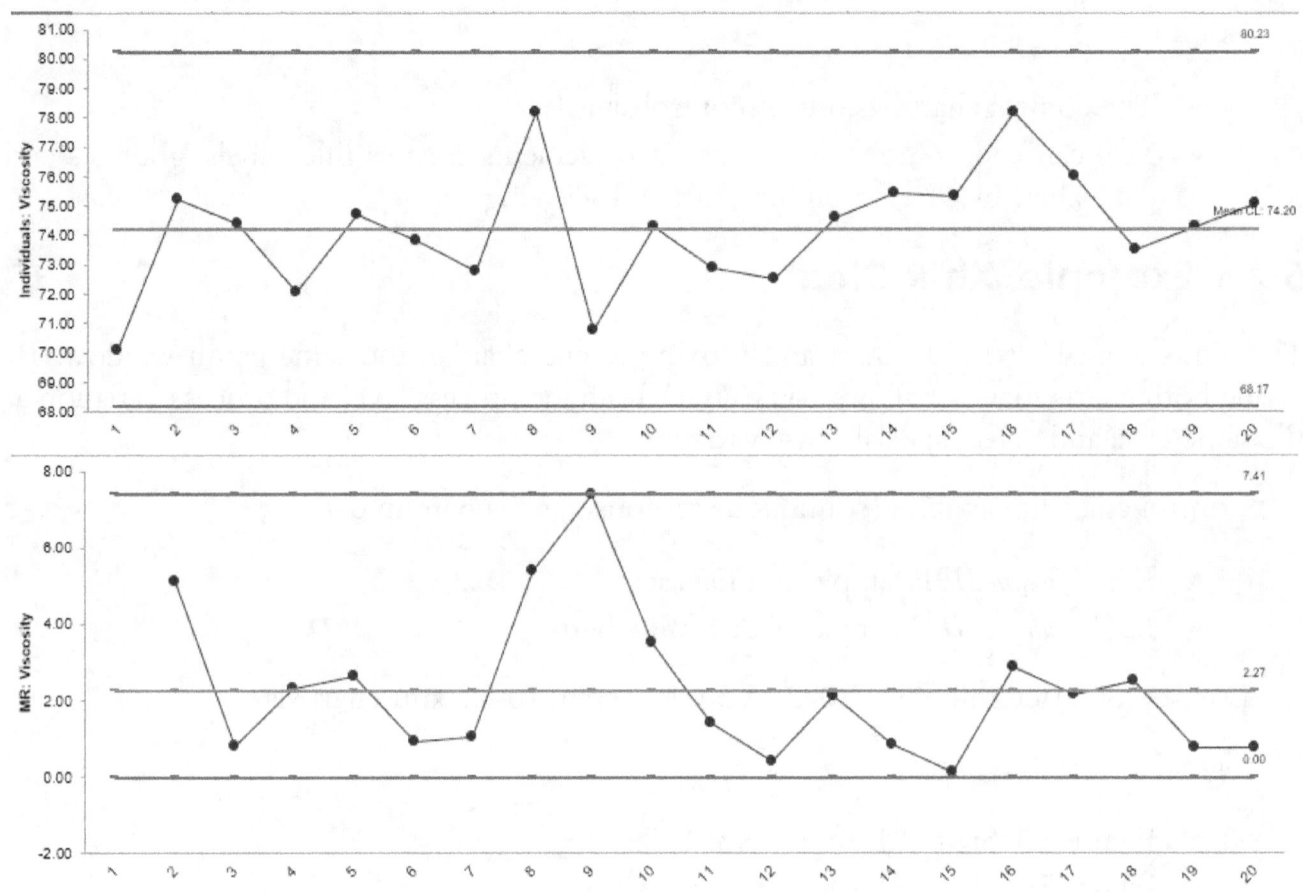

Figure 5.4: SigmaXL Output (XmR Chart)

Comment

- The control chart does not show any out-of-control signals
- You can add, remove or change chart elements such as title, labels, gridlines and data labels by clicking on the chart and selecting "+".

5.3   Example: P-Chart

The P chart tracks the proportion defective and detects the presence of special causes.

Control chart of a non-conformance rate

IEE Volume III Example and Dataset

- *IEE Volume III* Example 10.3: p-chart
- Dataset (Smarter Solutions (2022): V3 C10, Exam 10-03, p chart
- SigmaXL Input/Output
- Figure 5.5: SigmaXL Input (p-chart)
- Figure 5.6: SigmaXL Output (p-chart)

SigmaXL Chart Function: Control Charts>Attribute Charts>P

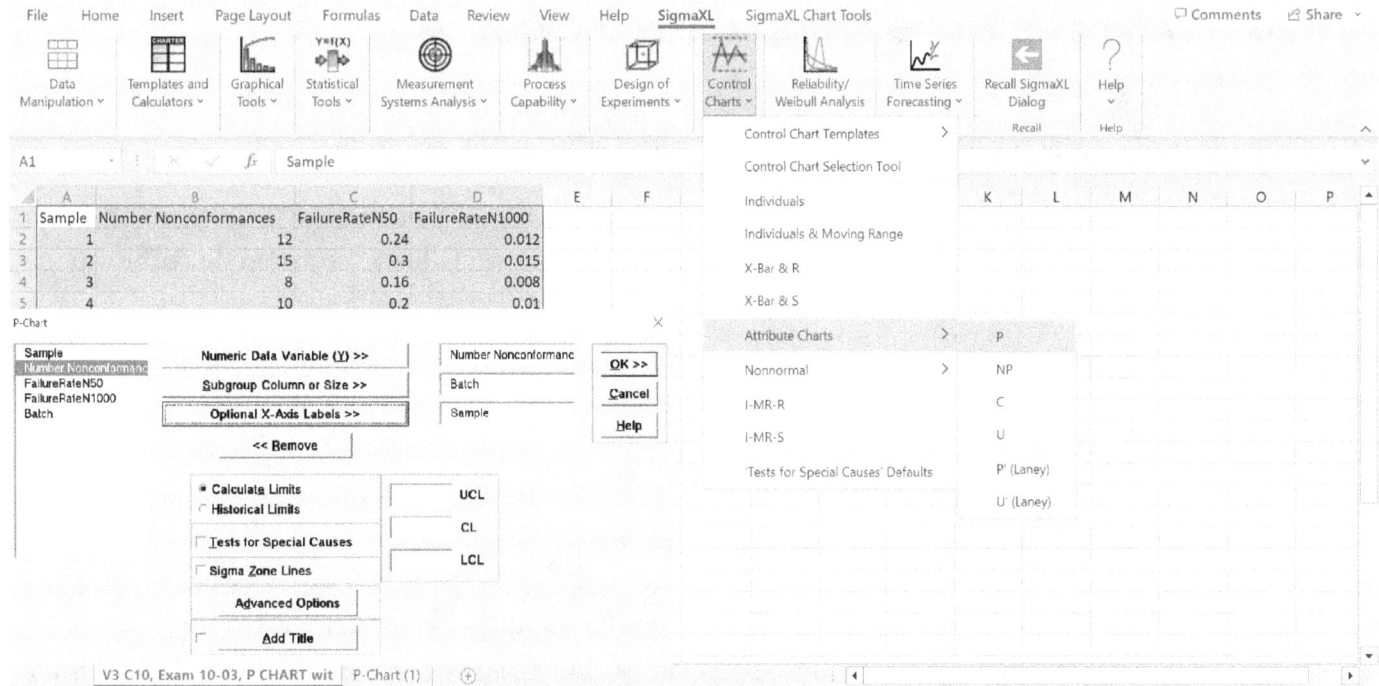

Figure 5.5: SigmaXL Input (p-chart)

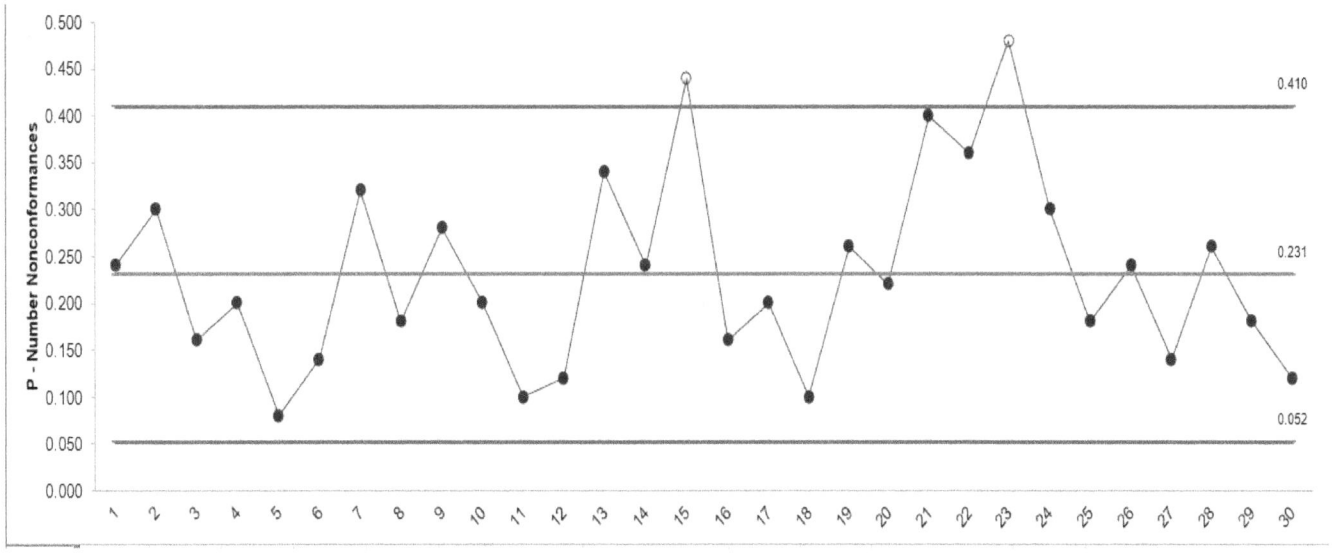

Figure 5.6: SigmaXL Output (p-chart)

Comment

- This control chart has two out-of-control signals.
- You can add, remove or change chart elements such as title, labels, gridlines and data labels by clicking on the chart and selecting "+".

5.4   Example: Process Capability Indices

A process is said to be capable when the $\pm$ 3 standard deviation points of the distribution of individual measurements are contained well within the specification limits.

You can use capability analysis when your data are from a normal distribution. If data is non normal, you will typically need to transform your data to follow a normal distribution (see non normal data section of the book).

The SigmaXL capability report includes: the histogram and capability statistics (within and overall).

Process Capability Indices for Continuous Data

IEE Volume III Example and Dataset

- *IEE Volume III* Example 11.1: Process Capability/Performance Indices
- Dataset (Smarter Solutions (2022): V3 C11, Exam 11-01, process capability.xlsx

SigmaXL Input/Output

- Figure 5.7: SigmaXL Input (Process Capability Indices – Specifications Limits of 24 and 50)
- Figure 5.8: SigmaXL Output (Process Capability Indices – Specifications Limits of 24 and 50)

SigmaXL Chart Function: Process Capability>Capability Combination Report (Subgroups)

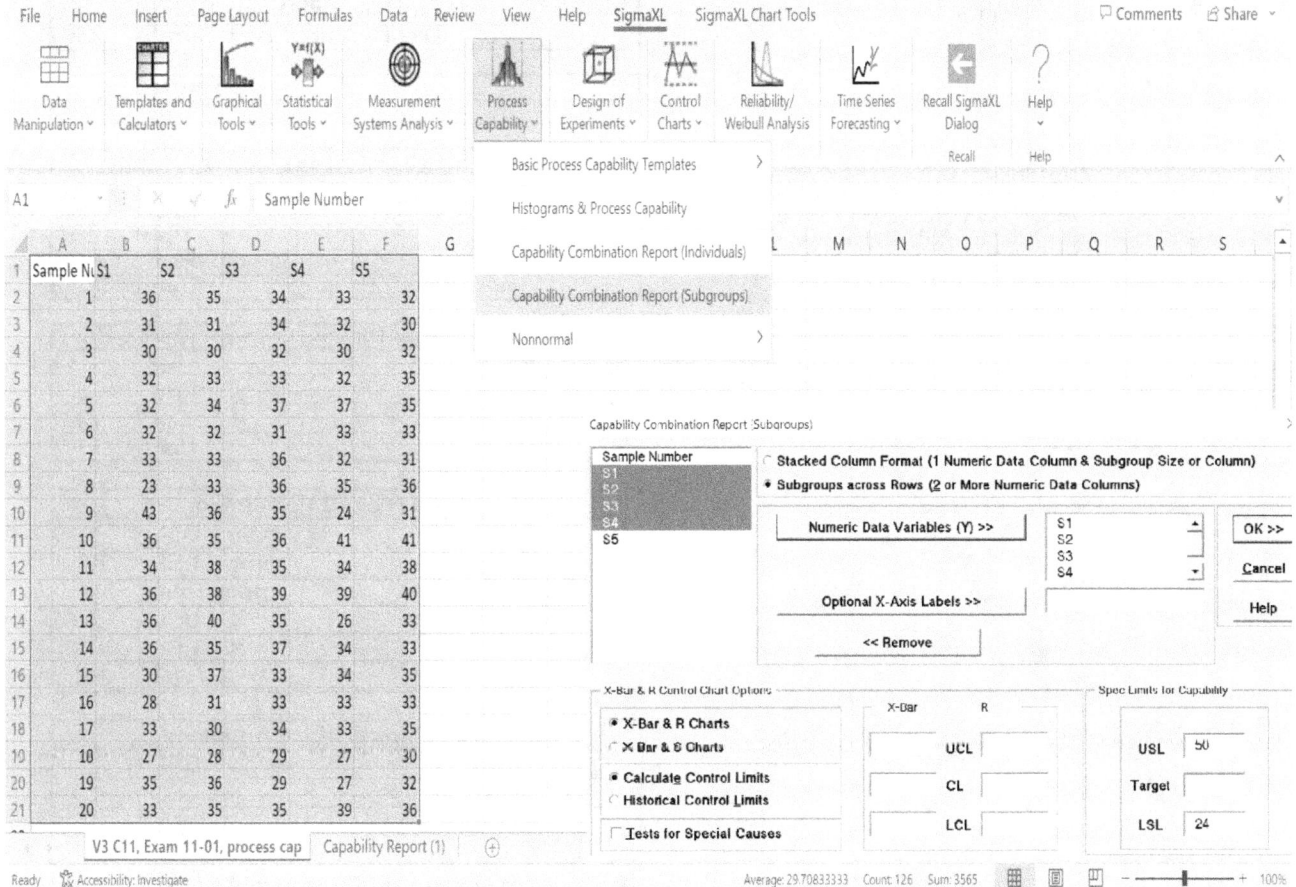

Figure 5.7: SigmaXL Input (Process Capability Indices – Specifications Limits of 24 and 50)

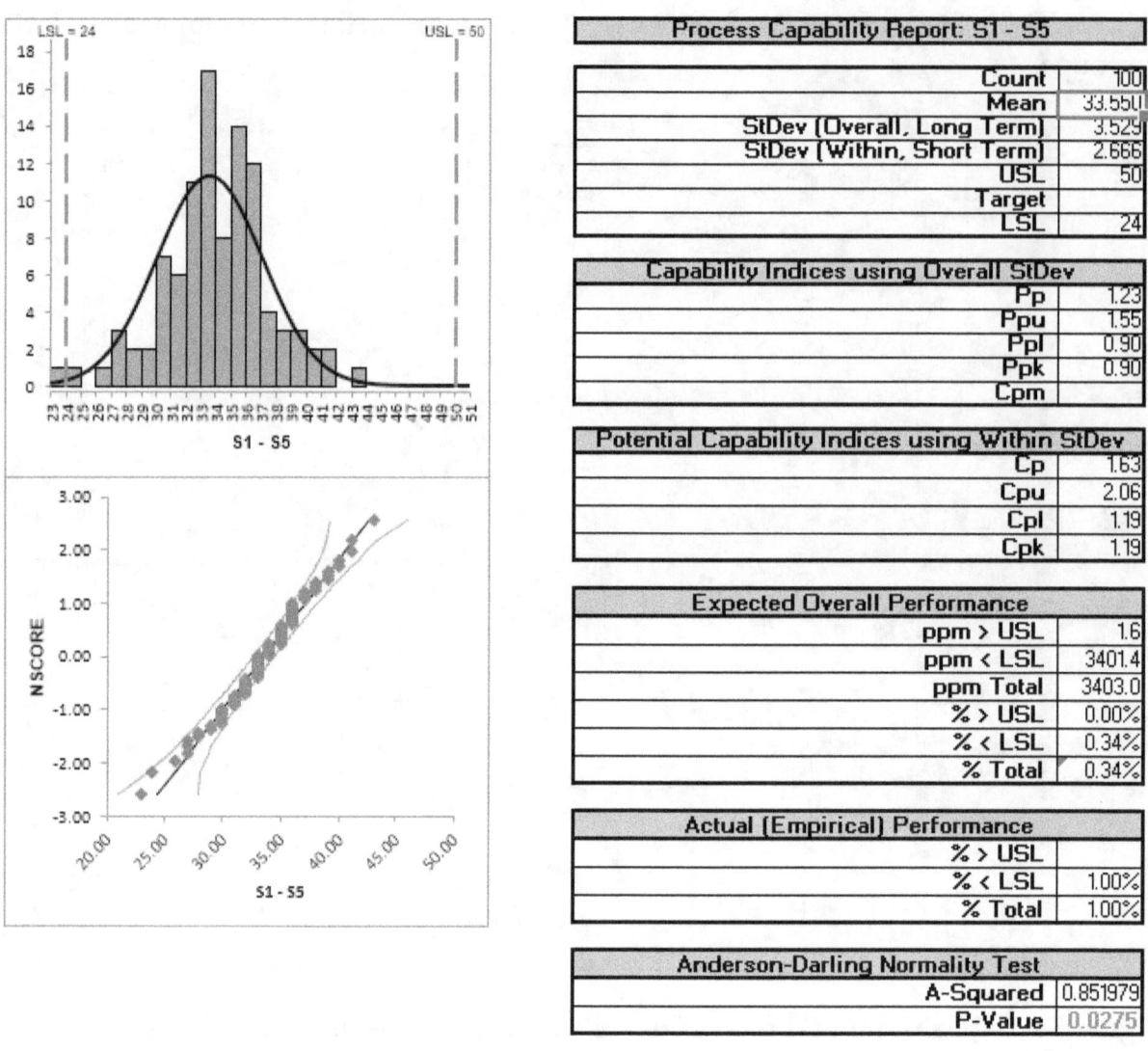

Figure 5.8: SigmaXL Output (Process Capability Indices – Specifications Limits of 24 and 50)

Comments

- This process capability report provides process capability indices statements (i.e., Cp=1.63, Cpk=1.19, Pp=1.23, Ppk=0.90), which people typically have difficulty understanding and can be dependent upon the sampling procedure from the monitored process.

- The results from a probability plot are easier to understand and do not have the sample-collection issues that traditional process capability indices have.

- You can add, remove or change chart elements such as title, labels, gridlines and data labels by clicking on the chart and selecting "+".

5.5 Traditional Control Charts and Process Capability Indices Reporting Versus 30,000-foot-level Reports

In the second half of the 1920s, when Dr. Walter A. Shewhart of Bell Telephone Laboratories developed a theory of statistical quality control, he concluded that there were two components to variations displayed in all manufacturing processes. The first component was steady, i.e., a random variation response that appeared to be inherent in the process. The second component was an intermittent variation to assignable causes.

Shewhart concluded that assignable causes could be economically discovered and removed with a practical diagnostic program incorporating fundamental process changes. Dr. Shewhart is given credit for developing the standard control chart test based on 3σ limits to separate the steady component of variation from assignable causes. Because of war production efforts, in the 1940s, Shewhart control charts were widely used.

Deming notes (Deming 1986): "A fault in the interpretation of observations, seen everywhere, is to suppose that every event (defect, mistake, accident) is attributable to someone (usually the one nearest at hand), or is related to some special event. The fact is that most troubles with service and production lie in the system." Dr. Deming adds: "We shall speak of faults of the system as common causes of trouble and faults from fleeting events as special causes." Dr. Deming elaborates further: "Confusion between common causes and special causes leads to frustration of everyone, and leads to greater variability and higher costs, exactly contrary to what is needed. I should estimate that in my experience, most troubles and possibilities for improvement add up to proportions something like this: 94% belong to the system (responsibility of management), 6% special."

Control charts offer the study of variation and its source over time. Control charts can provide monitoring and control and the time-stamp identification of improvements. Control charts can reflect either a Shewhart or Deming point of view, which are:

- Shewhart: Control charts can identify assignable causes that could be internal or external to the system.
- Deming: Control charts can separate a process's special from common cause issues, where special causes originate from fleeting events experienced by the system and common causes arise from the natural variation of the process that is both internal and external to the system.

There can be a significant difference in identifying out-of-control conditions for a given process situation for these two charting approaches. This two-chart difference is a substantial issue since reacting to fix the problem of the day when it is a common cause issue as though it were a special-cause event adds little, if any, value to the long-term performance of the process. The high-level viewpoint for a process-output response using an IEE 30,000-foot-level reporting methodology aligns with Dr. Deming's philosophy. With 30,000-foot-level reporting, process stability is determined using an individuals chart, not an x-bar and R chart, p-chart, or c-chart. The reasons for using an individuals chart instead of other control charting methodologies is described in

- "Issues and Resolution to xbar and R chart Formula Problems" (Smarter Solutions 2015c)
- "Issues and Resolution to P-chart Control Limits Formula False Signals" (Smarter Solutions 2015b)
- "Issues and Resolution to C-chart Formula Problems" (Smarter Solutions 2015d)

A traditional Shewhart explanation of the value of control charts is that control charts can give early identification of special causes for timely resolution before producing many poor-quality parts/transactions. This timely reaction can be beneficial; however, organizations often focus only on the output of a process when applying control charts. This measurement type does not control the process and may not offer timely problem identification. We prefer to monitor the key process input variables to manage a process using control charts. The process flow should then be stopped for timely resolution when the variable goes out of control or at an undesirable level (See pre-control charts in *IEE Volume III*, Chapter 38).

IEE discourages the use of sigma quality-level metrics. In addition, there can be much confusion about traditional process capability and process performance indices such as Cp, Cpk, Pp, and Ppk. Sometimes, I am asked bizarre questions about how to calculate, transform, or interpret a process capability or process performance indices. I typically ask the person how long she has worked with these metrics. This person might give a response of three years. I reply, "I understand that you are confused, and I have no reason to doubt your intelligence. If you are confused by these indices after working with them for several years, how can we expect the CEO and line workers to understand and embrace this reporting?" I typically get the response that they are also confused about how to transition the report to the physical world. I then respond that she should use alternative metrics for this reporting.

The following two chapters describe implementing the IEE alternative high-level measurement system process for various situations, as summarized in *IEE Volume III* Figure 12.1. Individual measurement report tracking is accomplished through the IEE scorecard/dashboard metric reporting process as follows:

1. An infrequent subgroup/sampling plan is determined so that the typical variability from process input factors occurs between subgroups or periods, e.g., by day, week, or month.
2. An individuals-chart is used to determine whether the process response is stable. The process is considered predictable if the output response has a recent stability region.

3. When the process is considered predictable, a prediction statement is formulated for the latest stability region. The usual reporting format for this prediction statement is:

   a. When there is a specification requirement, report a nonconformance rate percentage.
   b. When there are no specification limits for a continuous response, report the expected mean or median response and 80% frequency of occurrence rate.

These techniques usually are associated with manufacturing processes. However, these analysis techniques are beneficial for assessing parameters in other business areas, e.g., the time required to process an invoice.

IEE uses the term process capability/performance metric to describe a process's predictive output in terms everyone can easily understand, i.e., step 3 in the above process. It is important to note that this metric reporting format is consistent for both continuous and attribute failure rate responses. This consistency is unlike traditional reporting, where continuous-response outputs lead to reporting process capability and process performance indices (See *IEE Volume III*, Chapter 11) and attribute responses lead to reporting a proportion rate for non-conformance.

Customers often ask for process capability and performance indices; hence, these metrics can be calculated and supplied to customers. However, organizations should strongly consider the IEE 30,000-foot-level reporting methods as the approach they use for their internal measurement reporting system. In addition, they should think about what they might do to educate their customers on the value of this alternative metric reporting methodology.

To reiterate, IEE utilizes individuals-charts to examine processes from a high-level viewpoint for assessing process-output response stability, which is consistent with Dr. Deming's philosophy. 30,000-foot-level reporting can offer much more value to an organization than current process control charting techniques.

As noted earlier, Dr. Deming stated that 94% of the troubles in a process belong to the system (common cause); only 6% are special-cause. With the IEE approach, an individuals-control chart might illustrate to management and others that past firefighting activities have resulted from reacting to common cause issues as though they were special-cause events. This overreacting to typical process noise up-and-down variation is an expensive approach with little value.

The IEE approach does not view typical short-term variation as special-cause excursions but as noise to the overall process response. If the process is determined to be predictable, and the response level is undesirable, there is a pull for an improvement project creation. Within IEE improvement projects, inputs and their magnitudes are examined collectively over the process's stable/predictable period to determine areas to give focus for process improvement opportunities.

6

IEE-DMAIC — Measure Phase (Baseline Project): IEE 30,000-foot-level Report (Continuous Response)

6.1 IEE-DMAIC Roadmap Component

Book 1 Reference: *IEE Volume III*, Chapter 12

Book 2 Reference: Lean Six Sigma Project Execution Guide – Section 3

Internet: www.smartersolutions.com/roadmap (clicking on highlighted area provides the flowchart below)

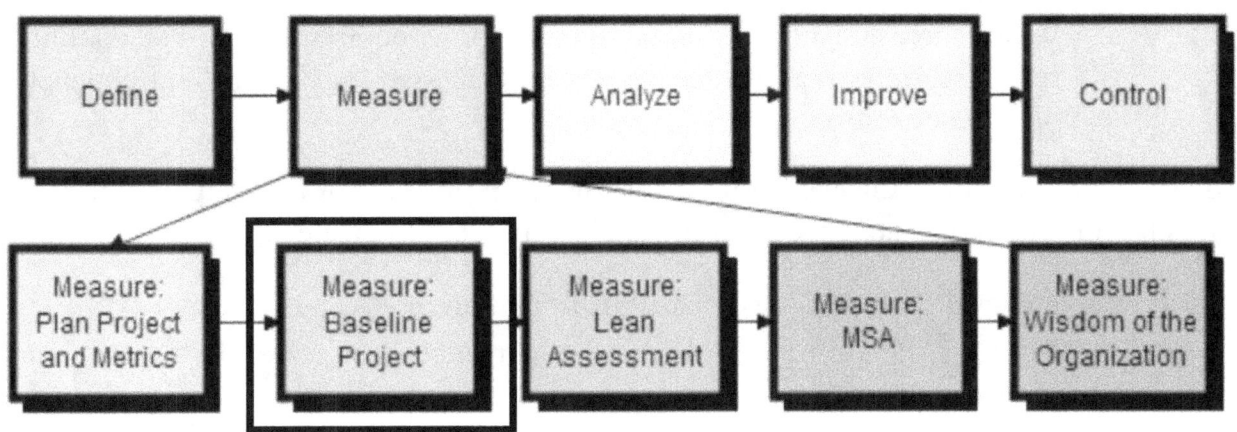

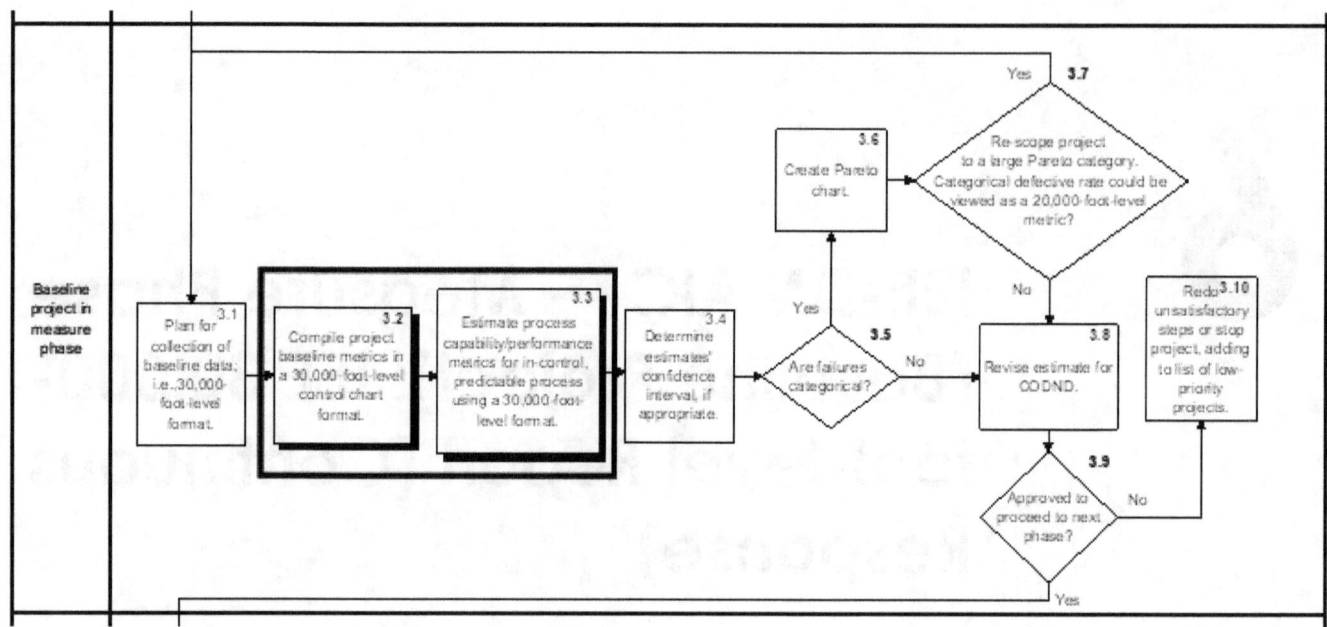

The above graphic highlights the IEE-DMAIC roadmap steps described in this chapter.

This chapter and the next chapter elaborate more on the IEE scorecard/dashboard two-step creation process, which is:

1. Assess the process for stability. If the process is stable, the process response is considered predictable.
2. When the process is predictable, formulate a prediction statement for the latest stability region. The usual reporting format for this statement is:

   a. When there is a specification requirement, report the non-conformance percentage rate
   b. When there are no functional specification requirements for a continuous response, report a median or mean response and an 80% frequency of occurrence rate

This chapter describes the execution of this two-step process for a variety of continuous-output charting situations; i.e., this chapter will illustrate how to create a:

- Satellite-level scorecard/dashboard profit margin plot
- 30,000-foot-level on-time delivery performance scorecard/dashboard metric reporting statement

In this assessment, the initial data compiling describes the voice of the process (VOP). A gap assessment compares the voice of the process to the voice of the customer expectations, e.g., specifications. This chapter describes how to use an individuals-30,000-foot-level report to assess process stability and then, if a process is stable, provide a prediction statement as to how well the voice of the process meets the voice of the customer desires.

The baseline project in the measure phase 3.2 and 3.3 drill-down steps shown above provides the decision trees for 30,000-foot-level individuals charting and process capability/performance metric reporting. Figures 12.1 and 12.2 in *IEE Volume III* describe these drill-downs, highlighting the continuous-data branch. A similar drill down is available through the clickable www.smartersolutions.com/roadmap link.

This chapter describes the IEE 30,000-foot-level reporting of these drill downs for continuous process output data, while the next chapter describes the use of these drill downs for non-conformance rate attribute data.

Figure 6.1 shows the drill-down of step 3.2 of the IEE-DMAIC project execution roadmap for a continuous output response option highlighted.

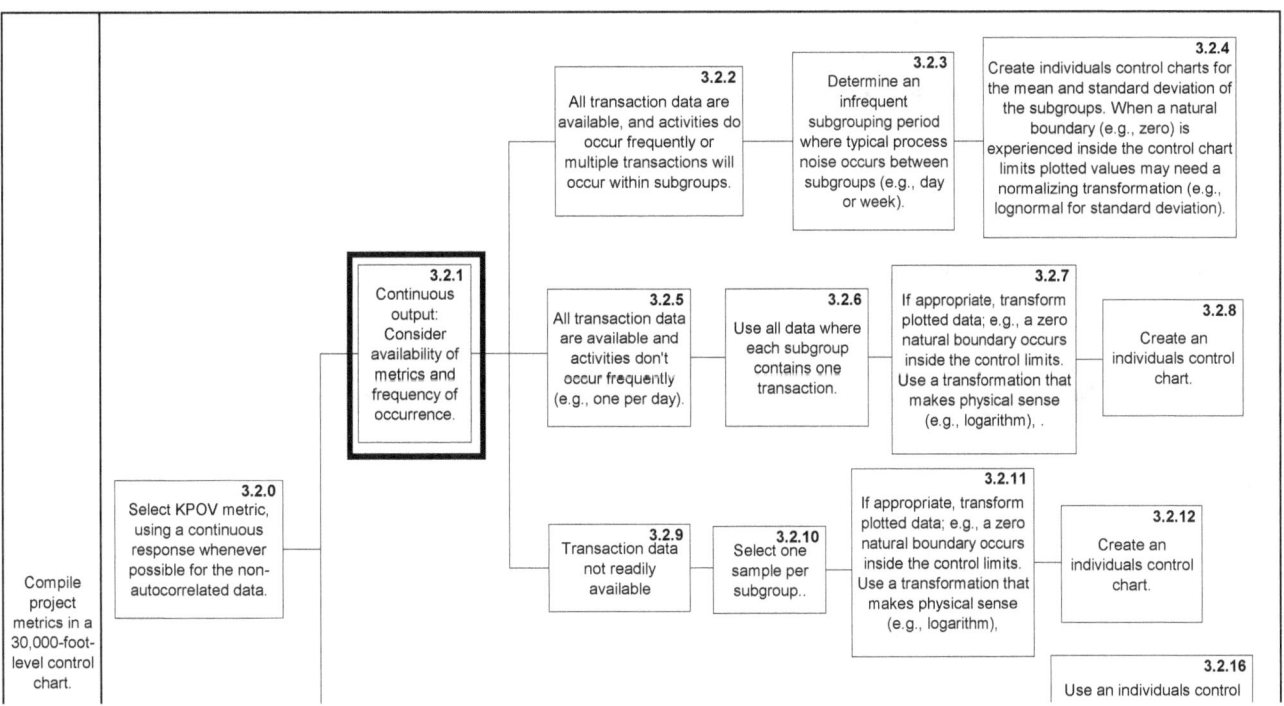

Figure 6.1: Process Stability Assessment Chart Selection for a Continuous Response

Figure 6.2 shows the IEE 30,000-foot-level process capability/performance metric decision tree for stable processes, i.e., a drill-down of step 3.3 of the IEE-DMAIC project execution roadmap with a continuous output response option highlighted.

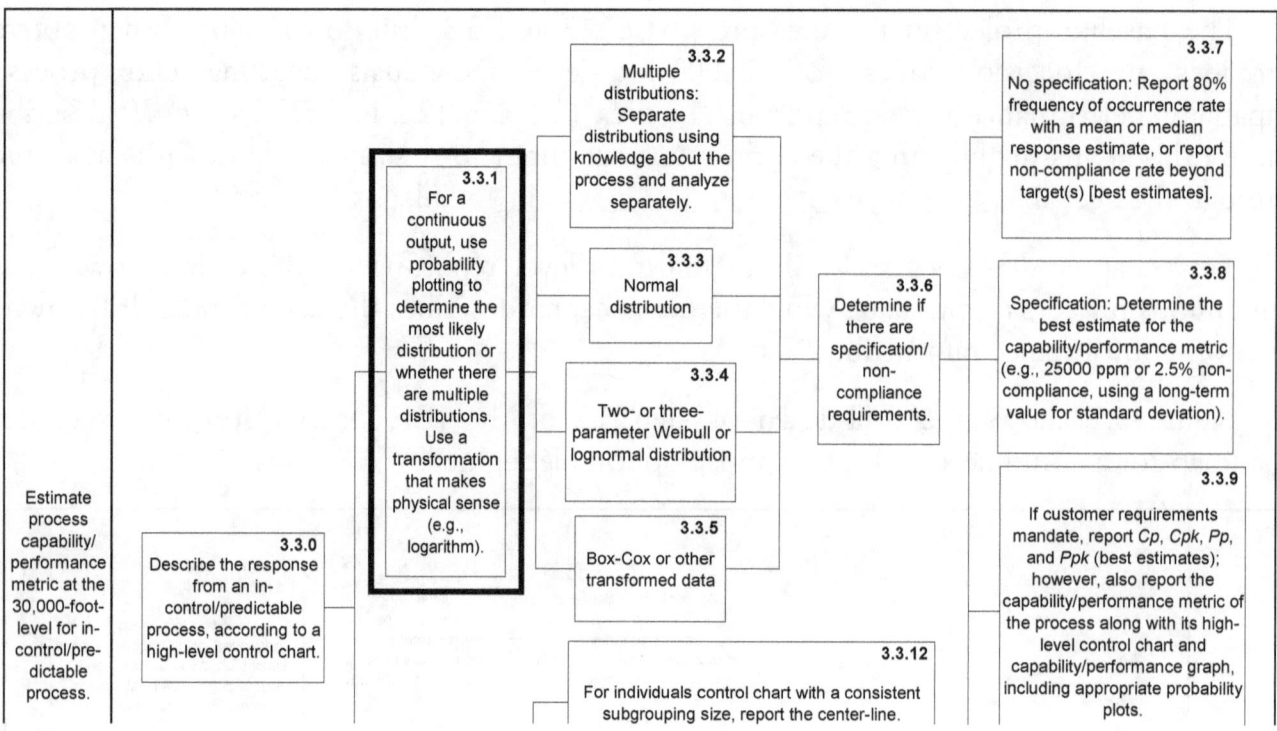

Figure 6.2: Process Capability/Performance Statement from Stable Processes for a Continuous Response

6.2   30,000-foot-level Reporting for a Continuous Response

Application: The methodologies described in this section apply to the creation of 30,000-foot-level reports for the following process assessments that have specification requirements (Reference Figures 6.1 and 6.2):

- One sample per chemical batch where there are upper and lower specifications
- DSO (days sales outstanding) when there is an upper criterion for the number of days late beyond a due date
- Duration of all infrequent equipment changeover times when there is an upper criterion for task completion time
- Hold time in a call center when there is an upper criterion for the time to complete the task
- Time in the checkout line at a store when there is a lower- and upper-time criterion
- One sampled part/process measurement daily, where the part has an upper and lower specification
- The time for filling one weekly-sampled customer order, where there is a maximum time requirement

The roadmap steps for this IEE application are:

1. Assess process stability using a 30,000-foot-level individuals chart(s) (Figure 6.1):

   o Continuous output [3.2.1] – All transaction data are available, and activities don't occur frequently (e.g., one per day)

      ▪ [3.2.5] – Use all data where each subgroup contains one transaction
      ▪ [3.2.6] – If appropriate, transform the data
      ▪ [3.2.7] – Create an individuals control chart [3.2.8]

   o Continuous output [3.2.1] – Not readily available transaction data

      ▪ [3.2.9] – Transaction data that are not readily available
      ▪ [3.2.10] – Select one sample per group
      ▪ [3.2.11] – If appropriate, transform the data
      ▪ [3.2.12] – Create an individuals control chart

2. Determine process capability/performance for stable (predictable processes) (Figure 6.2). For a continuous output, use probability plotting to determine the most likely distribution or whether there are multiple distributions and reporting capability/performance for stable processes

   o [3.3.1] – Use probability plot to determine distribution
   o [3.3.6] – Determine if there are specification/non-compliance requirements
   o 3.3.8] (for example) – Specification: Determine the best estimate for the capability/performance metric (e.g., 25,000 ppm or 2.5% non-compliance, using a long-term value for standard deviation).

6.3 Application Examples: IEE 30,000-foot-level and Satellite Metric Reports

- Satellite-level metric: The last three-year EBITDA (i.e., earnings before interest, taxes, depreciation, and amortization) for a company was reported monthly with an individuals-control chart where no values were beyond the individuals-chart upper control limit (UCL) and lower control limit (LCL) lines and no trends appeared. This measured over-time response is considered stable; hence, predictable. Data in the probability plot followed a straight line. The system's process capability/performance metric was determined from the report's probability plot as a best-estimate mean monthly value with an 80% frequency of occurrence. The organization then set a goal to improve the measurement response—a strategic plan to improve this metric aligned with the organizational objective to improve this satellite-level metric. The organization selected 30,000-foot-level operational metrics to improve and created IEE-DMAIC execution plans to enhance these metrics.

- Transactional 30,000-foot-level metric: There was a selection of one random paid invoice every day from the last fifteen months of invoices from a stable process, i.e., days sales outstanding (DSO), with a reporting of the number of days beyond the due date. There was a report of the difference in payment date from its scheduled date for each sample in a lognormal individuals chart; there was no datum point beyond the individuals' chart UCL and LCL lines. A lognormal probability plot fits the data well. Data in the probability plot followed a straight line. The lognormal probability plot provided an estimate for the proportion of invoices beyond 30 days late at the bottom of the report-out. Since this percentage value was unacceptable, an IEE project was initiated to improve this DSO metric.

- Transactional 30,000-foot-level metric: There was the tracking of the mean and standard deviation response of all DSOs using a weekly subgrouping in two individual control charts. No datum point was beyond the individuals' chart UCL and LCL lines. At the bottom of the report, the process's long-term process capability/performance metric was reported as the percentage of individual transactions beyond 30 days. If this futuristic projection is not acceptable, there is a need for process improvement.

- Manufacturing 30,000-foot-level metric: One random sample of a manufactured part was selected daily over the last year. The diameter of the production part was measured and plotted in an individuals chart, where no value was beyond the individuals chart UCL and LCL lines. Data in the probability plot followed a straight line. The long-term process capability/performance metric was reported at the bottom of the chart as the estimated percentage non-conformance rate beyond the specification limits, as determined from the chart's probability plot. If this futuristic projection is not acceptable, there is a need for process improvement.

- Transactional and Manufacturing 30,000-foot-level lead time metric (i.e., a Lean metric): One transaction was randomly selected each day over the last year, where there was a measurement and reporting of the time from order entry to fulfillment. No value was beyond the individuals-chart UCL and LCL lines, and data in the probability plot followed a straight line. The long-term process capability/performance metric was stated at the bottom of the report as an estimated mean and 80% frequency of occurrence rate. If this futuristic projection is not acceptable, there is a need for process improvement.

- Transactional and Manufacturing 30,000-foot-level inventory metric or satellite-level TOC metric (i.e., a Lean metric): There was tracking and reporting of monthly inventory in an individuals-chart. No values were beyond the individuals' chart UCL and LCL lines, and data in the probability plot followed a straight line. The long-term process capability/performance metric was reported as the mean expected inventory levels with an 80% month-to-month occurrence rate. If this futuristic projection is not acceptable, there is a need for process improvement.

6.4 Using a Free App to Create 30,000-foot-level and Satellite-level Reports

Figures 1.17 and 1.19 provide examples of 30,000-foot-level reports. This section introduces the usage of an Enterprise Performance Reporting System (EPRS) metric app that one can freely apply to create 30,000-foot-level reports for their Excel spreadsheet-formatted datasets. This app generated the 30,000-foot-level and satellite-level reports in this chapter and other chapters within this book.

An organization can also create and automatically update 30,000-foot-level reports behind its firewall. See "Integrated Enterprise Excellence (IEE) Business Management System Software" (Smarter Solutions 2019) for information about how to develop automatically updated 30,000-foot-level reports and more.

"Free Business Process Management Software" (Smarter Solutions 2020) provides access to the free EPRS metric-app. In addition to app access, more than ten instructional videos on how to use this app are provided, as shown in Figure 6.3.

Figure 6.3: Free 30,000-foot-level Reporting App Webpage

After signing up for the app, Figure 6.4 will appear on the user's computer. Figures 6.4 – 6.10 include how-to-use statements for this app.

EPRS Metrics Tool App
EPRS Metrics Tool App
View Instructions
View Instructional Videos
View Example Datasets
20 example Excel data sets are available through this tab. When clicking a dataset, the Excel file is downloaded to your computer.
IEE Chart Builder
File input data can be from an Excel spreadsheet of an attribute failure rate or continuous (no-subgrouped or subgrouped) response data.

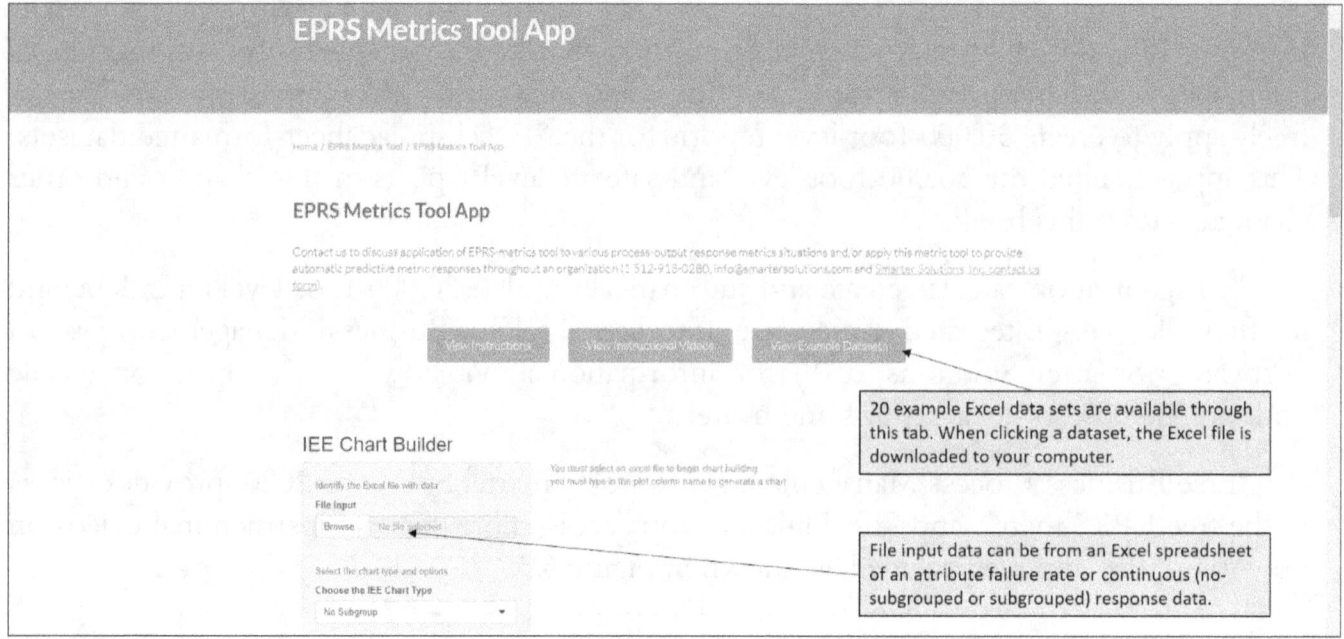

Figure 6.4: EPRS Metric-App – Image 1 of 7

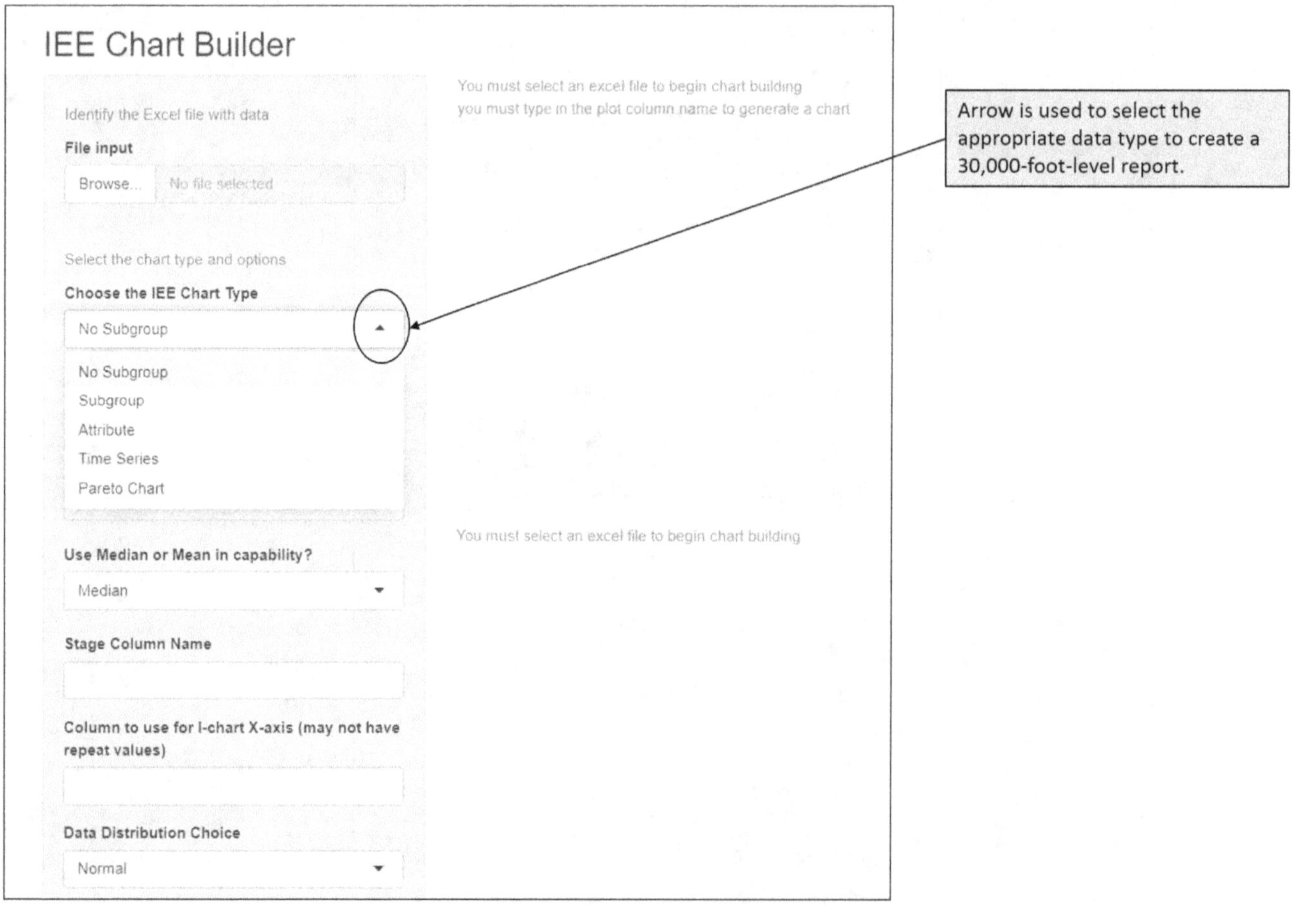

IEE Chart Builder
Identify the Excel file with data
File input
Browse...
No file selected
You must select an excel file to begin chart building
you must type in the plot column name to generate a chart
Arrow is used to select the appropriate data type to create a 30,000-foot-level report.
Select the chart type and options
Choose the IEE Chart Type
No Subgroup
No Subgroup
Subgroup
Attribute
Time Series
Pareto Chart
You must select an excel file to begin chart building
Use Median or Mean in capability?
Median
Stage Column Name
Column to use for I-chart X-axis (may not have repeat values)
Data Distribution Choice
Normal

Figure 6.5: EPRS Metric-App – Image 2 of 7

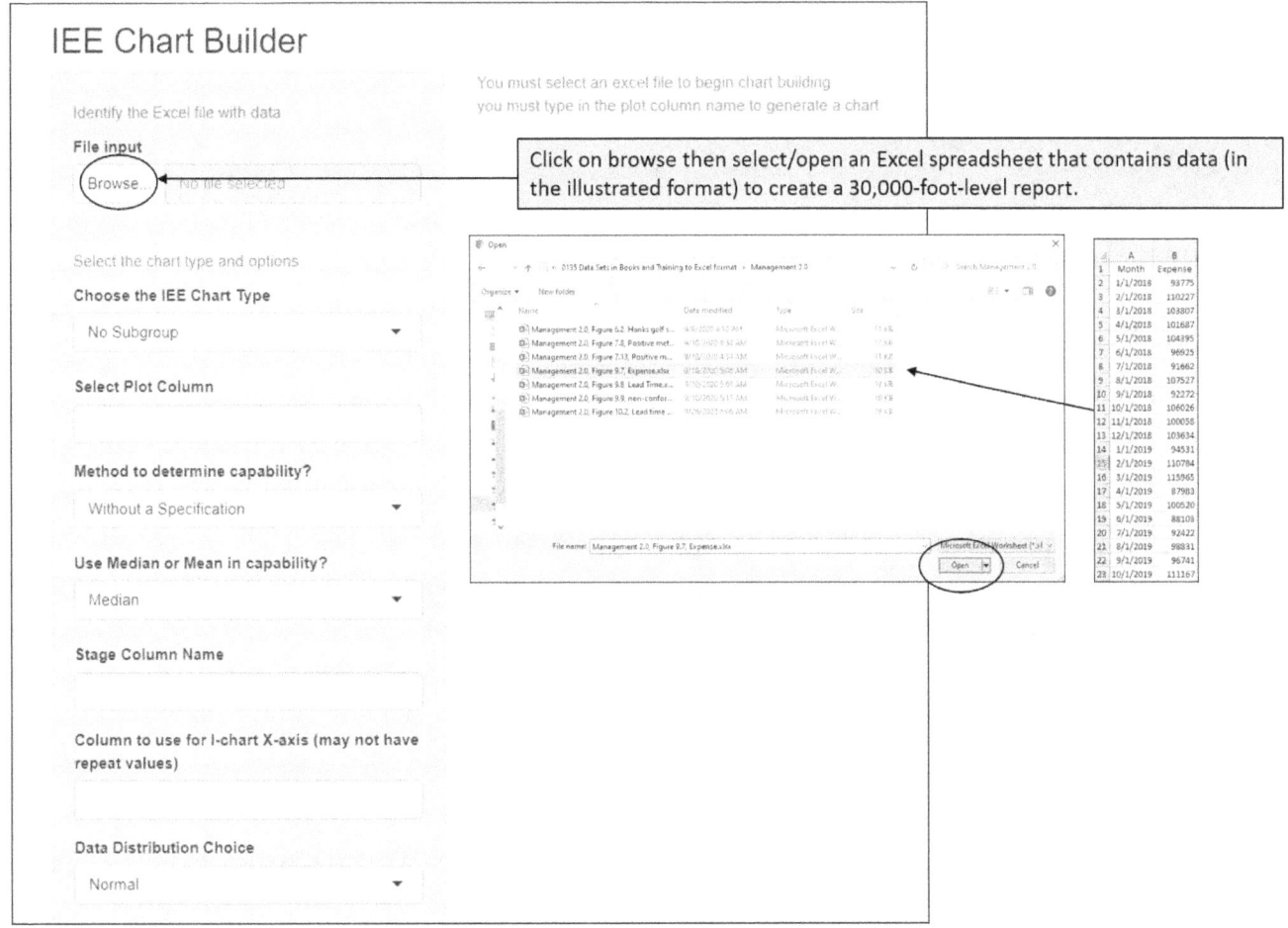

Figure 6.6: EPRS Metric-App – Image 3 of 7

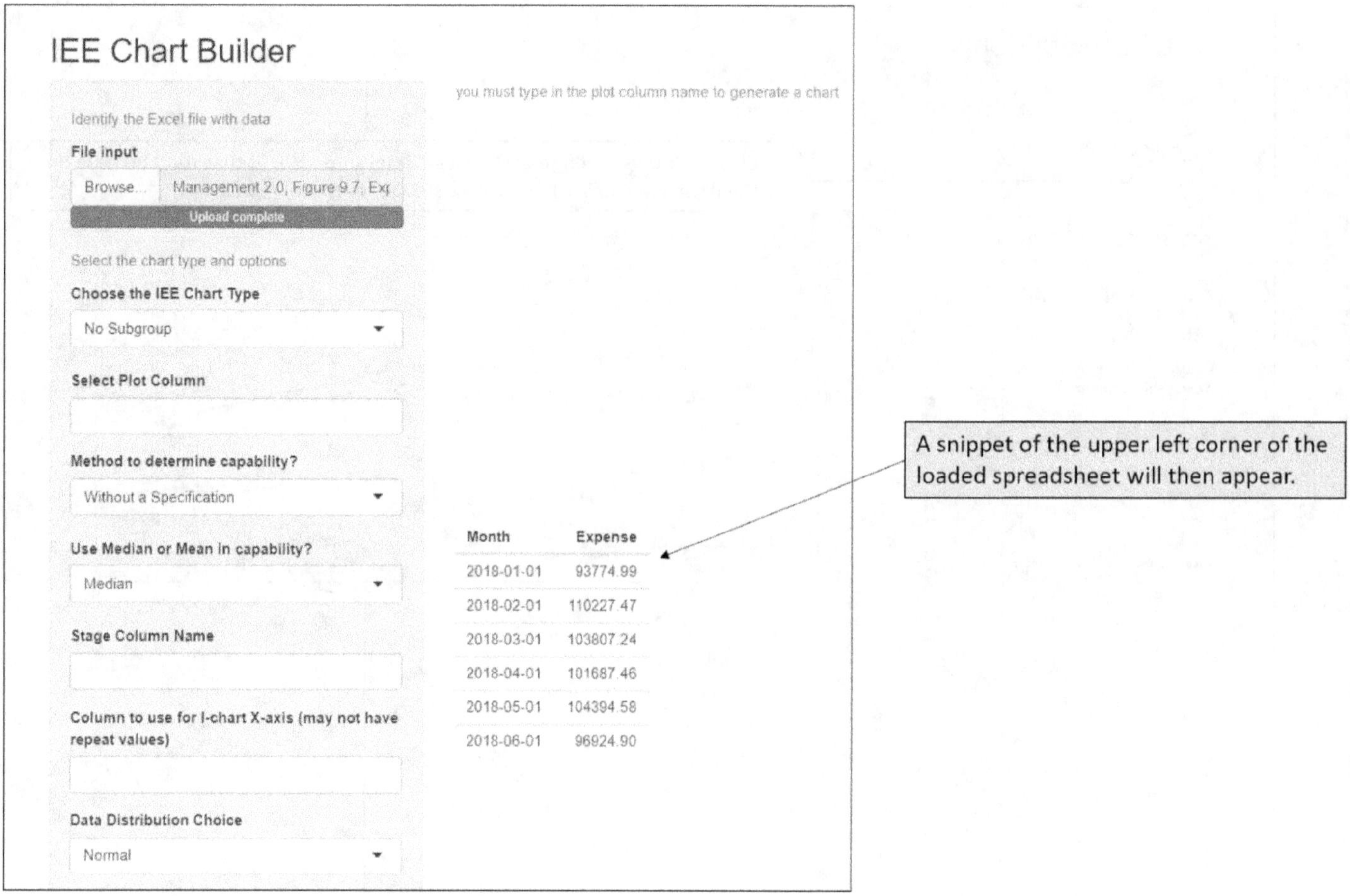

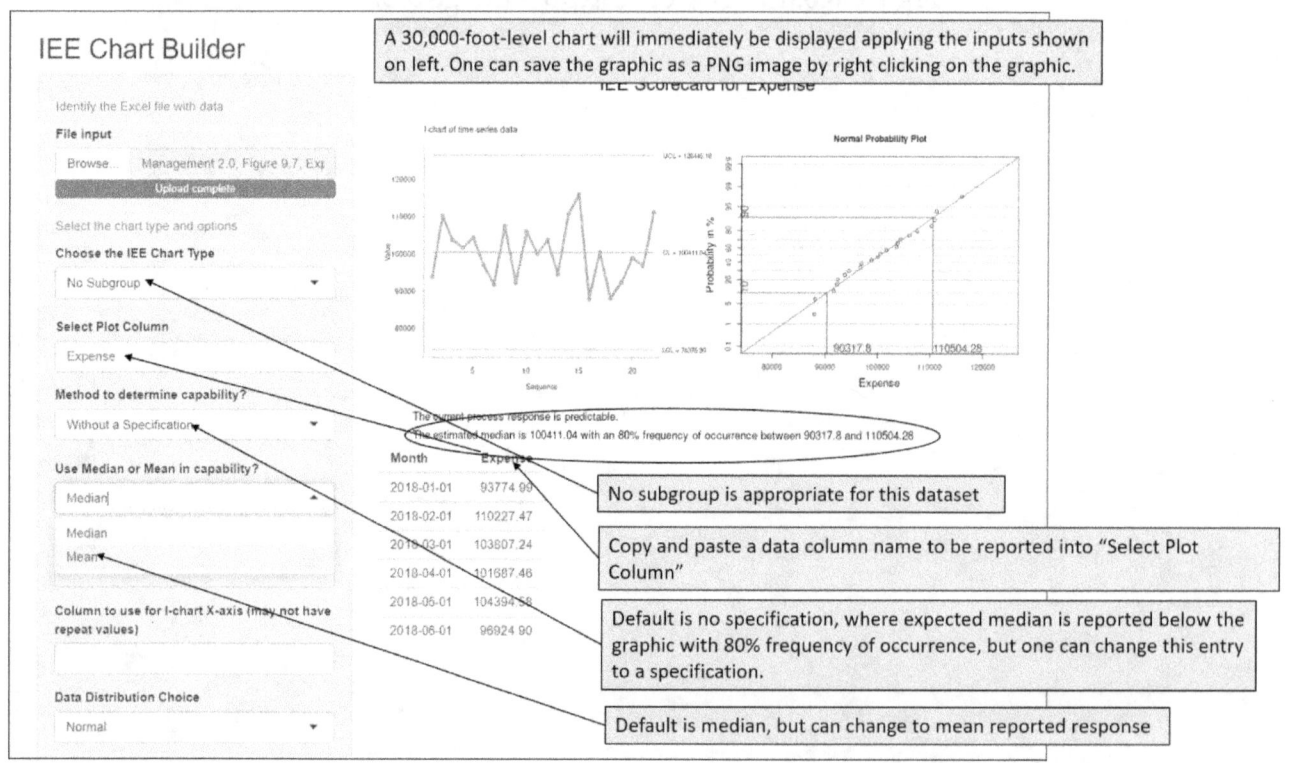

Figure 6.7: EPRS Metric-App – Image 4 of 7

Figure 6.8: EPRS Metric-App – Image 5 of 7

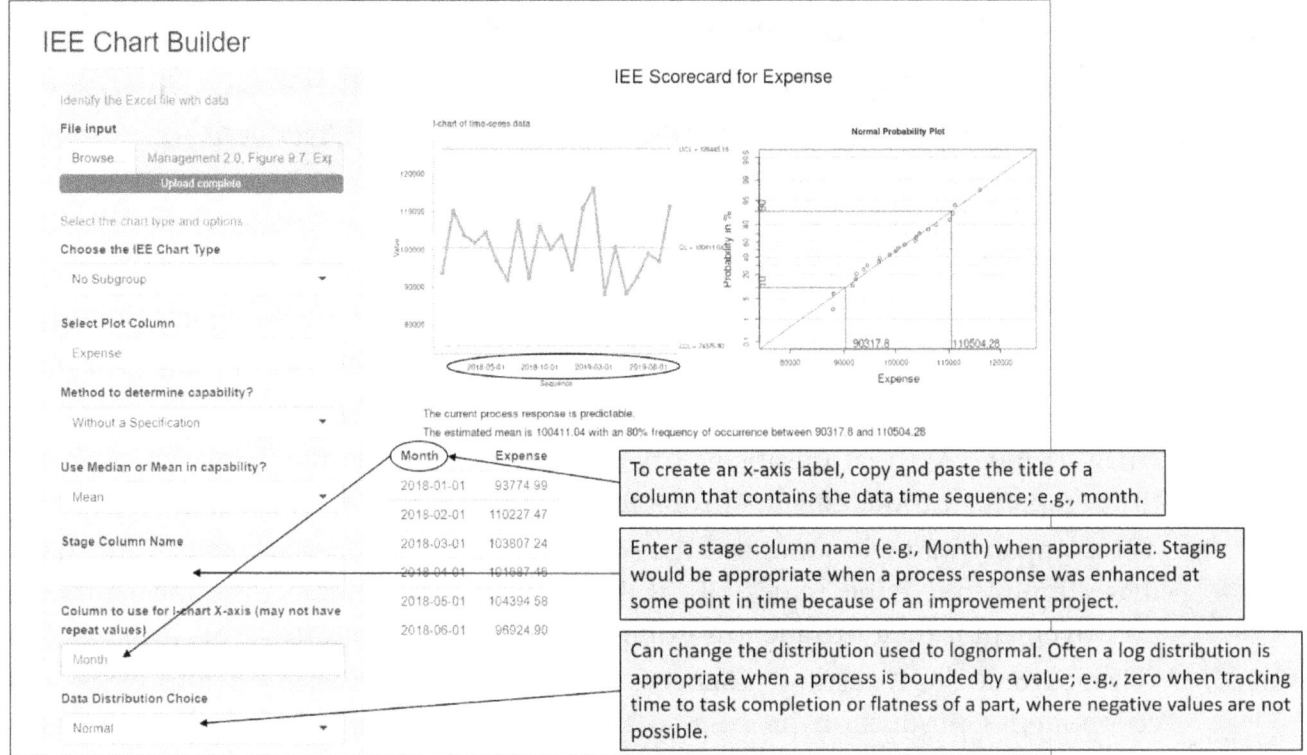

Figure 6.9: EPRS Metric-App – Image 6 of 7

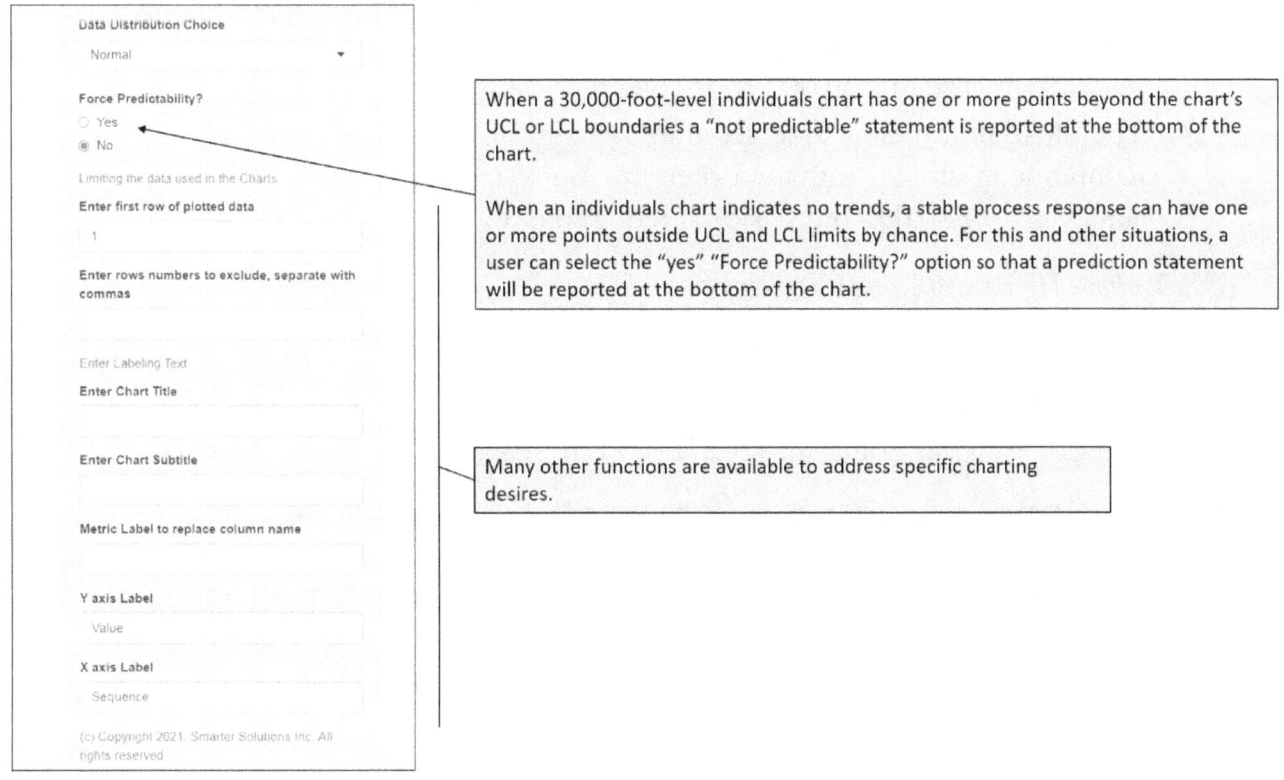

Figure 6.10: EPRS Metric-App – Image 7 of 7

6.5 Example: 30,000-foot-level reporting using EPRS Metric-App (Continuous Response – One Measurement for each time-series increment with a Specification Requirement)

Applications

- A company's Acceptable Quality Level (AQL) inspection process for achieving a supplier's component requirements was not going well relative to providing satisfactory component input quality to the production process. Production from the company often did not meet its specification requirement.

- Analysis indicated that unsatisfactory supplier quality was the primary reason for the company's product quality problem of a product they produced.

- The company wanted to monitor the supplier's part's dimension using an approach that circumvented the issues of AQL testing and encouraged supplier-process improvement if their production's output response was unsatisfactory.

- With current AQL testing practices, there was no emphasis on improving the component's production process so that the process will produce better quality components in the future. A 30,000-foot-level reporting approach addresses this need.

- A team recorded one critical requirement response for each production lot in an Excel spreadsheet and used the EPRS metric-app to report this component-response metric in a 30,000-foot-level reporting format.

- The illustration below assesses the viscosity of a supplier's product; however, the technique is similar to many other situations, e.g., how well a specific component achieves a +/- 0.005-dimensional requirement.

IEE Volume III Example and Dataset

- *IEE Volume III* Example 12.1: 30,000-foot-level Report – One Measurement for Each Time-series Increment, with Specification
- Dataset (Smarter Solutions (2022): V3 C10, Exam 10-02, xmr chart.xlsx

SigmaXL or EPRS [Smarter Solutions (2020)] Metric-App Input/Output

- Figure 6.11: EPRS Metric-App Input (30,000-foot-level Report, Specifications are 72 and 78)
- Figure 6.12: EPRS Metric-App Output (30,000-foot-level Report, Specifications are 72 and 78)

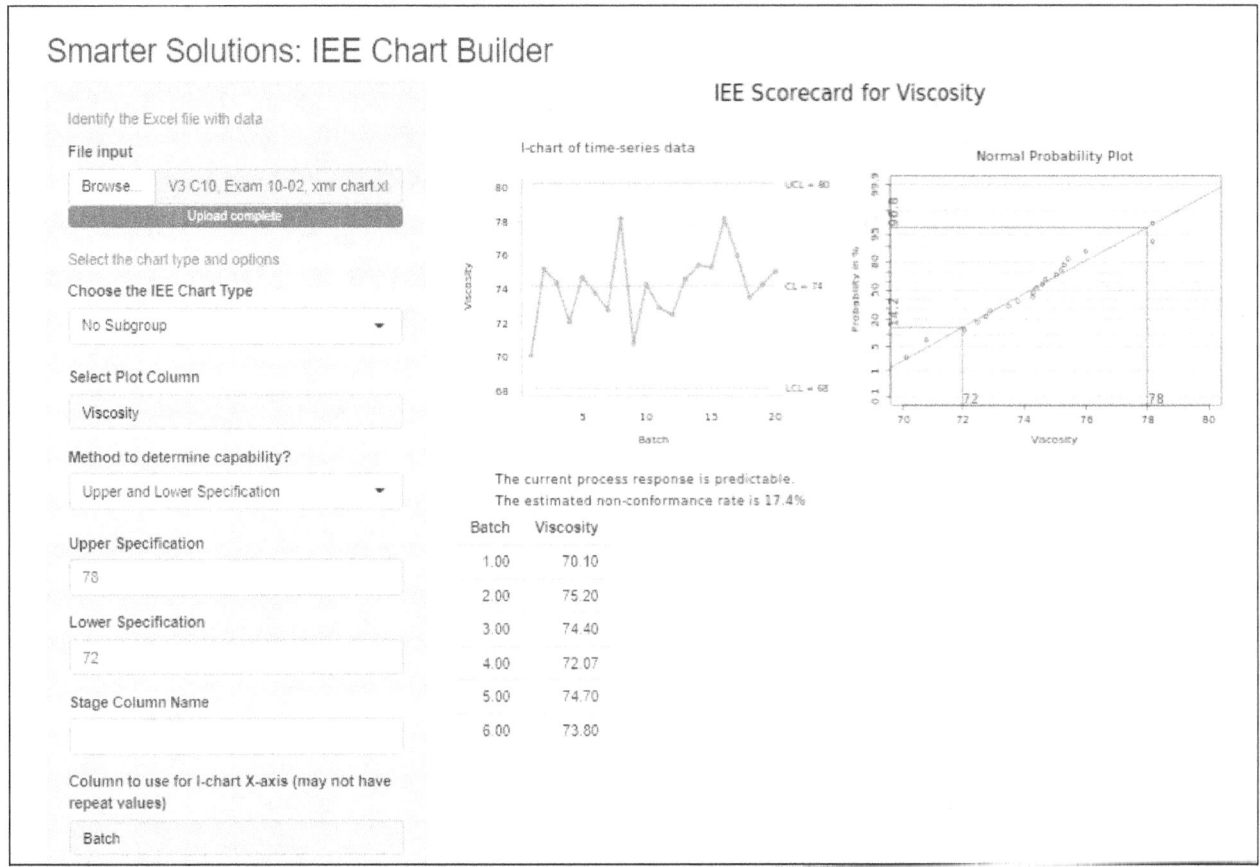

Figure 6.11: EPRS Metric-App Input (30,000-foot-level Report, Specifications are 72 and 78)

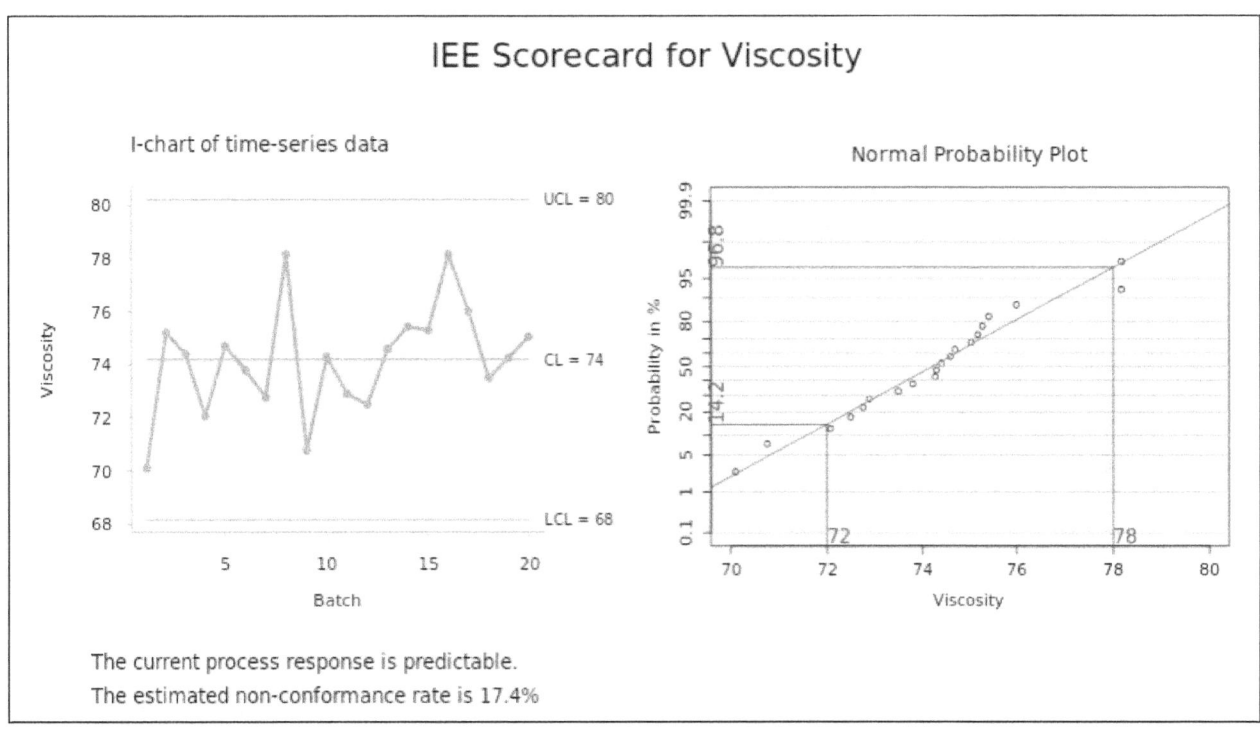

Figure 6.12: EPRS Metric-App Output (30,000-foot-level Report, Specifications are 72 and 78)

Comment

- If this estimated 17.4% non-conformance rate is unacceptable, there is a need for process improvement.

6.6   Example: 30,000-foot-level reporting using EPRS Metric-App (Continuous Response – Multiple Samples in Subgroup for each time-series increment with Specification Requirement)

Application: Continuous Response – Multiple measurements for each time-series increment subgroup

IEE Volume III Example and Dataset

- *IEE Volume III* Example 12.2: 30,000-foot-level Report – Multiple Measurements for Each Time-series Increment, with Specification
- Dataset (Smarter Solutions (2022): V3 C12, Exam 12-02.1, subgroup5

SigmaXL or EPRS Metric-App [Smarter Solutions (2020)] Input/Output

- Figure 6.13: EPRS Metric-App Input (30,000-foot-level Report, Specifications are 95 and 105)
- Figure 6.14: EPRS Metric-App Output (30,000-foot-level Report, Specifications are 95 and 105)

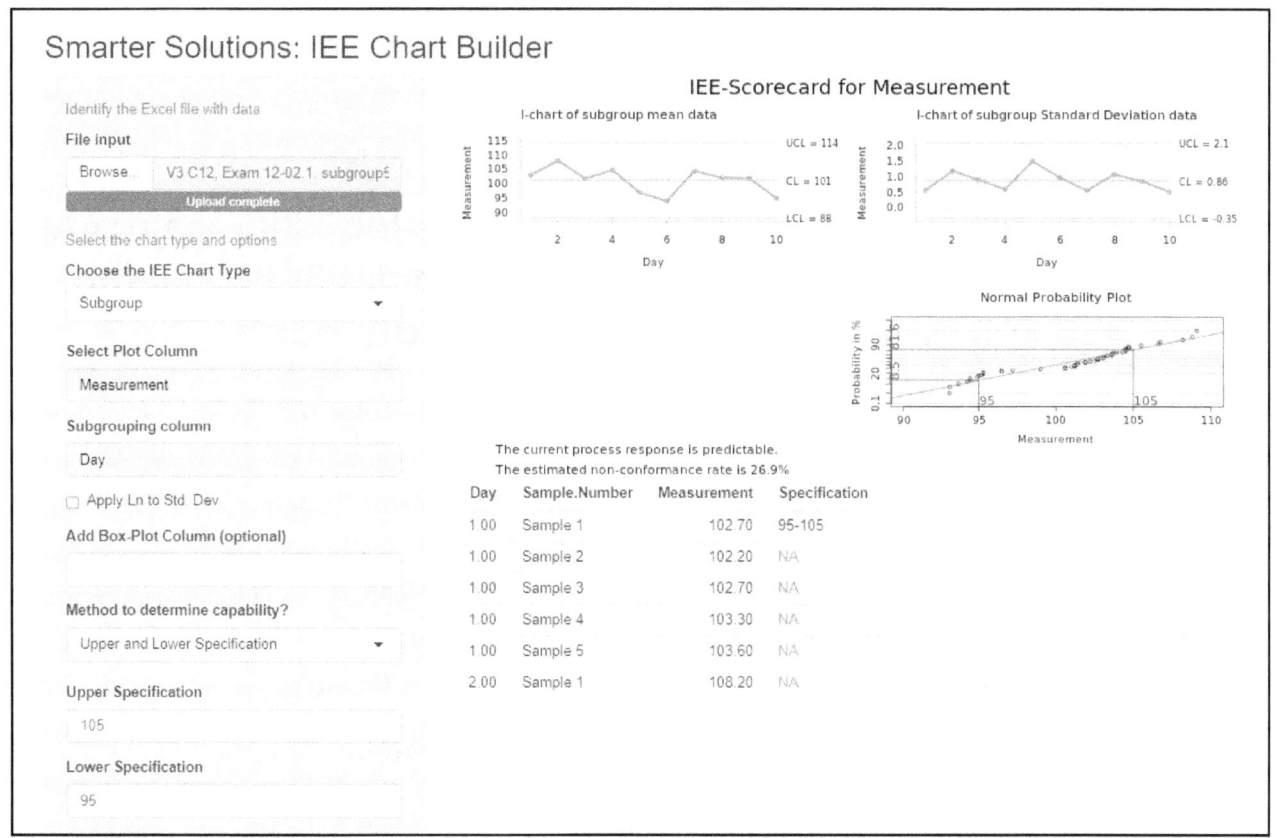

Figure 6.13: EPRS Metric-App Input (30,000-foot-level Report, Specifications are 95 and 105)

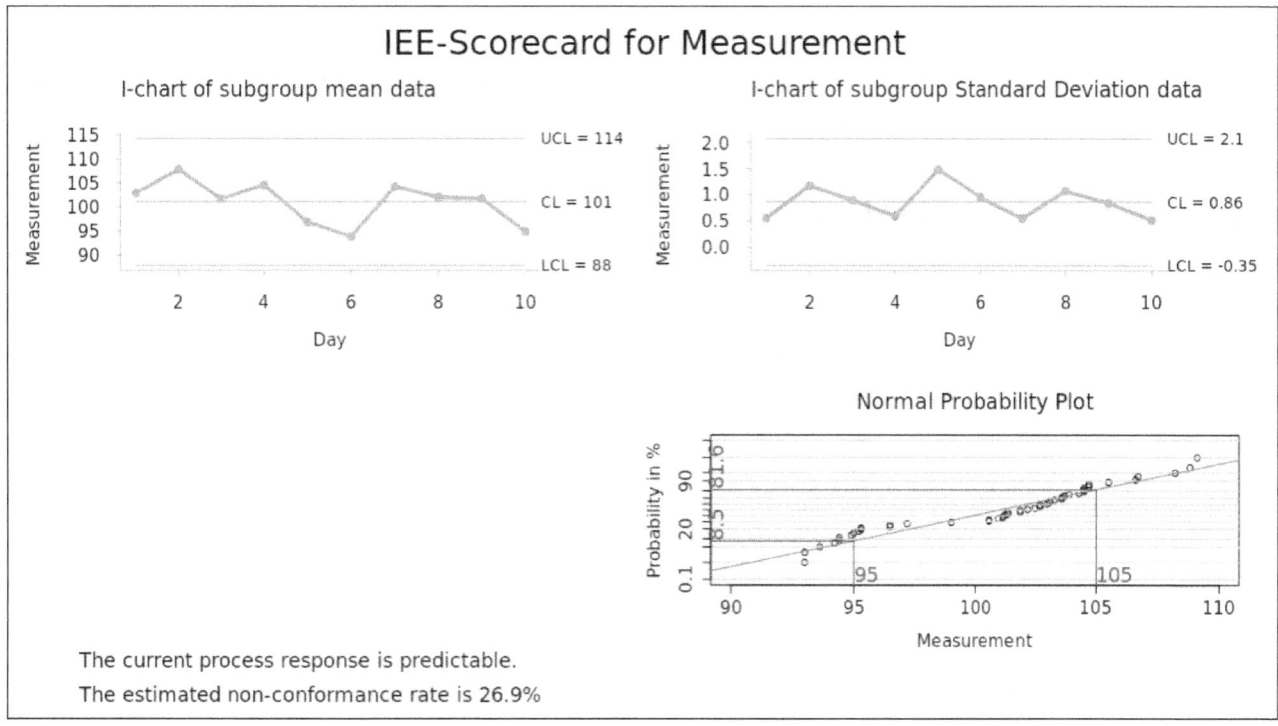

Figure 6.14: EPRS Metric-App Output (30,000-foot-level Report, Specifications are 95 and 105)

Comment

- If this estimated 26.9% non-conformance rate is unacceptable, there is a need for process improvement.

6.7 Example: 30,000-foot-level reporting using EPRS Metric-App (Continuous Response – The Implication of Subgrouping Period Selection on Process Stability Statements)

Application: Continuous Response – The Implication of Subgrouping Period Selection on Process Stability Statements

IEE Volume III Example and Dataset

- *IEE Volume III* Example 12.4: 30,000-foot-level Report – The Implication of Subgrouping Period Selection on Process Stability Statements
- Dataset (Smarter Solutions (2022): V3 C12, Exam 12-04, subgrouping period

SigmaXL or EPRS Metric-App [Smarter Solutions (2020)] Input/Output

- Figure 6.15: EPRS Metric-App Input (30,000-foot-level Report, No subgrouping, upper specification limit of 305)
- Figure 6.16: EPRS Metric-App Output (30,000-foot-level Report, No subgrouping, upper specification limit of 305)
- Figure 6.17: EPRS Metric-App Input (30,000-foot-level Report, Subgrouping, upper specification limit of 305)
- Figure 6.18: EPRS Metric-App Output (30,000-foot-level Report, Subgrouping, upper specification limit of 305)

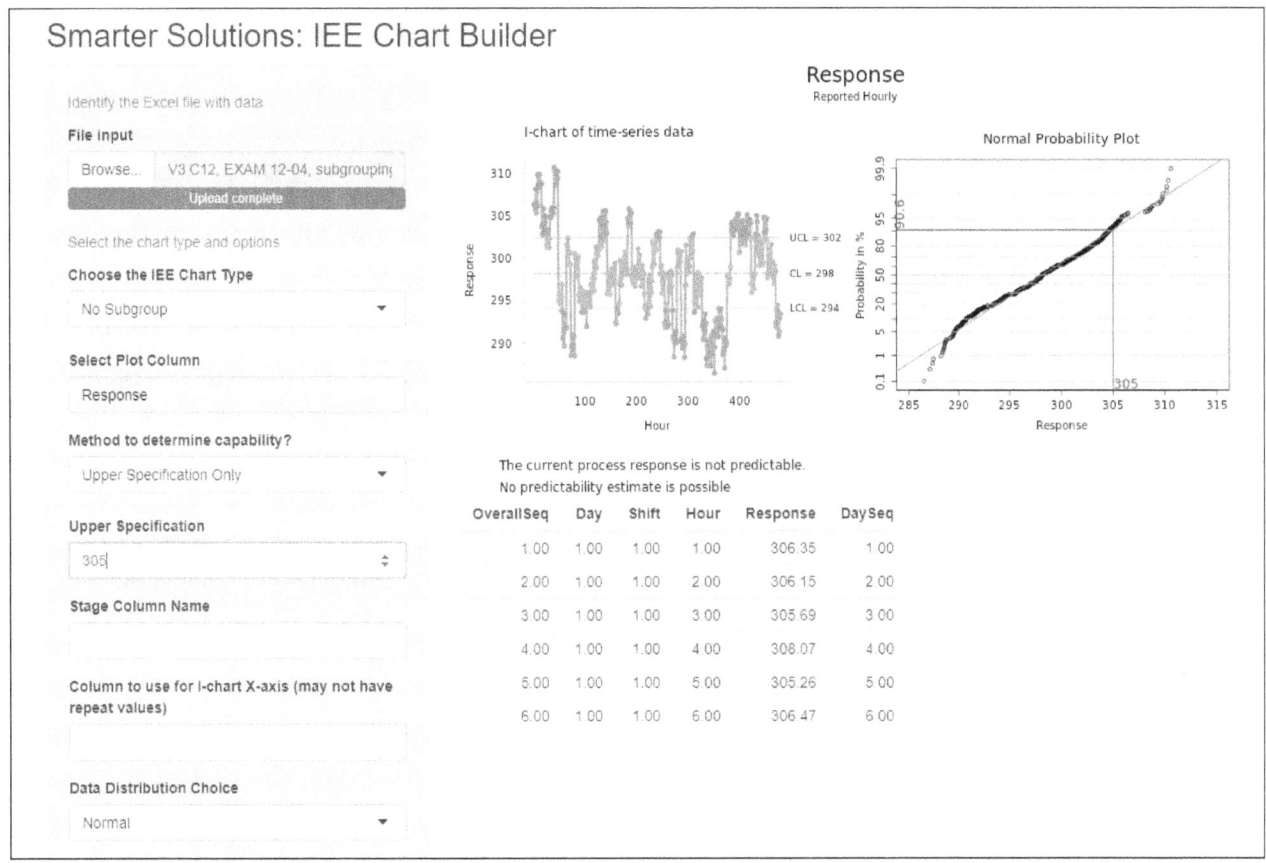

Figure 6.15: EPRS Metric-App Input (30,000-foot-level Report, No subgrouping, upper specification limit of 305)

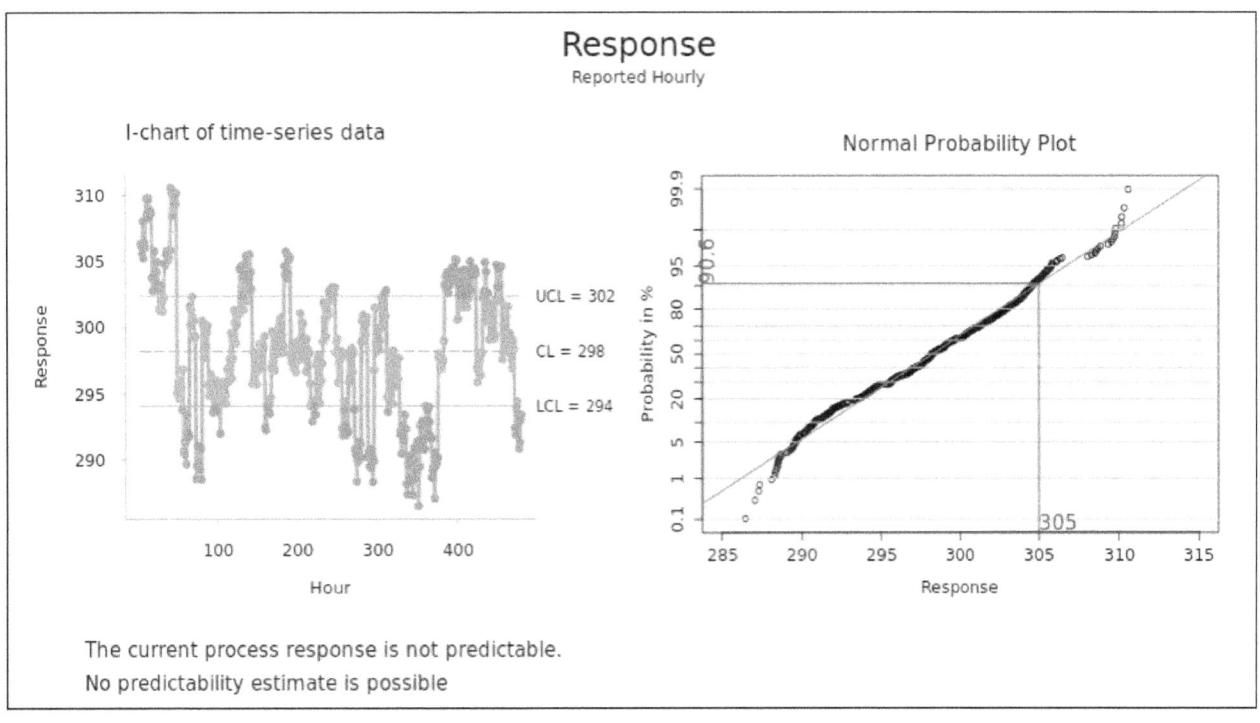

Figure 6.16: EPRS Metric-App Output (30,000-foot-level Report, No subgrouping, upper specification limit of 305)

Comments

- Because many points are beyond the UCL and LCL lines, the process is considered not stable; hence, a prediction statement cannot be made
- However, the reporting frequency is hourly, and there appears to be a clustering of points, which suggests that there could be differences by the hour of the day as a source of X "process noise" output response variation
- A less frequent reporting frequency may be appropriate, e.g., daily subgrouping
- The following two figures illustrate the creation of a 30,000-foot-level report with a daily subgrouping for this dataset

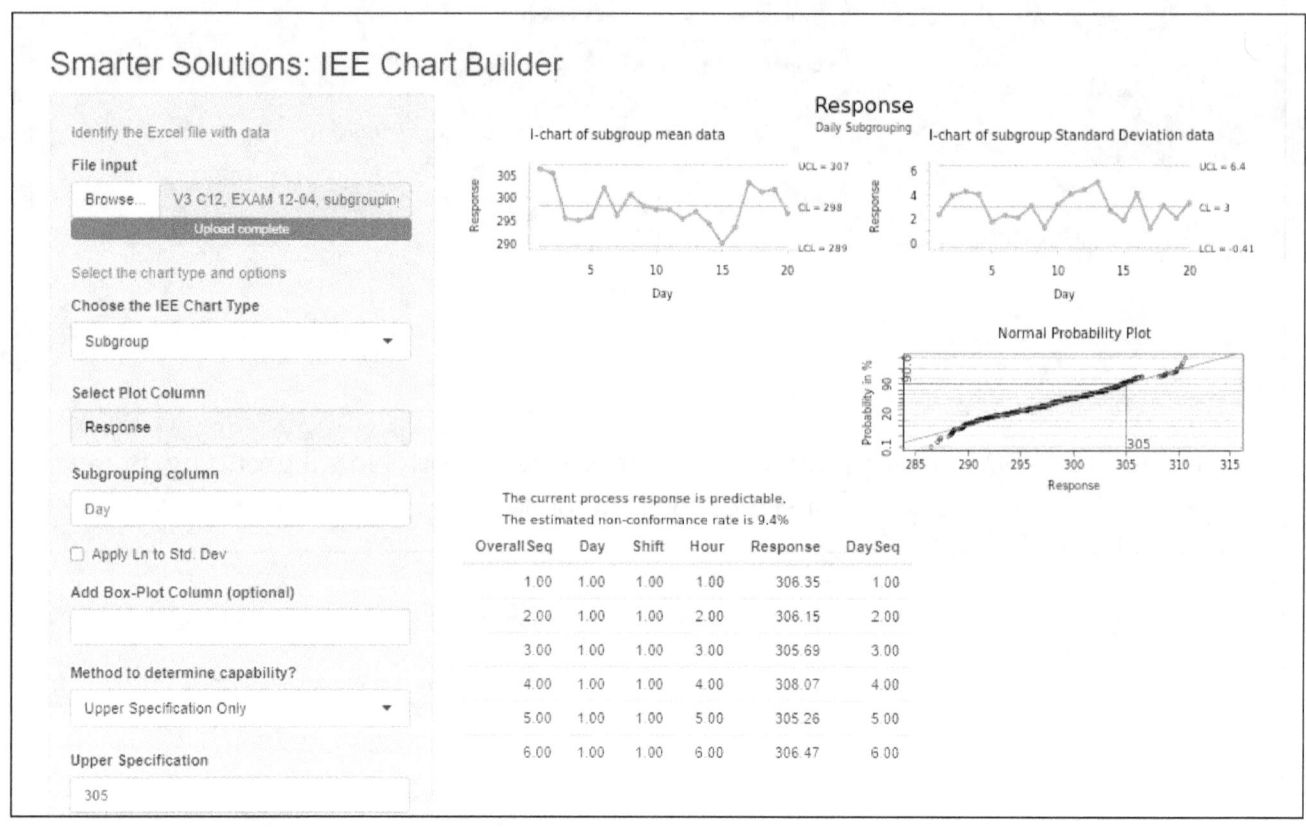

Figure 6.17: EPRS Metric-App Input (30,000-foot-level Report, Subgrouping, upper specification limit of 305)

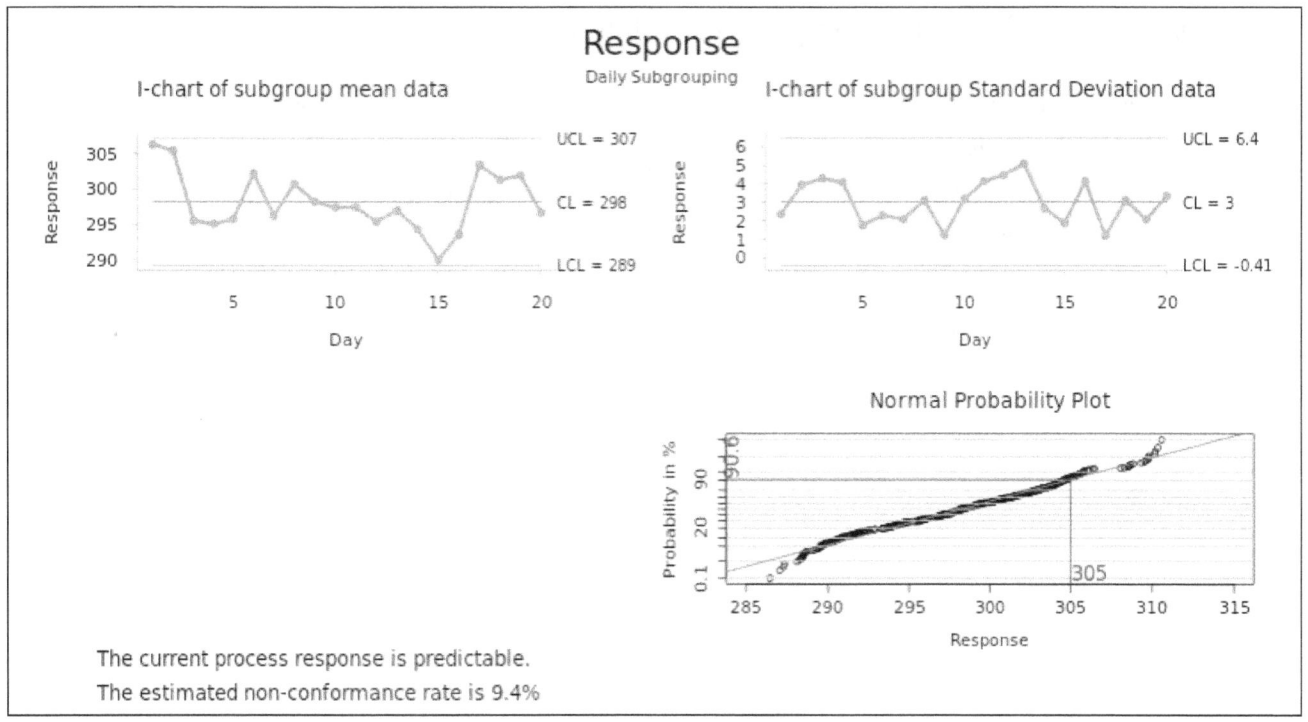

Figure 6.18: EPRS Metric-App Output (30,000-foot-level Report, Subgrouping, upper specification limit of 305)

Comments

- With a daily subgrouping, the process now appears stable and predictable, with an estimated non-conformance rate of 9.4%
- If this 9.4% estimated non-conformance rate is unacceptable, there is a need for process improvement.
- This example illustrates the importance of subgrouping for some 30,000-foot-level reporting situations

6.8 Example: 30,000-foot-level Reporting using EPRS Metric-App (Continuous Response – One Time-Series Value, No Specification)

Application: Continuous Response – No Subgroup, No Specification

IEE Volume III Example and Dataset

- *IEE Volume III* Example 12.5: 30,000-foot-level Report – Continuous Response, No Subgroups, No Specification
- Dataset (Smarter Solutions (2022): V3 C12, Exam 12-05, Early Attendance.xlsx

SigmaXL or EPRS Metric-App [Smarter Solutions (2020)] Input/Output

- Figure 6.19: EPRS Metric-App Input (30,000-foot-level Report, No Subgrouping, No Specification)
- Figure 6.20: EPRS Metric-App Output (30,000-foot-level Report, No subgrouping, No Specification)

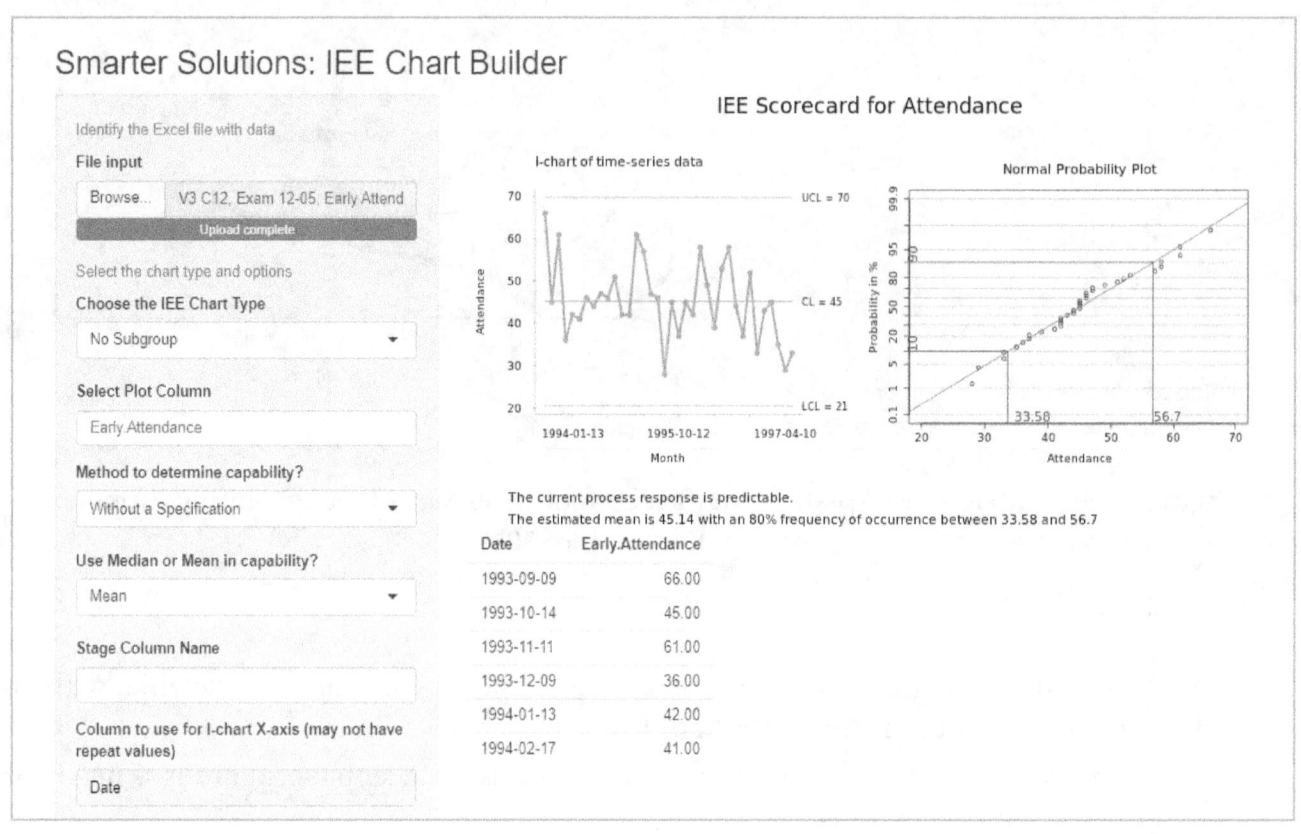

Figure 6.19: EPRS Metric-App Input (30,000-foot-level Report, No Subgrouping, No Specification)

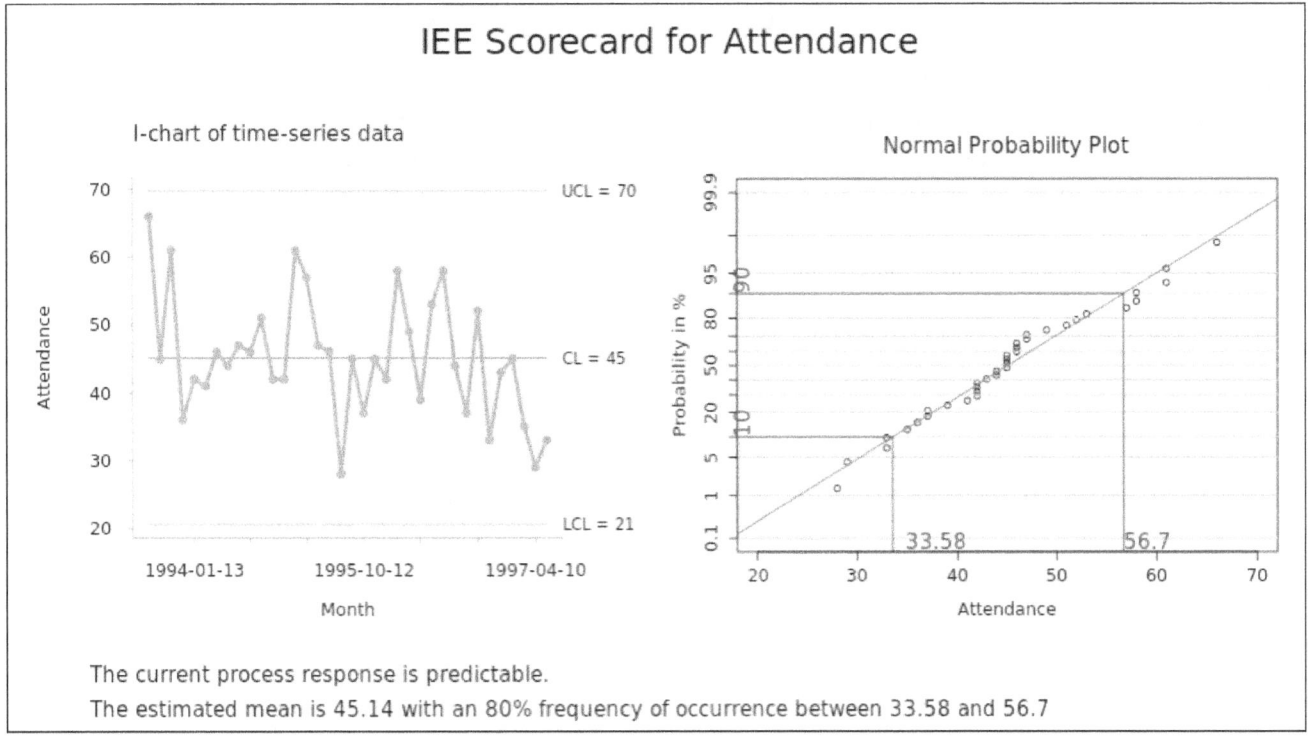

Figure 6.20: EPRS Metric-App Output (30,000-foot-level Report, No subgrouping, No Specification)

Comment

- If this estimated mean and 80% frequency of occurrence rate is unacceptable, there is a need for process improvement.

6.9 Example: 30,000-foot-level Reporting using EPRS Metric-App (Continuous Response – One Time-Series Value, Non-normal Distribution, with Specification)

Application: Continuous Response – No Subgroup, Lognormal Distribution, Specification

IEE Volume III Example and Dataset

- *IEE Volume III* Example 12.6: 30,000-foot-level Report – Continuous Response, Box-Cox Transformation, Specification
- Dataset (Smarter Solutions (2022): V3 C12, Exam 12-06, Chemical Residue.xlsx

SigmaXL or EPRS Metric-App [Smarter Solutions (2020)] Input/Output

- Figure 6.21: EPRS Metric-App Input (30,000-foot-level Report, No Subgrouping, No Transformation, Specification)
- Figure 6.22: EPRS Metric-App Input (30,000-foot-level Report, No Subgrouping, Lognormal Transformation, Specification)

- Figure 6.23: EPRS Metric-App Input (30,000-foot-level Report, No Subgrouping, Lognormal Transformation with Forced Predictability, Specification)
- Figure 6.24: EPRS Metric-App Output (30,000-foot-level Report, No Subgrouping, Lognormal Transformation with Forced Predictability, Specification)

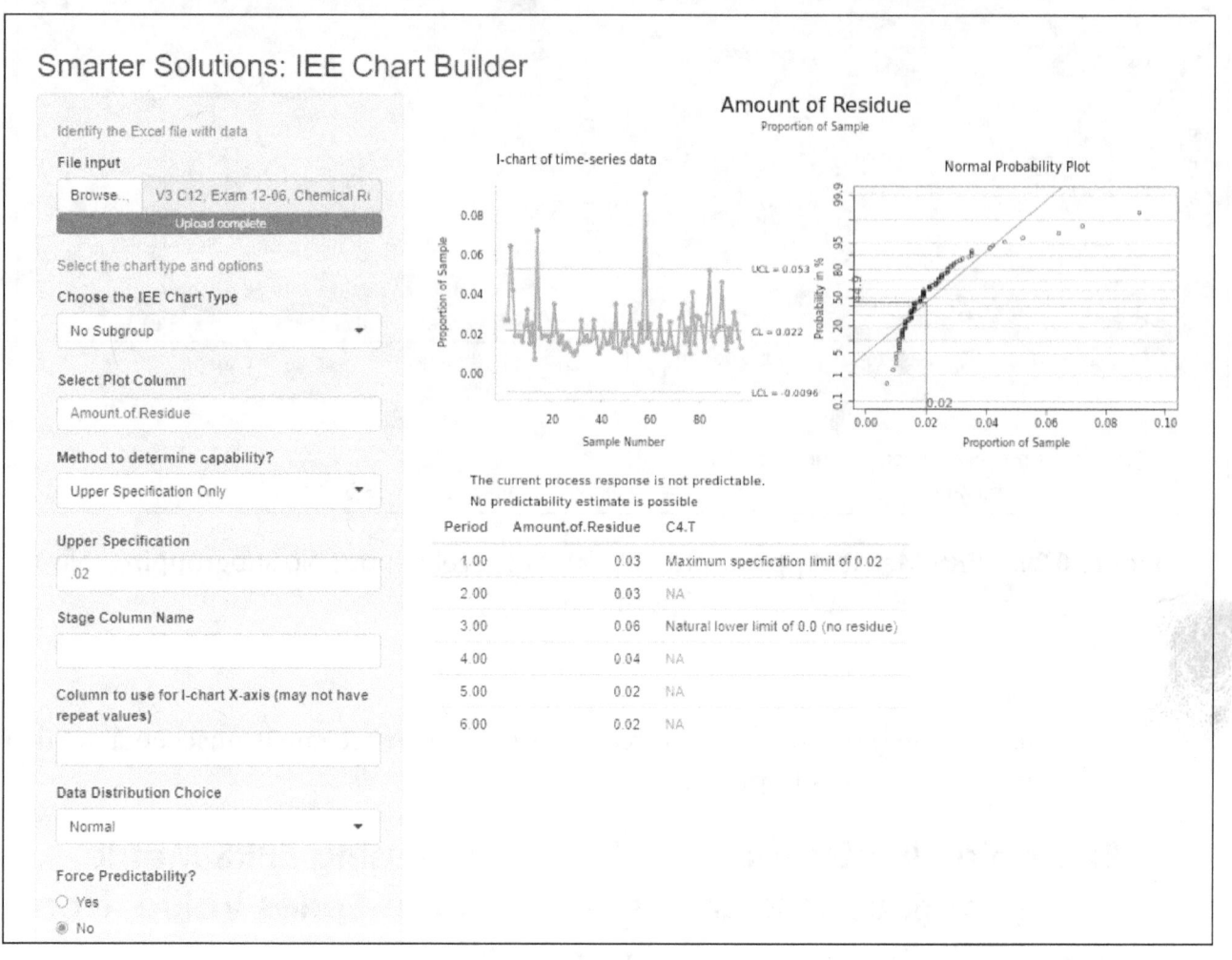

Figure 6.21: EPRS Metric-App Input (30,000-foot-level Report, No Subgrouping, No Transformation, Specification)

Comment: Figure 21 – 30,000-foot-level report creation

- The proportion of residue cannot be below zero
- The probability plot has a convex shape that approaches zero as a lower boundary
- Zero is within the LCL line in the individuals-chart (i.e., physically not possible to have less than zero values)
- There is a need for a lognormal data transformation. Figures 6.22, 6.23, and 6.24 shows the result of this transformation

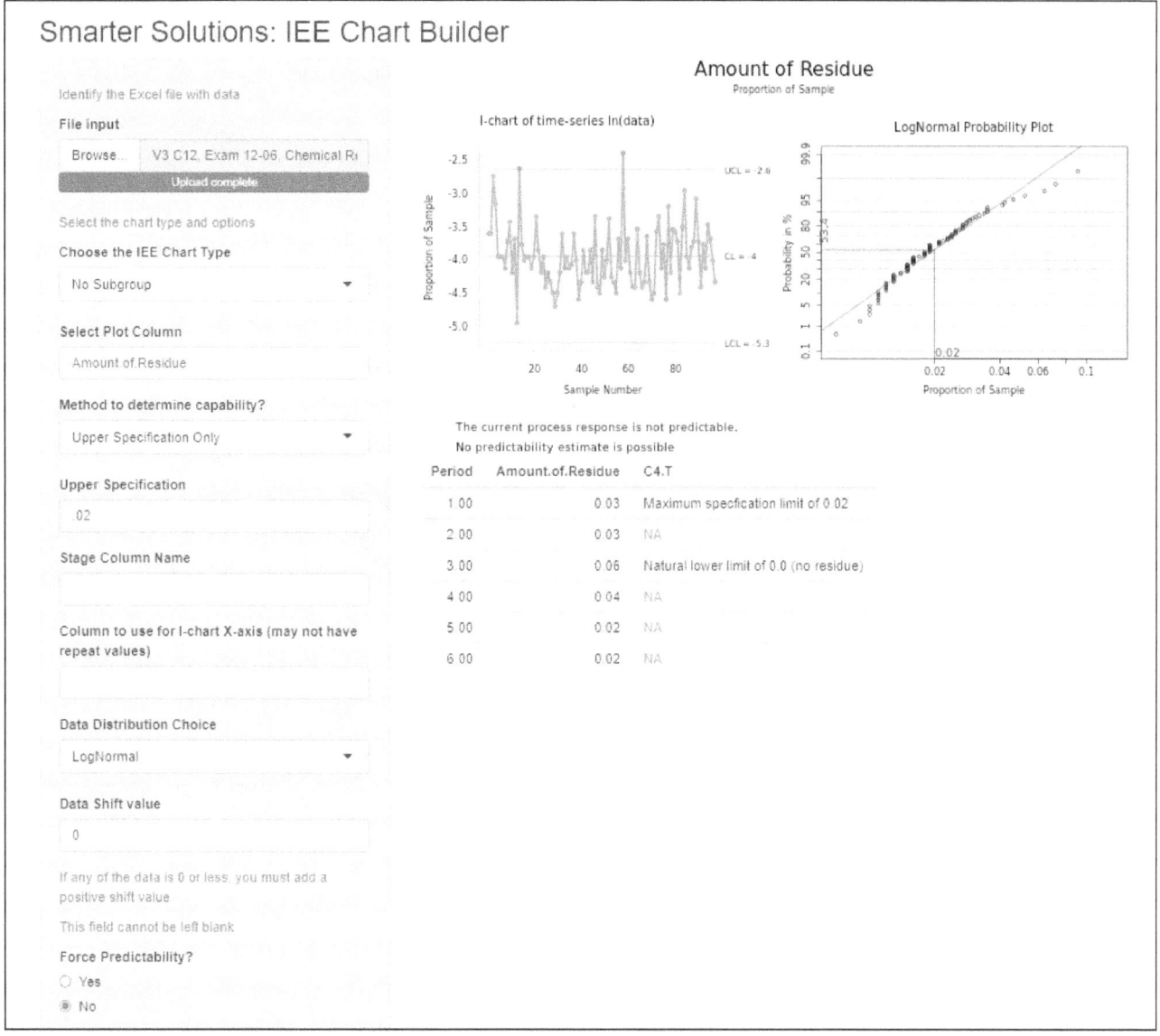

Figure 6.22: EPRS Metric-App Input (30,000-foot-level Report, No Subgrouping, Lognormal Transformation, Specification)

30,000-foot-level report chart-creation comments

- The lognormal probability plot provides a better distribution fit than a normal-probability plot, i.e., the lognormal line best-estimate line closely follows the datum points
- There was no prediction statement on the report because there were a couple of values beyond the UCL line
- The two points beyond the individuals-chart UCL line are close to the line. There was no reason to believe these datum points were not from common-cause variation
- The following two figures will apply the "force predictability" option

83

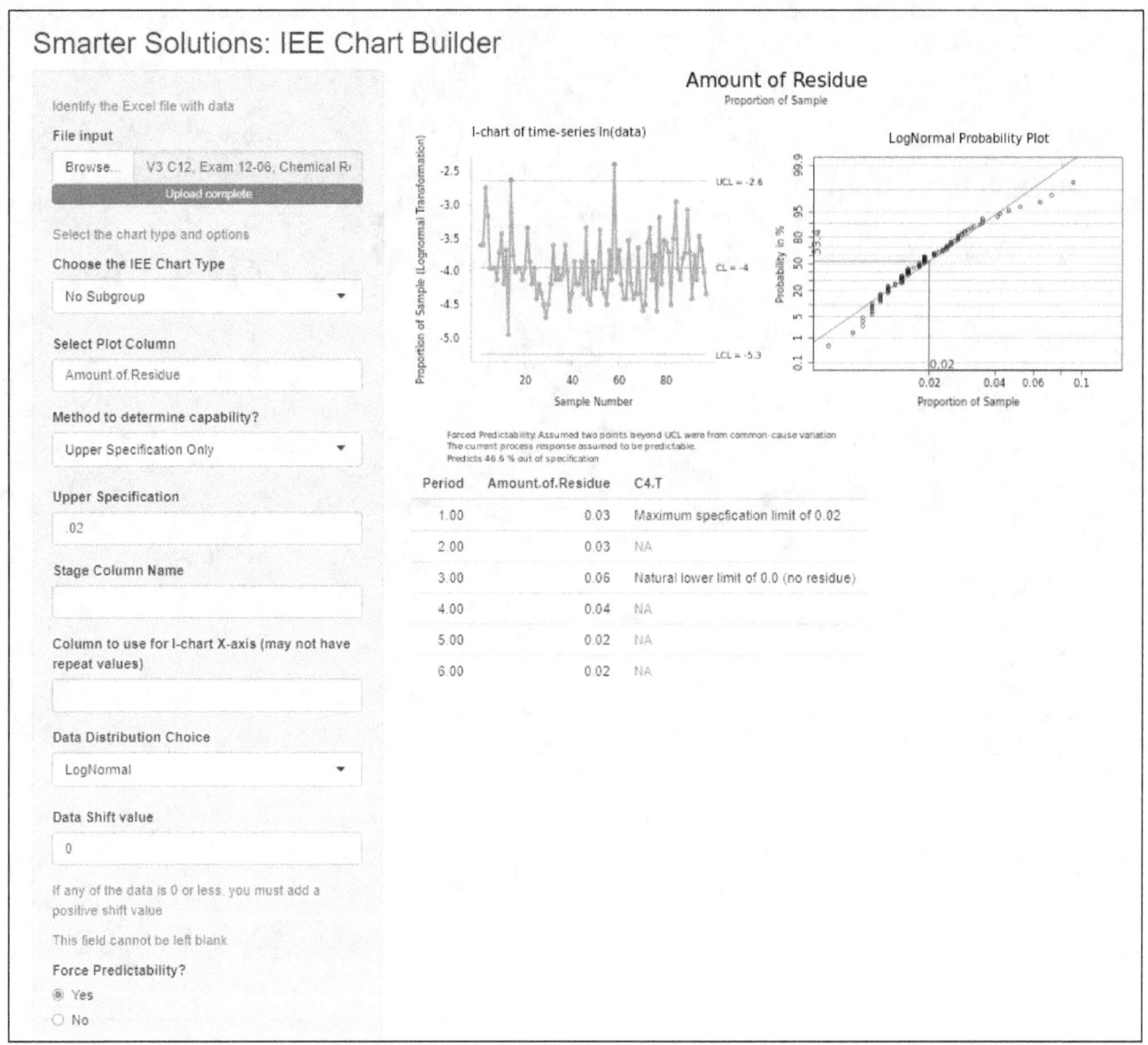

Figure 6.23: EPRS Metric-App Input (30,000-foot-level Report, No Subgrouping, Lognormal Transformation with Forced Predictability, Specification)

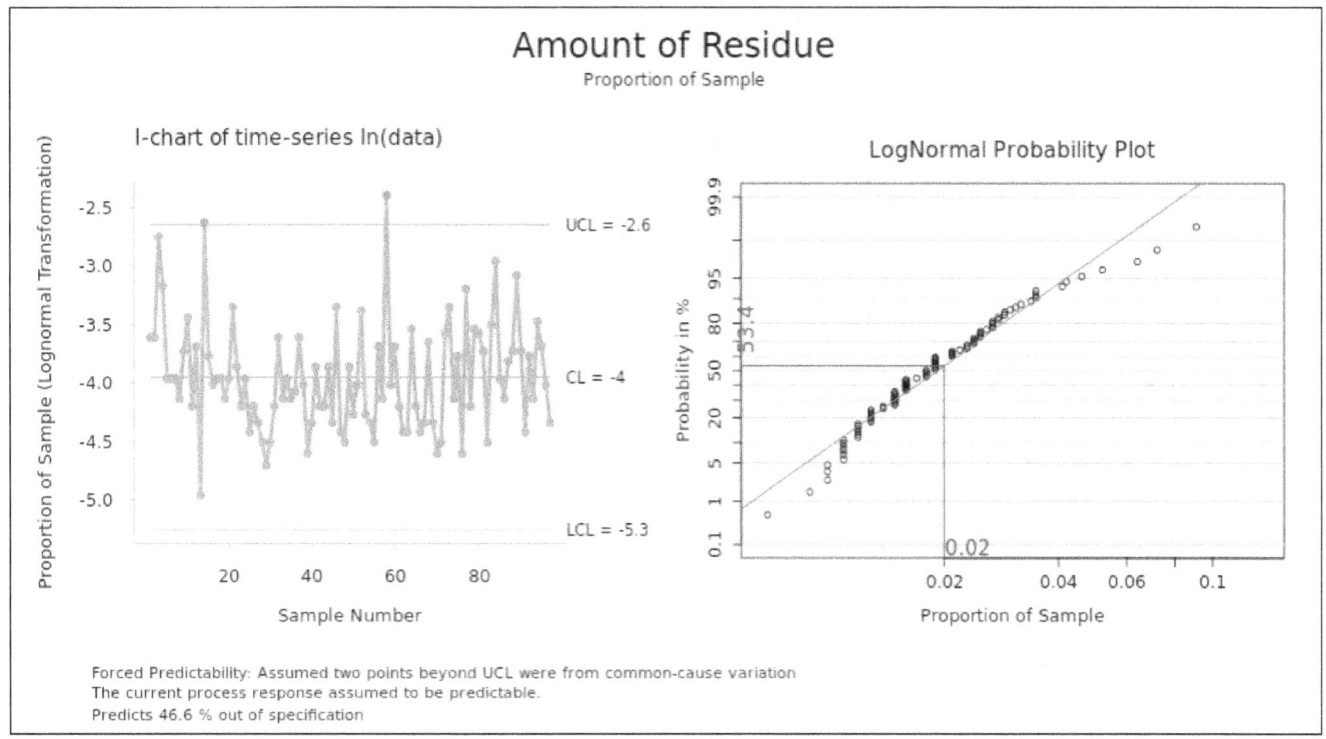

Figure 6.24: EPRS Metric-App Output (30,000-foot-level Report, No Subgrouping, Lognormal Transformation with Forced Predictability, Specification)

Comments: 30,000-foot-level report creation

- The predicted 30,000-foot-level report indicates that about 47% of the measurement in the future will not meet the 0.02 proportion upper limit residue specification
- If this amount of predicted residue is unsatisfactory, there is a need for process improvement

6.10 Example: 30,000-foot-level Reporting using EPRS Metric-App (Continuous Response – One Time-Series Value, Non-normal Distribution, Negative Values, No Specification)

Application: Continuous Response – No Subgroup, Lognormal Distribution, Negative Values, No Specification

IEE Volume III Example and Dataset

- *IEE Volume III* Example 12.7: 30,000-foot-level Report – Continuous Response, Box-Cox Transformation, Negative Values, No Specification
- Dataset (Smarter Solutions (2022): V3 C12, Exam 12-07, DSO with Negatives.xlsx

SigmaXL or EPRS Metric-App [Smarter Solutions (2020)] Input/Output

- Figure 6.25: EPRS Metric-App Input (30,000-foot-level Report, No Subgroup, No Transformation, No Specification)
- Figure 6.26: SigmaXL Creation of 3-Parameter Lognormal Distribution to Determine EPRS Metric-App Shift from Zero Value
- Figure 6.27: SigmaXL 3-Parameter Lognormal Distribution Plot
- Figure 6.28: EPRS Metric App-Input (30,000-foot-level Report, No Subgroup, Lognormal Transformation with Shift Value)
- Figure 6.29: EPRS Metric App-Output (30,000-foot-level Report, No Subgroup, Lognormal Transformation with Shift Value)

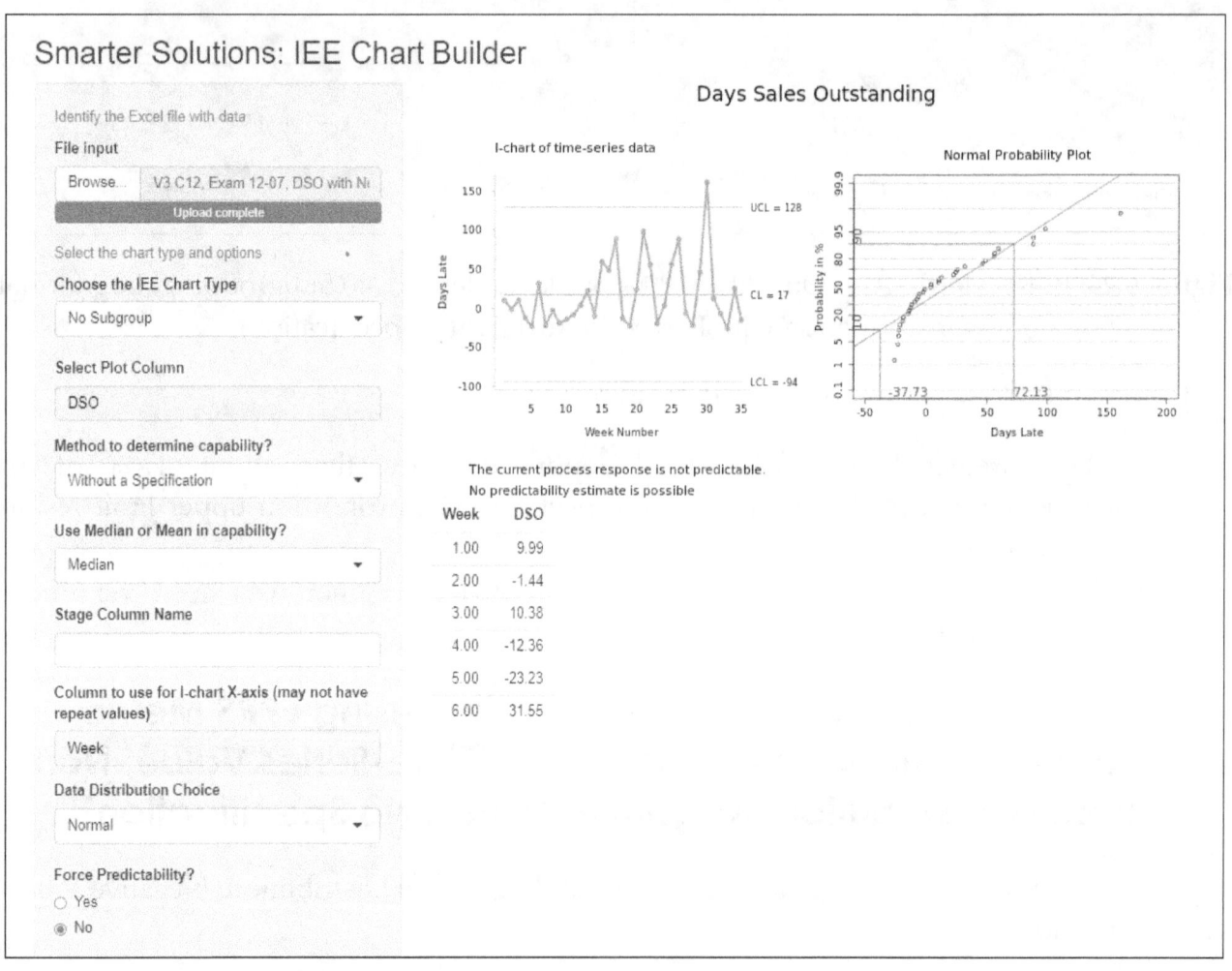

Figure 6.25: EPRS Metric-App Input (30,000-foot-level Report, No Subgroup, No Transformation, No Specification)

Comments: Figure 6.25, 30,000-foot-level report creation

- The normal-probability plot in the report-out has a convex curvature that approaches a negative value.

- A lognormal distribution seems appropriate for this DSO response situation, but a lognormal distribution cannot have negative values. Because of this, a 3-parameter lognormal distribution is proper. The EPRS metric-app needs a *data shift value* for an entry, i.e., the absolute value of a negative number, which data asymptotically approaches. SigmaXL can provide this "threshold" value for a 3-parameter lognormal distribution.

SigmaXL Chart Function: Control Charts>Nonnormal>Distribution Fitting

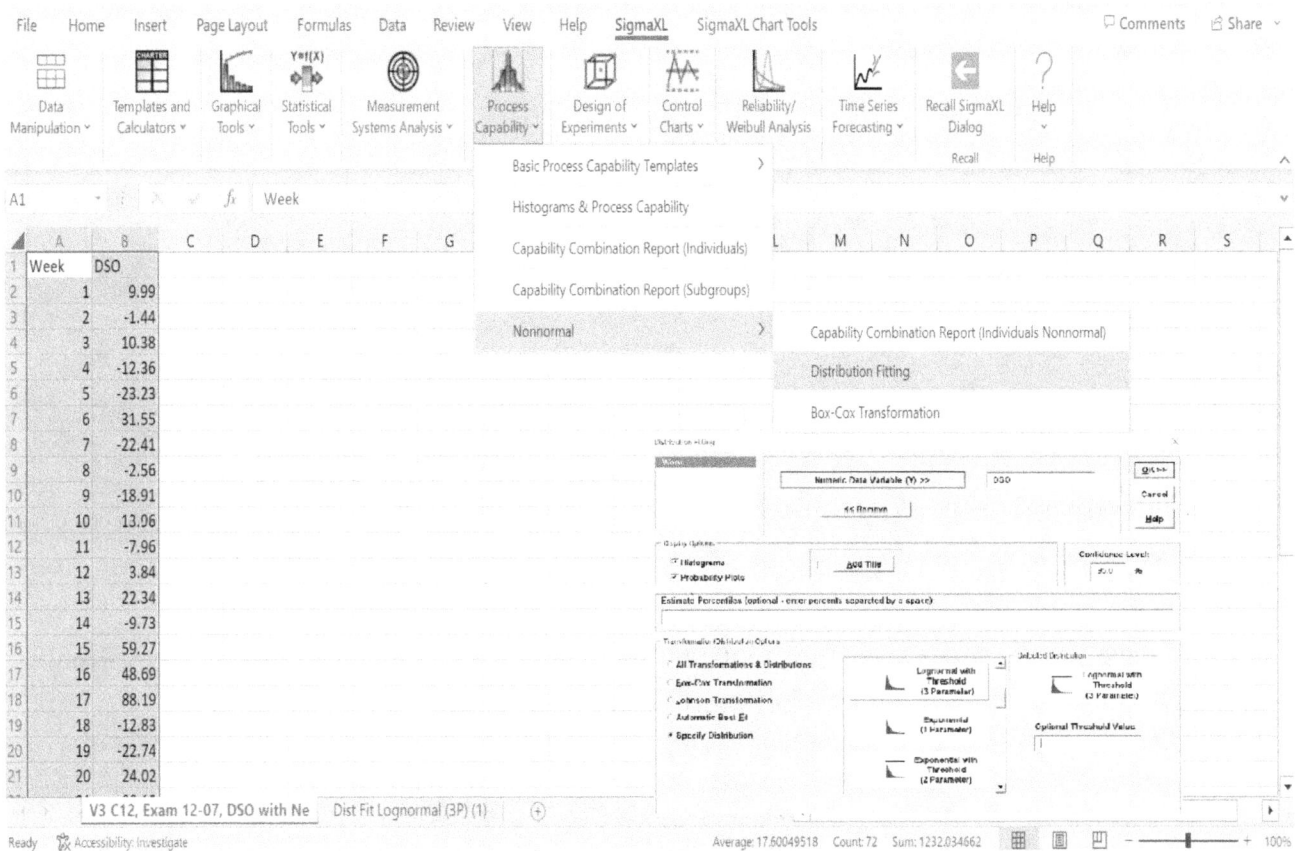

Figure 6.26: SigmaXL Creation of 3-Parameter Lognormal Distribution to Determine EPRS Metric-App Shift from Zero Value

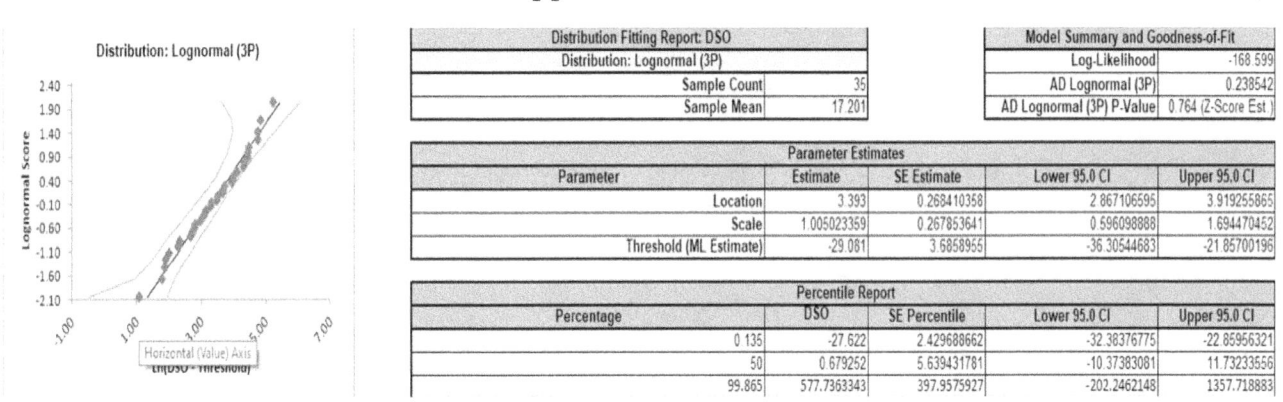

Figure 6.27: SigmaXL 3-Parameter Lognormal Distribution Plot

Comments: Figure 6.27, SigmaXL 3-parameter log-normal plot

- The 3-parameter lognormal-probability plot provides a good distribution fit, i.e., data follows a straight line
- The threshold value noted in the upper right of the plot is -29.081
- An appropriate EPRS metric-app lognormal distribution "shift value" is +29.081

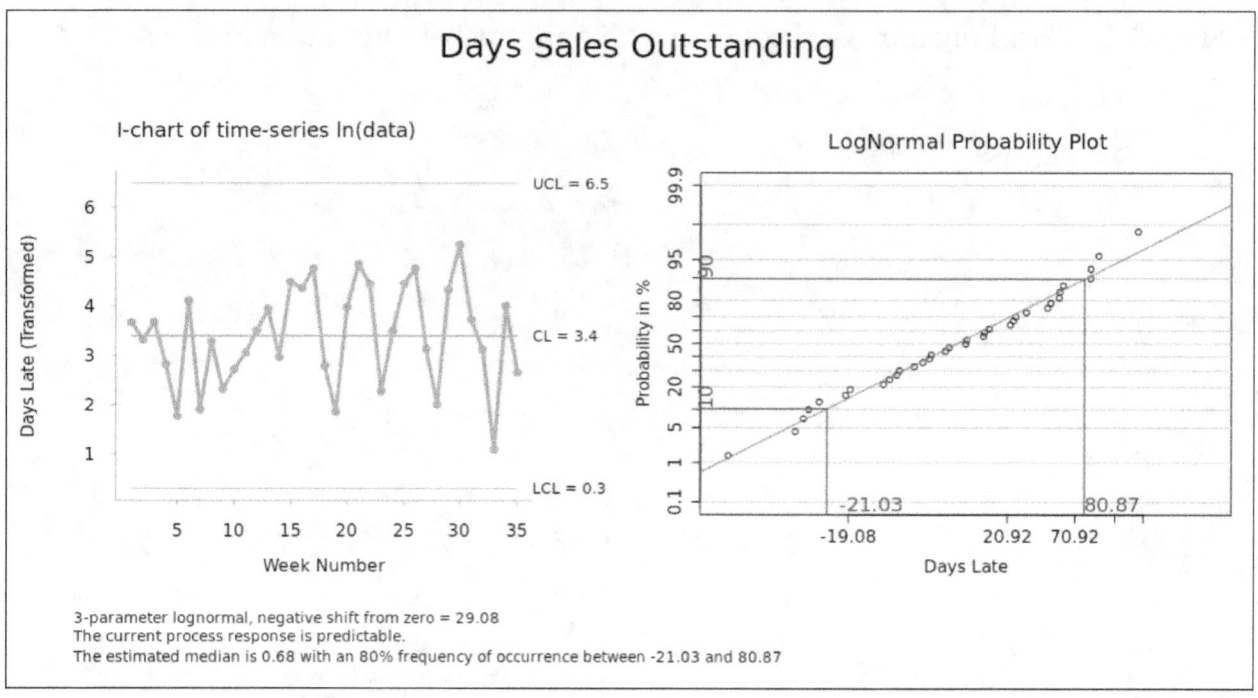

Figure 6.28: EPRS Metric-App Input (30,000-foot-level Report, No Subgroup, Lognormal Transformation with Shift Value)

IEE Scorecard for DSO

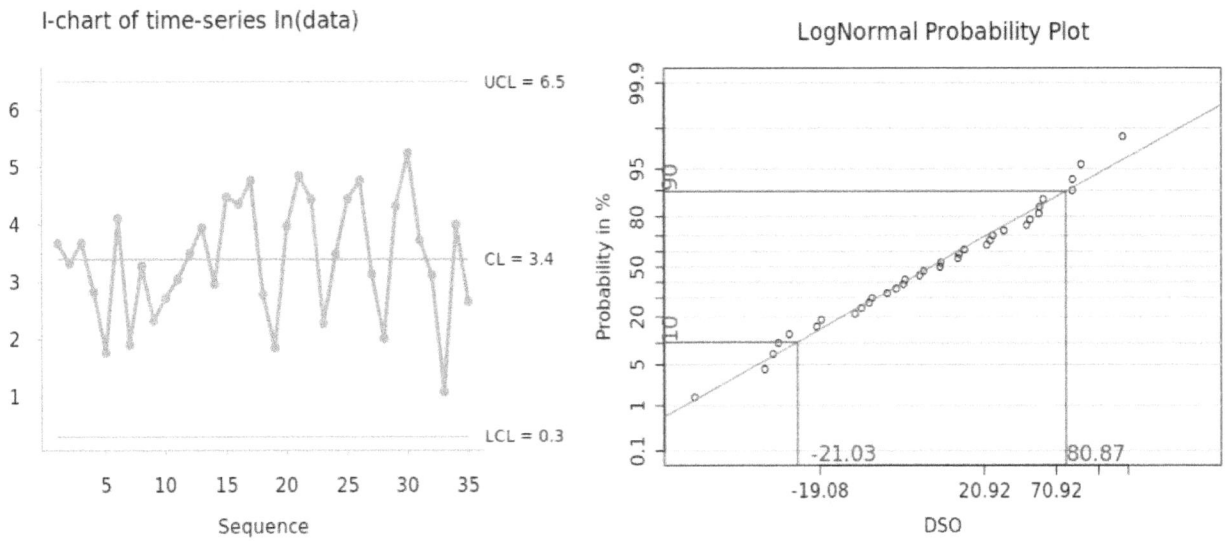

The current process response is predictable.

The estimated median is 0.68 with an 80% frequency of occurrence between -21.03 and 80.87

Figure 6.29: EPRS Metric-App Output (30,000-foot-level Report, No Subgroup, Lognormal Transformation with Shift Value)

Comment

- If this estimated median and 80% frequency of occurrence rate is unacceptable, there is a need for process improvement.
- You can add, remove or change chart elements such as title, labels, gridlines and data labels by clicking on the chart and selecting "+".

7

IEE-DMAIC — Measure Phase (Baseline Project): IEE 30,000-foot-level Report (Attribute Failure Rate Response)

7.1 IEE-DMAIC Roadmap Component

Book 1 Reference: *IEE Volume III* – Chapter 13

Book 2 Reference: *Lean Six Sigma Project Execution Guide* – Section 3

Internet: www.smartersolutions.com/roadmap (clicking on highlighted area provides the flowchart below)

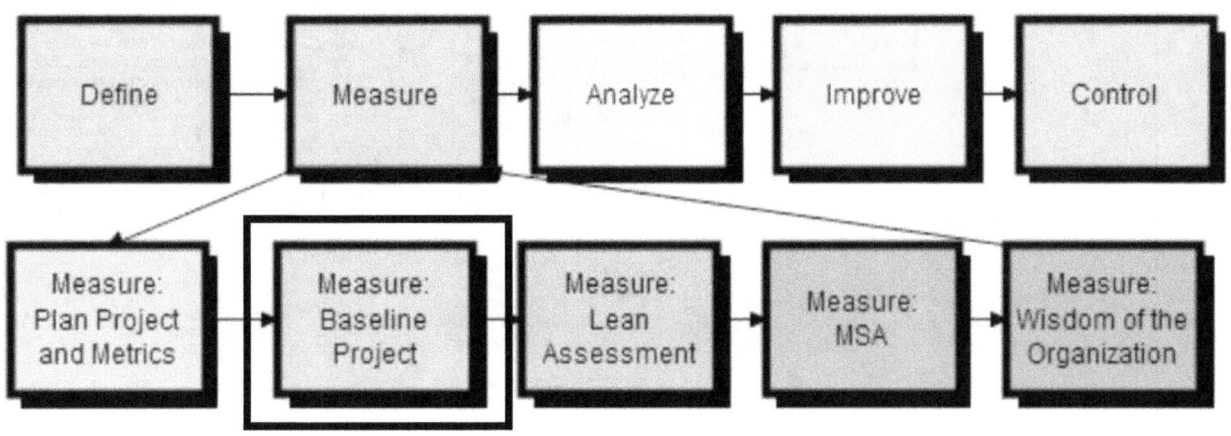

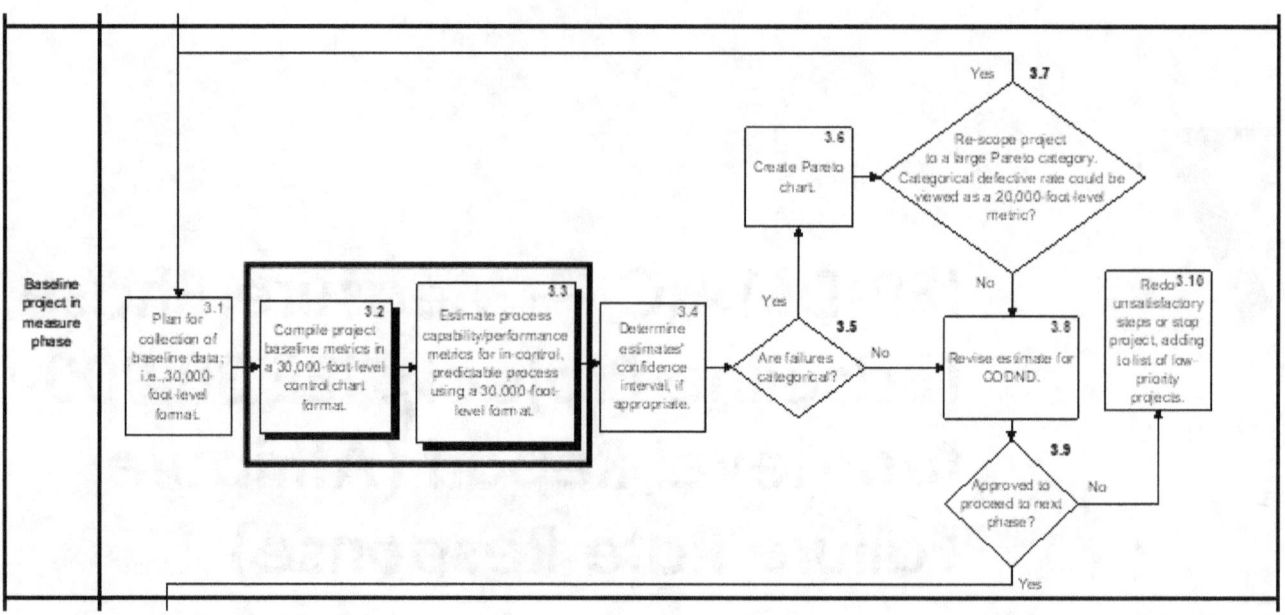

Figure 7.1 shows a step 3.2 drilldown of the IEE DMAIC project execution roadmap where the attribute (failure rate) output response is highlighted in this process-stability assessment decision tree.

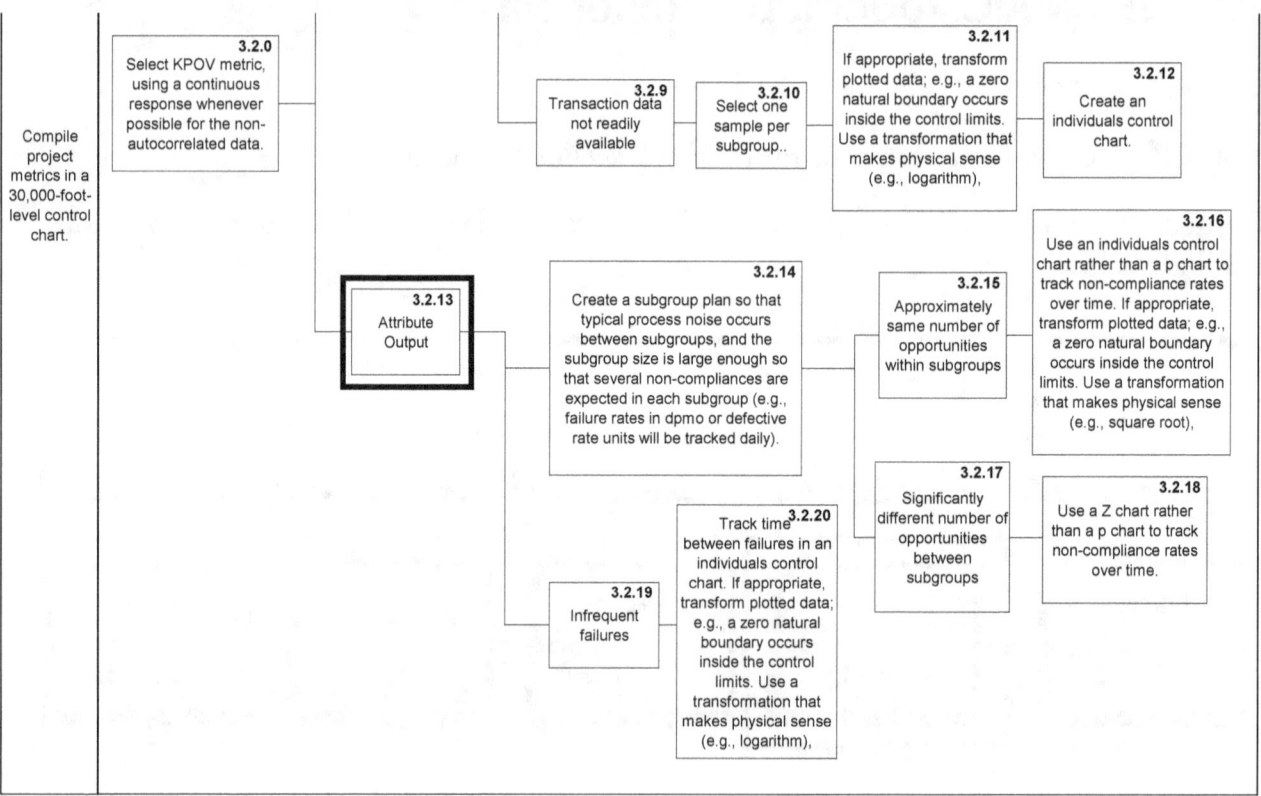

Figure 7.1: Process Stability Assessment Chart Selection for an Attribute Failure Rate Response

Figure 7.2 shows a step 3.3 drill-down of the IEE DMAIC project execution roadmap where the attribute (failure rate) output response is highlighted in this process-stability assessment decision tree.

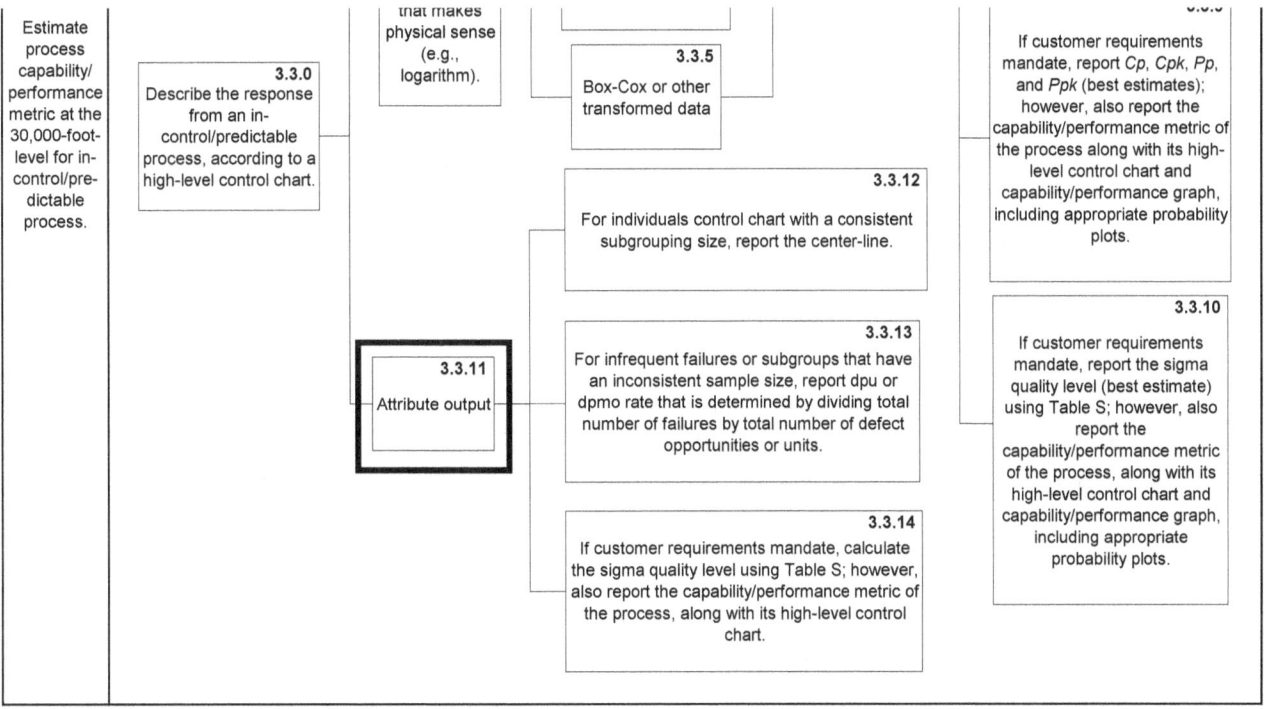

Figure 7.2: Process Capability/Performance Statement from Stable Processes for an Attribute Failure Rate Response

7.2   IEE 30,000-foot-level Reporting: Attribute Failure Rate Output

The methodologies described in this section apply to the creation of 30,000-foot-level reports for the following process assessments:

- The daily defective rate for transaction execution; e.g., insurance claims or manufactured parts
- The daily process DPMO rate when there are multiple defect opportunities when completing a variety of transactions, e.g., completing an invoice or manufacturing a printed circuit board

Input data provides a standard deviation for calculating the control chart limits for continuous data. However, the binomial and Poisson distribution equations show that standard deviation is dependent on the mean of the data, not data dispersion, as with continuous data. Hence, the standard deviation for an attribute control that uses the binomial or Poisson distribution originates from a formula based on the mean.

An in-control process considers that the underlying probabilities remain fixed over time for the binomial-distribution-based and Poisson-distribution-based control charts. This probability-over-time consistency does not often occur, dramatically impacting the binomial-distribution-based and Poisson-distribution-based control-chart limits, especially when the sample size gets large.

For large sample sizes, batch-to-batch variation can be more significant than the prediction of traditional theory because of the violation of an underlying assumption. This assumption is that the sum of one or more binomial-distributed random variables will follow a binomial distribution. This assumption is not valid if these random variables have differing values. The implication is that with substantial sample sizes, classical control chart formulas squeeze limits toward the centerline of the charts and can result in many points falling outside the control limits. The implication is that the process is out of control most of the time (unpredictable process) when in reality, the control limits do not reflect the true common-cause variability of the process.

A remedy for this problem is to plot the attribute failure rates as individual measurements. One problem with this approach is that the failure rate for the time of interest can be meager. For this situation, the control chart limit might be less than zero, which is not physically possible. One approach to get around this problem is to use an individuals-control chart to track the time between failures.

Another problem with plotting failure rates directly as individual measurements is that there can be a difference in batch sample size. Situations described in this book assume that subgroup sample sizes are similar.

The steps to perform this IEE analysis under various situations are:

1. Control chart creation steps (see Figure 7.1)

   o   Attribute (failure rate) output [3.2.14] – Create a subgroup plan so that typical process noise occurs between subgroups, and the subgroup size is large enough so that there is an expectation that several non-compliances will happen in each subset, e.g., defective rates tracked weekly. Each subgroup should have approximately the same number of opportunities. Use an individuals-chart rather than a p-chart to track non-compliance rates over time, where the data may need an appropriate normalizing transformation.

   o   Attribute (failure rate) output [3.2.19], [3.2.20] – When failures occur infrequently (e.g., Safety occurrences in an organization), use an individuals-chart for tracking the time between events.

2. Process capability/performance metric creation steps for predictable processes (Figure 7.2):

   o   Attribute (failure rate) output [3.3.12] – For an individuals-chart with a consistent subgrouping size where there is no transformation, a 30,000-foot-level reporting at the bottom of the chart will be the same as the chart's center-line non-conformance rate o   Attribute (failure rate) output [3.3.13] – For infrequent failures, report a mean and 80% frequency-of-occurrence rate between failures or a division of the total number of failures by the total number of defect opportunities or units.

7.3   Example: Comparing P-chart Reporting to 30,000-foot-level Reporting using EPRS Metric-App (Attribute Failure Rate Response)

SigmaXL: p-chart

EPRS Metric-App: Attribute Failure Rate Response

IEE Volume III Example and Dataset

- *IEE Volume III* Example 13.1: Attribute Failure Rate Response, Comparing SigmaXL p-chart with a 30,000-foot-level report
- Dataset (Smarter Solutions (2022): V3 C13, Exam 13-01, IEE pass-fail predictability.xlsx

SigmaXL or EPRS Metric-App [Smarter Solutions (2020)] Input/Output

- Figure 7.3: SigmaXL Input p-chart Creation
- Figure 7.4: SigmaXL Output p-chart
- Figure 7.5: EPRS Metric-App Input 30,000-foot-level Report of p-chart Data
- Figure 7.6: EPRS Metric-App Output 30,000-foot-level Report of p-chart Data

SigmaXL Chart Function: Control Charts>Attributes Charts>P

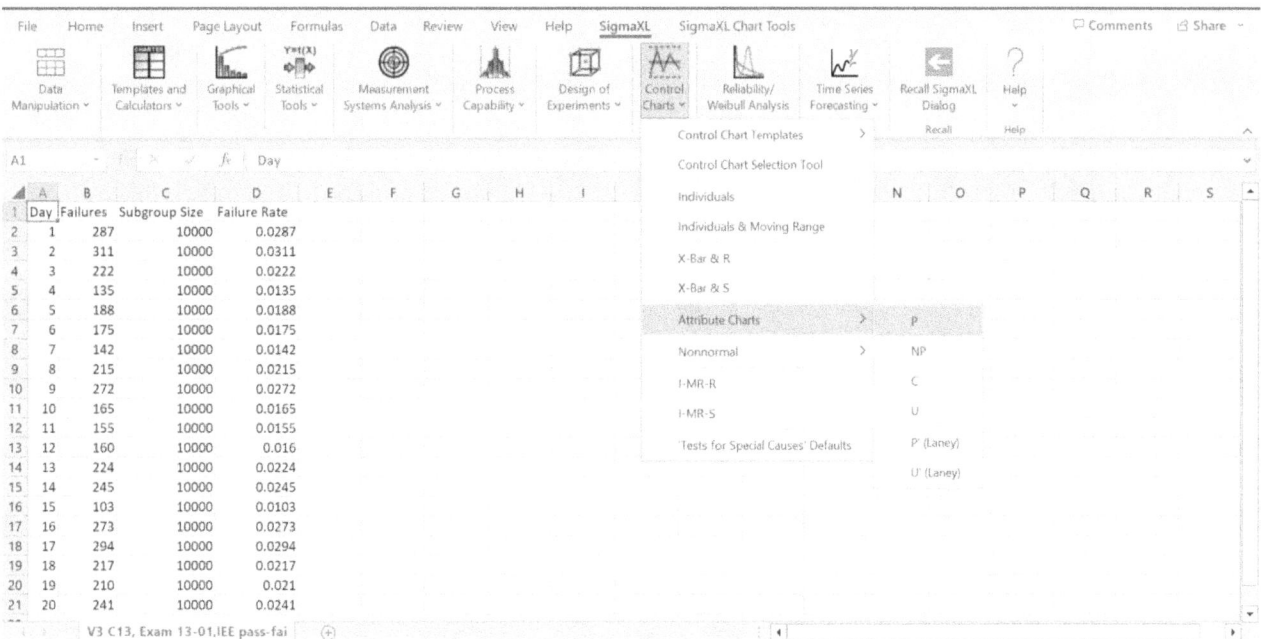

Figure 7.3: Creating SigmaXL p-chart

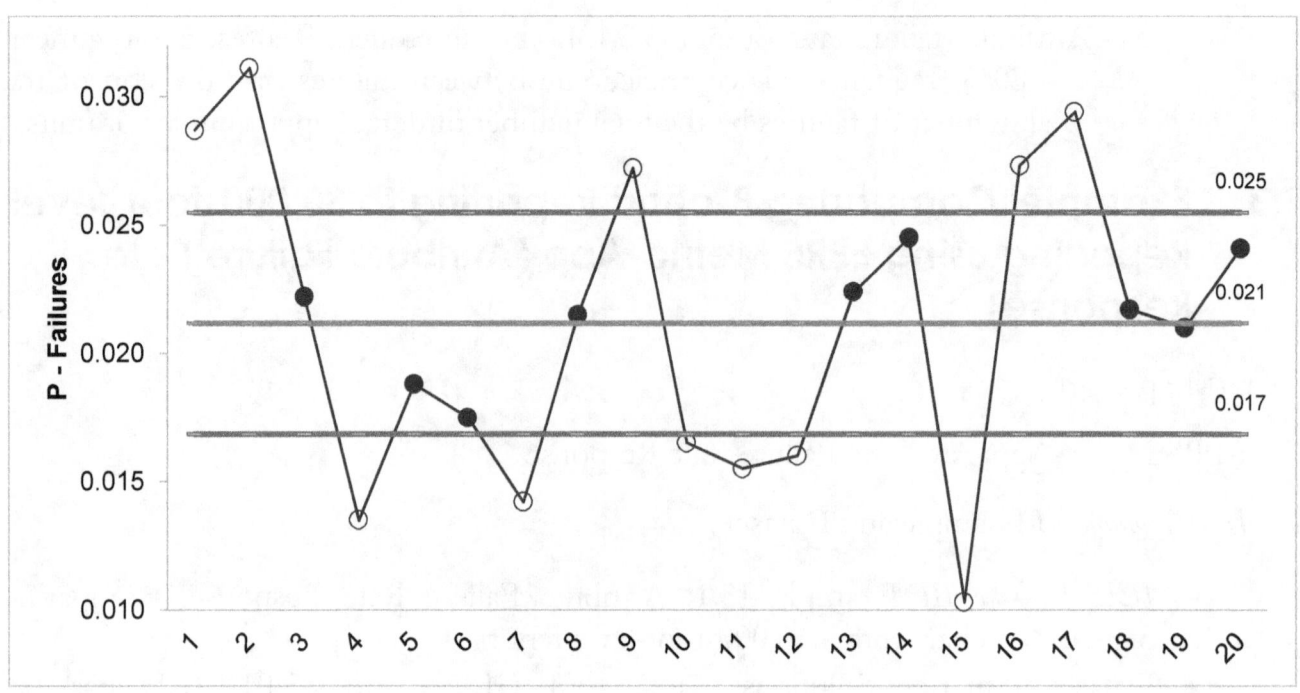

Figure 7.4: SigmaXL p-chart

Comment

- There are many out-of-control signals that should be addressed
- You can add, remove or change chart elements such as title, labels, gridlines and data labels by clicking on the chart and selecting "+".

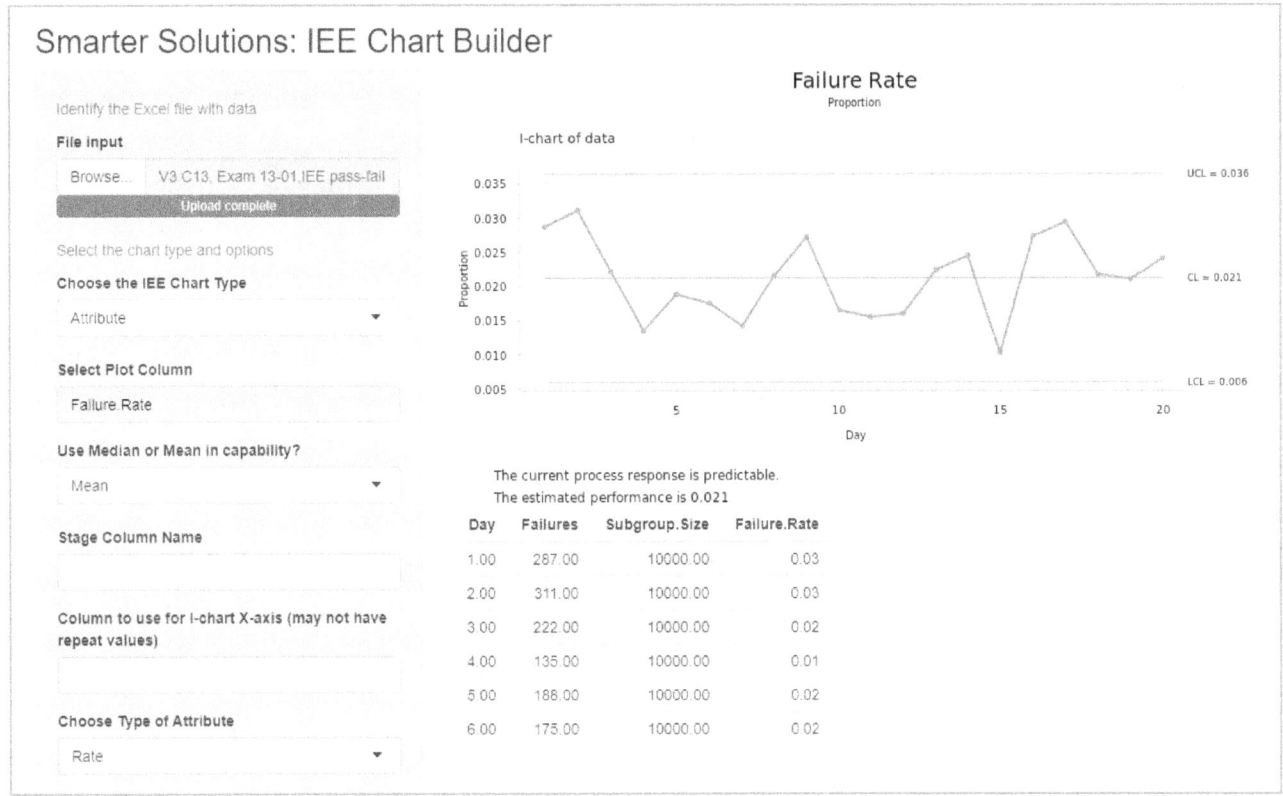

Figure 7.5: EPRS Metric-App Input 30,000-foot-level Report of p-chart Data

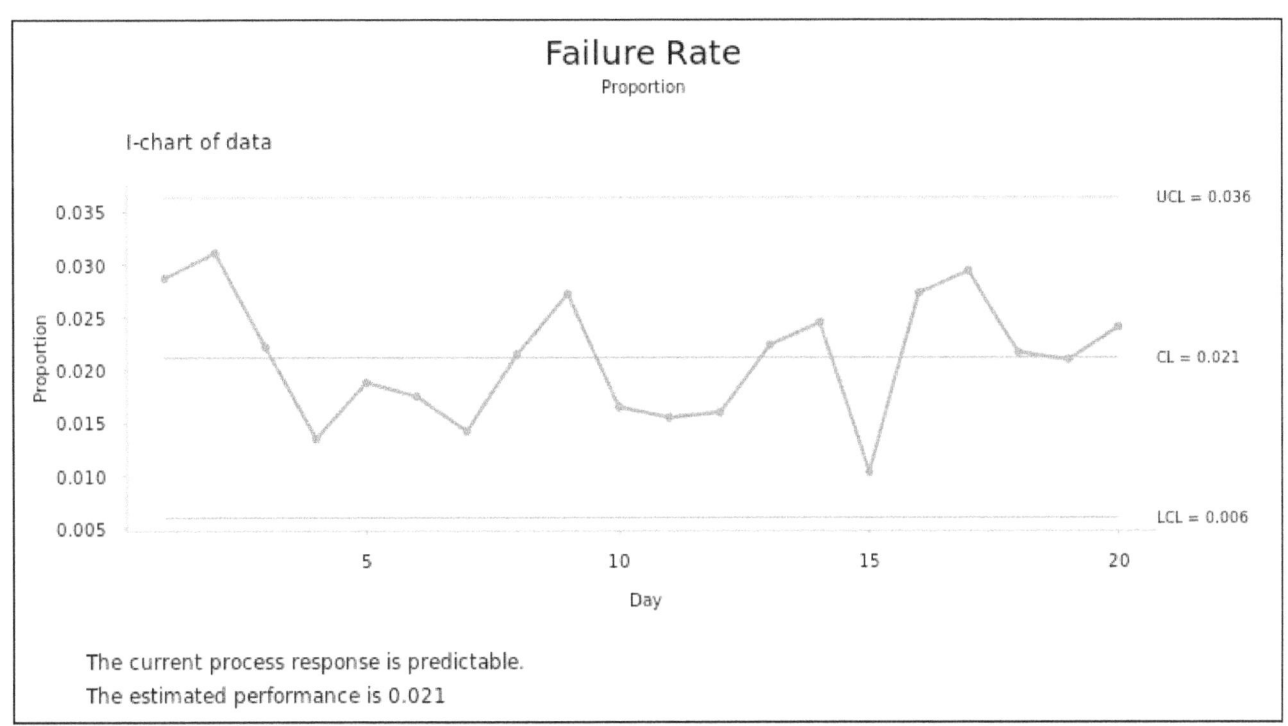

Figure 7.6: EPRS Metric-App Output 30,000-foot-level Report of p-chart Data

Comments

- The 30,000-foot-level report in Figure 7.6 indicates process stability. It provides an estimated predictive non-conformance rate statement for the process of 0.021, while a traditional p-chart in Figure 7.4 shows that the process is out-of-control. The reason for this reporting difference and why the Figure 7.6 report is a better reporting methodology is described in "Issues and Resolution to p-chart Control Limits Formula False Signals" (Smarter Solutions 2015b).

- If the estimated failure rate of 0.021 shown in Figure 7.6 is unacceptable, there is a need for process improvement.

- You can add, remove or change chart elements such as title, labels, gridlines and data labels by clicking on the chart and selecting "+".

7.4 Example: 30,000-foot-level Reporting using EPRS Metric- App (Attribute Failure Rate Response)

Application: Attribute Failure Rate Response

IEE Volume III Example and Dataset

- *IEE Volume III* Example 13.2: 30,000-foot-level Report – Attribute Failure Rate Response
- Dataset (Smarter Solutions (2022): V3 C13, Exam 13-02, Orange Juice.xlsx

SigmaXL or EPRS Metric-App [Smarter Solutions (2020)] Input/Output

- Figure 7.7: EPRS Metric-App Input (Attribute Failure Rate)
- Figure 7.8: EPRS Metric-App Output (Attribute Failure Rate)

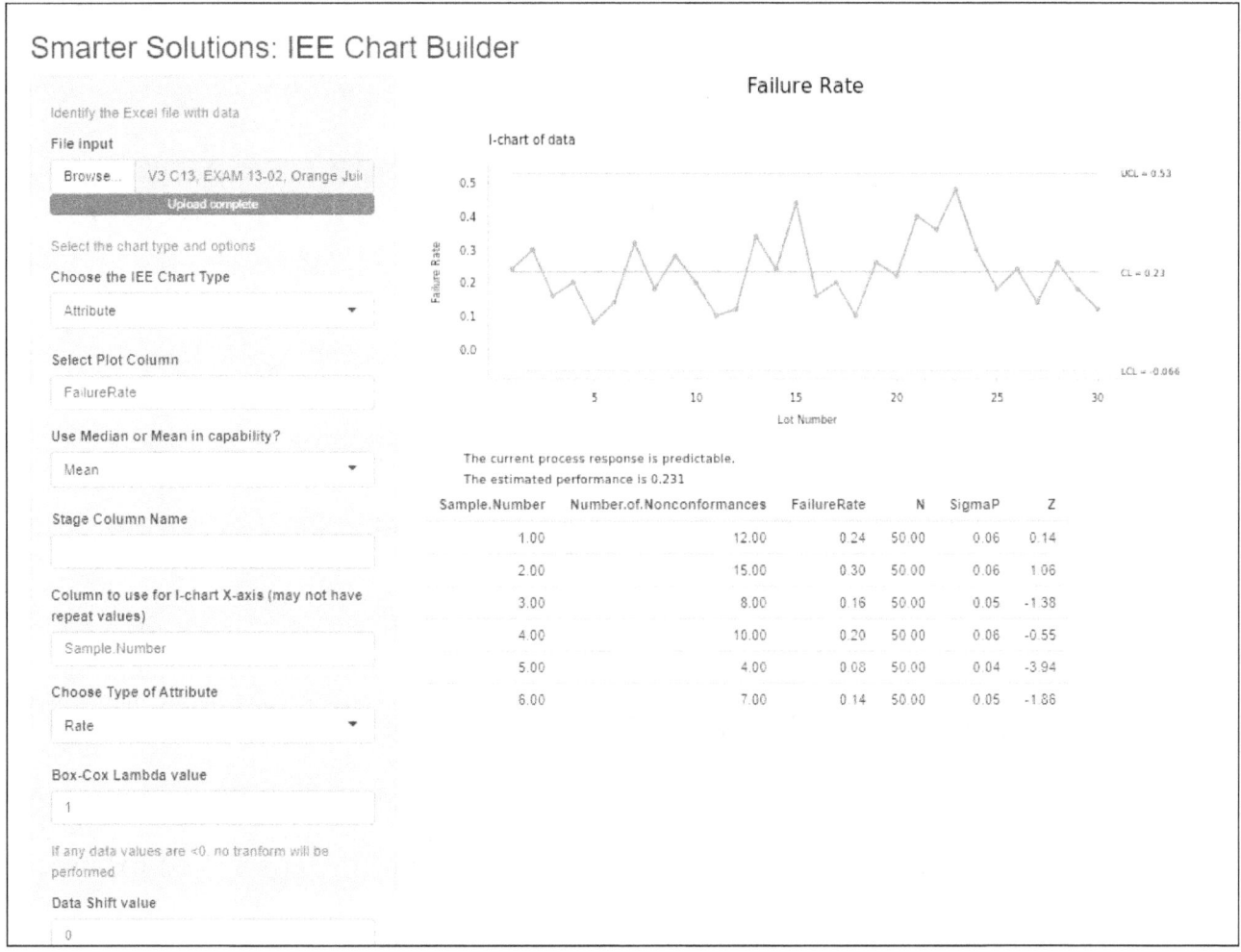

Figure 7.7: EPRS Metric-App Input (Attribute Failure Rate)

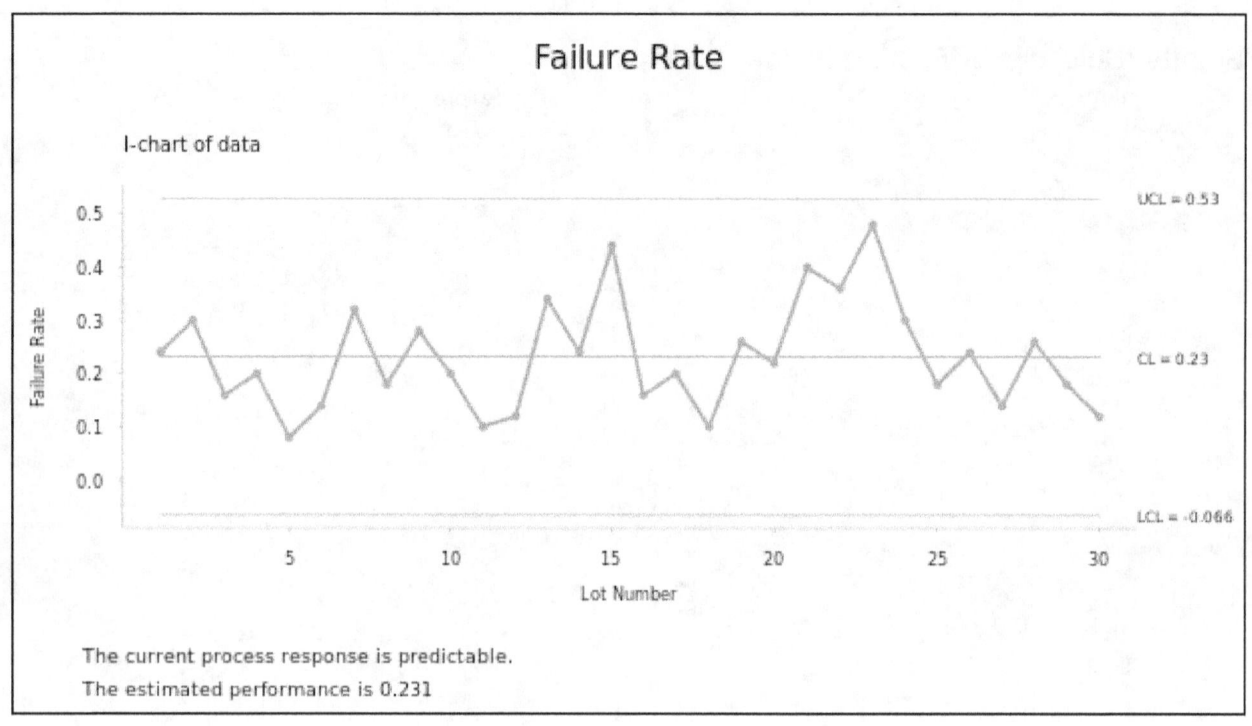

Figure 7.8: EPRS Metric-App Output (Attribute Failure Rate)

Comment

- If this estimated failure rate of 23.1% is unacceptable, there is a need for process improvement.

7.5   Example: 30,000-foot-level Reporting using EPRS Metric-App (Infrequent Failures)

Application: Attribute response when failures are infrequent

IEE Volume III Example and Dataset

- *IEE Volume III* Example 13.3: 30,000-foot-level Report – Attribute Infrequent Failures
- Dataset (Smarter Solutions (2022): V3 C13, Exam 13-03, IEE Infrequent Events.xlsx

SigmaXL or EPRS Metric-App [Smarter Solutions (2020)] Input/Output

- Figure 7.9: EPRS Metric-App Input (30,000-foot-level Report, Infrequent Failures, Before Process Change)
- Figure 7.10: EPRS Metric-App Output (30,000-foot-level Report, Infrequent Failures, Before Process Change)
- Figure 7.11: EPRS Metric-App Input (30,000-foot-level Report, Infrequent Failures, Before and After Process Change)

- Figure 7.12: EPRS Metric-App Output (30,000-foot-level Report, Infrequent Failures, Before and After Process Change)

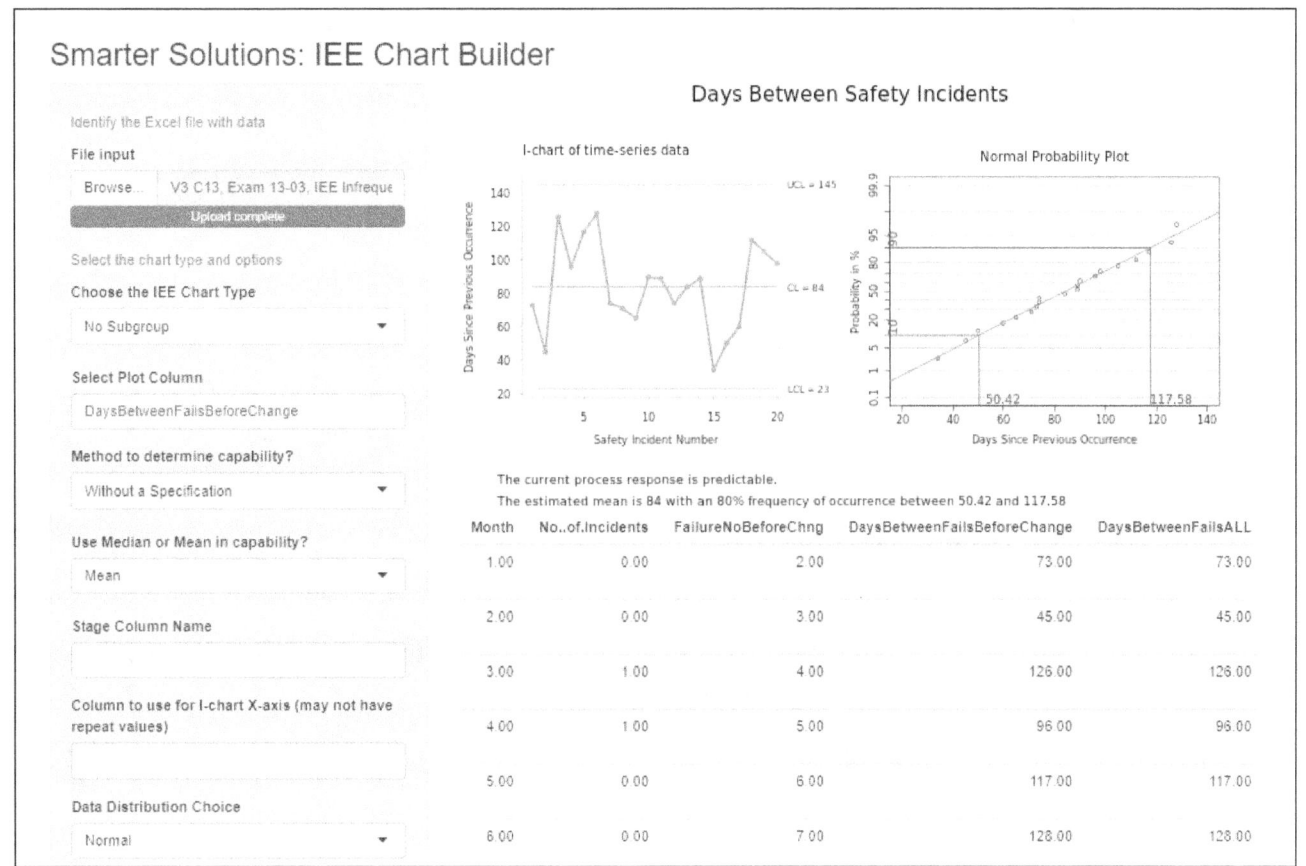

Figure 7.9: EPRS Metric-App Input (30,000-foot-level Report, Infrequent Failures, Before Process Change)

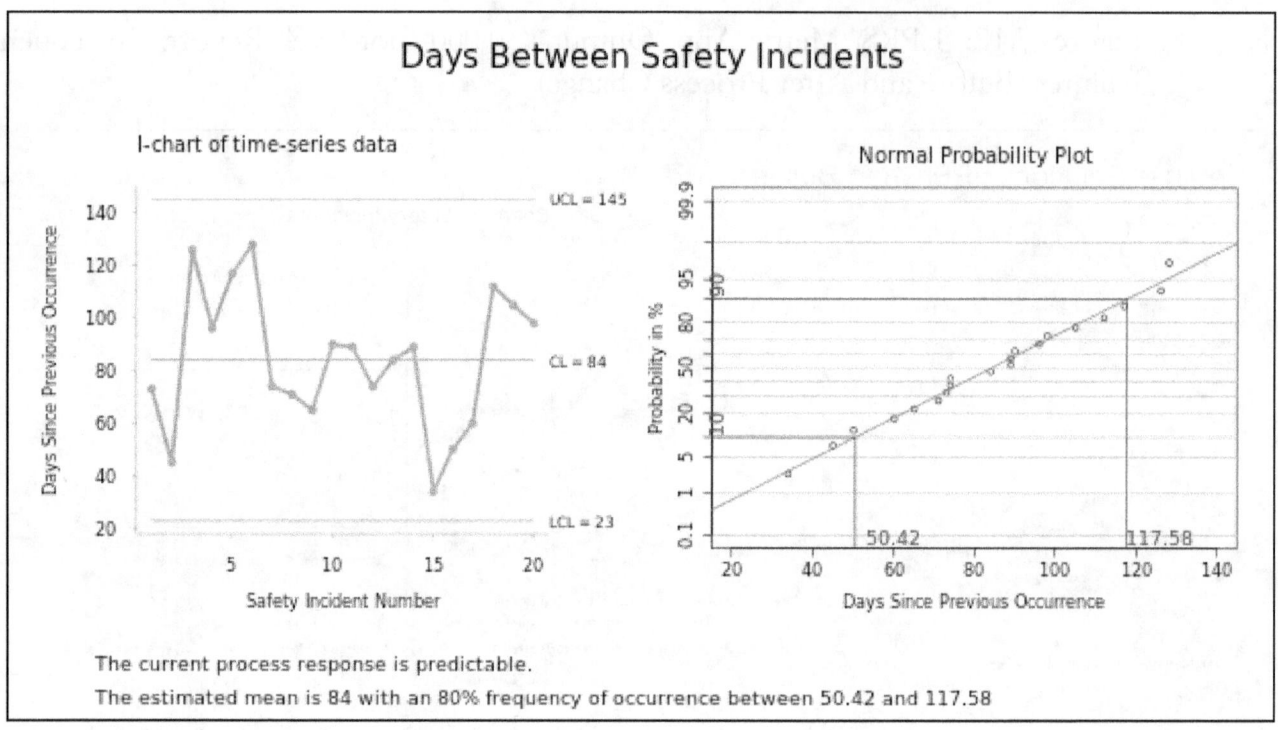

Figure 7.10: EPRS Metric-App Output (30,000-foot-level Report, Infrequent Failures, Before Process Change)

Comments: 30,000-foot-level report

- The process is stable
- Could report a mean of 84 days between failures and 80% (4 out of 5 incidents) between 50 and 117 days
- Could also report an estimated daily safety occurrence rate of $1/84 = 0.0119$ daily safety occurrence rate
- If this occurrence rate is unsatisfactory, there is a need for improvements
- Figures 7.11 and 7.12 show the results of a process improvement effort

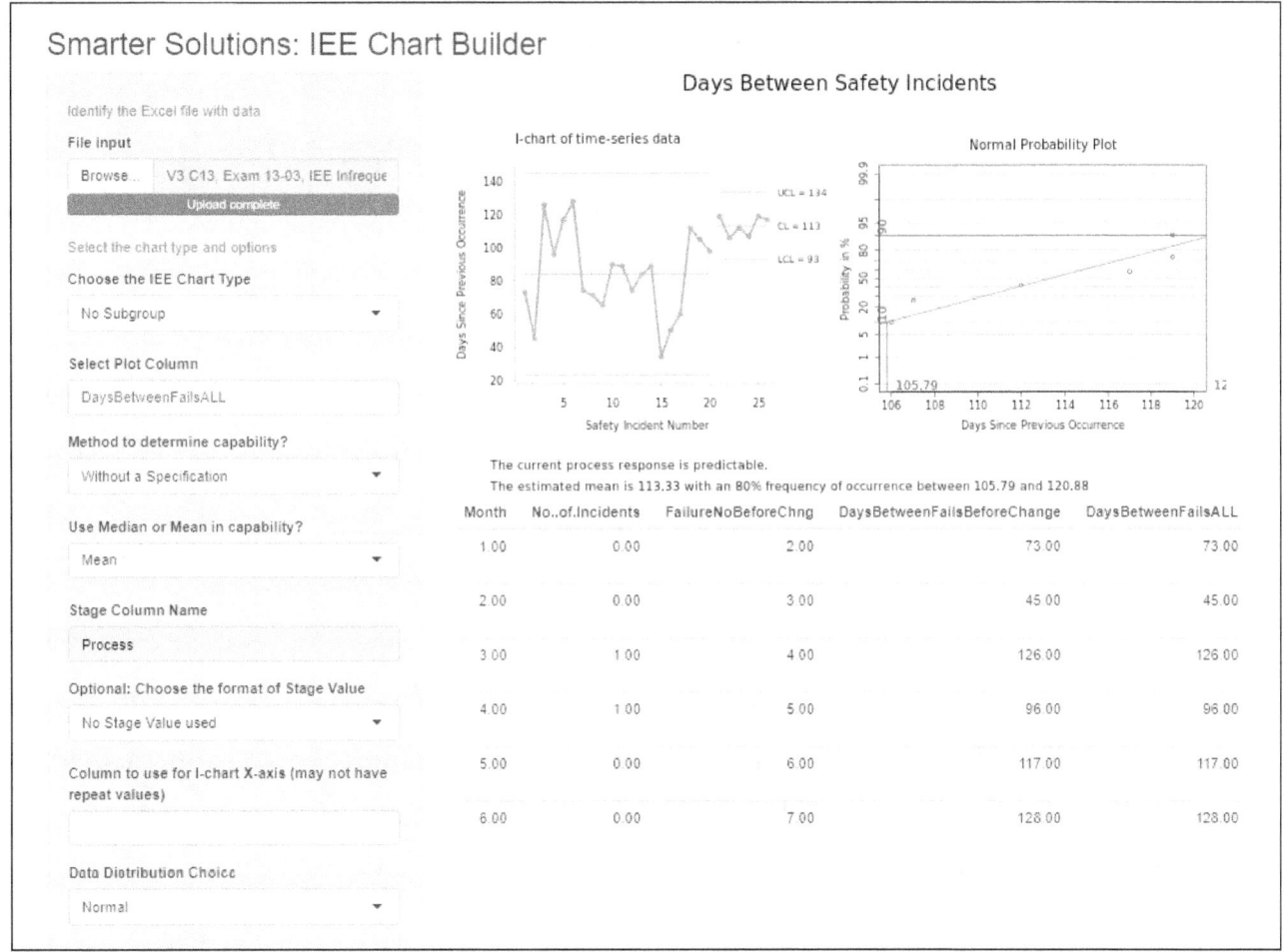

Figure 7.11: EPRS Metric-App Input (30,000-foot-level Report, Infrequent Failures, Before and After Process Change)

Comments

- Stage Column Name "Process" is not seen in the Excel worksheet upper left corner snippet shown in Figure 7.11
- Open the Excel spreadsheet to see the name "Process" further to the right of this snippet spreadsheet view

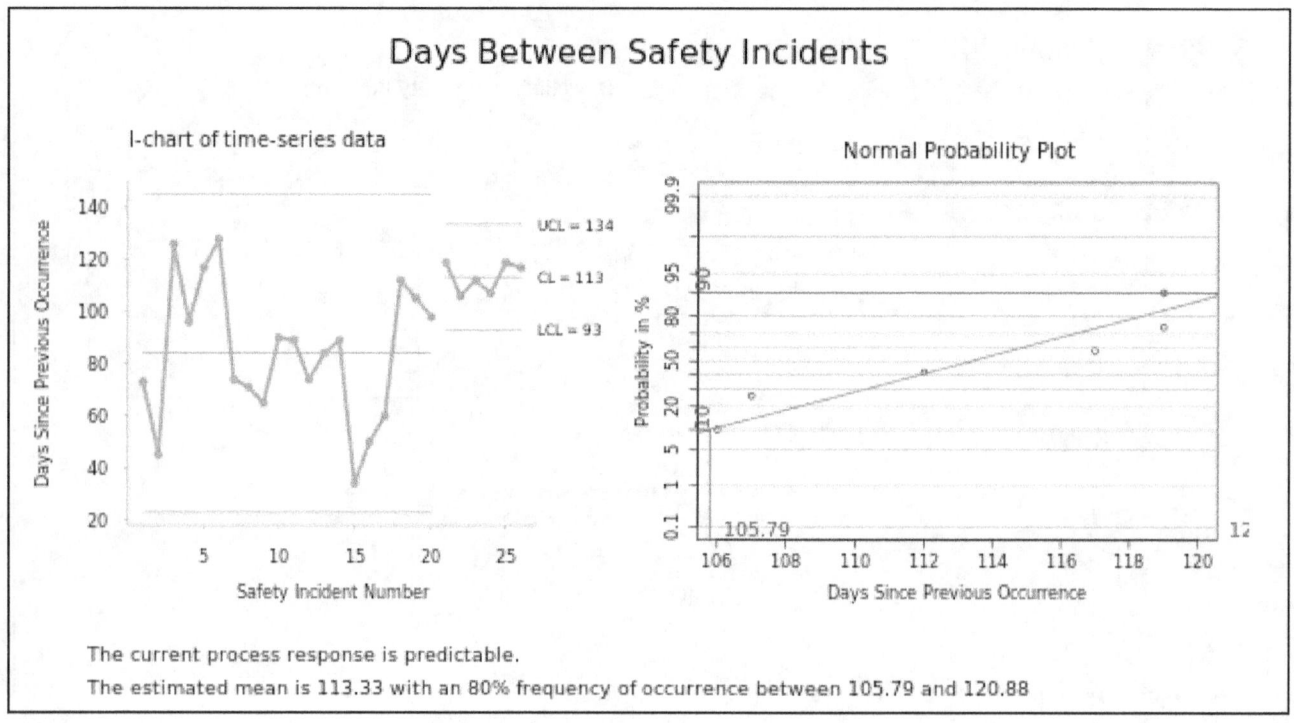

Figure 7.12: EPRS Metric-App Output (30,000-foot-level Report, Infrequent Failures, Before and After Process Change)

Comments: 30,000-foot-level report

- The organization created a process improvement project to increase the time between safety incidents

- Because of this improvement project, the process has a new (staged), improved level of stable process performance

- The new process predicted mean-time-between-safety-incidents is 113 days with an 80% frequency of occurrence between 106 and 121 days.

- This safety occurrence rate is an improvement of the previously reported mean time between incident rate of 84 days between failures with an 80% frequency of occurrence between 50 and 117 days

- If this occurrence rate is still unsatisfactory, there is a need for further process improvements

7.6 Example: 30,000-foot-level Reporting using EPRS Metric-App (Attribute Failure Rate Assessment with Pareto Chart)

Application: Attribute Failure Rate (Y) Response and Pareto Chart

IEE Volume III Example and Dataset

- *IEE Volume III* Example 13.5: 30,000-foot-level Report – Attribute Failure Rate Assessment and Pareto Chart

- Dataset (Smarter Solutions (2022): V3 C13, Exam 13-05, 30000 ft Attribute.xlsx

SigmaXL or EPRS Metric-App [Smarter Solutions (2020)] Input/Output

- Figure 7.13: EPRS Metric-App Input (30,000-foot-level Report, Attribute Failure Rate, No Staging)
- Figure 7.14: EPRS Metric-App Input (30,000-foot-level Report, Attribute Failure Rate, Staging)
- Figure 7.15: EPRS Metric-App Output (30,000-foot-level Report, Attribute Failure Rate, Staging)
- Figure 7.16: EPRS Metric-App Input/Output (Pareto Chart – Frequency of Occurrence)
- Figure 7.17: EPRS Metric-App Input/Output (Pareto Chart – Cost of Doing Nothing Differently [CODND])

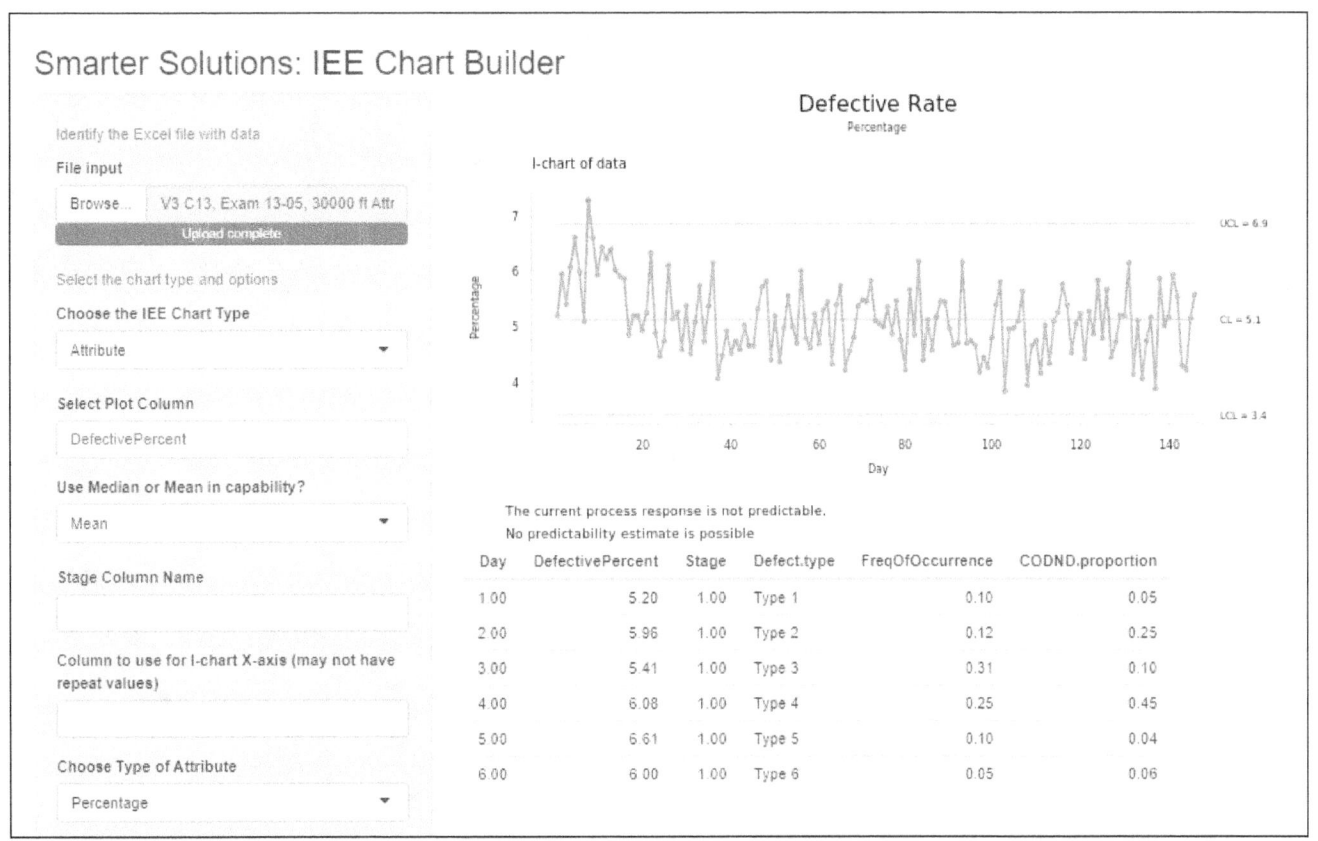

Figure 7.13: EPRS Metric-App Input (30,000-foot-level Report, Attribute Failure Rate, No Staging)

Comment

- On day 17 the process appears to have a significantly lesser failure rate
- Figure 7.14 shows the staging of this process output response on this day

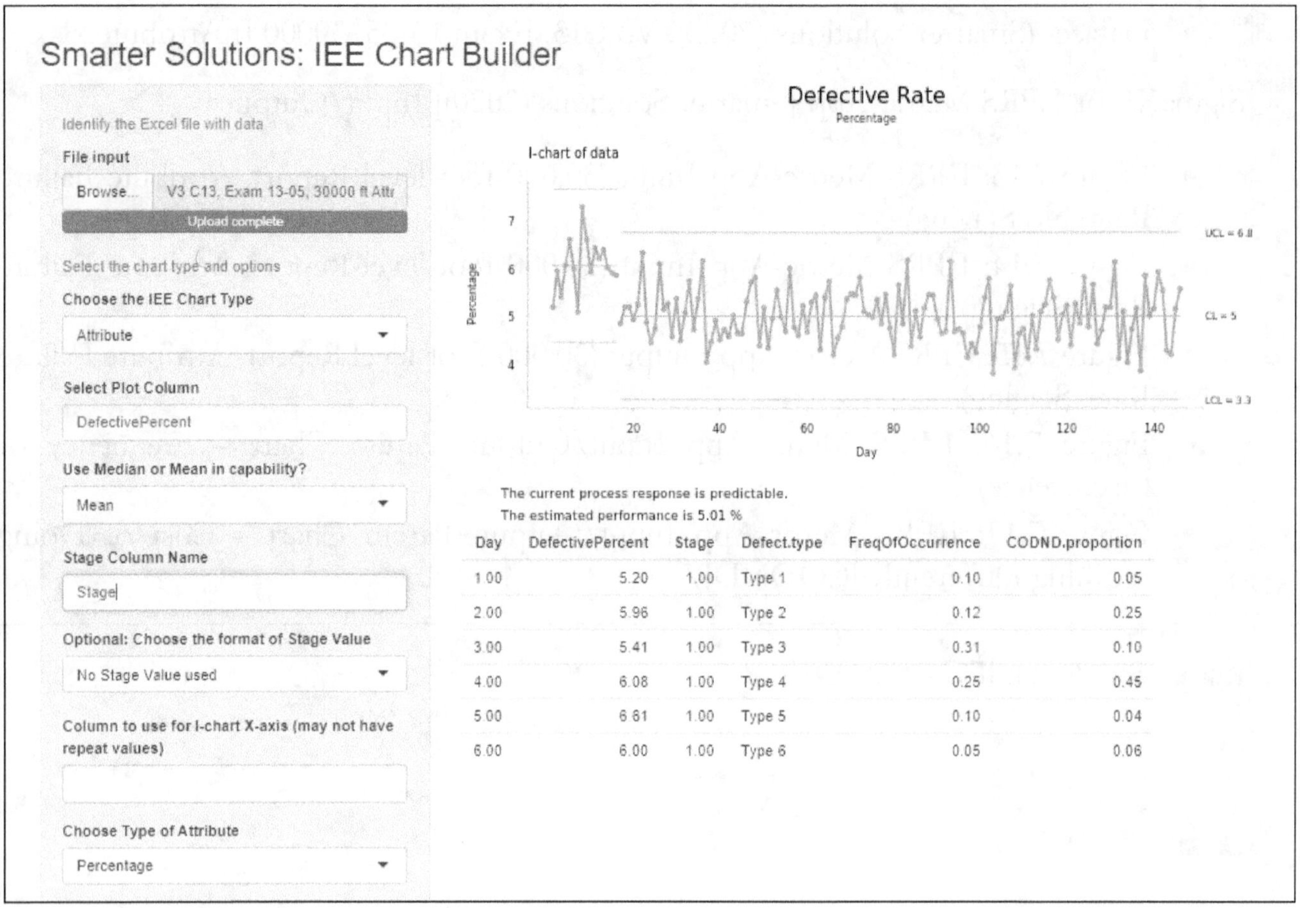

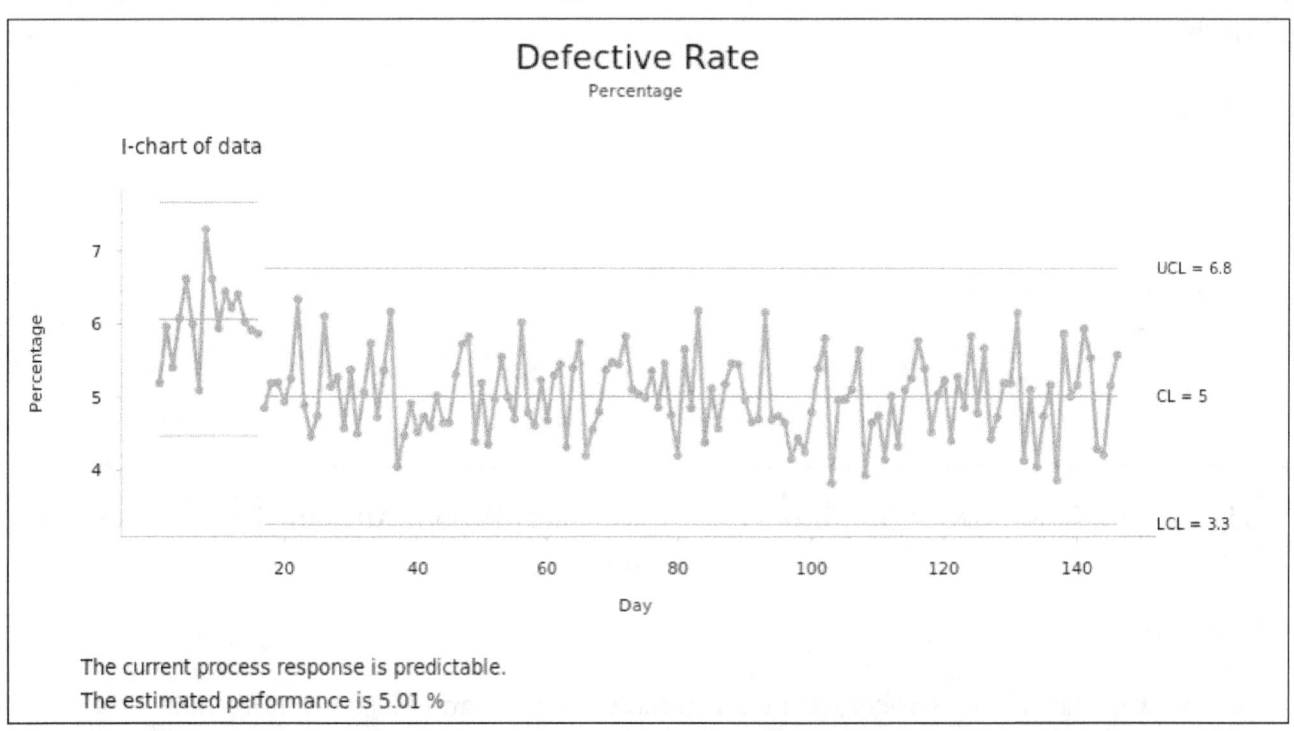

Figure 7.14: EPRS Metric-App Input (30,000-foot-level Report, Attribute Failure Rate, Staging)

Figure 7.15: EPRS Metric-App Output (30,000-foot-level Report, Attribute Failure Rate, Staging)

Comments: Figure 7.15

- The process staging on day 17 appeared to be the right thing to do
- The organization considered that the new estimated predicted performance of 5.01% was unacceptable
- Pareto charts of the frequency and CODND by failure type can provide insight of where to focus process improvement efforts, as illustrated in Figures 7.16 and 7.17

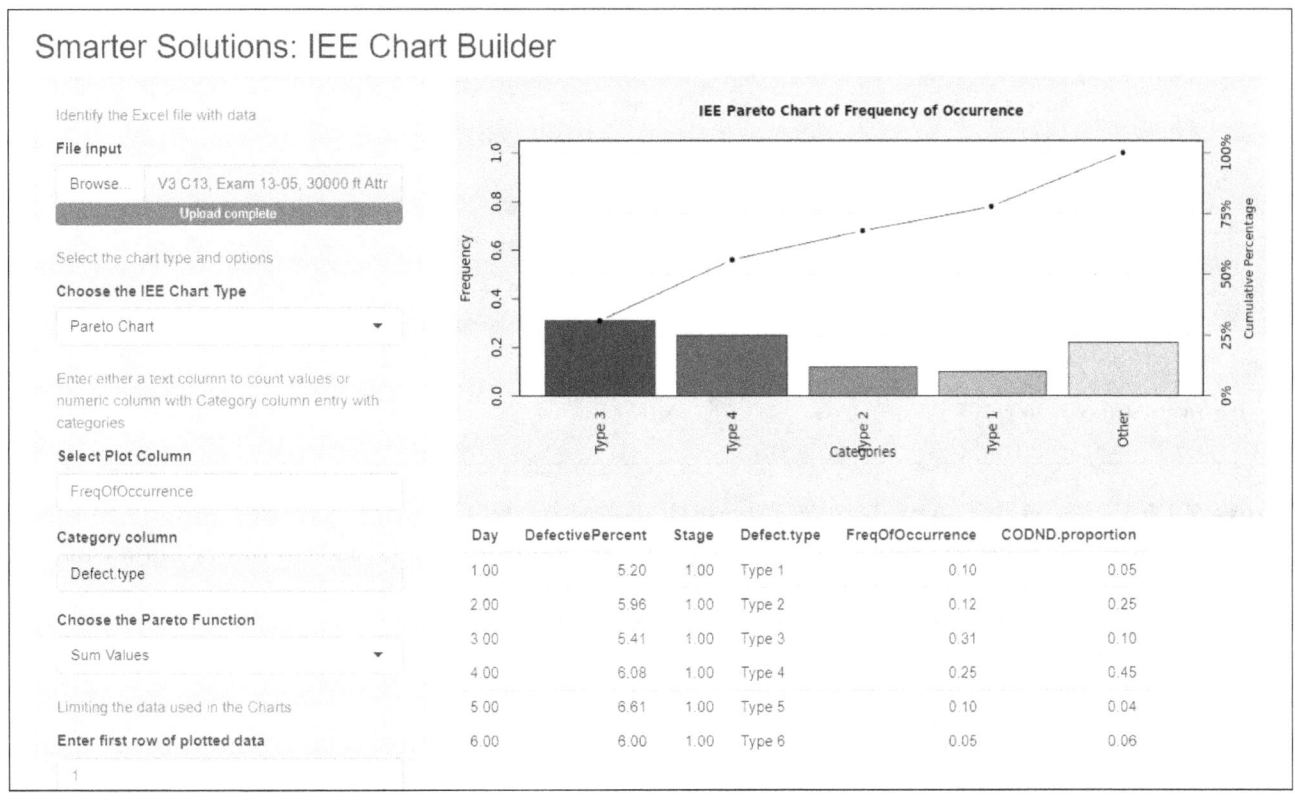

Figure 7.16: EPRS Metric-App Input/Output (Pareto Chart – Frequency of Occurrence)

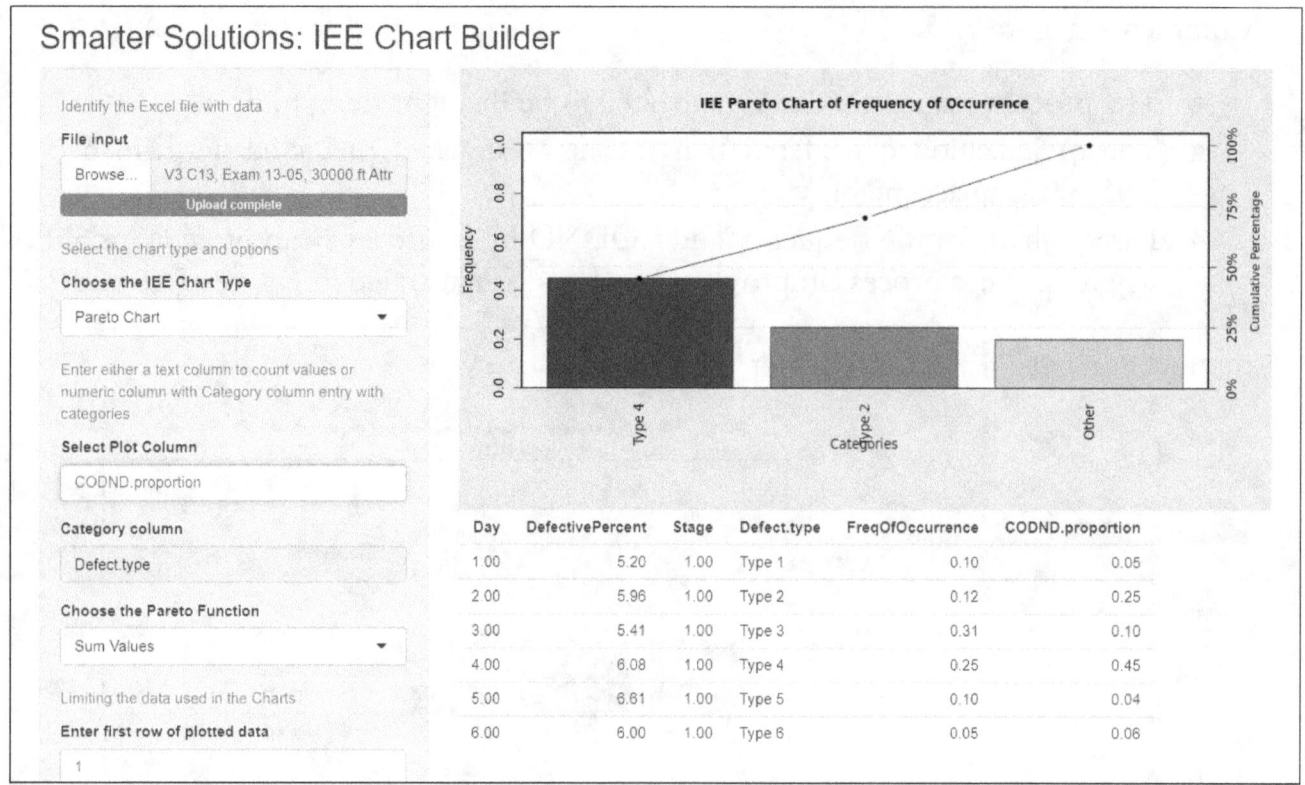

Figure 7.17: EPRS Metric-App Input/Output (Pareto Chart – Cost of Doing Nothing Differently [CODND])

Comments: Figures 7.16 and 7.17

- For process improvement efforts to reduce the frequency of non-conformance rate, Figure 7.16 indicates to focus first on what to do differently to minimize defective Type 3 and then on Type 4 failures
- For process improvement efforts to reduce the Cost of Doing Nothing Differently (CODND) amount, Figure 7.17 indicates to focus first on what to do differently to minimize defective Type 4 failures

8 IEE-DMAIC — Measure Phase (Measurement Systems Analysis)

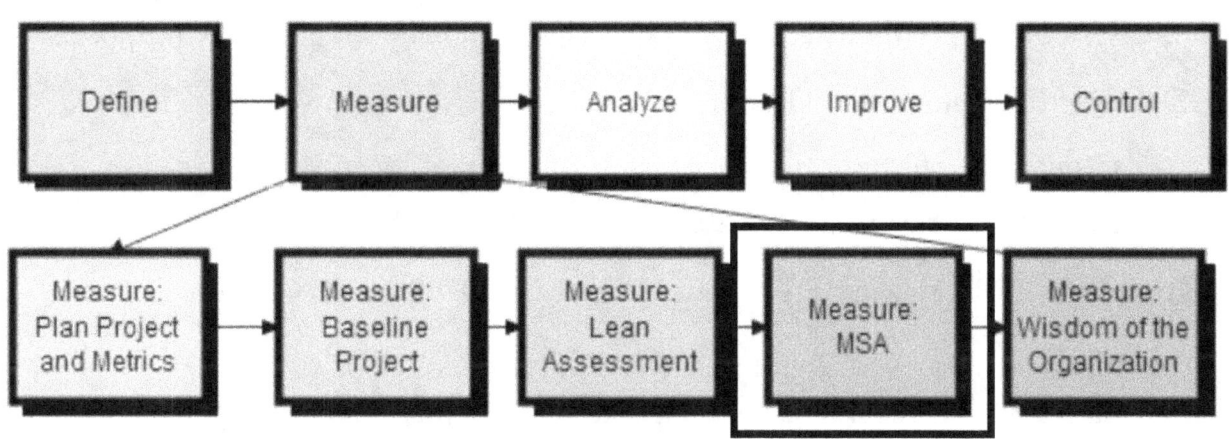

8.1 IEE-DMAIC Roadmap Component

Book 1 Reference: *IEE Volume III* – Chapter 15

Book 2 Reference: *Lean Six Sigma Project Execution Guide* – Section 5

Internet: www.smartersolutions.com/roadmap (clicking on highlighted area provides the flowchart below)

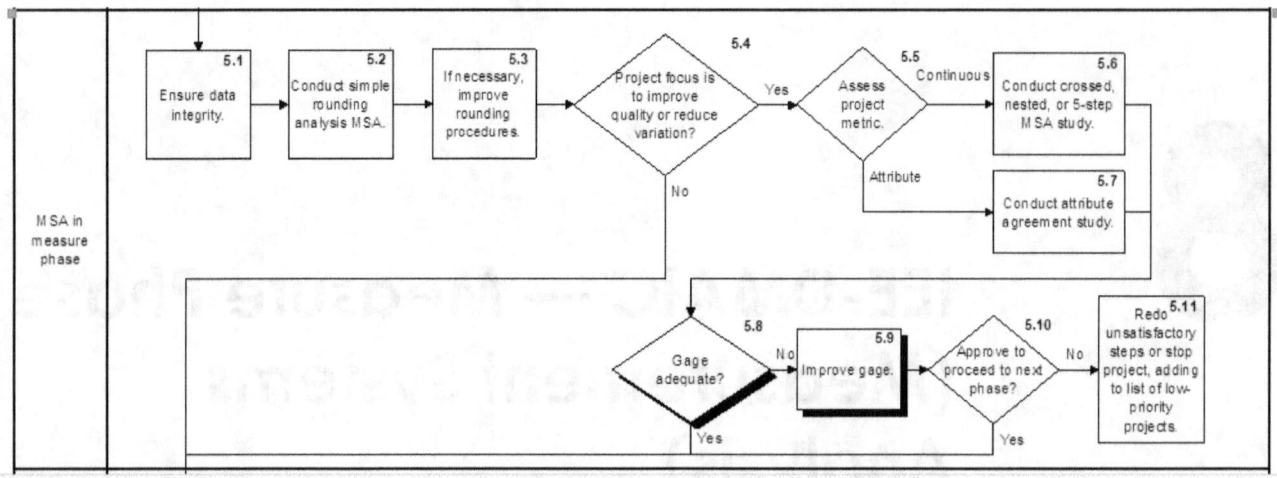

8.2 Example: Gage Repeatability and Reproducibility (Gage R&R) Study

The Gage R&R Study is a method of quantifying the repeatability and reproducibility of a measuring system and is conducted to evaluate a gage suitability for a specific purpose.

EE Volume III Example and Dataset

- *IEE Volume III* Example 15.1: Gage R&R Study
- Dataset (Smarter Solutions (2022): V3 C15, Exam 15-01, gage r&r

SigmaXL or EPRS Metric-App [Smarter Solutions (2020)] Input/Output

- Figure 8.1: SigmaXL Input (Gage R&R Study)
- Figure 8.2: SigmaXL Output (Gage R&R Study [Part 1])
- Figure 8.3: SigmaXL Output (Gage R&R Study [Part 2])
- Figure 8.4: SigmaXL Output (Gage R&R Study [Part 3])

SigmaXL Chart Function: Measurement System Analysis>Create Gage R&R Study (Crossed) Worksheet

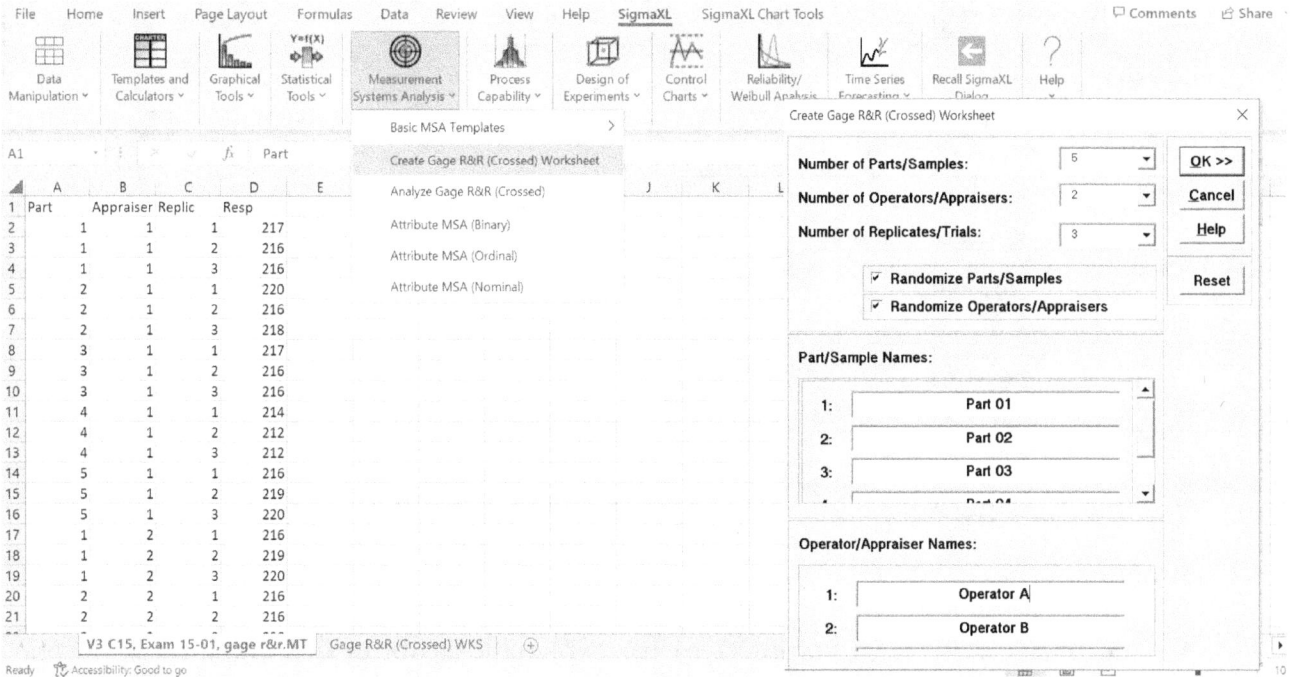

Figure 8.1: SigmaXL Input (Gage R&R Study)

Analysis of Variance with Part * Operator Interaction:

Source	DF	SS	MS	F	P
Part:	4	129.47	32.367	13.676	0.0133
Operator:	1	2.700	2.700	1.141	0.3456
Part * Operator:	4	9.467	2.367	0.922078	0.4706
Repeatability:	20	51.333	2.567		
Total:	29	192.97	6.654		

Analysis of Variance without Part * Operator Interaction (P for Interaction >= 0.1):

Source	DF	SS	MS	F	P
Part:	4	129.47	32.367	12.776	0.0000
Operator:	1	2.700	2.700	1.065789474	0.3122
Repeatability:	24	60.800	2.533		
Total:	29	192.9666667	6.654022989		

Figure 8.2: SigmaXL Output (Gage R&R Study [Part 1])

Comment

- See *IEE Volume III*, Example 15.1 for explanations about this Gage R&R output
- You can add, remove or change chart elements such as title, labels, gridlines and data labels by clicking on the chart and selecting "+".

Gage R&R Metrics	StDev	StDev Lower 90% CI	StDev Upper 90% CI	6 * StDev	% Total Variation (TV)	% TV Lower 90% CI	% TV Upper 90% CI
Gage R&R:	1.595	1.314	6.941	9.571	58.18	27.74	95.58
Operator (AV Appraiser Variation):	0.105409255	0	6.752	0.632456	3.84		
Part * Operator (INT Interaction):	0	0	0	0	0.00		
Reproducibility (SQRT(AV^2 + INT^2)):	0.105409255	0	6.752	0.632456	3.84		
Repeatability (EV Equipment Variation):	1.592	1.292	2.095	9.550	58.05		
Part Variation (PV):	2.230	1.353	5.470	13.379	81.33		
Total Variation (TV):	2.742	2.079	7.715	16.450	100.00		

Gage R&R Metrics	Variance Component	% Contribution of Variance Component
Gage R&R:	2.544	33.85
Operator:	0.011111111	0.15
Part * Operator:	0	0.00
Reproducibility:	0.011111111	0.15
Repeatability:	2.533	33.70
Part Variation:	4.972	66.15
Total Variation:	7.517	100.00

Figure 8.3: SigmaXL Output (Gage R&R Study [Part 2])

Comment

- See *IEE Volume III*, Example 15.1 for explanations about this Gage R&R output

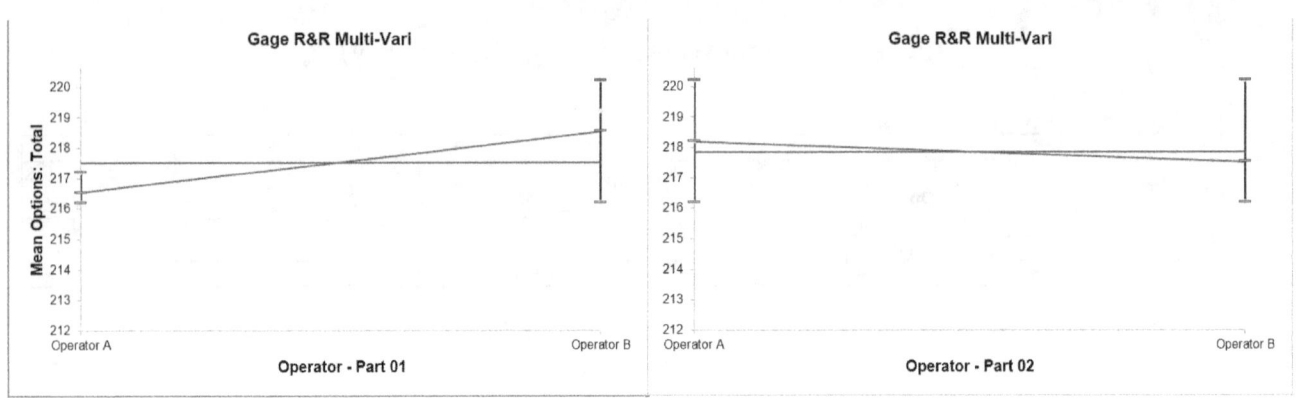

Figure 8.4: SigmaXL Output (Gage R&R Study [Part 3a])

Comment

- See *IEE Volume III*, Example 15.1 for detailed explanations about this Gage R&R output
- The Gage R&R multi-vari charts show each part as a separate graph. The measurements fore each operator are denoted as a vertical line with the top tick corresponding to the maximum reading and the bottom tick is the minimum. The middle tick is the mean reading and the horizontal line across each graph is the overall average for each part.
- You can add, remove or change chart elements such as title, labels, gridlines and data labels by clicking on the chart and selecting "+".

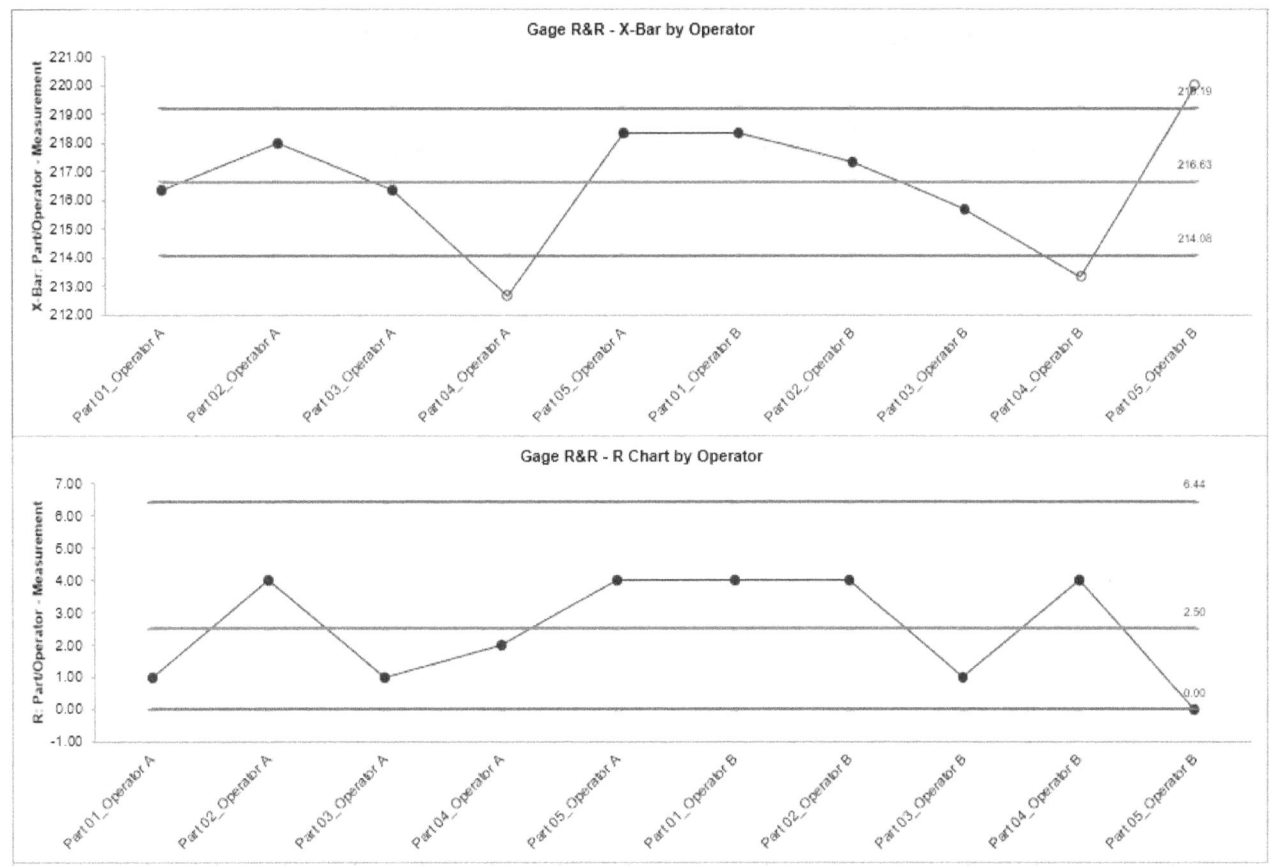

Figure 8.4: SigmaXL Output (Gage R&R Study [Part 3b])

Comment

- See *IEE Volume III*, Example 15.1 for detailed explanations about this Gage R&R output
- You can add, remove or change chart elements such as title, labels, gridlines and data labels by clicking on the chart and selecting "+".

8.3   Example: Attribute Agreement Analysis

IEE Volume III Example and Dataset

- *IEE Volume III* Example 15.3: Attribute Agreement Analysis
- Dataset (Smarter Solutions (2022): V3 C15, Exam 15-03, attribute essay evaluation MSA.xlsx

SigmaXL or EPRS Metric-App [Smarter Solutions (2020)] Input/Output

- Figure 8.5: SigmaXL Input (Attribute Agreement study)
- Figure 8.6: SigmaXL Output (Attribute Agreement study [Part 1])
- Figure 8.7: SigmaXL Output (Attribute Agreement study [Part 2])
- Figure 8.8: SigmaXL Output (Attribute Agreement study [Part 3])

- Figure 8.9: SigmaXL Output (Attribute Agreement study [Part 4])
- Figure 8.10: SigmaXL Output (Attribute Agreement study [Part 5])

SigmaXL Chart Function: Measurement System Analysis>Attribute MSA (Nominal)

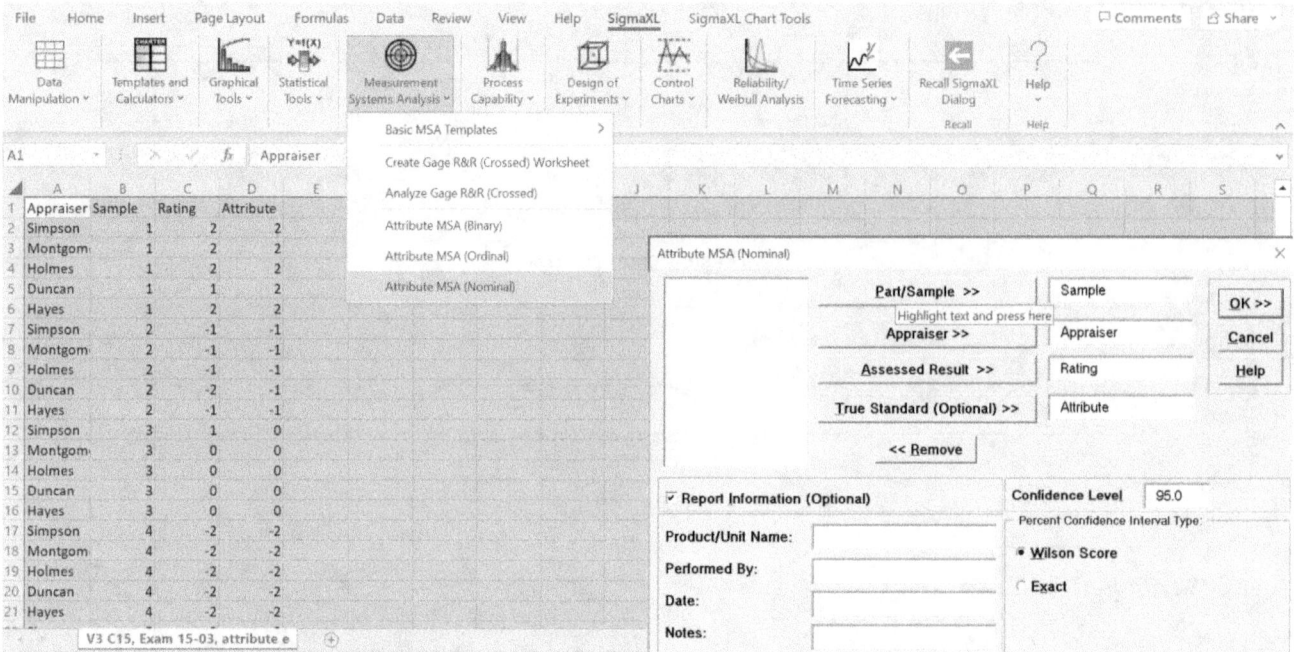

Figure 8.5: SigmaXL Input (Attribute Agreement study)

Each Appraiser vs. Standard Agreement	# Inspected	# Matched	Percent	95.0% LC (Score)	95.0% UC (Score)
Duncan	15	8	53.33	30.12	75.13
Hayes	15	13	86.67	62.12	96.26
Holmes	15	15	100.00	79.61	100.00
Montgomery	15	15	100.00	79.61	100.00
Simpson	15	14	93.33	70.18	98.81

Between Appraiser Agreement	# Inspected	# Matched	Percent	95.0% LC (Score)	95.0% UC (Score)
	15	6	40.00	19.82	64.25

All Appraisers vs. Standard Agreement	# Inspected	# Matched	Percent	95.0% LC (Score)	95.0% UC (Score)
	15	6	40.00	19.82	64.25

Attribute Effectiveness Report:

Each Appraiser vs. Standard Effectiveness	# Inspected	# Matched	Percent	95.0% LC (Score)	95.0% UC (Score)
Duncan	15	8	53.33	30.12	75.13
Hayes	15	13	86.67	62.12	96.26
Holmes	15	15	100.00	79.61	100.00
Montgomery	15	15	100.00	79.61	100.00
Simpson	15	14	93.33	70.18	98.81

All Appraisers vs. Standard Effectiveness	# Inspected	# Matched	Percent	95.0% LC (Score)	95.0% UC (Score)
	75	65	86.67	77.17	92.53

Figure 8.6: SigmaXL Output (Attribute Agreement study [Part 1])

Comment

- See *IEE Volume III*, Example 15.3, for explanations about this attribute agreement analysis

- You can add, remove or change chart elements such as title, labels, gridlines and data labels by clicking on the chart and selecting "+".

Fleiss' Kappa Overall Response	Fleiss' Kappa Overall Response P-Value	Fleiss' Kappa Overall Response 35.0% LC	Fleiss' Kappa Overall Response 35.0% UC	Fleiss' Kappa Response (1)	Fleiss' Kappa Response (1) P-Value	Fleiss' Kappa Response (1) 35.0% LC	Fleiss' Kappa Response (1) 35.0% UC
0.4118	0.0008	0.1552	0.6684	0.5833	0.0119	0.0773	1.0000
0.8295	0.0000	0.5666	1.0000	0.6296	0.0074	0.1236	1.0000
1.0000	0.0000	0.7426	1.0000	1.0000	0.0001	0.4939	1.0000
1.0000	0.0000	0.7426	1.0000	1.0000	0.0001	0.4939	1.0000
0.3160	0.0000	0.6594	1.0000	1.0000	0.0001	0.4939	1.0000

Fleiss' Kappa Overall Response	Fleiss' Kappa Overall Response P-Value	Fleiss' Kappa Overall Response 35.0% LC	Fleiss' Kappa Overall Response 35.0% UC	Fleiss' Kappa Response (1)	Fleiss' Kappa Response (1) P-Value	Fleiss' Kappa Response (1) 35.0% LC	Fleiss' Kappa Response (1) 35.0% UC
0.5730	0.0000	0.5921	0.7538	0.6804	0.0000	0.5204	0.8404

Fleiss' Kappa Overall Response	Fleiss' Kappa Overall Response P-Value	Fleiss' Kappa Overall Response 35.0% LC	Fleiss' Kappa Overall Response 35.0% UC	Fleiss' Kappa Response (1)	Fleiss' Kappa Response (1) P-Value	Fleiss' Kappa Response (1) 35.0% LC	Fleiss' Kappa Response (1) 35.0% UC
0.8315	0.0000	0.7160	0.9463	0.8426	0.0000	0.6163	1.0000

Fleiss' Kappa Overall Response	Fleiss' Kappa Overall Response P-Value	Fleiss' Kappa Overall 35.0% LC	Fleiss' Kappa Overall 35.0% UC	Fleiss' Kappa Response (1)	Fleiss' Kappa Response (1) P-Value	Fleiss' Kappa Response (1) 35.0% LC	Fleiss' Kappa Response (1) 35.0% UC
0.4118	0.0008	0.1552	0.6684	0.5833	0.0113	0.0773	1.0000
0.8295	0.0000	0.5666	1.0000	0.6296	0.0074	0.1236	1.0000
1.0000	0.0000	0.7426	1.0000	1.0000	0.0001	0.4939	1.0000
1.0000	0.0000	0.7426	1.0000	1.0000	0.0001	0.4939	1.0000
0.3160	0.0000	0.6594	1.0000	1.0000	0.0001	0.4939	1.0000

Fleiss' Kappa Overall Response	Fleiss' Kappa Overall Response P-Value	Fleiss' Kappa Overall Response 35.0% LC	Fleiss' Kappa Overall Response 35.0% UC	Fleiss' Kappa Response (1)	Fleiss' Kappa Response (1) P-Value	Fleiss' Kappa Response (1) 35.0% LC	Fleiss' Kappa Response (1) 35.0% UC
0.8320	0.0000	0.7173	0.9466	0.8339	0.0000	0.6076	1.0000

Figure 8.7: SigmaXL Output (Attribute Agreement study [Part 2])

Comment

- See *IEE Volume III*, Example 15.3, for explanations about this attribute agreement analysis
- You can add, remove or change chart elements such as title, labels, gridlines and data labels by clicking on the chart and selecting "+".

Fleiss' Kappa Response (4)	Fleiss' Kappa Response (4) P-Value	Fleiss' Kappa Response (4) 95.0% LC	Fleiss' Kappa Response (4) 95.0% UC	Fleiss' Kappa Response (5)	Fleiss' Kappa Response (5) P-Value	Fleiss' Kappa Response (5) 95.0% LC	Fleiss' Kappa Response (5) 95.0% UC
0.4410	0.0438	-0.0651	0.3471	0.4231	0.0507	-0.0830	0.3231
0.7600	0.0016	0.2539	1.0000	0.8137	0.0008	0.3076	1.0000
1.0000	0.0001	0.4939	1.0000	1.0000	0.0001	0.4939	1.0000
1.0000	0.0001	0.4939	1.0000	1.0000	0.0001	0.4939	1.0000
0.8137	0.0008	0.3076	1.0000	1.0000	0.0001	0.4939	1.0000

Fleiss' Kappa Response (4)	Fleiss' Kappa Response (4) P-Value	Fleiss' Kappa Response (4) 95.0% LC	Fleiss' Kappa Response (4) 95.0% UC	Fleiss' Kappa Response (5)	Fleiss' Kappa Response (5) P-Value	Fleiss' Kappa Response (5) 95.0% LC	Fleiss' Kappa Response (5) 95.0% UC
0.6425	0.0000	0.4824	0.8025	0.7365	0.0000	0.5765	0.8966

Fleiss' Kappa Response (4)	Fleiss' Kappa Response (4) P-Value	Fleiss' Kappa Response (4) 95.0% LC	Fleiss' Kappa Response (4) 95.0% UC	Fleiss' Kappa Response (5)	Fleiss' Kappa Response (5) P-Value	Fleiss' Kappa Response (5) 95.0% LC	Fleiss' Kappa Response (5) 95.0% UC
0.8023	0.0000	0.5766	1.0000	0.8473	0.0000	0.6210	1.0000

Fleiss' Kappa Response (4)	Fleiss' Kappa Response (4) P-Value	Fleiss' Kappa Response (4) 95.0% LC	Fleiss' Kappa Response (4) 95.0% UC	Fleiss' Kappa Response (5)	Fleiss' Kappa Response (5) P-Value	Fleiss' Kappa Response (5) 95.0% LC	Fleiss' Kappa Response (5) 95.0% UC
0.4410	0.0438	-0.0651	0.3471	0.4231	0.0507	-0.0830	0.3231
0.7600	0.0016	0.2539	1.0000	0.8137	0.0008	0.3076	1.0000
1.0000	0.0001	0.4939	1.0000	1.0000	0.0001	0.4939	1.0000
1.0000	0.0001	0.4939	1.0000	1.0000	0.0001	0.4939	1.0000
0.8137	0.0008	0.3076	1.0000	1.0000	0.0001	0.4939	1.0000

Fleiss' Kappa Response (4)	Fleiss' Kappa Response (4) P-Value	Fleiss' Kappa Response (4) 95.0% LC	Fleiss' Kappa Response (4) 95.0% UC	Fleiss' Kappa Response (5)	Fleiss' Kappa Response (5) P-Value	Fleiss' Kappa Response (5) 95.0% LC	Fleiss' Kappa Response (5) 95.0% UC
0.7367	0.0000	0.5704	1.0000	0.8718	0.0000	0.6454	1.0000

Figure 8.8: SigmaXL Output (Attribute Agreement study [Part 3])

Comment

- See *IEE Volume III*, Example 15.3, for explanations about this attribute agreement analysis
- You can add, remove or change chart elements such as title, labels, gridlines and data labels by clicking on the chart and selecting "+".

Effectiveness and Misclassification Summary	Standard (1)	Standard (2)	Standard (3)	Standard (4)	Standard (5)
Appraiser Response (1)	9	2	0	0	0
Appraiser Response (2)	1	13	2	0	0
Appraiser Response (3)	0	0	17	1	0
Appraiser Response (4)	0	0	1	13	2
Appraiser Response (5)	0	0	0	1	13

Sample	Attribut	Duncan	Hayes 1	Holmes 1	Montgomery 1	Simpson 1
1	2	1	2	2	2	2
2	-1	-2	-1	-1	-1	-1
3	0	0	0	0	0	1
4	-2	-2	-2	-2	-2	-2
5	0	-1	0	0	0	0
6	1	1	1	1	1	1
7	2	1	2	2	2	2
8	0	0	0			0
9	-1	-2	-1			-1
10	1	0	2	1	1	1
11	-2	-2	-1	-2	-2	-2
12	0	-1	0	0	0	0
13	2	2	2	2	2	2
14	-1	-1	-1	-1	-1	-1
15	1	1	1	1	1	1

Figure 8.9: SigmaXL Output (Attribute Agreement study [Part 4])

Comment

- See *IEE Volume III*, Example 15.3, for explanations about this attribute agreement analysis
- You can add, remove or change chart elements such as title, labels, gridlines and data labels by clicking on the chart and selecting "+".

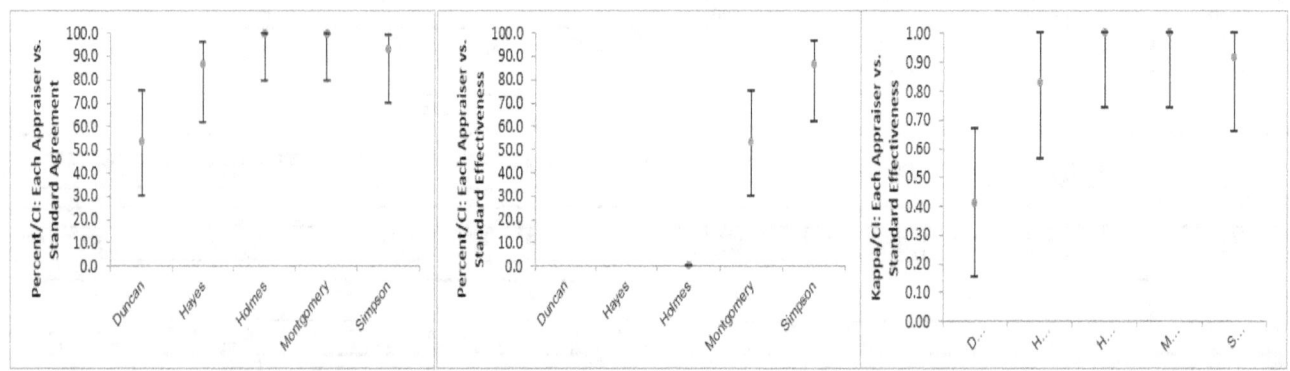

Figure 8.10: SigmaXL Output (Attribute Agreement study [Part 5])

Comment

- See *IEE Volume III*, Example 15.3, for explanations about this attribute agreement analysis
- You can add, remove or change chart elements such as title, labels, gridlines and data labels by clicking on the chart and selecting "+".

IEE-DMAIC — Measure Phase (Wisdom of the Organization)

9.1 IEE-DMAIC Roadmap Component

Book 1 Reference: *IEE Volume III* – Chapter 16

Book 2 Reference: *Lean Six Sigma Project Execution Guide* – Section 6

Internet: www.smartersolutions.com/roadmap (clicking on highlighted area provides the flowchart below)

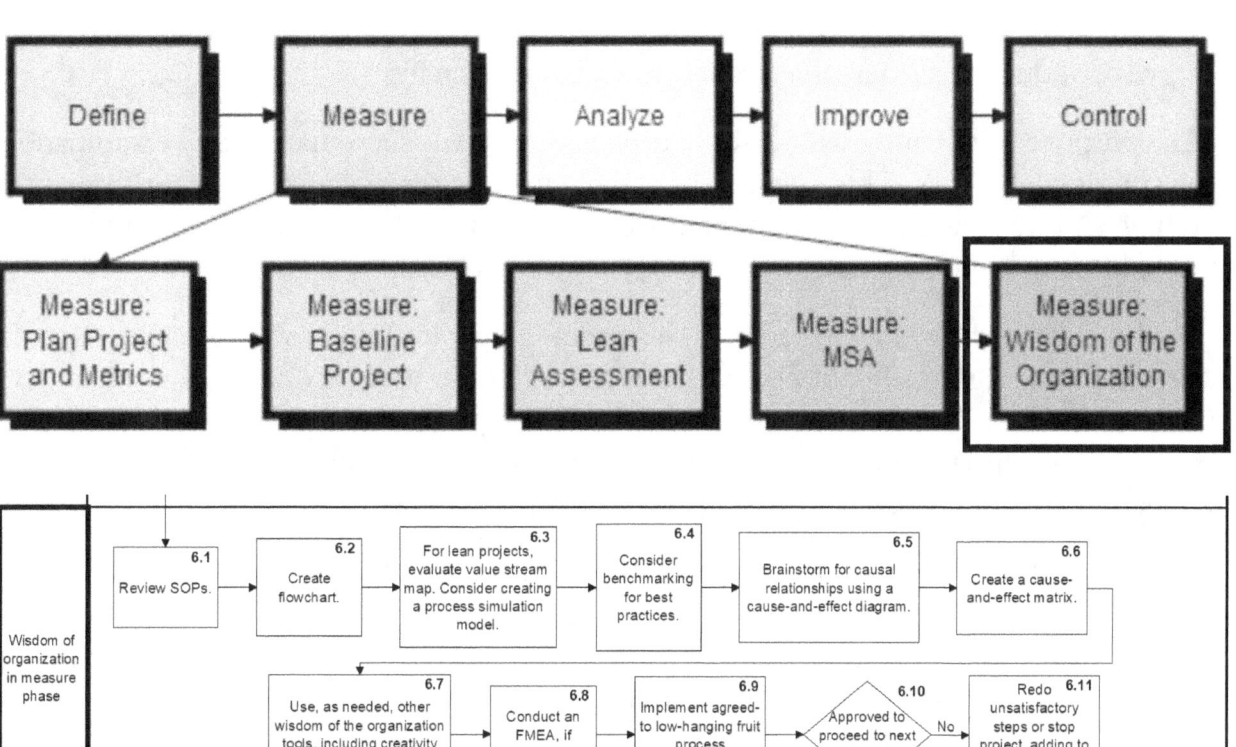

IEE Lean Six Sigma improvement projects have a 30,000-foot-level response (Y) that needs improvement. This Y can be significantly affected by the Xs within the process, i.e., $Y=f(X)$. In the Wisdom of the Organization (WOTO) project execution phase, a process improvement team brainstorms for the purpose of compiling thoughts on to where to look or focus for improvement opportunities.

One IEE aspect is the use of data to gain insight to what might be done differently to improve. This is analogous to a murder mystery where information is gathered that can generate insightful clues to help determine "who dunnit". Similarly, during the execution of a project, we want to gain insight to where focus efforts and data collection should concentrate.

Often when starting a project, the team lead has biases, which can hinder effectiveness in finding a solution. Rather than the project lead's immediately starting the collecting-data process upon project initiation, it is much more effective to create a system for using teams to help gain this insight. This is accomplished using the wisdom of the organization drill down process.

A traditional DMAIC basic suggested tool flow to capture the team's wisdom of the organization inputs is:

- Flow chart the as-is process, i.e., the detailed steps described in the project's SIPOC (Supplier-input-process-output-customer)
- Create a cause-and-effect diagram
- Create a cause-and-effect matrix
- Conduct an FMEA (Failure mode and effects analysis)

The purpose of initiating with flowcharting is that the documentation and examination of current process activities. This assessment often surprises many, since the team thought that something else was being done. Other brainstorming tools such as affinity diagramming, could also be added, when appropriate, to the above 4-step process.

This wisdom of the organization assessment could lead to some apparent beneficial process changes, e.g., standardized work practices. These agree-to changes need not have formal statistical analyses to prove their worth. This type of change should be implemented when most appropriate. If these changes truly improve the process, the 30,000-foot-level individuals chart will change to a new, improved response level.

However, often it is not clear whether some brainstormed "Xs" currently impact or would impact the overall process. We create from the wisdom of the organization effort hypotheses that can be tested in the project execution analyze phase. The result of these analyses can then lead to process changes during the improve phase roadmap step.

9.2 Example: Cause-and-Effect Diagram

The Cause-and-Effect Diagram (Fishbone Diagram) is a problem solving tool and a key step in process improvement as it helps identifying more difficult to discover causes.

IEE Volume III Example and Dataset

- *IEE Volume III* Section 16.6 Cause-and-Effect Diagram
- Dataset (Smarter Solutions (2022): V3 C16, Sec 16-06. cause and effect.xlsx

SigmaXL or EPRS Metric-App [Smarter Solutions (2020)] Input/Output

- Figure 9.1: SigmaXL Input (Cause-and-Effect Diagram)
- Figure 9.2: SigmaXL Output (Cause-and-Effect Diagram)

SigmaXL Chart Function: DMAIC & DFSS Templates>Cause & Effect (Fishbone) Template

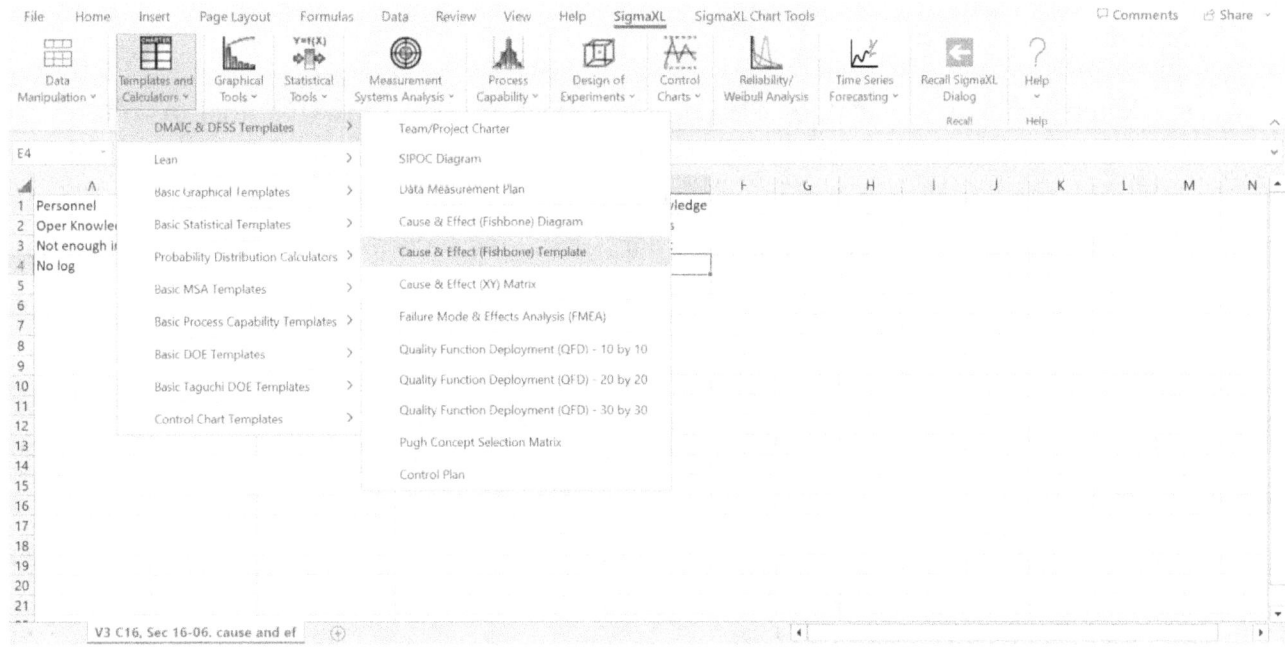

Figure 9.1: SigmaXL Input (Cause-and-Effect Diagram)

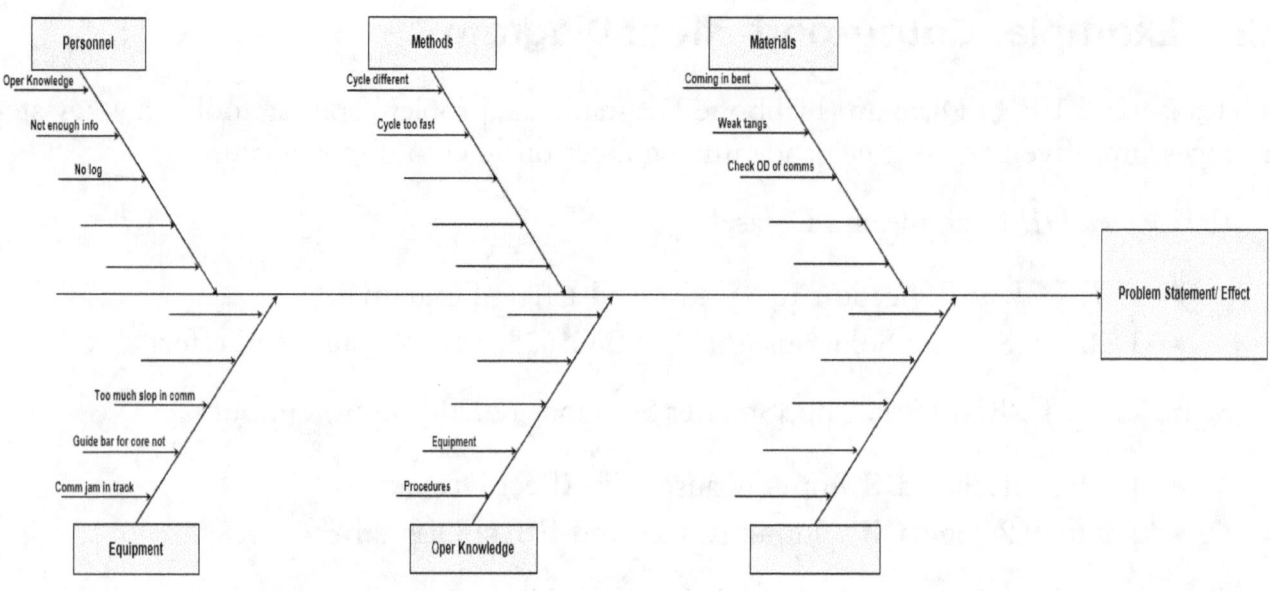

Figure 9.2: SigmaXL Output (Cause-and-Effect Diagram)

Comment

- When data are available, a hypothesis test in the DMAIC analyze-phase can statistically assess whether an improvement idea is statistically significant and should be a focus for making process improvements
- You can add, remove or change chart elements such as title, labels, gridlines and data labels by clicking on the chart and selecting "+".

10 IEE-DMAIC — Analyze Phase: Visualization of Data

10.1 IEE-DMAIC Roadmap Component

Book 1 Reference: *IEE Volume III* – Chapter 18

Book 2 Reference: *Lean Six Sigma Project Execution Guide* – Section 7

Internet: www.smartersolutions.com/roadmap (clicking on highlighted area provides the flowchart below)

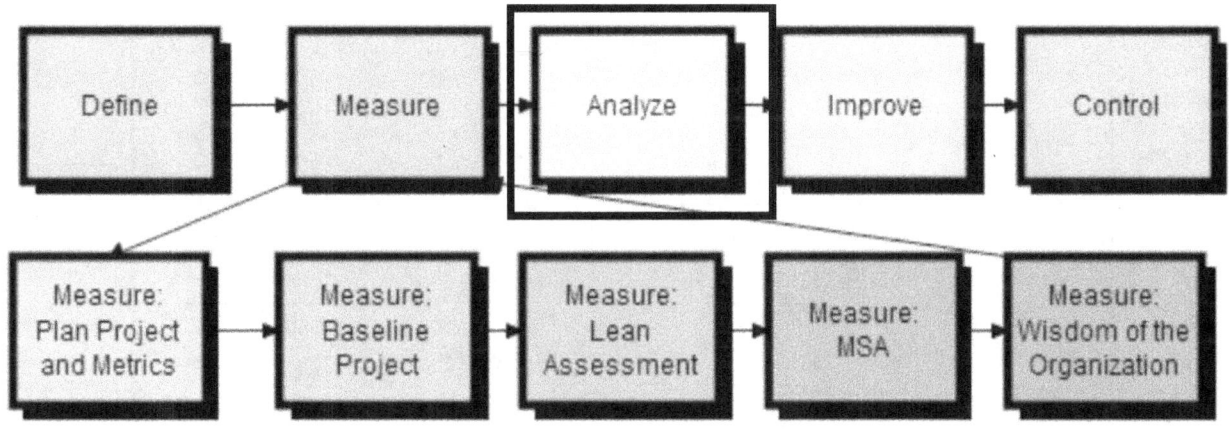

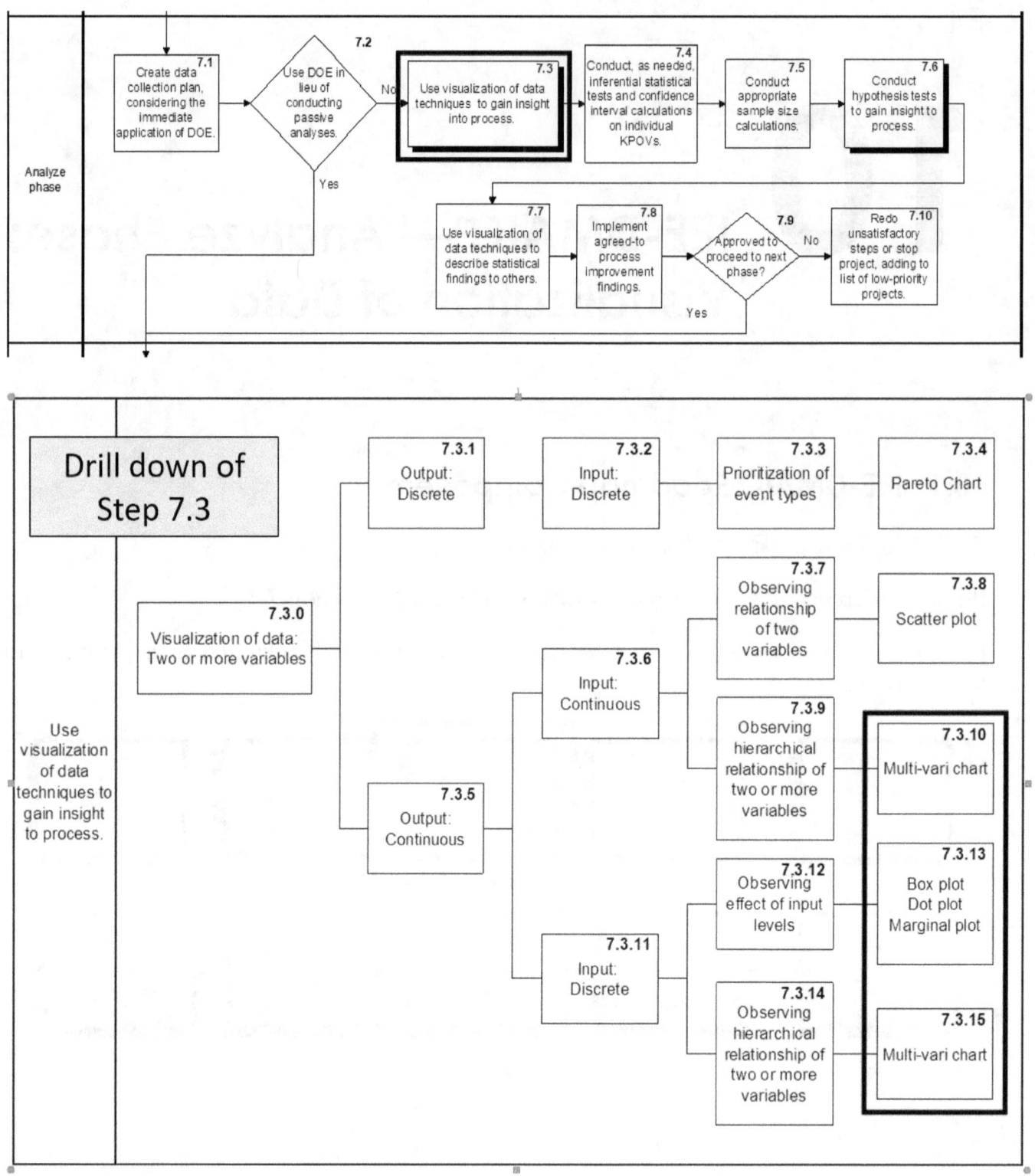

10.2 Improvement Project Roadmap: Analyze Phase

An output of the IEE DMAIC roadmap WOTO drill-down is a list of ideas (Xs) where a team might focus to gain insight for improvements efforts for enhancing the project's 30,000-foot-level report response (Y). One can both visually and statistically assess WOTO hypothesized causal relationship. This chapter provides tools for making a visual assessment. Later chapters describe statistical techniques for testing significance in a variety of situations.

Information gained from this work can provide insight into the sources of variability and unsatisfactory performance, and help improve processes. The tools in this phase are primarily passive. The reason for this is that within this phase the level of input variables from the wisdom of the organization are observed passively to see whether a relationship can be detected between them. If there is an observed relationship, this knowledge can help focus improvement efforts. When data are not readily available, it may be appropriate in the analyze phase to start conducting proactive Design of Experiments (DOE) tests immediately. DOE techniques are described in later chapters of this book.

10.3 Example: Visualization of Data

Application

- The non-conformance rate (Y) diameter of a manufactured part relative to its specification is unsatisfactory, as shown in a 30,000-foot-level report
- X assessment in Y=f(X) relationship: A team in the WOTO phase thought that there might be a difference between the cavities of the mold that produced the product and the measurement position in the delivered product.

IEE Volume III Example and Dataset

- *IEE Volume III* Example 18.1: Box Plot, Marginal Plot, Main Effects Plot and Interaction Plot
- Dataset (Smarter Solutions (2022): V3 C18, Exam 18-01, injection molding data.xlsx

SigmaXL or EPRS Metric-App [Smarter Solutions (2020)] Input/Output

- Figure 10.1: SigmaXL Input (Box Plot)
- Figure 10.2: SigmaXL Output (Box Plot)
- Figure 10.3: SigmaXL Input (Dot Plot)
- Figure 10.4: SigmaXL Output (Dot Plot)
- Figure 10.5: SigmaXL Input (Categorical Grouped Scatterplot)
- Figure 10.6: SigmaXL Output (Categorical Grouped Scatterplot)
- Figure 10.7: SigmaXL Input (Mean with 95% CI Plot)
- Figure 10.8: SigmaXL Output (Mean with 95% CI Plot)
- Figure 10.9: SigmaXL Input (Interaction Plot)
- Figure 10.10: SigmaXL Output (Interaction Plot)

The boxplot is a graphical representation of the distribution of a sample. It shows the distribution shape, central tendency, and variability.

SigmaXL Chart Function: Graphical Tools>Boxplots

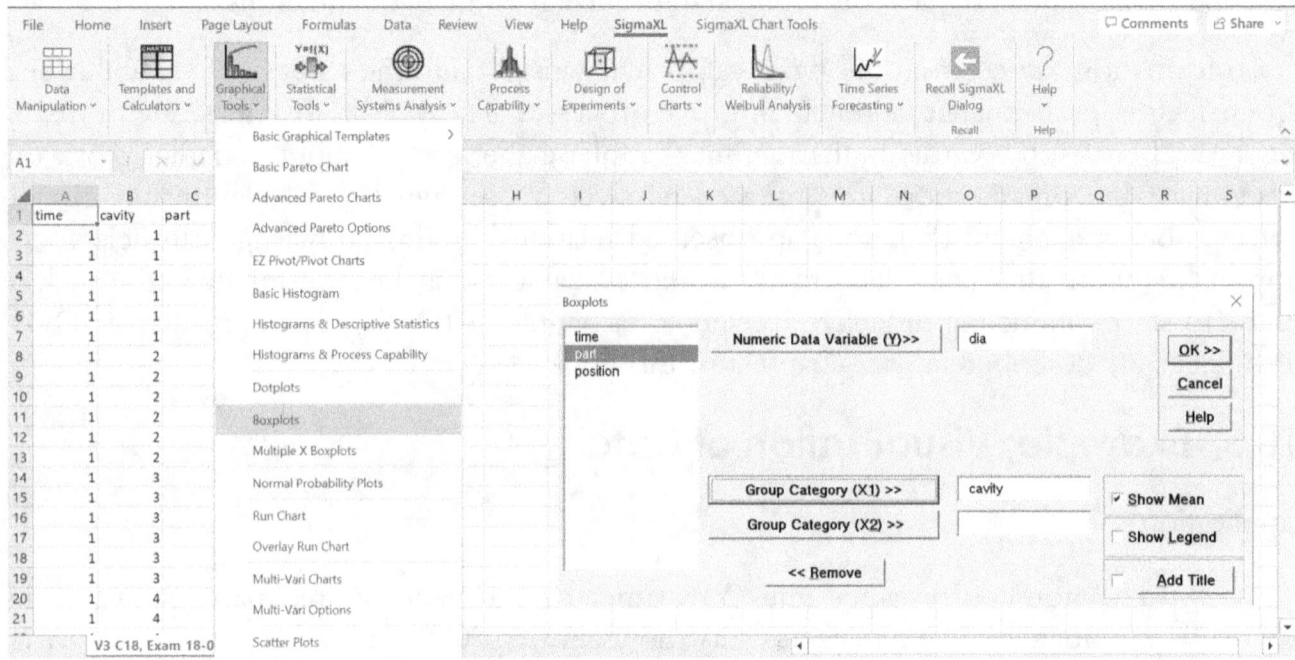

Figure 10.1: SigmaXL box plot creation SigmaXL Input (Box Plot)

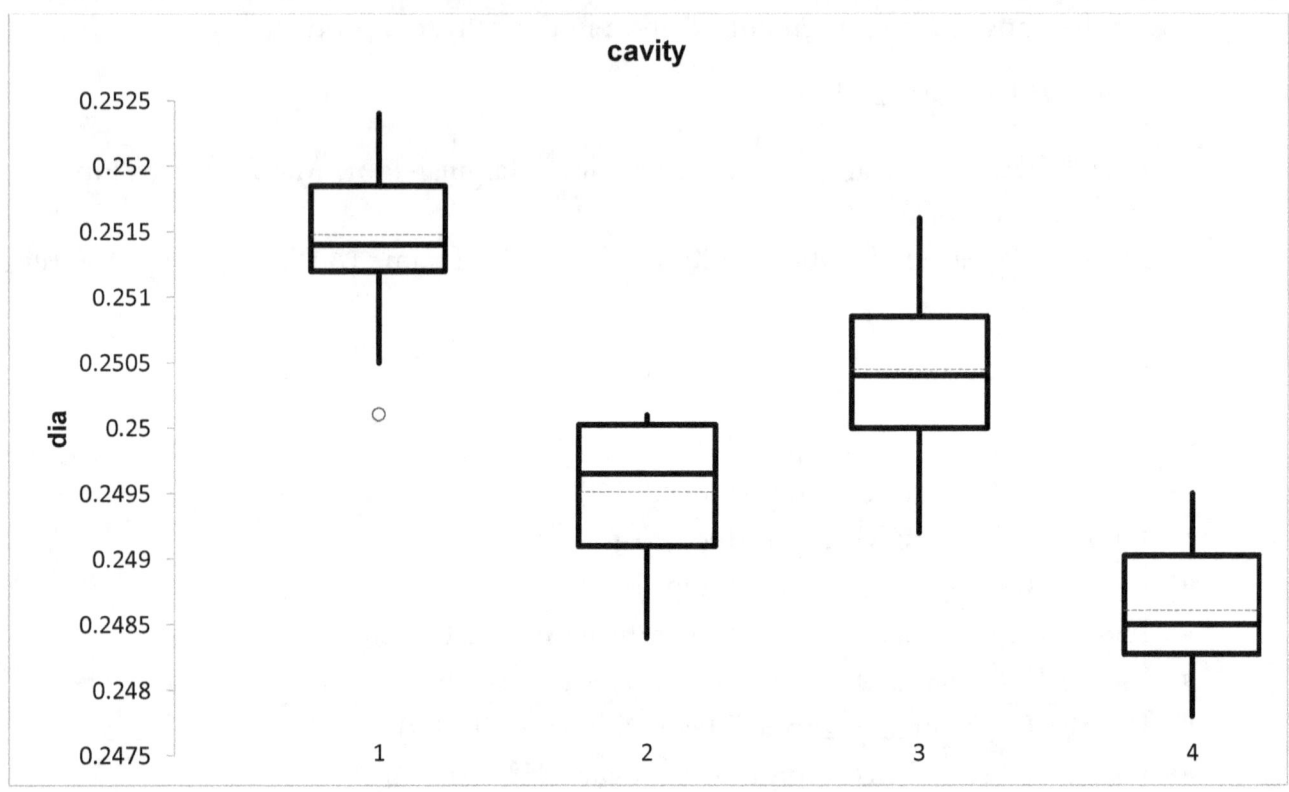

Figure 10.2: SigmaXL Output (Box Plot)

Comment

- It appears there are differences in the diameter of parts (Y) as a function of the cavity number (X)
- You can add, remove or change chart elements such as title, labels, gridlines and data labels by clicking on the chart and selecting "+".

The dotplots show the distribution of a continuous data set.

SigmaXL Chart Function: Graphical Tools>Dotplots

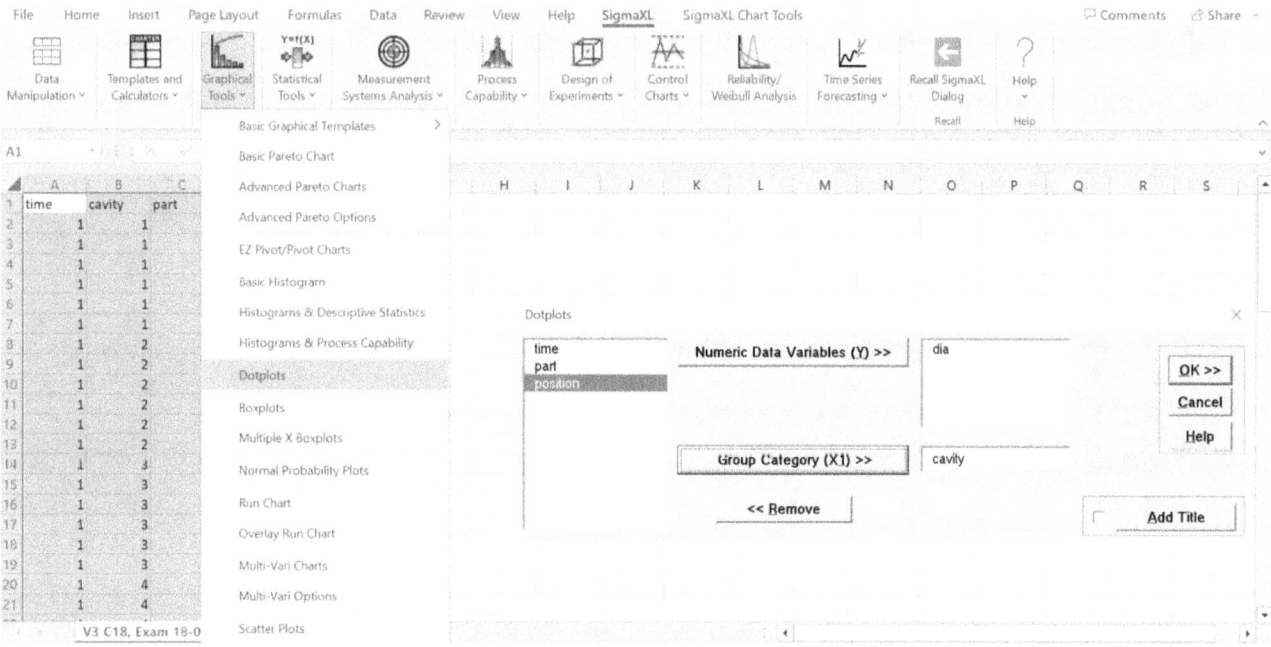

Figure 10.3: SigmaXL Input (Dot Plot)

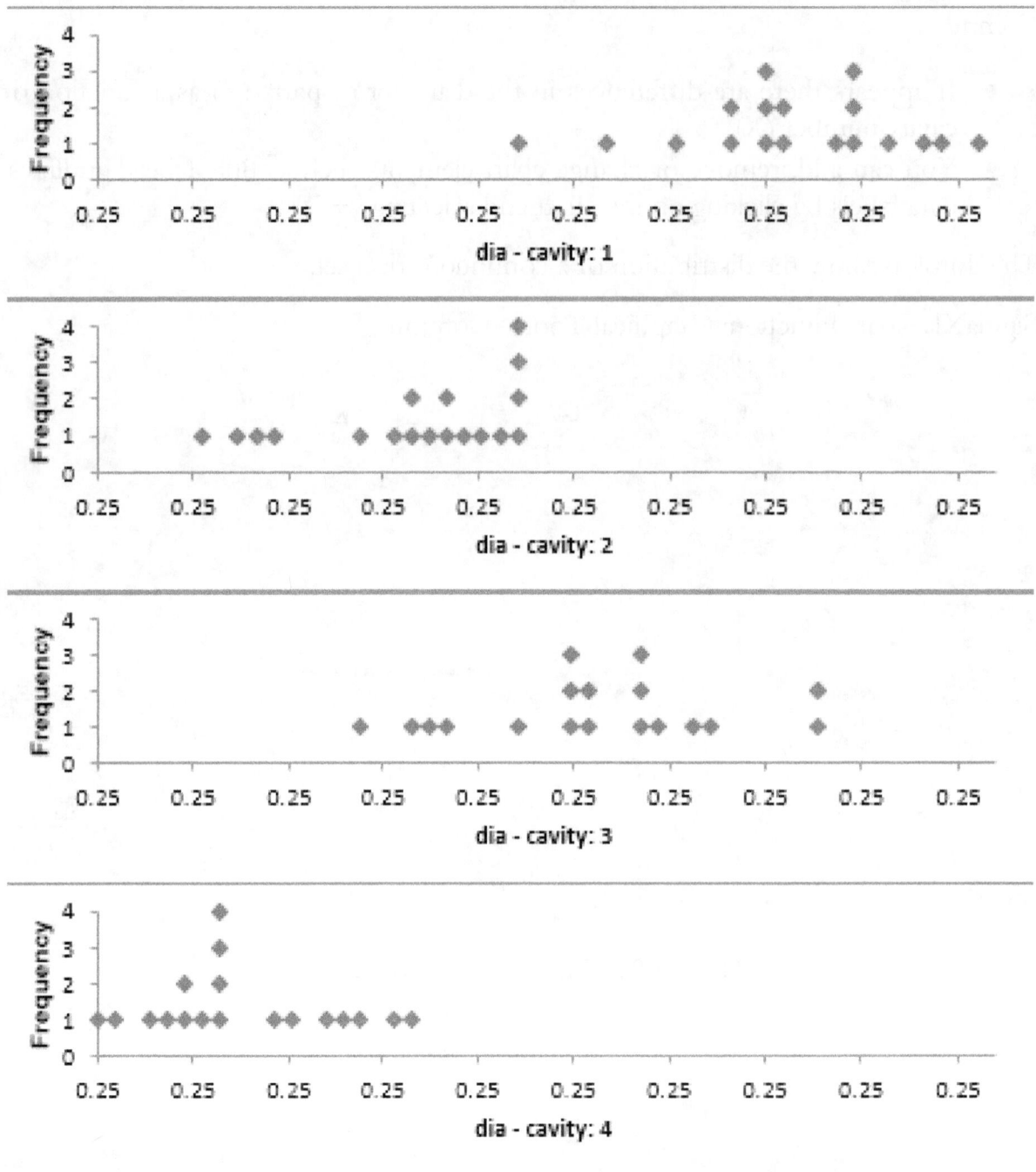

Figure 10.4: SigmaXL Output (Dot Plot)

Comment

- It appears there are differences in the diameter of parts (Y) as a function of the cavity number (X)
- You can add, remove or change chart elements such as title, labels, gridlines and data labels by clicking on the chart and selecting "+".

Note: you can also use a scatterplot to create a categorical grouped scatterplot.

SigmaXL Chart Function: Graphical Tools>Scatter Plots

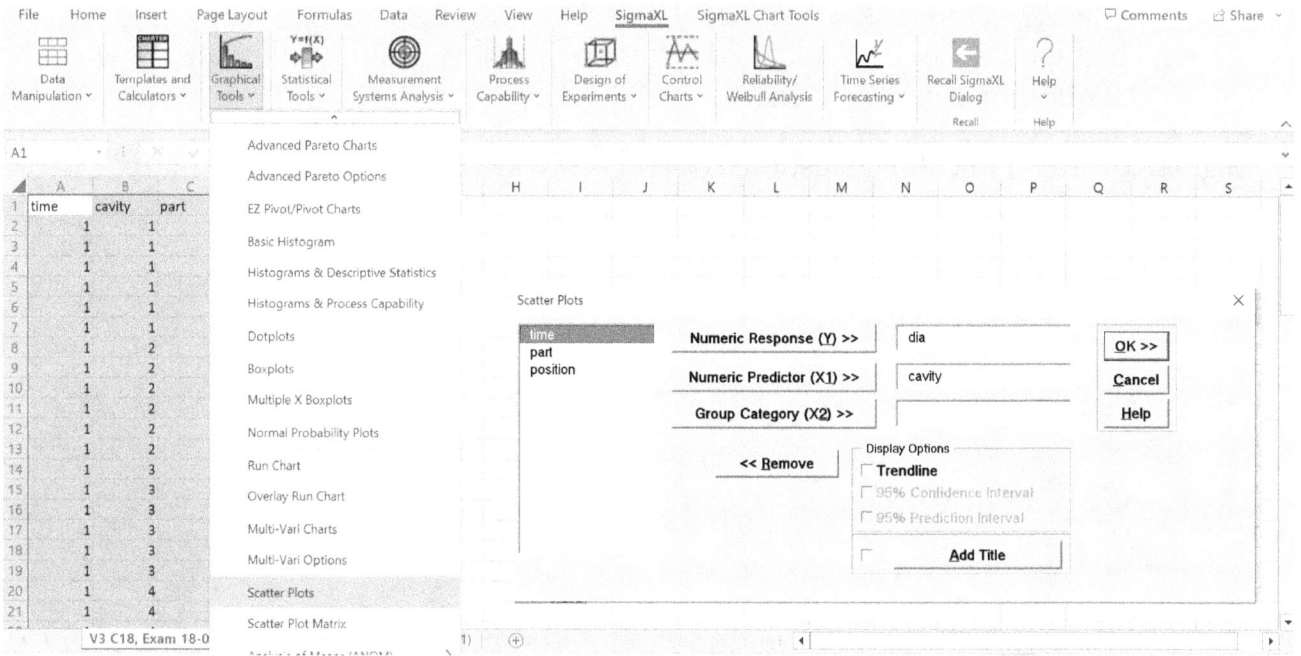

Figure 10.5: SigmaXL Input (Categorical Grouped Scatterplot)

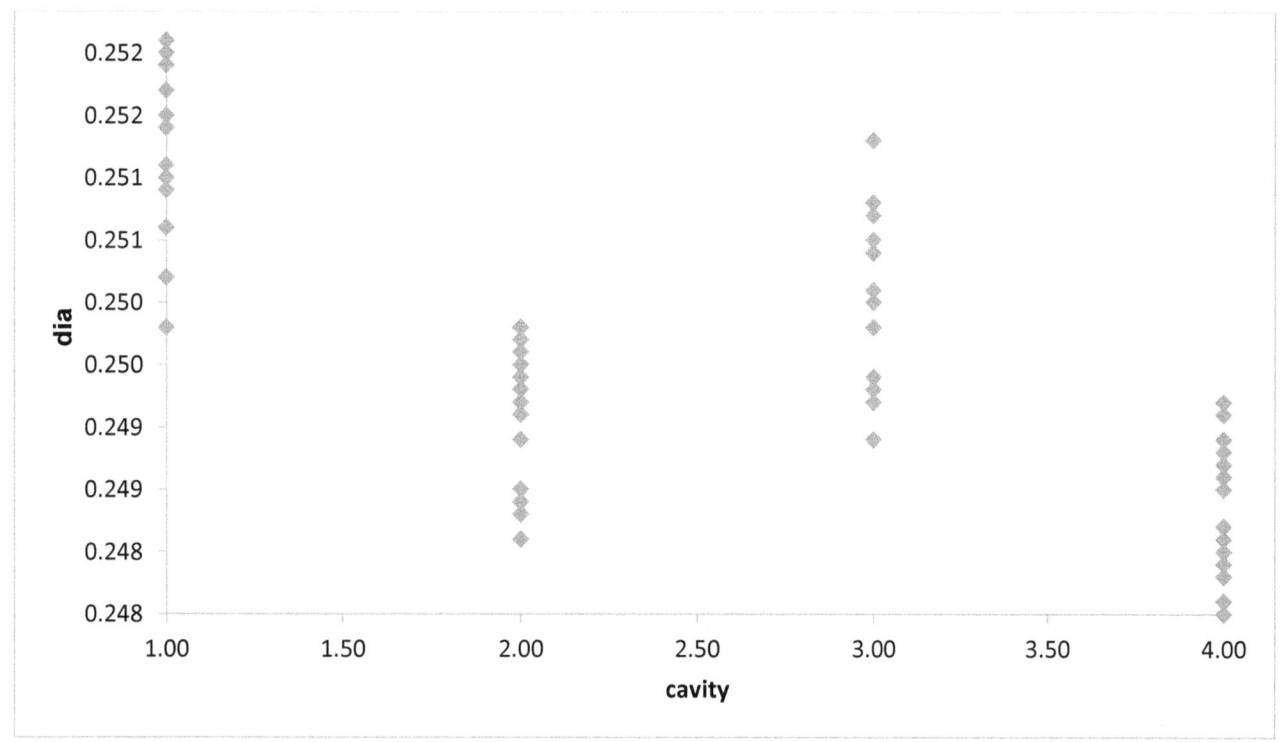

Figure 10.6: SigmaXL Output (Categorical Grouped Scatterplot)

Comment

- It appears there are differences in the diameter of parts (Y) as a function of the cavity number (X)

- You can add, remove or change chart elements such as title, labels, gridlines and data labels by clicking on the chart and selecting "+".
- The One-Way ANOVA is used to test the equality of population means when the classification is by one variable.

SigmaXL Chart Function: Statistical Tools>One-Way ANOVA & Means Matrix

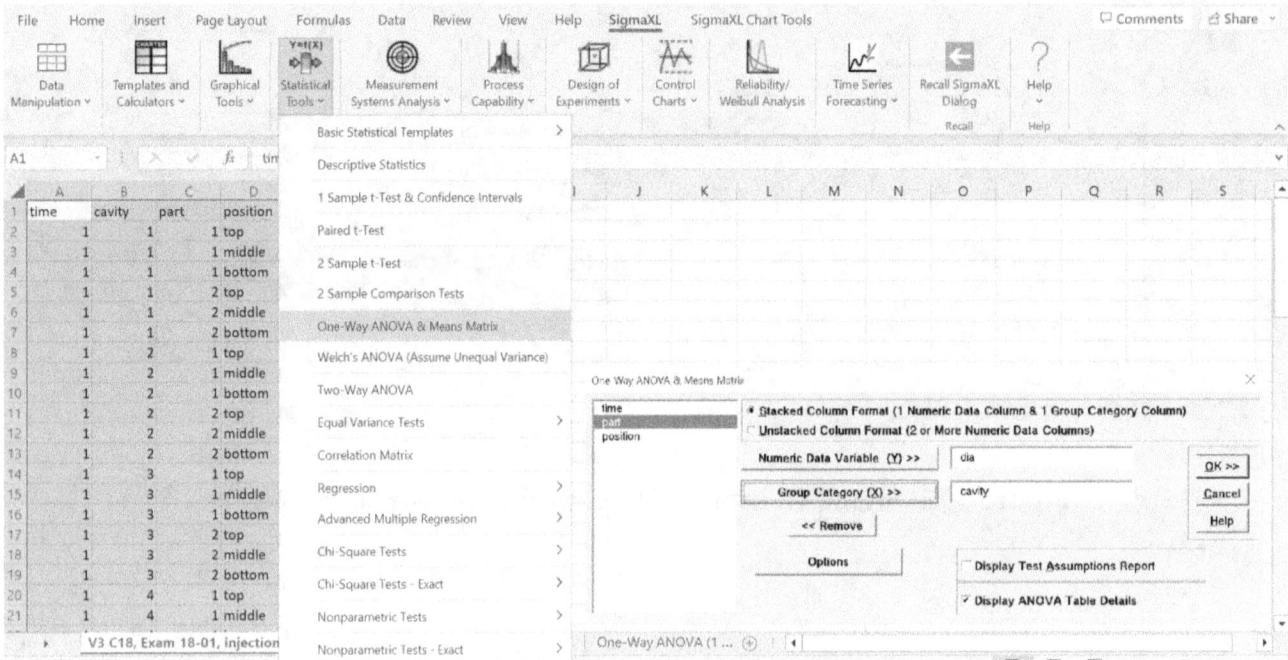

Figure 10.7: SigmaXL Input (Main effects Plot)

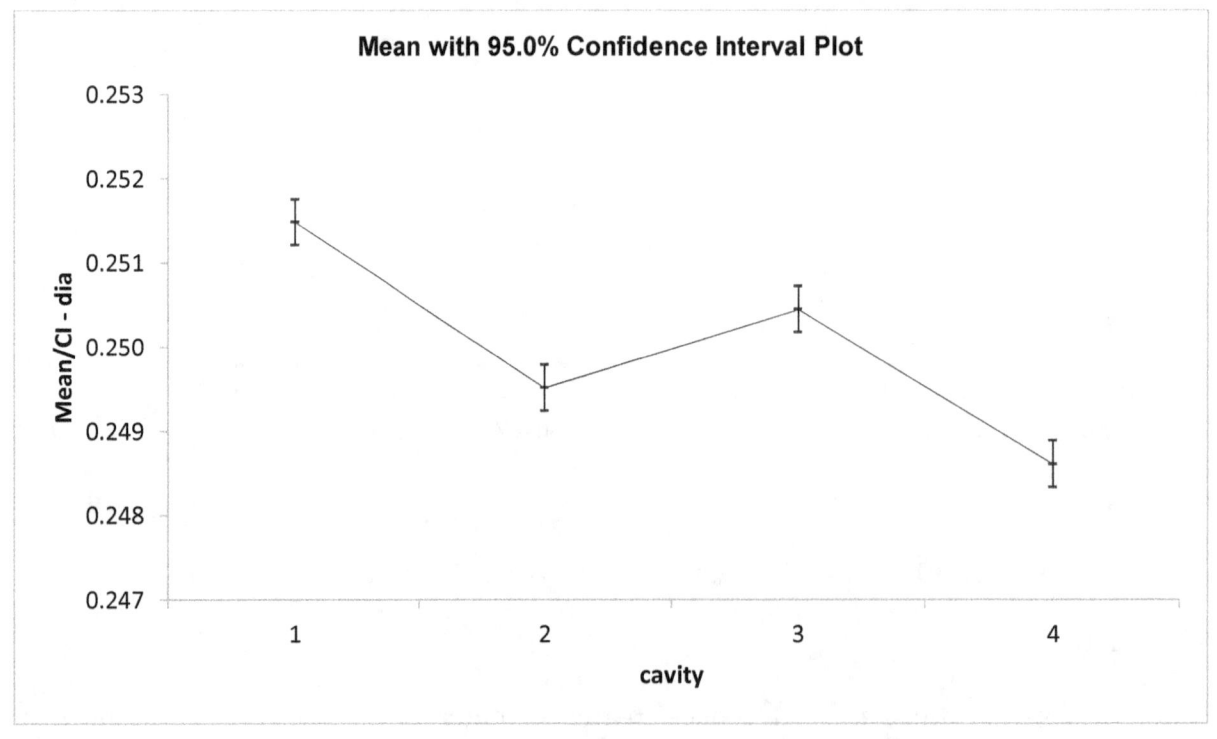

Figure 10.8: SigmaXL Output (Main Effects Plot)

Comment

- It appears there are differences in the diameter of parts (Y) as a function of the cavity number (X)
- Similar with previous figures, this figure includes the variability within each cavity
- Main effect plots are more beneficial in report-outs from a conducted DOE
- You can add, remove or change chart elements such as title, labels, gridlines and data labels by clicking on the chart and selecting "+".

The Two-Way ANOVA performs an analysis of variance to test the equality of population means when the classification is by two factors or variables.

SigmaXL Chart Function: Statistical Tools>Two-Way ANOVA

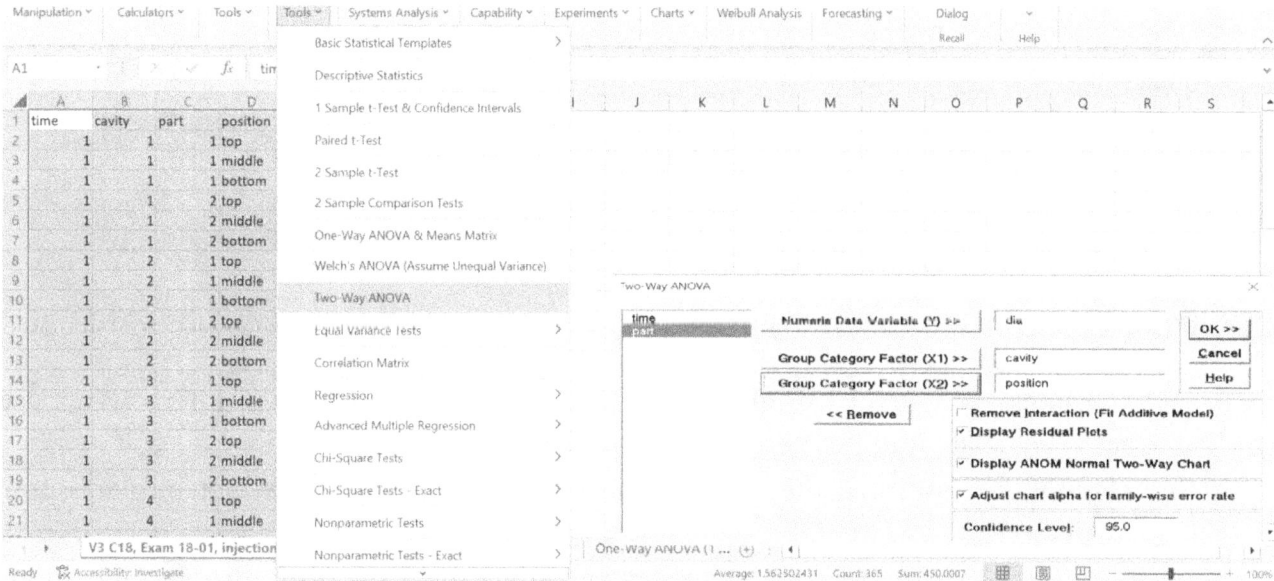

Figure 10.9: SigmaXL Input (Interaction Plot)

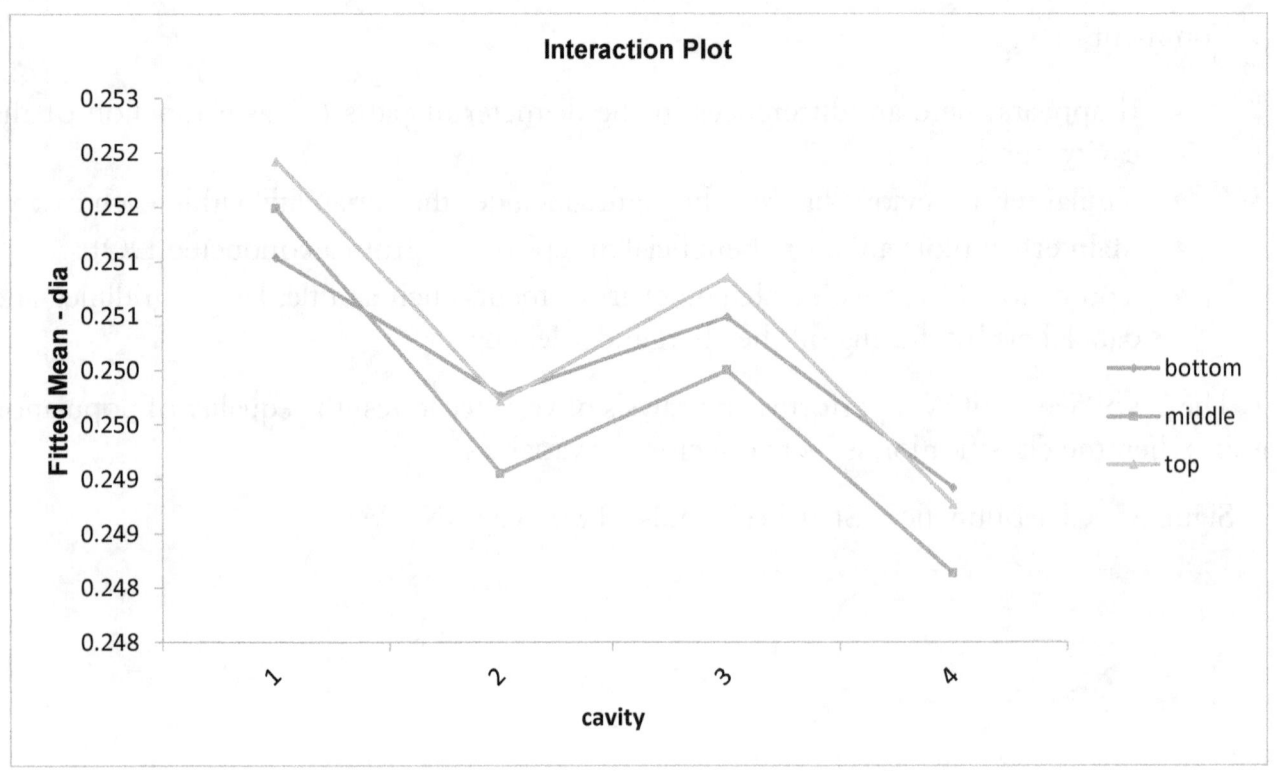

Figure 10.10: SigmaXL Output (Interaction Plot)

Comments

- The lines in Figure 10.10 are not parallel, which implies that an interaction exists between cavity number and position
- The middle position is the lowest value for cavities 2, 3, and 4, which implies a cone shaped part
- For cavity 1, the middle position is between the top and bottom measured positions, which implies an hour-glass shaped part
- You can add, remove or change chart elements such as title, labels, gridlines and data labels by clicking on the chart and selecting "+".

10.4 Example: Analyze Phase (Visualization of Data – Multi-Vari Chart)

Application: 30,000-foot-level reporting of Y in Y=f(X) relationship

- A team is to improve the 30,000-foot-level report non-conformance rate to specification of a plastic part's diameter (i.e., Y) via an IEE DMAIC project.
- X possibilities from the project team's WOTO work with the Y=f(X) relationship were mold cavity and measurement position within the manufactured part.

IEE Volume III Example and Dataset

- *IEE Volume III* Example 18.2: Multi-vari chart
- Dataset (Smarter Solutions (2022): V3 C18, Exam 18-01, injection molding data.xlsx

SigmaXL or EPRS Metric-App [Smarter Solutions (2020)] Input/Output

- Figure 10.11: SigmaXL Input (Multi-vari Chart)
- Figure 10.12: SigmaXL Output (Multi-vari Chart)

The multi-vari charts are typically used in preliminary analysis as a visual alternative to the analysis of variance.

SigmaXL Chart Function: Graphical Tools>Multi-Vari Charts

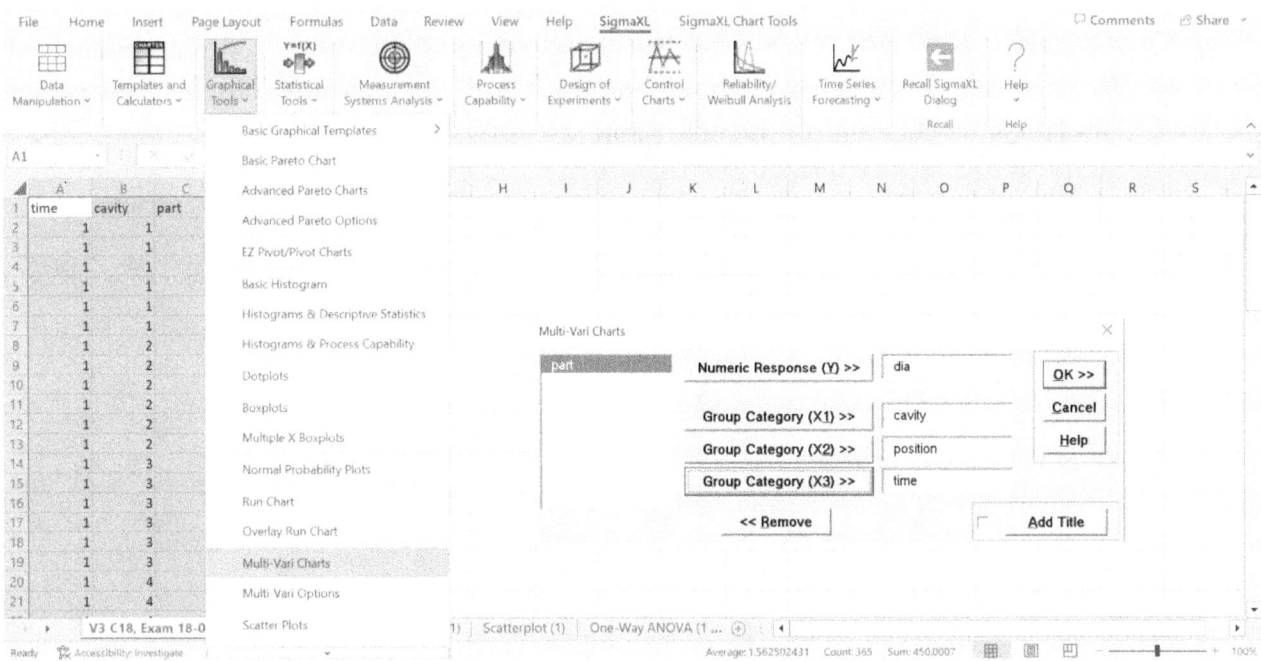

Figure 10.11: SigmaXL Input (Multi-vari Chart)

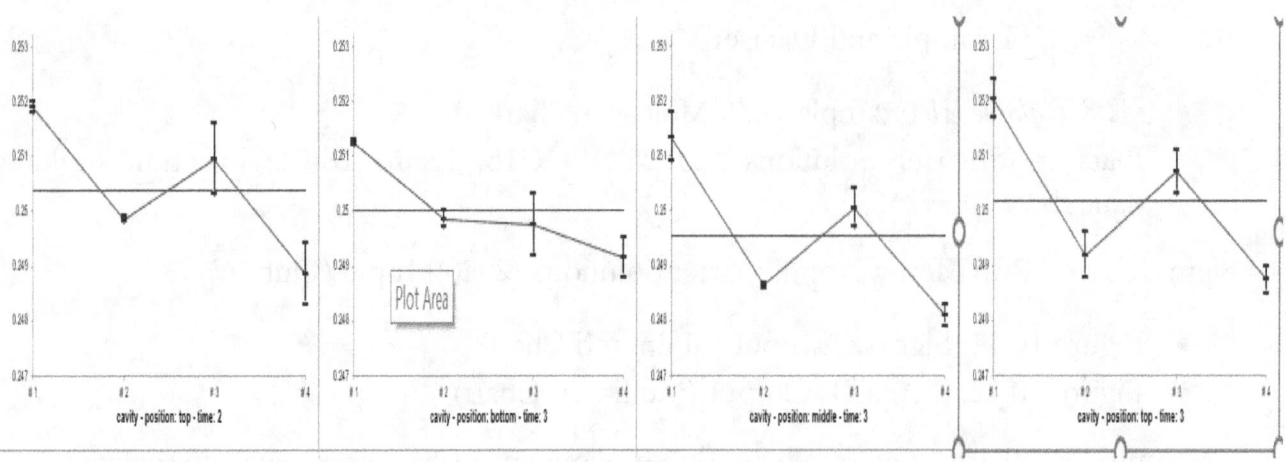

Figure 10.12: SigmaXL Output (Multi-vari Chart)

Comment

- See *IEE Volume III* Section 18.6 for this chart's explanation
- You can add, remove or change chart elements such as title, labels, gridlines and data labels by clicking on the chart and selecting "+".

11

Inferences: Continuous Response

Reference: *IEE Volume III*, Chapter 20

The last chapter described visualization tools. This chapter provides the foundation for conducting statistical tests for the improvement project's DMAIC "analyze" and "improve" phases. This foundation also applies to investigations at the enterprise level.

Statistically, a population is a group of data from a single distribution where a single category can be the source of the population's samples. There may be the uncovering of multiple data-populations sources using statistical tools and techniques, e.g., different sources, locations, or machines.

Descriptive statistics help pull beneficial information from data, whereas probability provides a basis for inferential statistics and sampling plans. This chapter focuses on inferential statistics, where we will bridge from sample data to statements about the population, i.e., inference of properties from the sampled population.

11.1 Hypothesis Testing

A hypothesis test starts with two opposing hypotheses: Ho, the null hypothesis which states that some property of a population (such as the mean, variance) is not different from a specified value or from another population and Ha, the alternative hypothesis that states that the null hypothesis is wrong, and can also specify the direction of the difference.

In industrial situations, a team may want to determine whether the parameters of a statistical distribution (e.g., normal distribution) have particular values or relationships. The team may want to test a hypothesis that a distribution's mean or standard deviation has a specific value or that the difference between two means is zero. Hypothesis testing procedures are used for these situations.

11.2 Example: Sample Size Determination for a Mean Criterion

IEE Volume III Example 20.1: Sample Size Determination for a Mean

A stereo-amplifier-output power level specification average is at least 100 watts (W) per channel. Determine the sample size that is needed to verify this criterion given the following:

$\alpha = 0.1$
$\beta = 0.05$
$\delta = 0.5\sigma$.

SigmaXL or EPRS Metric-App [Smarter Solutions (2020)] Input/Output

- Figure 11.1: SigmaXL Input (Sample Size Determination)
- Figure 11.2: SigmaXL Output (Sample Size Determination)

SigmaXL Chart Function: Statistical Tools>Power and Sample Size Calculator>1 Sample t-Test Calculator

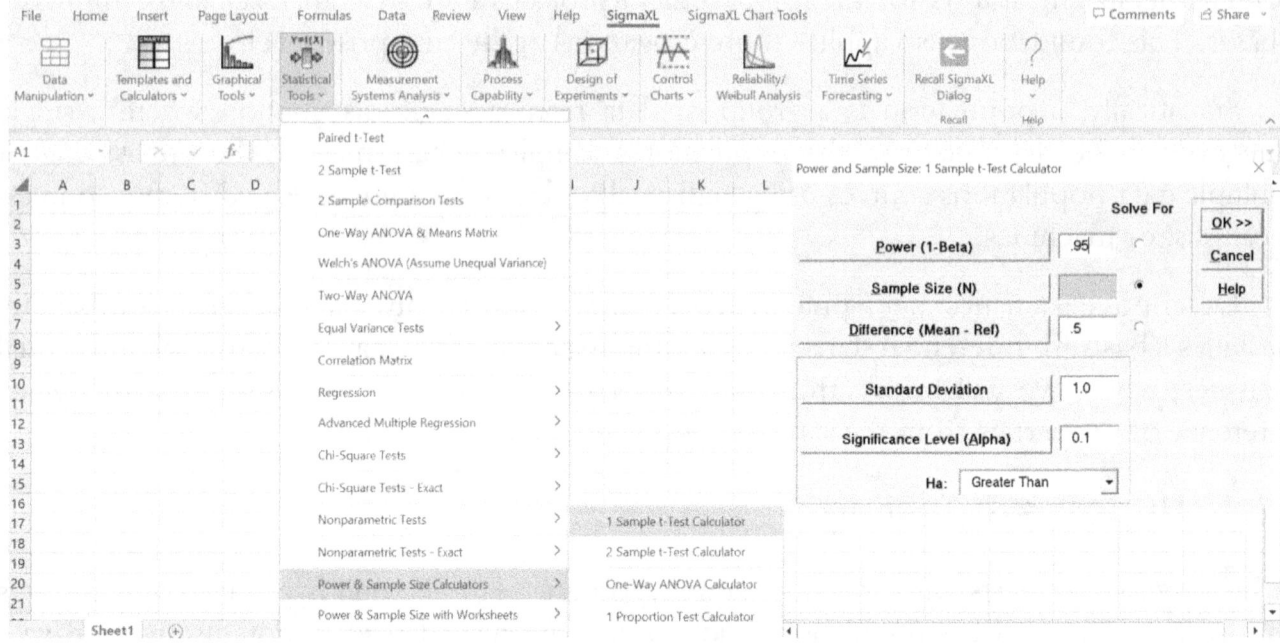

Figure 11.1: SigmaXL Input (Sample Size Determination)

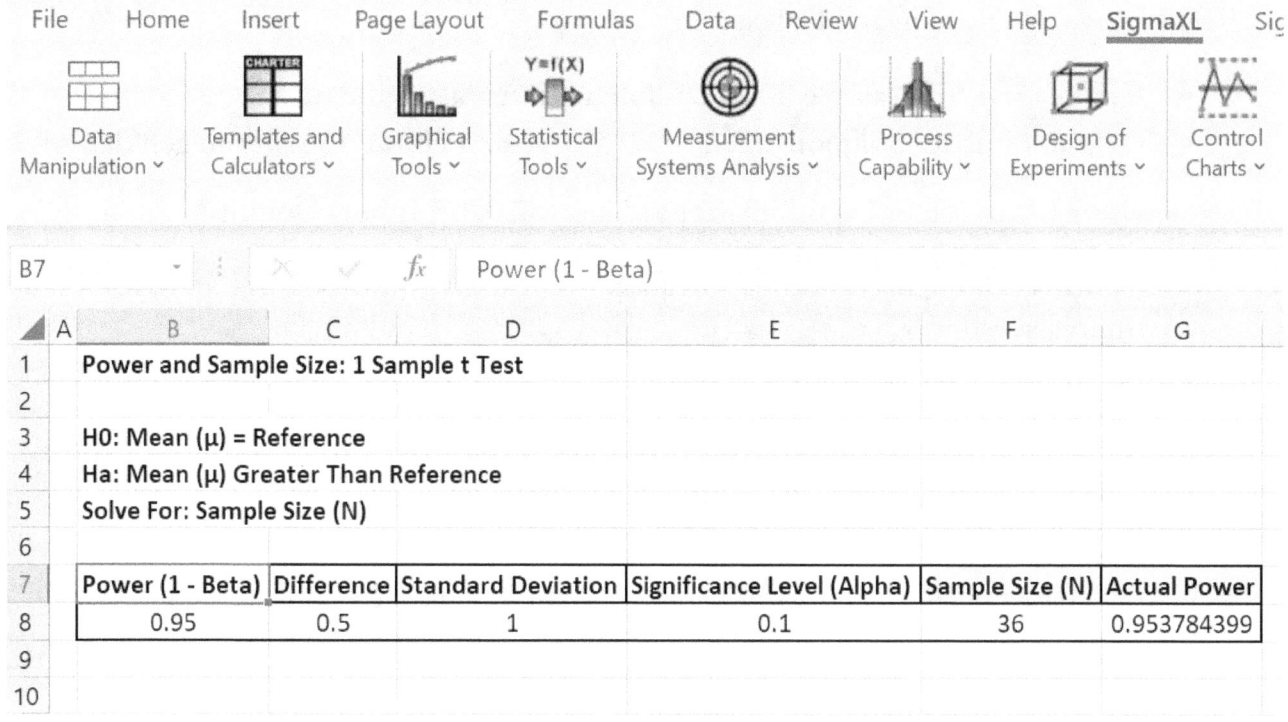

Figure 11.2: SigmaXL Output (Sample Size Determination)

Comments

- Sample size is 36
- Because individuals want to make sure they are making the correct decision, they often specify small α and β values with a small δ value. In some instances, this practice can lead to unrealistically large sample sizes with standard test times and resource constraints.
- When this happens, the experimenter may need to accept more risk than she was initially willing to tolerate.
- One should then recalculate the sample size, permitting the more significant risks (e.g., a higher α and β value) with increased uncertainty (i.e., a higher δ value).
- You can add, remove or change chart elements such as title, labels, gridlines and data labels by clicking on the chart and selecting "+".

11.3 Example: Hypothesis Tests and Confidence Intervals of a Sample's Mean

Application: 30,000-foot-level report (Y) and Y=f(X) relationship

- A confidence interval of a mean Y response from a stable 30,000-foot-level report where data are from the period of process-response stability
- A confidence interval of a mean X response from a stable 30,000-foot-level report where data are from the period of process-response stability

IEE Volume III Example and Dataset

- *IEE Volume III* Example 20.2: Confidence interval on the mean
- Dataset (Smarter Solutions (2022): V3 C20, exam 20-02, 16 random gen data.xlsx

SigmaXL or EPRS Metric-App [Smarter Solutions (2020)] Input/Output

- Figure 11.3: SigmaXL Input (Mean Response Hypothesis Tests and Confidence Intervals)
- Figure 11.4: SigmaXL Output (Mean Response Hypothesis Tests and Confidence Intervals)

The 1-Sample t-Test is used to determine whether the mean of a population is statistically different from a known or hypothesized value.

SigmaXL Chart Function: Statistical Tools>1 -Sample t-Test & Confidence Intervals

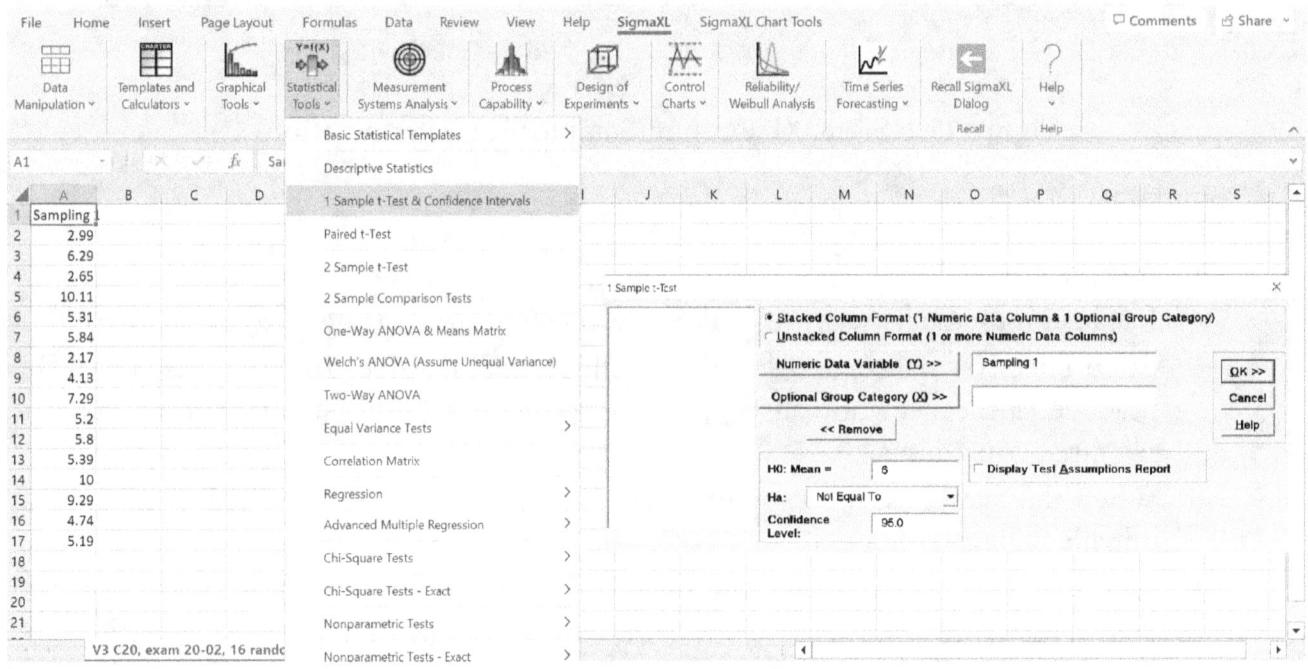

Figure 11.3: SigmaXL Input (Mean Response Hypothesis Tests and Confidence Intervals)

| File | Home | Insert | Page Layout | Formulas | D |

Data Manipulation ˅ | Templates and Calculators ˅ | Graphical Tools ˅ | Statistical Tools ˅ | Mea System

J14 | | ✕ | ✓ | fx

	A	B	C
1	**1 Sample t-Test**		
2			
3	**Test Information**		
4	H_0: Mean (Mu) = 6		
5	H_a: Mean (Mu) Not Equal To 6		
6			
7	**Results:**	**Sampling 1**	
8	Count	16	
9	Mean	5.774	
10	StDev	2.407	
11	SE Mean	0.601719	
12	t	-0.374967	
13	P-Value (2-sided)	0.7129	
14	UC (2-sided, 95%)	7.057	
15	LC (2-sided, 95%)	4.492	
16			
17			

Figure 11.4: SigmaXL Output (Mean Response Hypothesis Tests and Confidence Intervals)

Comments

- The descriptive statistics output shown in Figure 11.4 provides the outputs from statistical calculations, including a confidence interval
- If there were a hypothesis test selection in this SigmaXL function's input, the SigmaXL output shows under "Test," the result from this hypothesis test
- You can add, remove or change chart elements such as title, labels, gridlines and data labels by clicking on the chart and selecting "+".

11.4 Example: Standard Deviation Confidence Interval

Application: 30,000-foot-level report (Y) and Y=f(X) relationship

- A confidence interval of a standard deviation Y response from a stable 30,000-foot-level report where data are from the period of process-response stability.
- A confidence interval of a standard deviation X input from a stable 30,000-foot-level report where data are from the period of process-response stability.

IEE Volume III Example and Dataset

- *IEE Volume III* Example 20.4: Standard Deviation Confidence Statement
- Dataset (Smarter Solutions (2022): V3 C20, exam 20-02, 16 random gen data.xlsx

SigmaXL or EPRS Metric-App [Smarter Solutions (2020)] Input/Output

- Figure 11.5: SigmaXL Input (Standard Deviation Confidence Interval)
- Figure 11.6: SigmaXL Output (Standard Deviation Confidence Interval)

SigmaXL Chart Function: Statistical Tools>Basic Statistical Templates>1 Sample Chi-Square Test and CI for Standard Deviation

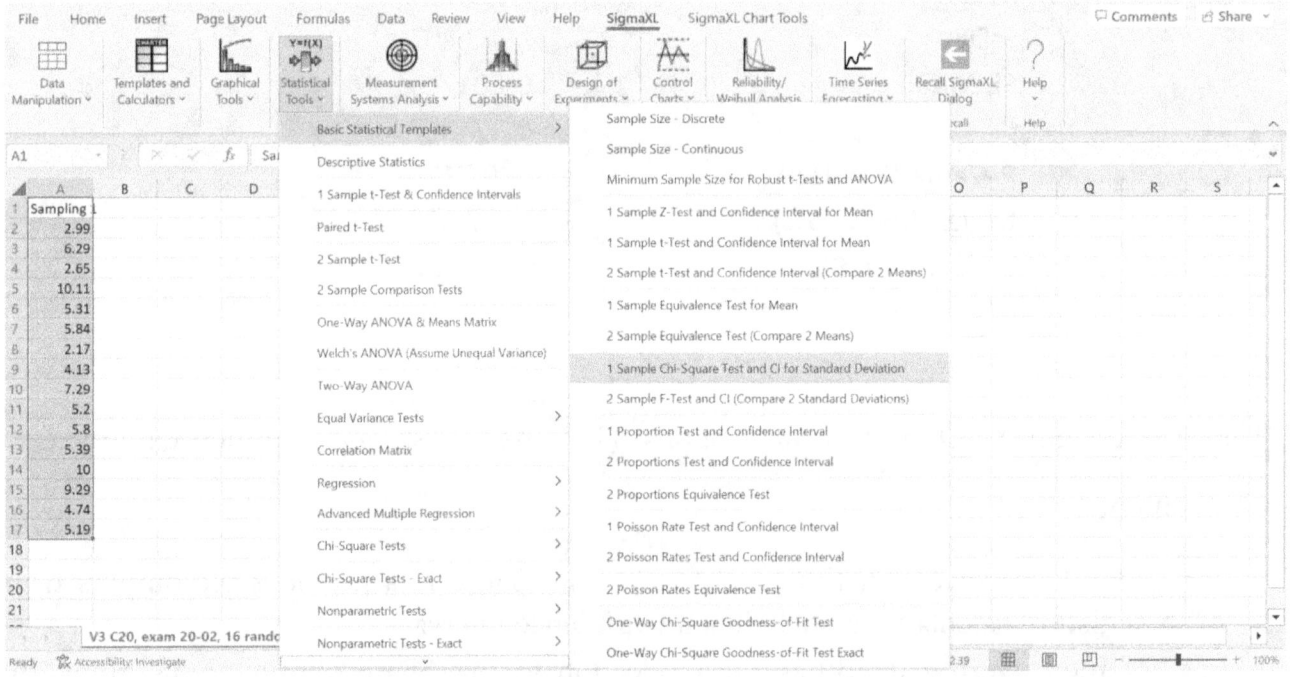

Figure 11.5: SigmaXL Input (Standard Deviation Confidence Interval)

Sigma XL	1 Sample Chi-Square Test and Confidence Interval for Standard Deviation		
Sample Data (user Inputs):			
Sample Size	n	·	16
Sample Standard Deviation	s		2.407
Null Hypothesis (hypothesized StDev)	H_0: Sigma (σ) =		0.5
Alternative Hypothesis	H_a: Sigma (σ)		Not Equal To
Confidence Level (enter .95 for 95%)	100*(1-α)%		95.0%

Results:	
Sample Variance	5.7936
DF	15
Chi-Square test statistic	347.6189
alpha	0.0500
P-Value (2 sided)	0.0000
Upper Confidence Limit (2 Sided)	3.7253
Lower Confidence Limit (2 Sided)	1.7781

Figure 11.6: SigmaXL Output (Standard Deviation Confidence Interval)

Comments

- The standard deviation in this calculation was from a random sample taken from a normal distribution where $\sigma = 2.0$.

- Note that this actual standard deviation value is contained in this confidence interval.

- When the confidence interval is 90%, one expects the confidence interval to have the actual value 90% of the time.

- You can add, remove or change chart elements such as title, labels, gridlines and data labels by clicking on the chart and selecting "+".

11.5 Percentage of the Population Assessments

Criteria sometimes assess the mean response of the product's population with no regard to the variability of the product response. Often what is needed is that all products be less than or greater than a criterion.

For example, a specification may exist that a product can withstand an electrostatic discharge (ESD) level of 700 volts (V). Is the intent of this specification that the mean of the population (if tested to failure) should be above 700 V? Or should all products built be able to resist a voltage level of 700 V?

Without testing every manufactured product, it is impossible to be 100% certain that every product will meet such a criterion. For criteria that require much certainty and a 100% population requirement, 100% testing to a level that anticipates field performance degradation may be required. However, a reduced confidence level may be acceptable with a lower percent confidence requirement (e.g., 95% of the population). Depending on the situation, the initial criterion may need adjustment to reflect the basic test strategy.

Another possible approach is a "best estimate" probability plot, which can give visual indications of population characteristics that may not otherwise be apparent. For example, a normal-distribution probability plot may indicate that data outliers are present or that a normal-distribution assumption is inappropriate. SigmaXL Descriptive Statistics can calculate the confidence intervals.

11.6 Example: Percentage of the Population Assessments

Application: 30,000-foot-level report (Y) and Y=f(X) relationship

- A percentage of population assessment of a Y response from a stable 30,000-foot-level report where data are from a period of process-response stability
- A percentage of population assessment of an X response from a stable 30,000-foot-level report where data are from a period of process-response stability

IEE Volume III Example and Dataset

- *IEE Volume III* Example 20.5: Percentage of the Population Statements
- Dataset (Smarter Solutions (2022): V3 C20, exam 20-02, 16 random gen data.xlsx

SigmaXL or EPRS Metric-App [Smarter Solutions (2020)] Input/Output

- Figure 11.7a: SigmaXL Input (Probability Plot)
- Figure 11.7b: SigmaXL Input (Descriptive Statistics)
- Figure 11.8: SigmaXL Output (Probability Plot and Descriptive Statistics)

SigmaXL Chart Function: Graphical Tools>Normal Probability Plots

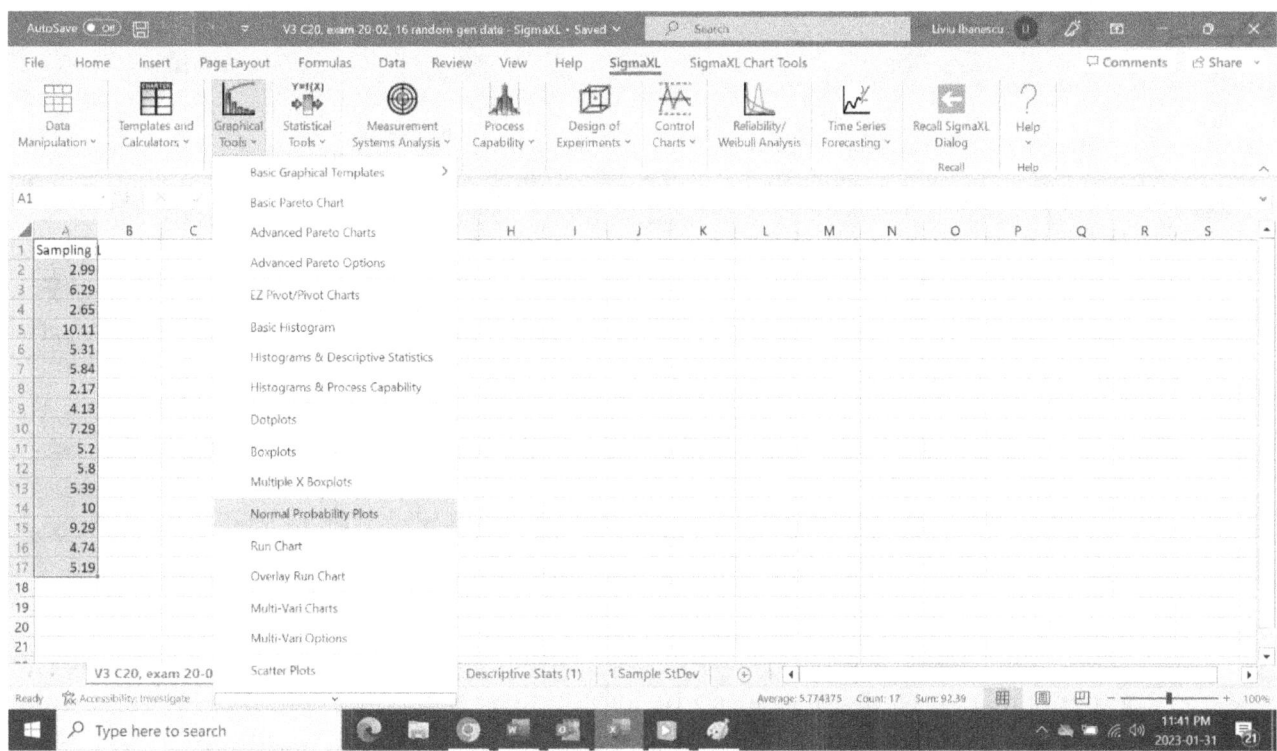

Figure 11.7a: SigmaXL Input (Normal Probability Plot)

SigmaXL Chart Function: Statistical Tools>Descriptive Statistics

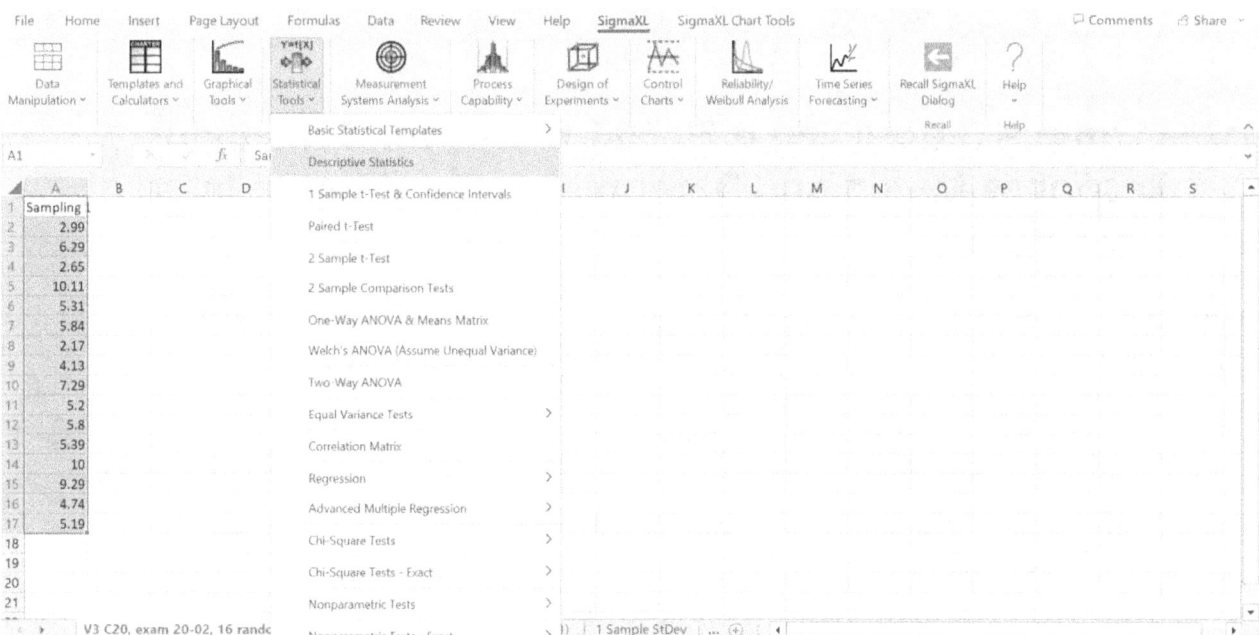

Figure 11.7b: SigmaXL Input (Descriptive Statistics)

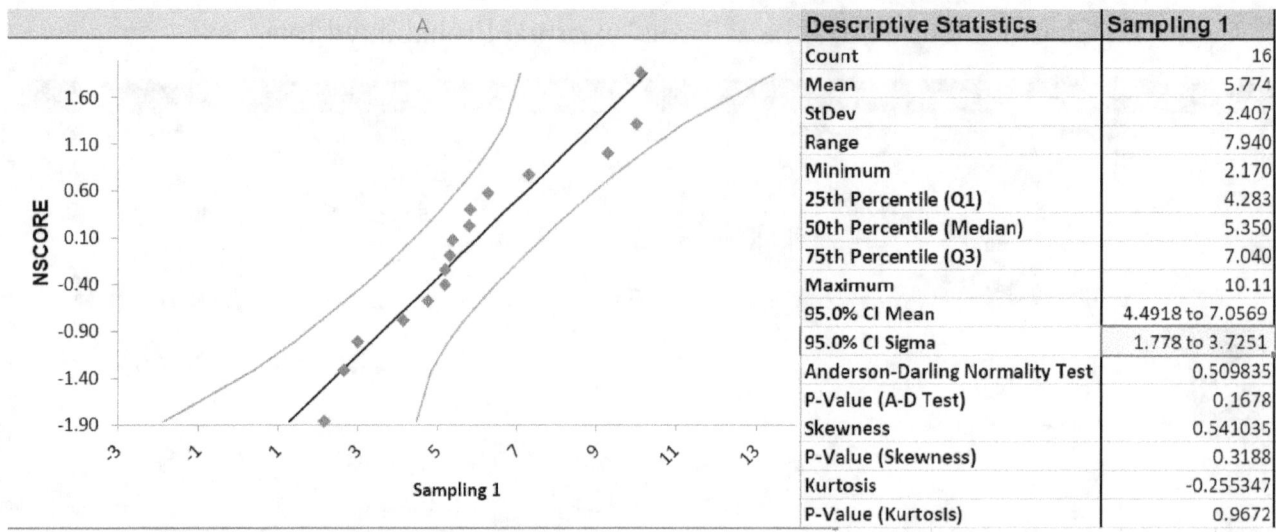

Descriptive Statistics	Sampling 1
Count	16
Mean	5.774
StDev	2.407
Range	7.940
Minimum	2.170
25th Percentile (Q1)	4.283
50th Percentile (Median)	5.350
75th Percentile (Q3)	7.040
Maximum	10.11
95.0% CI Mean	4.4918 to 7.0569
95.0% CI Sigma	1.778 to 3.7251
Anderson-Darling Normality Test	0.509835
P-Value (A-D Test)	0.1678
Skewness	0.541035
P-Value (Skewness)	0.3188
Kurtosis	-0.255347
P-Value (Kurtosis)	0.9672

Figure 11.8: SigmaXL Output (Probability Plot and Descriptive Statistics)

Comments

- As a minimum, when choosing a sample size for deciding the population percentage, extrapolation should be avoided to reach the desired percentage value.
- Another valid concern can emerge from this type of experiment. If there is a selection of samples from a process over a short period, this sample does not necessarily represent what the process will do over a more extended period of time, e.g., in the future.
- You can add, remove or change chart elements such as title, labels, gridlines and data labels by clicking on the chart and selecting "+".

11.7 Example (Baselining a 30,000-foot-level Continuous Response Metric and Determining Confidence Interval Statements)

Application: A percentage of population assessment of a Y response in a stable 30,000-foot-level report where recent data are from a period of process-output-response stability

- *IEE Volume III* Example and Dataset
- *IEE Volume III* Example 20.6 Base-lining a 30,000-foot-level Continuous-Response Metric and Determining Process Confidence Interval Statements
- Dataset (Smarter Solutions (2022): V3 C20, Exam 20-06, Baseline & Conf Int.xlsx

SigmaXL or EPRS App Input/Output

- Figure 11.9: EPRS Metric-App Input (Continuous Response)
- Figure 11.10: EPRS Metric-App Output (Continuous Response)
- Figure 11.11: EPRS Metric-App Input (Continuous Response, Staged)

- Figure 11.12: EPRS Metric-App Output (Continuous Response, Staged)
- Figure 11.13: SigmaXL Input (Mean Confidence Interval)
- Figure 11.14: SigmaXL Output (Mean Confidence Interval)
- Figure 11.15: SigmaXL Input (Standard Deviation Confidence Interval)
- Figure 11.16: SigmaXL Output (Standard Deviation Confidence Interval)
- Figure 11.17: SigmaXL Input (Percent of Population Confidence Interval Statements [Part 1])
- Figure 11.18: SigmaXL Input (Percent of Population Confidence Interval Statements [Part 2])
- Figure 11.19: SigmaXL Output (Percent of Population Confidence Interval Statements)

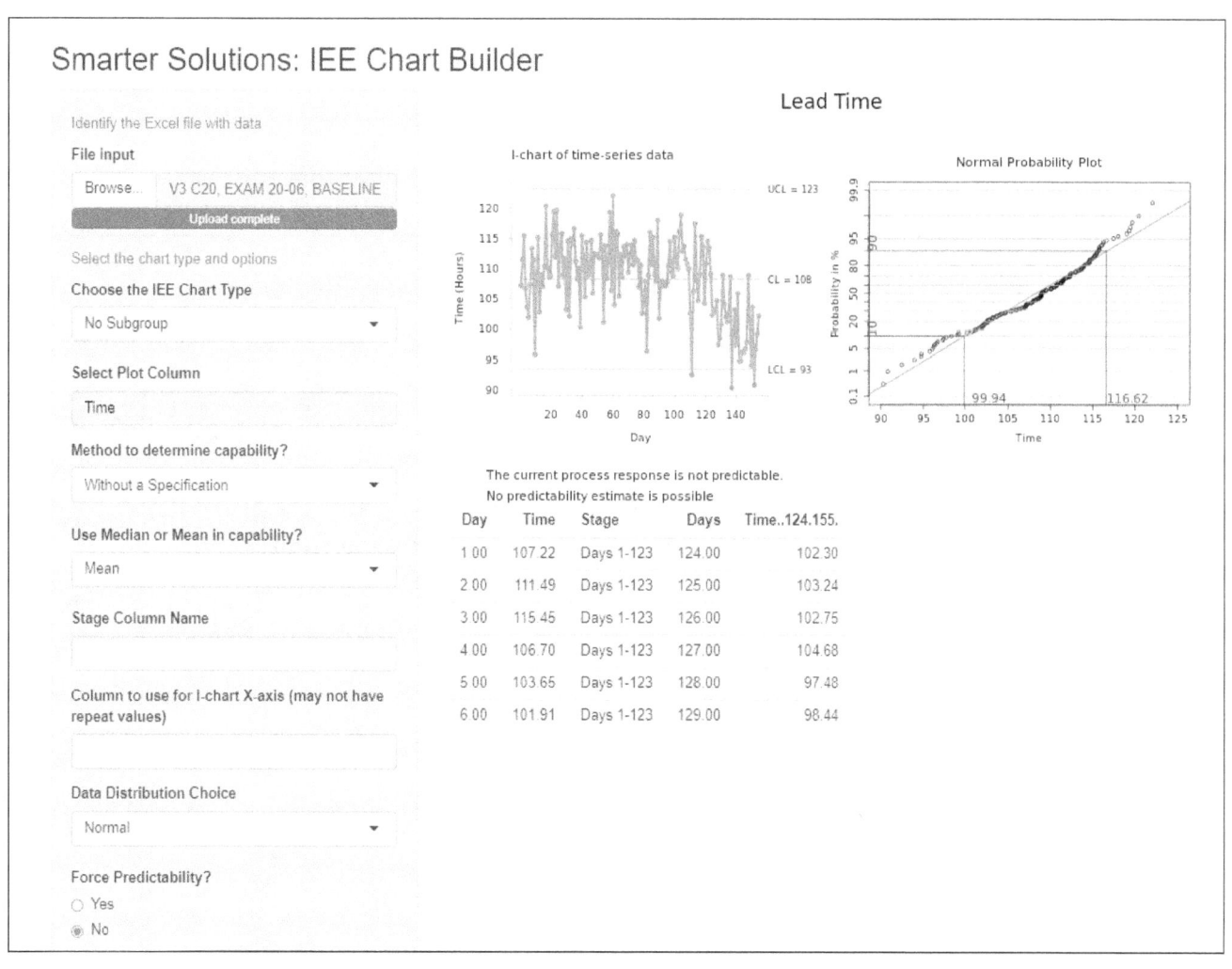

Figure 11.9: EPRS Metric-App Input (Continuous Response)

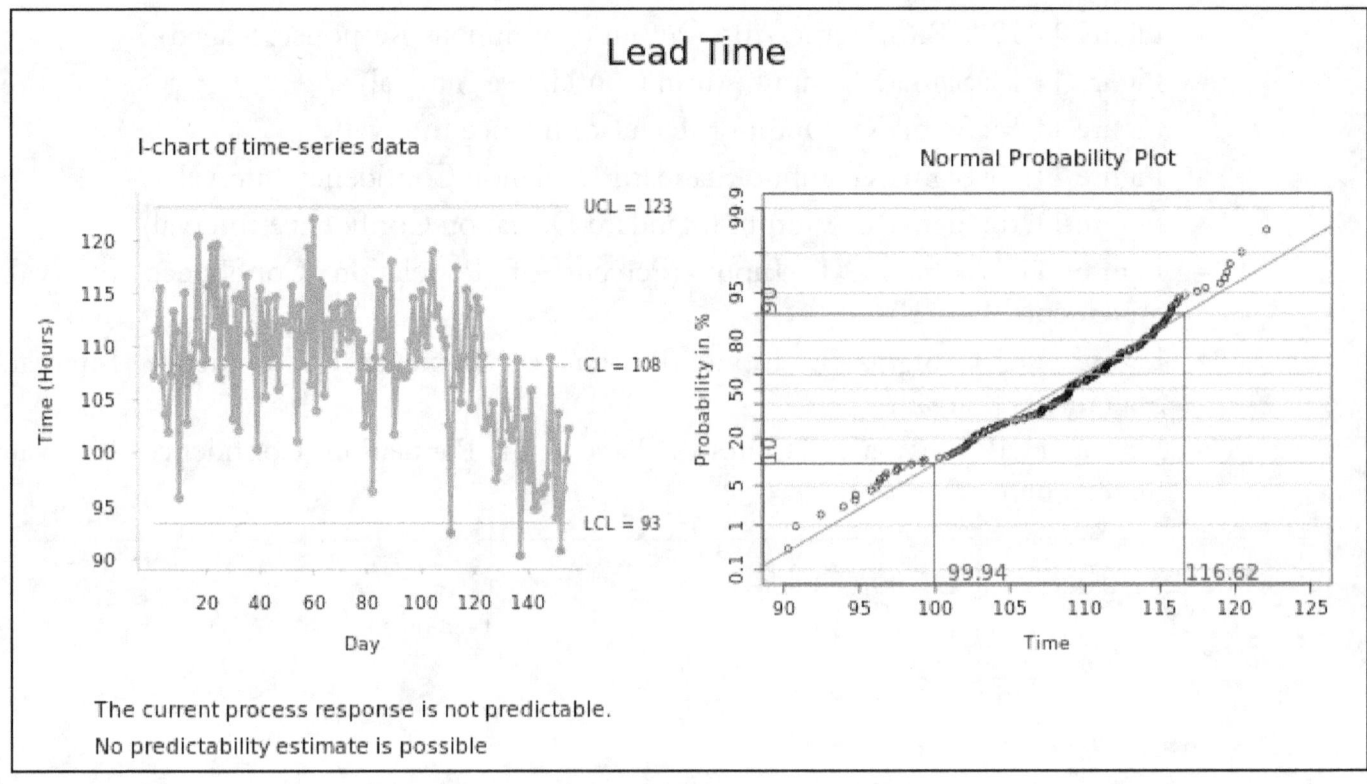

Figure 11.10: EPRS Metric-App Output (Continuous Response)

Comment

- The individuals chart indicates a process shift when there was a change to the process
- This 30,000-foot-level report individuals chart needs a staging when the process improvements occurred, which is shown in the following figures

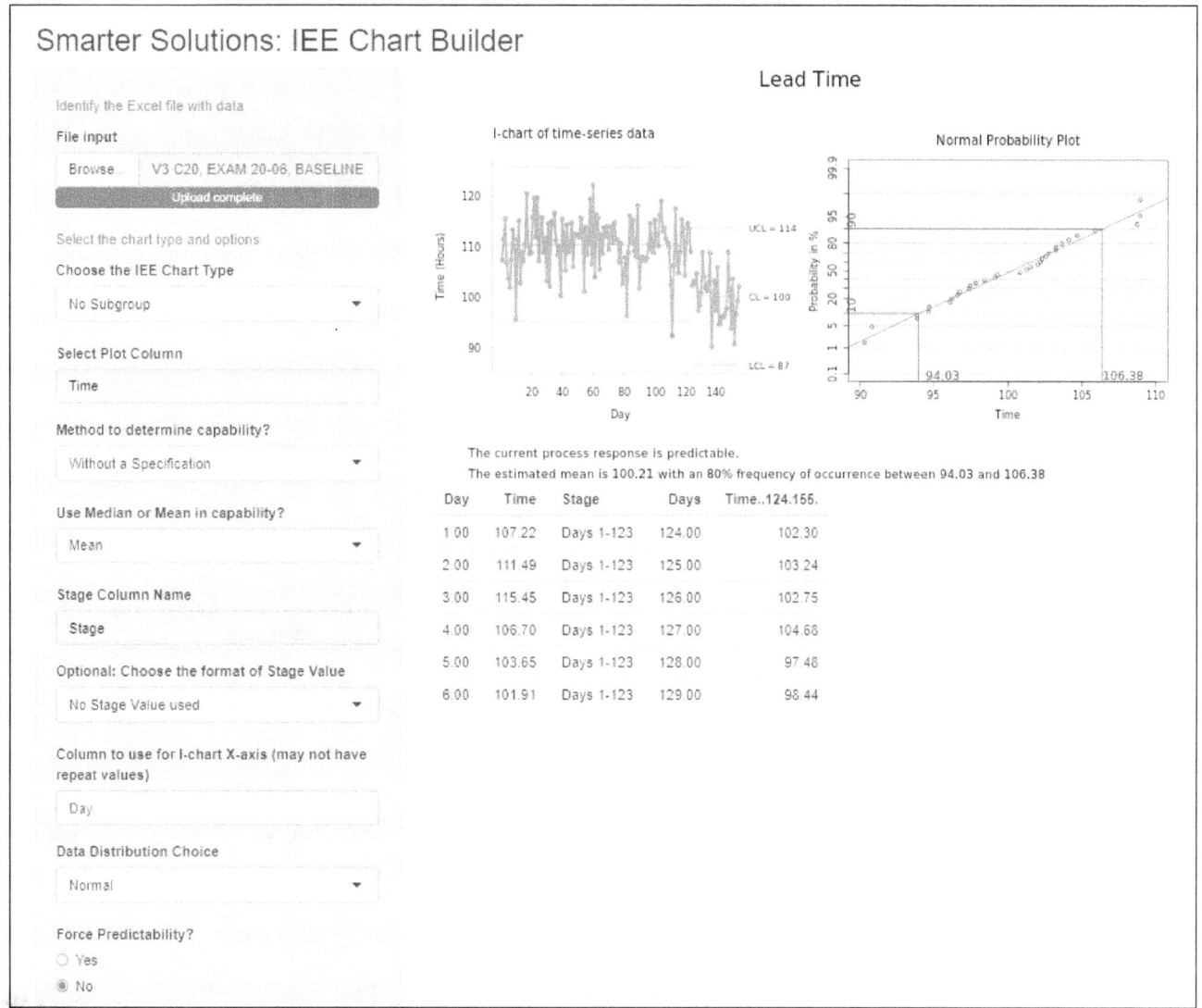

Figure 11.11: EPRS Metric-App Input (Continuous Response, Staged)

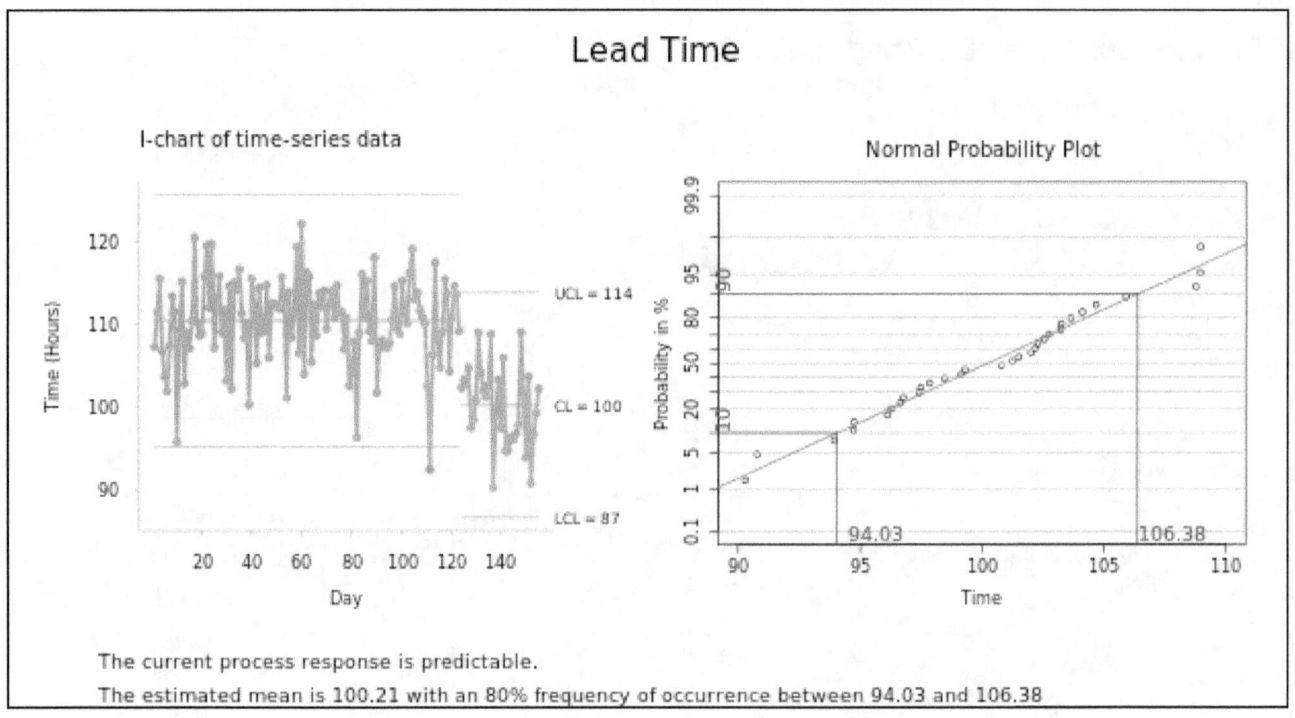

Figure 11.12: EPRS Metric-App Output (Continuous Response, Staged)

Comments

- Figure 11.12 indicates that there was a process response change. Because of this, it is appropriate to stage the individuals chart on day 124.
- The 30,000-foot-level reporting app calculates the individuals chart limits separately for the two stages.
- From the staged individuals chart shown in Figure 11.12, we have no reason to believe that the process is not predictable.
- Considering that data from day 124 to 155 are a random sample of the future, we can also calculate the confidence interval for the process population mean and standard deviation, as shown in the following figures.

SigmaXL Chart Function: Statistical Tools>1-Sample t-Test & Confidence Intervals

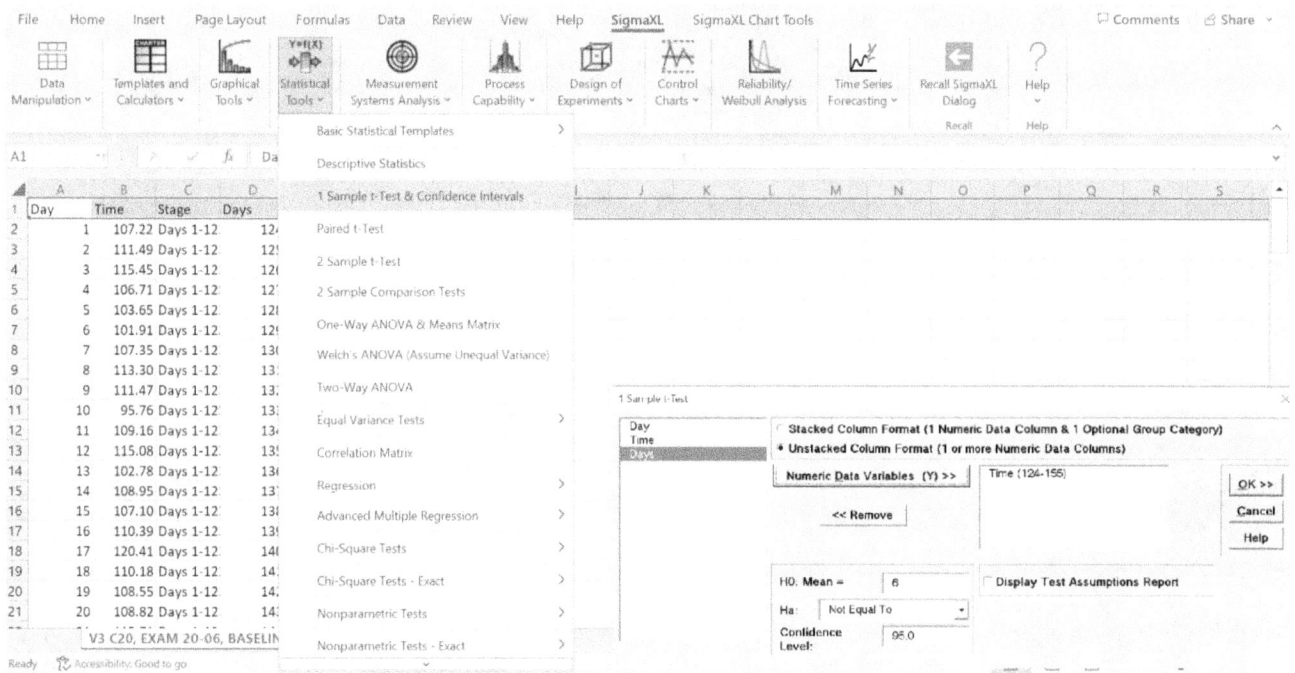

Figure 11.13: SigmaXL Input (Mean Confidence Interval)

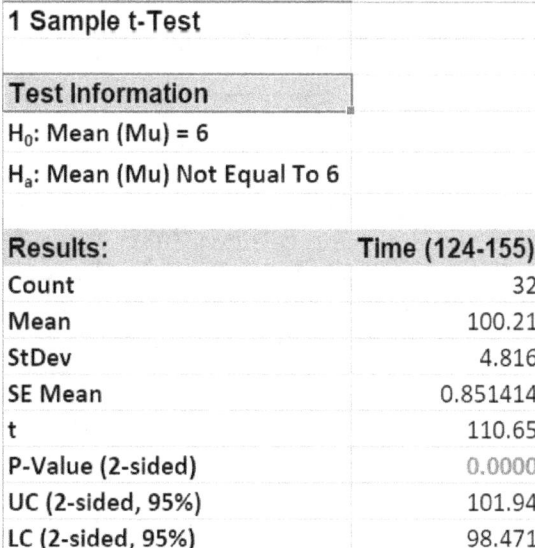

1 Sample t-Test	
Test Information	
H₀: Mean (Mu) = 6	
Hₐ: Mean (Mu) Not Equal To 6	
Results:	**Time (124-155)**
Count	32
Mean	100.21
StDev	4.816
SE Mean	0.851414
t	110.65
P-Value (2-sided)	0.0000
UC (2-sided, 95%)	101.94
LC (2-sided, 95%)	98.471

Figure 11.14: SigmaXL Output (Mean Confidence Interval)

Comments

- A 30,000-foot-level report provides a best-estimate for a mean process-output response
- Figure 11.14 provides a confidence interval for this mean process-output response
- You can add, remove or change chart elements such as title, labels, gridlines and data labels by clicking on the chart and selecting "+".

SigmaXL Chart Function: Statistical Tools>Basic Statistical Templates>1Sample Chi-Square Test and CI for Standard Deviation

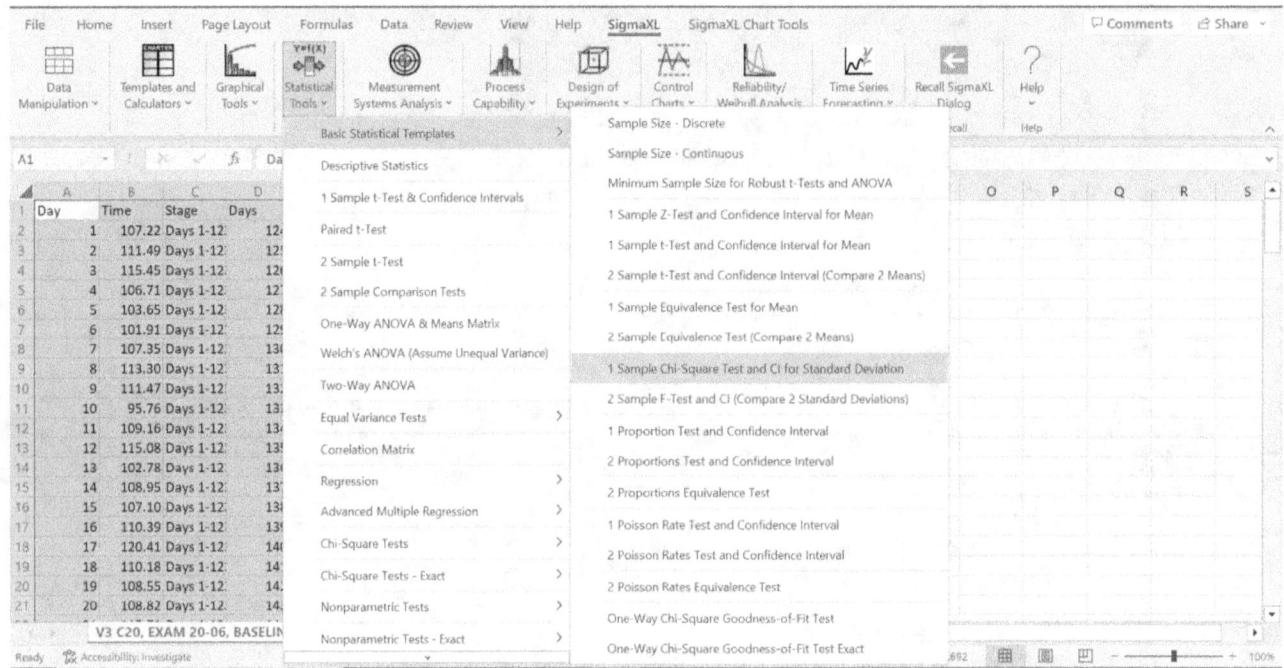

Figure 11.15: SigmaXL Input (Standard Deviation Confidence Interval)

1 Sample Chi-Square Test and Confidence Interval for Standard Deviation

Sample Data (user inputs):		
Sample Size	n	32
Sample Standard Deviation	s	4.816
Null Hypothesis (hypothesized StDev)	H_0: Sigma (σ) =	0.5
Alternative Hypothesis	H_a: Sigma (σ)	Not Equal To
Confidence Level (enter .95 for 95%)	100*(1-α)%	95.0%

Results:	
Sample Variance	23.1939
DF	31
Chi-Square test statistic	2876.0381
alpha	0.0500
P-Value (2 sided)	0.0000
Upper Confidence Limit (2 Sided)	6.4028
Lower Confidence Limit (2 Sided)	3.8610

Figure 11.16: SigmaXL Output (Standard Deviation Confidence Interval)

Comments

- A 30,000-foot-level report provides a best-estimate for a mean process-output response and an 80% frequency of occurrence rate

- Figure 11.16 provides a confidence interval for the standard deviation process-output response used when determining the 30,000-foot-level reported 80% frequency of occurrence rate

- You can add, remove or change chart elements such as title, labels, gridlines and data labels by clicking on the chart and selecting "+".

SigmaXL Chart Function: Graphical Tools>Normal Probability Plots

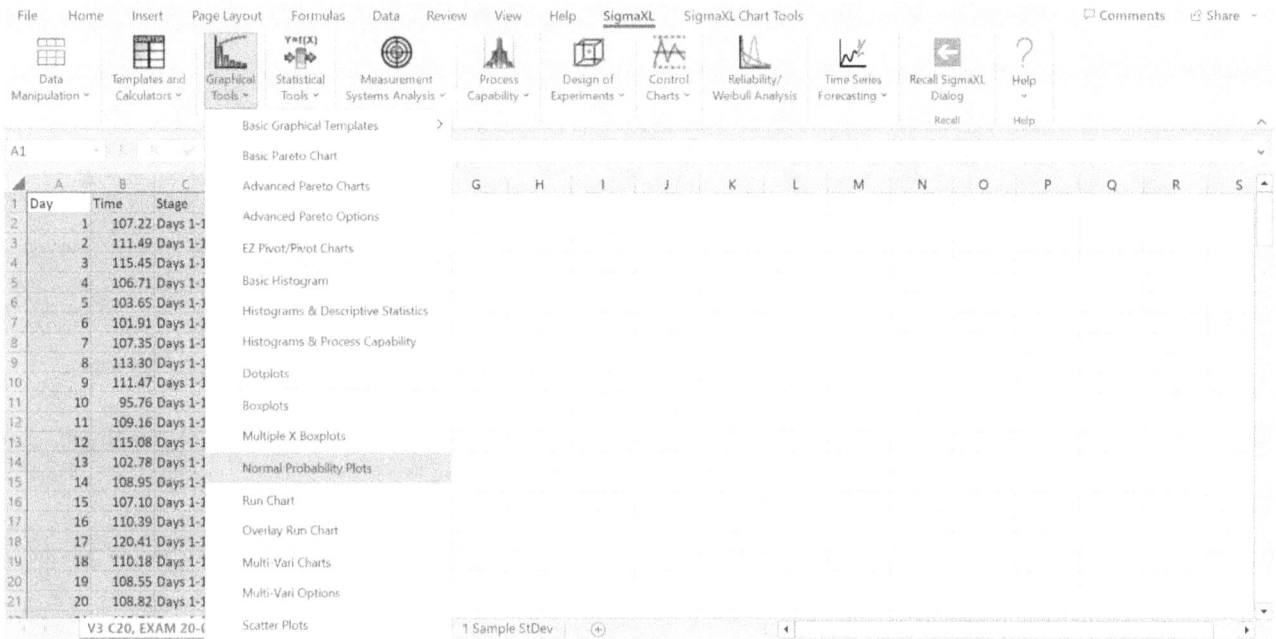

Figure 11.17: SigmaXL Input (Percent of Population Confidence Interval Statements [Part 1])

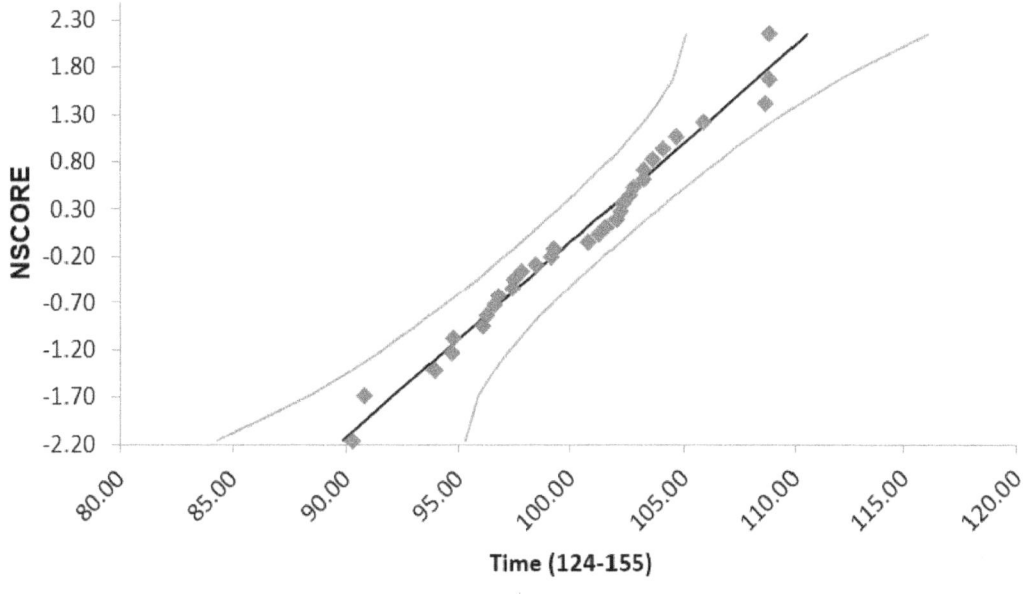

Figure 11.18: SigmaXL Input (Percent of Population Confidence Interval Statements [Part 2])

Scroll down to row 200, column AC to check the confidence bounds table:

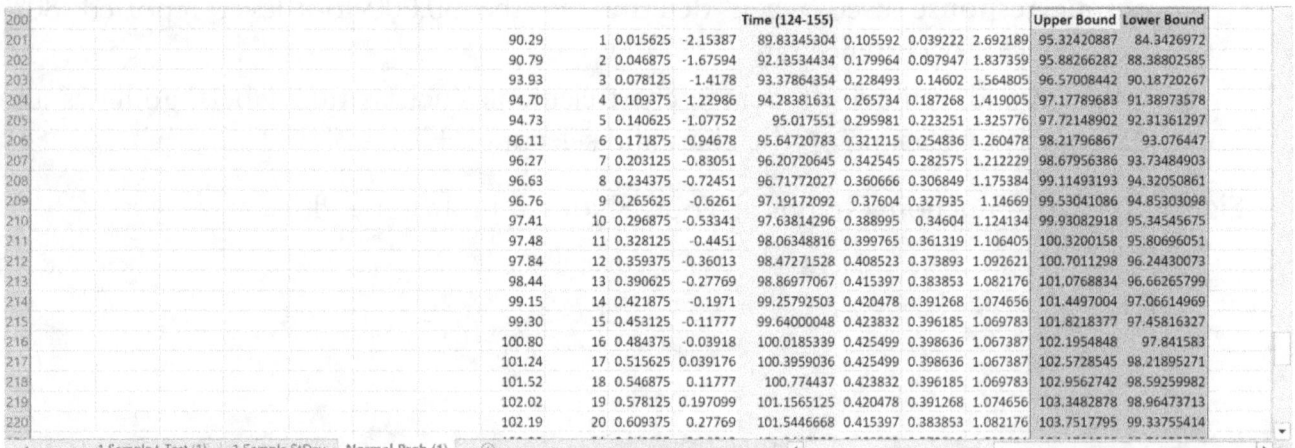

Figure 11.19: SigmaXL Output (Percent of Population Confidence Interval Statements)

Comments

- Figure 11.19 shows how to determine the confidence intervals
- You can add, remove or change chart elements such as title, labels, gridlines and data labels by clicking on the chart and selecting "+".

12 Inferences: Attribute Failure Rate Response

Reference: *IEE Volume III* – Chapter 21

This chapter and the previous chapter describe inferences for a one-sample population. The last chapter provides analyses for a continuous response, while this chapter addresses an attribute failure rate response.

Described is evaluating defective-count data (go/no-go attribute information). An example attribute (pass/fail or pass/nonconformance) situation is a copier fed or failed to feed individual sheets of paper satisfactorily; i.e., a copier may provide 999 sheets out of 1000 sheets of paper on average without a jam. The purpose of these experiments may be to assess with a confidence interval an attribute criterion or evaluate the proportion of parts beyond a continuous criterion value; e.g., 20% of the electrical measurements are less than 100,000 ohms.

With this chapter's described techniques, samples are evaluated to determine whether they will either pass or fail a requirement, i.e., a binary response. Experiments of this type can assess the proportion of a population that is defective through either a confidence interval statement or a hypothesis test of a criterion.

Tests of failure rate attribute information can require a much larger sample size than tests of continuous response.

12.1 Example: Sample Size (Hypothesis Test of an Attribute Failure Rate Criterion)

Application

- A supplier manufactures a component that is not to have more than one defective part for every 1000 parts, i.e., a 0.001 failure rate criterion.
- The supplier wants to determine a test sample size for assessing this criterion.

- The failure rate criterion is 1/1000 (0.001); however, a sample size calculation requires two failure rates (ρ_β and ρ_α).
- To determine values for ρ_β and ρ_α, let's presume a shift of 200 units was a minimal "important increment" from the above 1000-part criterion, along with $\alpha = \beta = 0.05$. The value for ρ_β would then be 0.00125, i.e., 1/(1000 - 200), while the value for ρ_α would be 0.000833, i.e., 1/(1000 + 200).

  - $\alpha = 0.05$
  - $\beta = 0.05$ (Power = 0.95)
  - $\rho_\beta = 0.00125$
  - $\rho_\alpha = 0.000833$

IEE Volume III Example and Dataset

- *IEE Volume III* Example 21.1 Sample Size – A Hypothesis Test of an Attribute Criterion
- Dataset: Not applicable

SigmaXL or EPRS Metric-App [Smarter Solutions (2020)] Input/Output

- Figure 12.1: SigmaXL Input (Sample Size – Hypothesis Test of a Defective Rate Criterion)
- Figure 12.2: SigmaXL Output (Sample Size – Hypothesis Test of a Defective Rate Criterion)
- The sample size depends on the level of significance, the desired power of the test, the variability of the outcome, and the effect size.

SigmaXL Chart Function: Statistical Tools>Power and Sample Size Calculators>1 Proportion Test Calculator

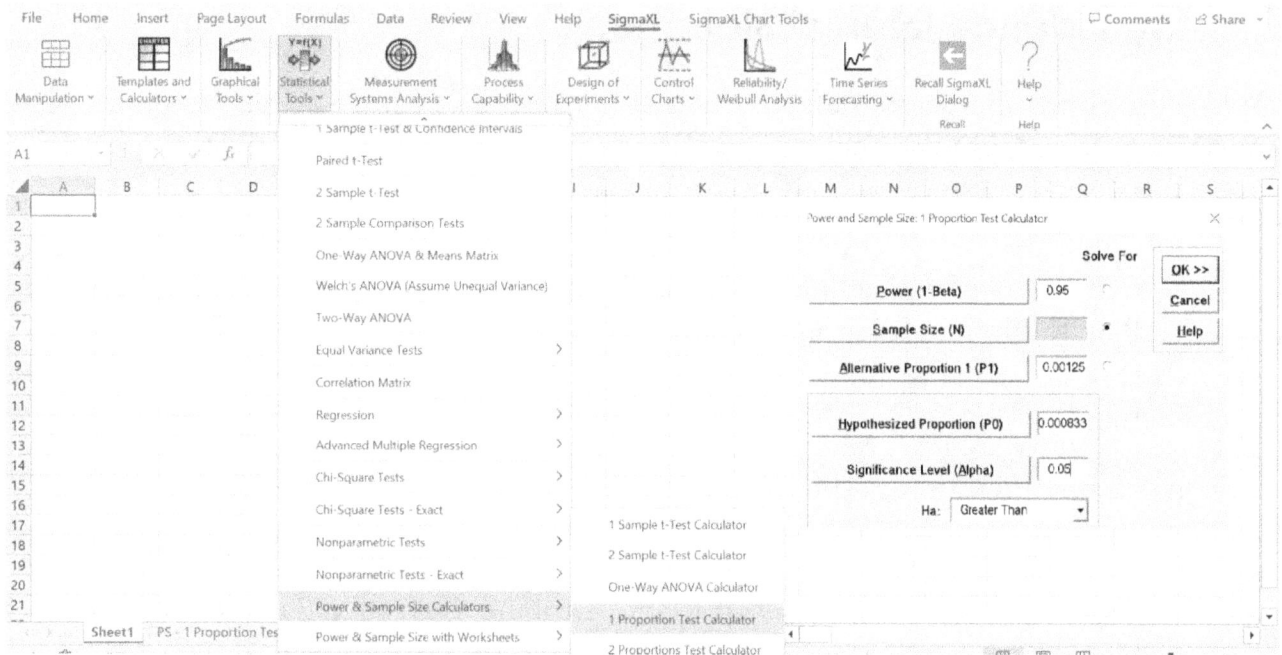

Figure 12.1: SigmaXL Input (Sample Size – Hypothesis Test of a Defective Rate Criterion)

Power and Sample Size: 1 Proportion Test

H0: P0 = 0.000833
Ha: P0 Greater Than 0.000833
Solve For: Sample Size (N)

Power (1 - Beta)	Alternative Proportion (P1)	Hypothesized Proportion (P0)	Significance Level (Alpha)	Sample Size (N)	Actual Power
0.95	0.00125	0.000833	0.05	64095	0.950000846

Figure 12.2: SigmaXL Output (Sample Size – Hypothesis Test of a Defective Rate Criterion)

Comments

- The sample size of 64,095 shown in Figure 12.2 is not reasonable for most situations.

- This considerable sample size is not atypical when developing an attribute defective-rate sampling plan.

- A relaxing of the test considerations for α, β, ρ_β, and ρ_α would reduce the calculated sample size, but the sample size would still be enormous for this situation.

- The sample size would be much smaller if this attribute non-conformance rate response could be changed to a continuous response

- *IEE Volume III* Section 21.5 describes reduced sample size testing for attribute defective-rate test situations.

- You can add, remove or change chart elements such as title, labels, gridlines and data labels by clicking on the chart and selecting "+".

12.2   Example: Baselining a 30,000-foot-level Attribute Defective Response Metric and Determining Process Output Confidence Interval Statements

Application: A process-output defective rate of a Y response from a stable 30,000-foot-level report where recent data are from a period of process-output-response stability.

IEE Volume III Example and Dataset

- *IEE Volume III* Example 21.4 Baselining a 30,000-foot-level Attribute Defective Rate Response Metric and Determining Process Confidence Interval Statement
- Dataset (Smarter Solutions (2022): V3 C21, Exam 21-04, Baseline Attr Conf Int.xlsx

SigmaXL or EPRS Metric-App [Smarter Solutions (2020)] Input/Output

- Figure 12.3: EPRS Metric-App Input (Attribute, Defective Rate, No Staging)
- Figure 12.4: EPRS Metric-App Input (Attribute, Defective Rate, Staging)
- Figure 12.5: EPRS Metric-App Output (Attribute, Defective Rate, Staging)
- Figure 12.6: SigmaXL Input (Defective rate Confidence Interval Statement, Recent Region of Stability)
- Figure 12.7: SigmaXL Output (Defective rate Confidence Interval Statement, Recent Region of Stability)

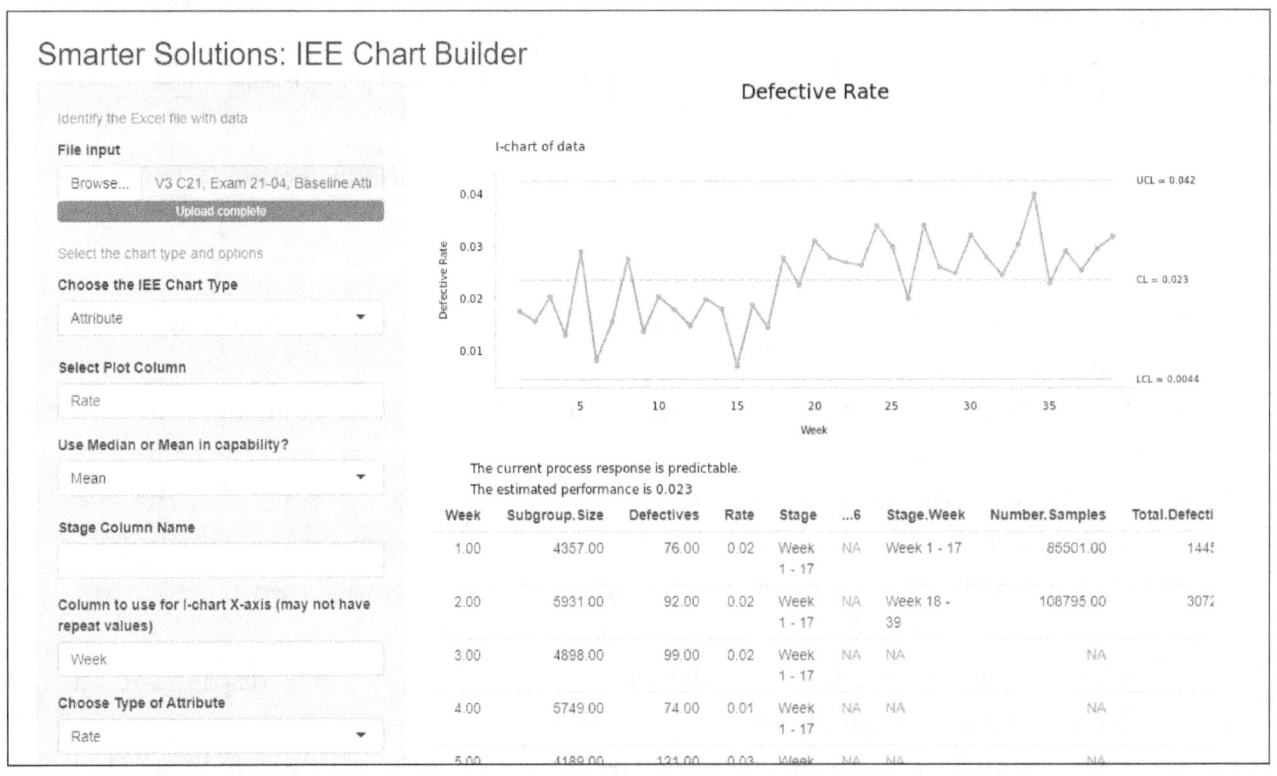

Figure 12.3: EPRS Metric-App Input (Attribute, Defective Rate, No Staging)

The individuals chart in Figure 12.3 indicates a shift in the response magnitude. Figure 12.4 shows an EPRS metric-app staging at the point in time where there was a degradation in the process output to a higher value.

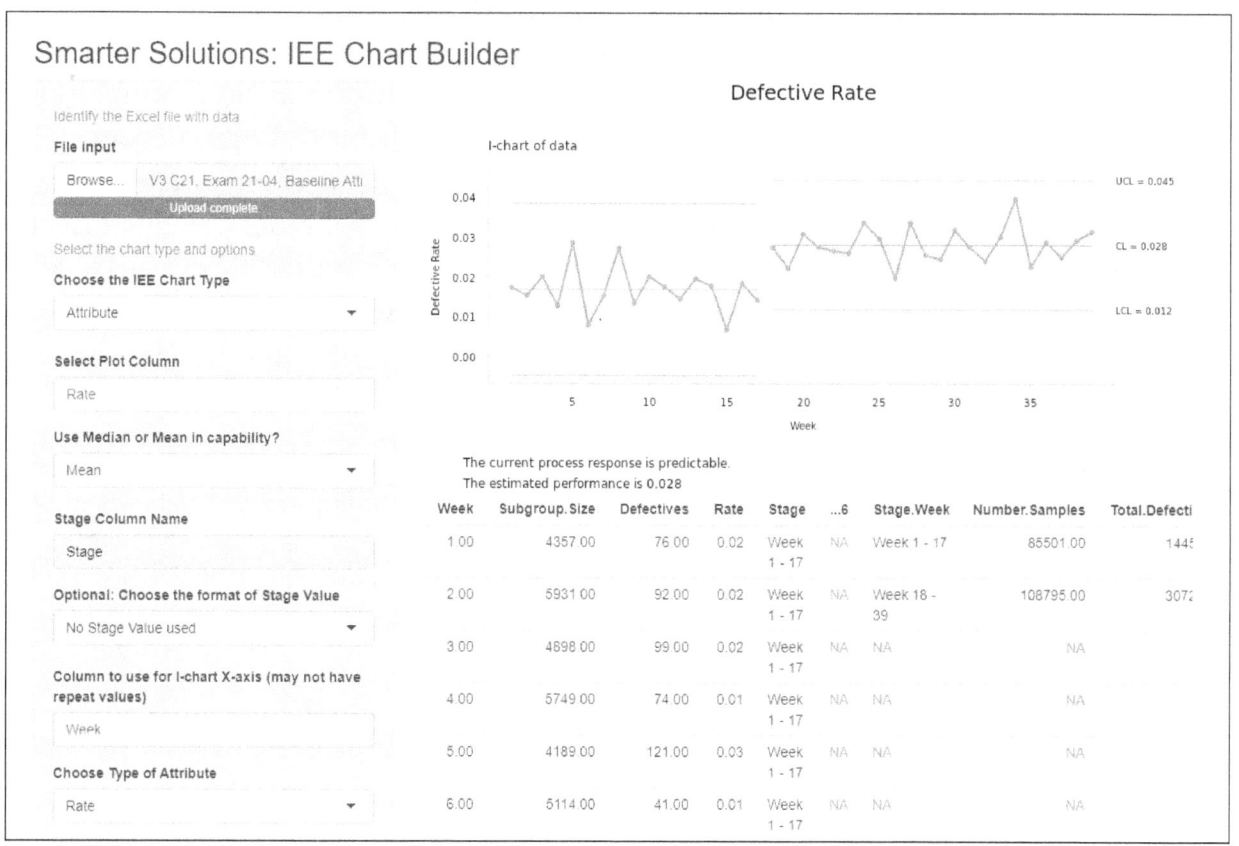

Figure 12.4: EPRS Metric-App Input (Attribute, Defective Rate, Staging)

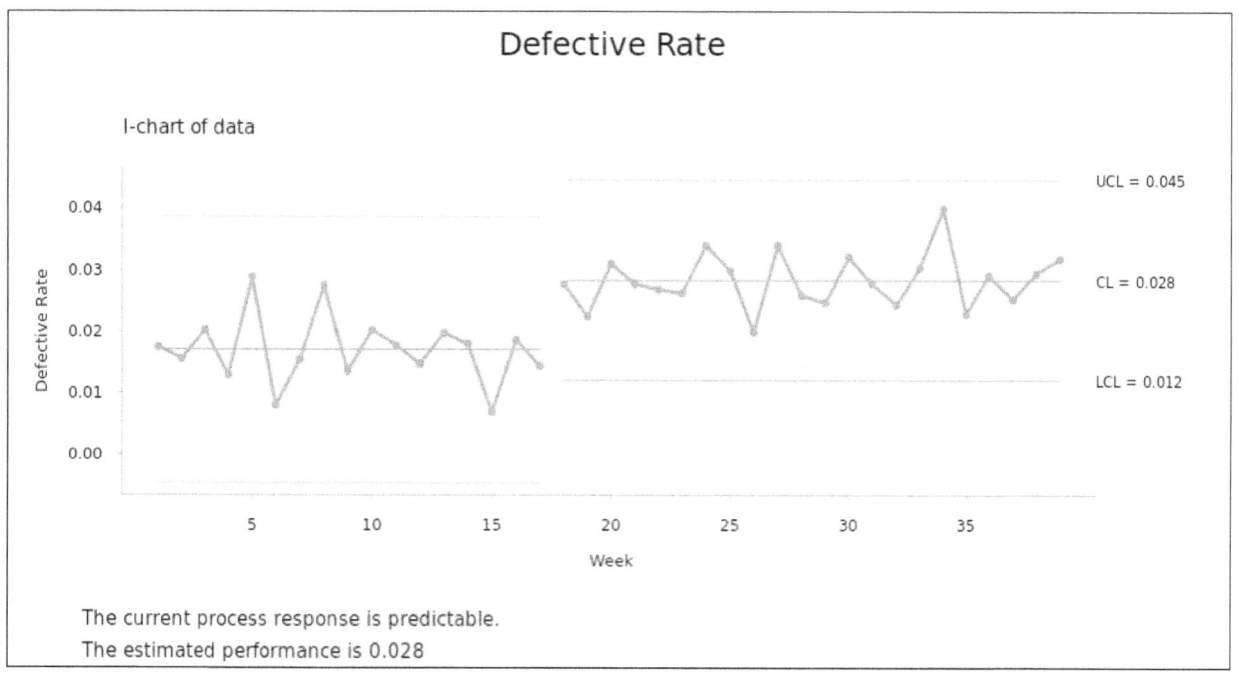

Figure 12.5: EPRS Metric-App Output (Attribute, Defective Rate, Staging)

Comments

- The process response changed
- The 30,000-foot-level report's individuals chart was staged
- Even though all pass/fail data that went through this process were captured, one can still consider the data from the latest stability region a future sample. If the magnitude of this estimate is undesirable, the process needs improvement.
- The overall process population defective rate confidence interval calculation is made by analyzing the raw data for the 30,000-foot-level report's individuals chart region of stability, i.e., a total of 3072 defective units out of 108795 transactions.
- There can also be a hypothesis test that the failure rate equals the mean failure rate from transactions before week 18. A later chapter describes the comparison of two proportions, which would be a better statistical assessment for this situation.

The 1 Proportion test calculates a confidence interval and performs a hypothesis test of the propotion.

SigmaXL Chart Function: Statistical Tools>Basic Statistical Templates>1 Proportion Test and Confidence Interval

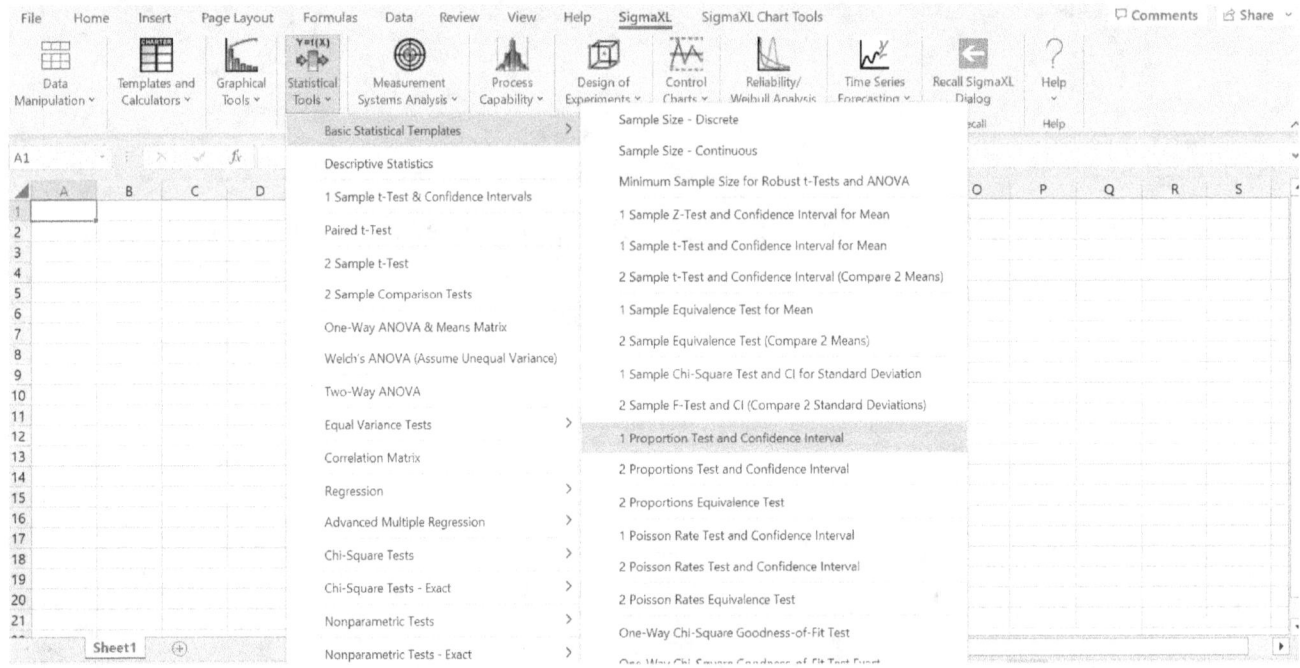

Figure 12.6: SigmaXL Input (Defective rate Confidence Interval Statement, Recent Region of Stability)

Sample Data (user inputs):		
Number of Events	x	3,072
Sample Size	n	108,379
Null Hypothesis (hypothesized proportion)	H₀: Proportion =	0.0169
Alternative Hypothesis	Hₐ: Proportion	Not Equal To
Confidence Level (enter .95 for 95%)	100*(1-α)%	95.0%
Hypothesis Test Method		Binomial Exact
Confidence Interval Method		Exact (Clopper-Pearson Beta)

Results:	
Sample proportion (x/n)	0.0283
alpha	0.0500
npq (npq should be >= 5 for normal approximation; q = 1-p)	2,984.9242
Z-statistic (normal)	29.2311
Binomial exact probability P-Value (2-sided)	0.0000
Upper Confidence Limit (2-sided)	0.0294
Lower Confidence Limit (2-sided)	0.0274

Figure 12.7: SigmaXL Output (Defective rate Confidence Interval Statement, Recent Region of Stability)

Comment

- The previous 30,000-foot-level report indicated that there was degradation in the process's defective rate.

- This analysis supports this conclusion since the P-value is less than 0.05, and the 0.0169 defective-non-conformance rate is below the population defective rate confidence interval.

- The process output response is now predictable with a best-estimate defective rate of 0.028, with a 95% confidence interval of 0.027 to 0.029.

- You can add, remove or change chart elements such as title, labels, gridlines and data labels by clicking on the chart and selecting "+".

12.3 Example: Acceptable Quality Level (AQL) Confidence Interval

This section shows how deceiving a product's AQL pass/fail sample-lot test strategy can be. A more effective approach is to monitor the 30,000-foot-level report's process-output response, where if a prediction statement is undesirable, there is a need for process improvement.

With AQL sampling plans, there is an inspection of the parts in a received lot to determine if the lot should be accepted or rejected. AQL sampling plan alternatives are available from tables as a function of an AQL criterion and other lot characteristics. Pass/fail decisions for an AQL evaluated lot are based only on the lot's performance, not on previous product performance from the process. AQL sampling plans do not show how a process is performing.

AQL sampling plans are inefficient and costly, especially when high levels of quality are needed. Often, organizations think they will achieve better quality with AQL sampling plans than they can. The trend is that organizations are moving away from AQL sampling plans; however, many organizations are slow to make the transition. The following describes the concepts and shortcomings of AQL sampling plans.

The sample-size risk statistics of AQL protect the producer, not the consumer. The following will illustrate this point by examining the confidence interval for an AQL test.

For N (lot size) = 75 and AQL = 4.0%, ANSI/ASQ Z1.4 yields for a general inspection level II a test plan in which

- Sample size = 13
- Acceptance number = 1
- Rejection number = 2

A SigmaXL confidence interval determination for one acceptance in a sample size of 13 is shown in

- Figure 12.8: SigmaXL Input (Defective Rate Confidence Interval)
- Figure 12.9: SigmaXL Output (Defective Rate Confidence Interval)

SigmaXL Chart Function: Templates and Calculators>1 Proportion Test and Confidence Interval

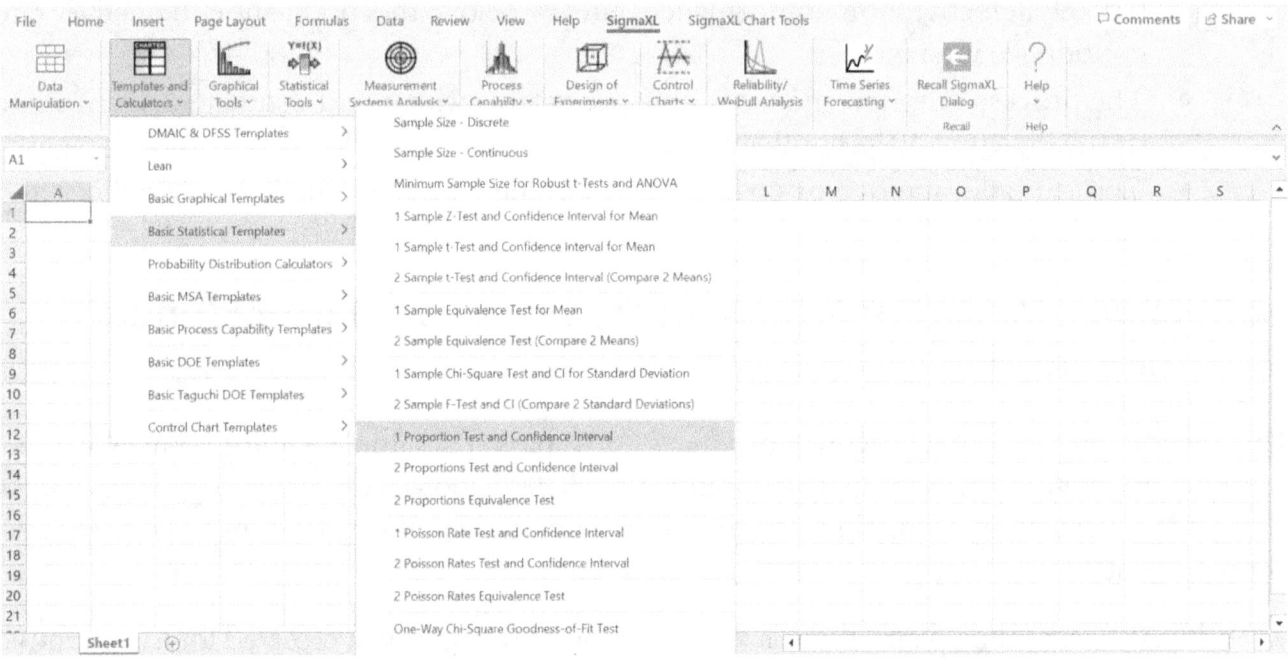

Figure 12.8: SigmaXL Input (Defective Rate Confidence Interval)

1 Proportion Test and Confidence Interval		
Sample Data (user inputs):		
Number of Events	x	1
Sample Size	n	13
Null Hypothesis (hypothesized proportion)	H_0: Proportion =	0.04
Alternative Hypothesis	H_a: Proportion	Less Than
Confidence Level (enter .95 for 95%)	100*(1-α)%	95.0%
Hypothesis Test Method		Binomial Exact
Confidence Interval Method		Exact (Clopper-Pearson Beta)
Results:		
Sample proportion (x/n)		0.0769
alpha		0.0500
npq (npq should be >= 5 for normal approximation; q = 1-p)		0.9231
Z-statistic (normal)		0.6794
Binomial exact probability P-Value (1-sided)		0.9068
Upper Confidence Limit (1-sided)		0.3163

Figure 12.9: SigmaXL Output (Defective Rate Confidence Interval)

Comment

- With a lot test sample size of 13 and one failure occurrence, the sample failure rate is 0.076923

- The 95% confidence interval upper boundary for this one failure rate occurrence with a sample lot size of 13 is 0.316 or 31.6%

- This 31.6% value is much larger than what one might expect with an AQL 4.0% test

- You can add, remove or change chart elements such as title, labels, gridlines and data labels by clicking on the chart and selecting "+".

13

IEE-DMAIC — Analyze Phase: Continuous Response Comparison Tests

13.1 IEE-DMAIC Roadmap Component

Book 1 Reference: *IEE Volume III* – Chapter 22

Book 2 Reference: *Lean Six Sigma Project Execution Guide* – Section 7

Internet: www.smartersolutions.com/roadmap (clicking on highlighted area provides the flowchart below)

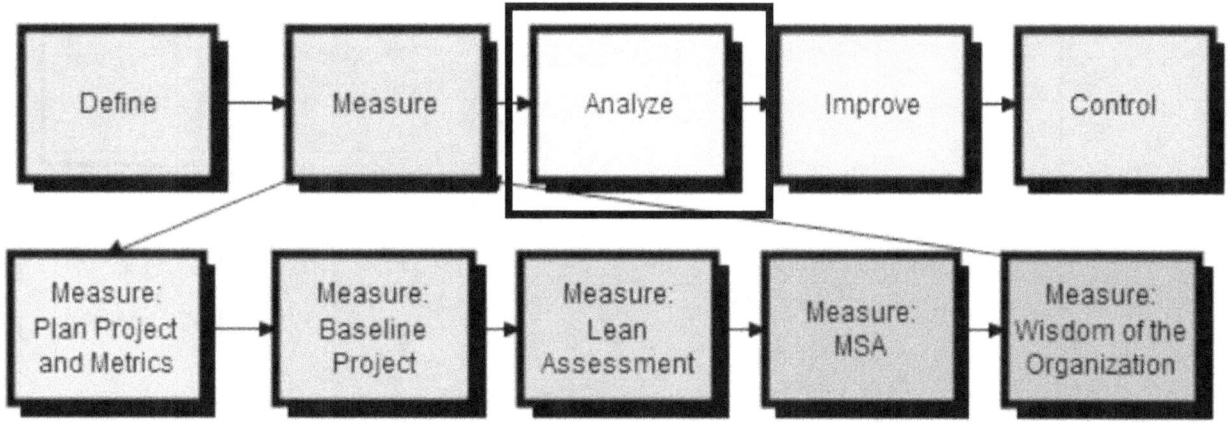

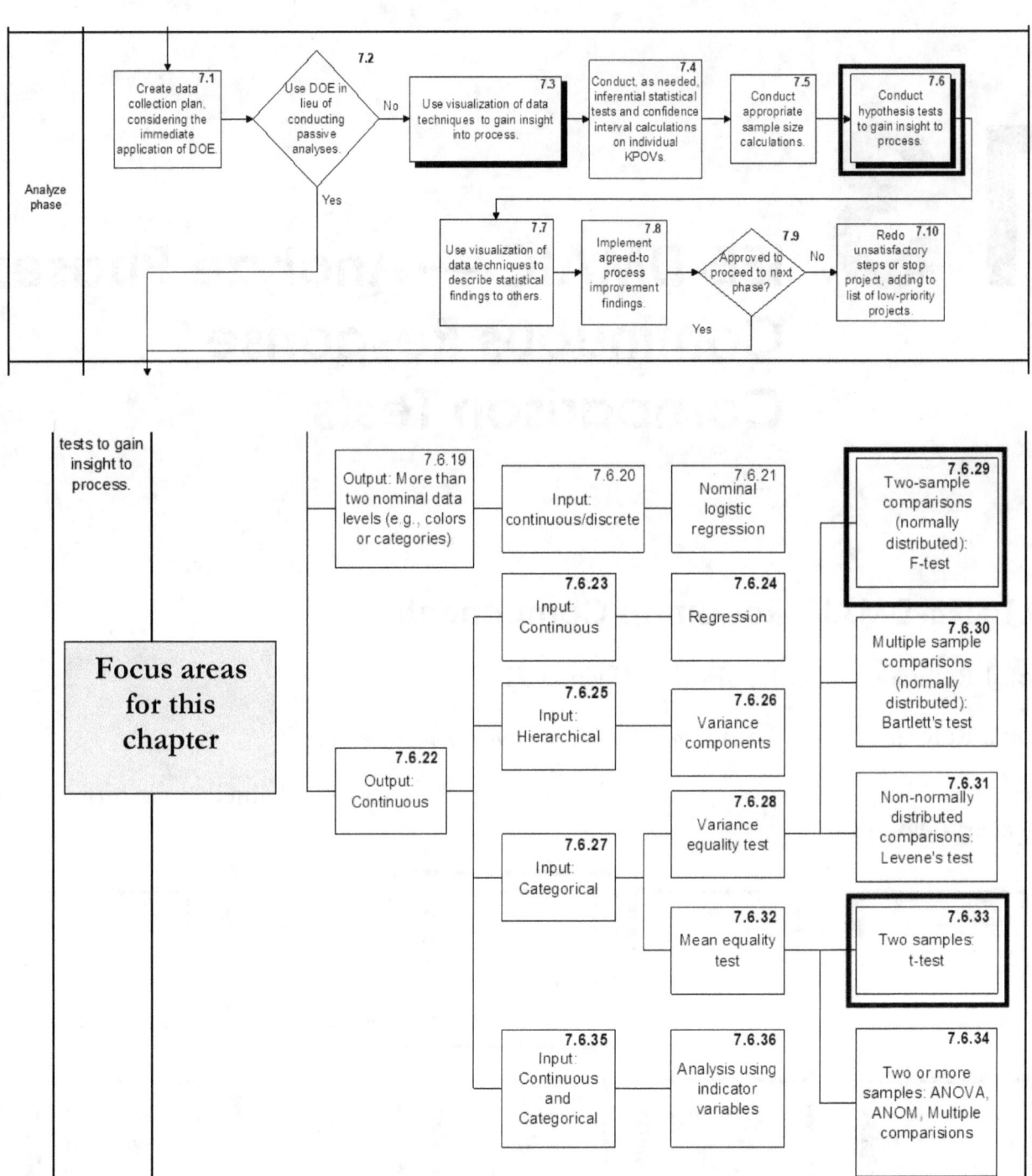

The previous two chapters described inferences from continuous and attribute population samples. This chapter and the next chapter extend these concepts to statistical inferences when comparing two populations, e.g., do two machines manufacture, on average, the diameter of a shaft to the same dimension? The next chapter focuses on attribute failure rate response situations, e.g., are the failure frequencies of completing a purchase order correctly the same between two departments?

When comparing the means of two samples, the null hypothesis is that there is no difference between the population means, while the alternative hypothesis is that there is a difference between the population means. A difference between two means could be single-sided, i.e., $\mu_1 > \mu_2$ or $\mu_1 < \mu_2$, or double-sided, i.e., $\mu_1 \neq \mu_2$.

In the IEE-DMAIC analysis phase, these tools can provide insight into inputs that affect an output response, i.e., the Xs in the equation $Y = f(X)$. This insight can then lead to improvement opportunities. In the DMAIC improve-phase of the IEE-DMAIC roadmap, these tools can also statistically assess the change impact on process output response.

13.2 Example: Comparing the Mean of Two Samples

IEE Volume III Example and Dataset

- *IEE Volume III* Example 22.1: Comparing the means of two samples
- Dataset (Smarter Solutions (2022): V3 C22, Exam 22-01, Two Samples.xlsx

SigmaXL or EPRS Metric-App [Smarter Solutions (2020)] Input/Output

- Figure 13.1: SigmaXL Input (Mean Hypothesis Comparison of Two Samples)
- Figure 13.2: SigmaXL Output (Mean Hypothesis Comparison of Two Samples)

The 2 sample t-Test performs and independent test and generates a confidence interval.

SigmaXL Chart Function: Statistical Tools>2 Sample t-Test

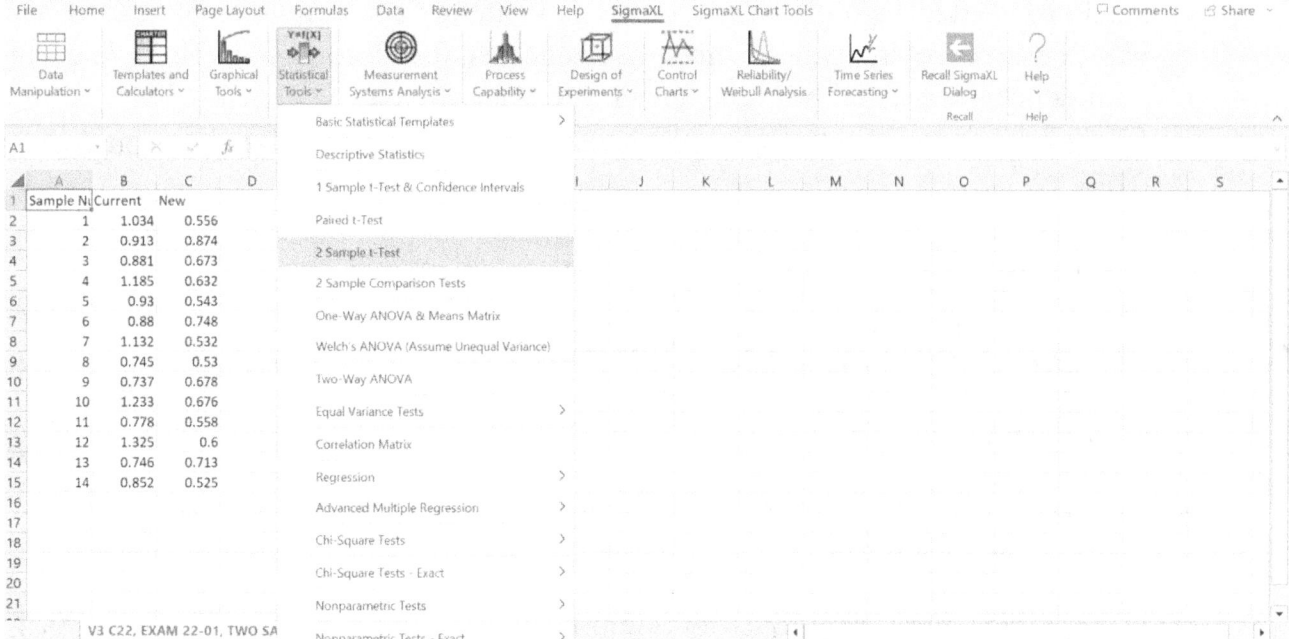

Figure 13.1: SigmaXL Input (Mean Hypothesis Comparison of Two Samples)

2 Sample t-Test		
Test Information		
H_0: Mean Difference = 0		
H_a: Mean Difference Not Equal To 0		
Assume Equal Variance		
Results:	**Current**	**New**
Count	14	14
Mean	0.955071	0.631286
Standard Deviation	0.195209	0.102415765
Mean Difference	0.323786	
Std Error Difference	0.058916209	
DF	26	
t	5.496	
P-Value (2-sided)	0.0000	
UC (2-sided, 95%)	0.444890	
LC (2-sided, 95%)	0.202682	

Figure 13.2: SigmaXL Output (Mean Hypothesis Comparison of Two Samples)

Comments

- From Figure 13.2, one can declare significance at an α decision level of 0.05, since the P-value of 0.000 is less than our 0.05 criteria.
- Also provided in Figure 13.2 is the best estimate for the difference of 0.3238. The 95% confidence interval for this difference is 0.202 to 0.444. Note that this confidence interval did not contain zero.
- If one of the confidence interval boundaries equals zero, the P-value would equal 0.05.
- You can add, remove or change chart elements such as title, labels, gridlines and data labels by clicking on the chart and selecting "+".

13.3 Example: Comparing the Variance of Two Samples

IEE Volume III Example and Dataset

- *IEE Volume III* Example 22.2: Comparing the variance of two samples
- Dataset (Smarter Solutions (2022): V3 C22, Exam 22-01, Two Samples.xlsx

SigmaXL or EPRS Metric-App [Smarter Solutions (2020)] Input/Output

- Figure 13.3 A: SigmaXL Input (Variance Hypothesis Comparison of Two Samples)
- Figure 13.3 B: SigmaXL Output (Variance Hypothesis Comparison of Two Samples)

- Figure 13.4 A: SigmaXL Output (2 Sample Comparison Tests)
- Figure 13.4 B: SigmaXL Output (2 Sample Comparison Tests)

Many statistical tests assume that samples have the same variance, therefore, this hypothesis needs to be tested.

The data from each group are normally distributed; therefore, we will use Bartlett's test as is more powerful than Levene's Test.

SigmaXL Chart Function: Statistical Tools>Equal Variance Test>Bartlett

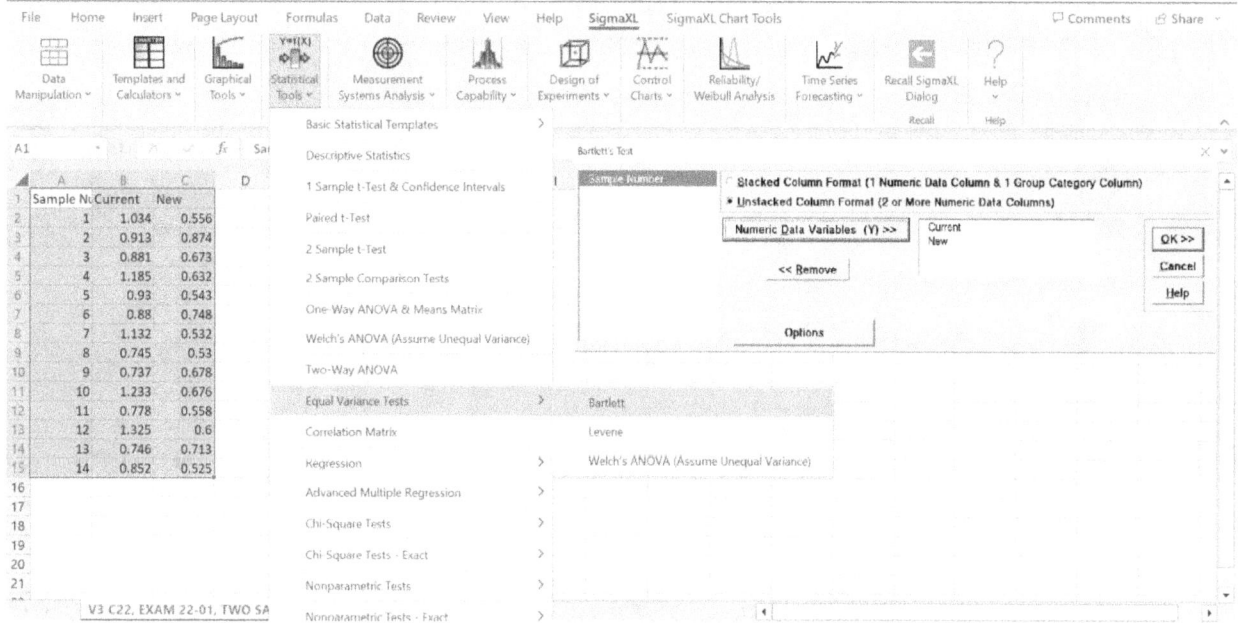

Figure 13.3 A: SigmaXL Input (Variance Hypothesis Comparison of Two Samples)

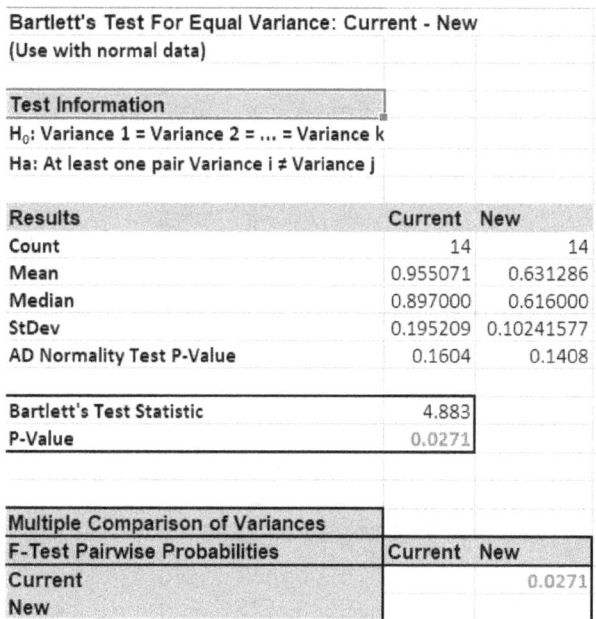

Figure 13.4 B: SigmaXL Output (Variance Hypothesis Comparison of Two Samples)

Another option is to use the 2 Sample Comparison Tests. The output in this case will include normality, means as well as variances tests.

SigmaXL Chart Function: Statistical Tools>2 Sample Comparison Tests

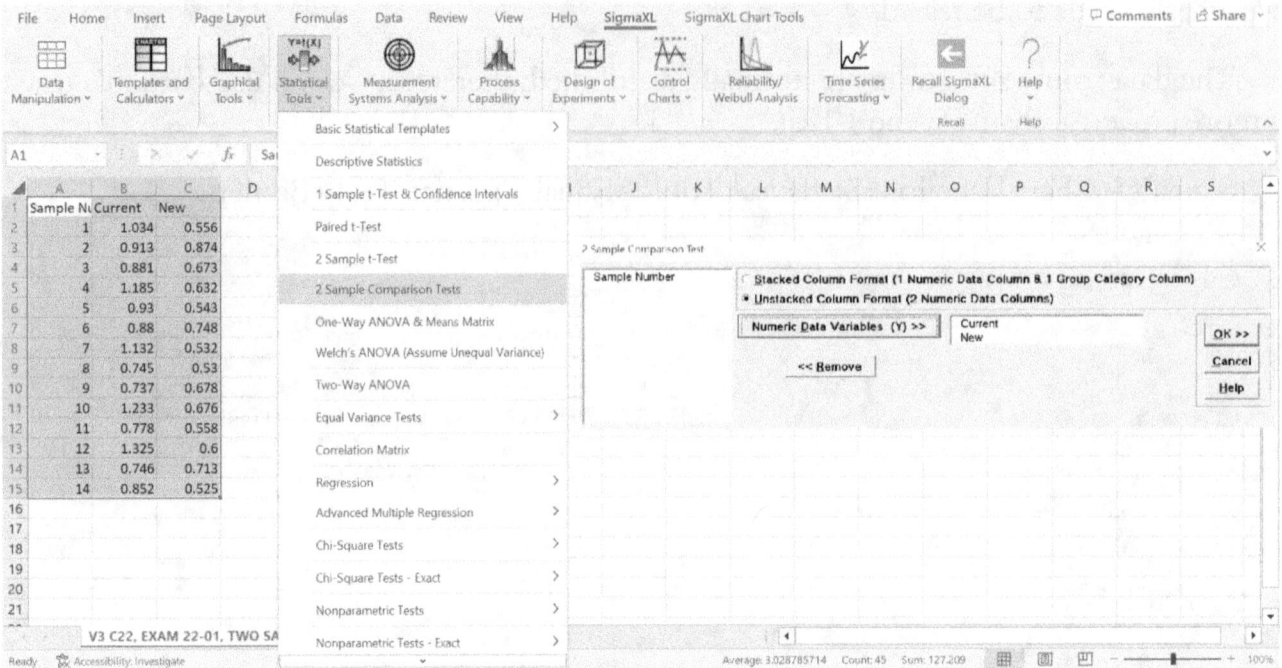

Figure 13.4 A: SigmaXL Input (2 Sample Comparison Tests)

2 Sample Comparison		
Results:	**Current**	**New**
Count	14	14
Mean	0.955071	0.631286
Median	0.897000	0.616000
Standard Deviation	0.195209	0.102415765
AD Normality Test P-Value	0.1604	0.1408
Test for Equal Variances:		
F-test (use with normal data):		
F (test statistic)	3.633	
P-Value (2-sided)	0.0271	
Levene's test		
(use with non-normal data):		
P-Value (2-sided)	0.0760	
2 Sample t-Test for means:		
Assume Equal Variance:		
t (test statistic)	5.496	
P-Value (2-sided)	0.0000	
P-Value (1-sided)	0.0000	
Assume Unequal Variance:		
t (test statistic)	5.496	
P-Value (2-sided)	0.0000	
P-Value (1-sided)	0.0000	
2 Sample Mann-Whitney test for medians:		
P-Value (2-sided)	0.0000	
P-Value (1-sided)	0.0000	

Figure 13.4 B: SigmaXL Output (2 Sample Comparison Tests)

Comments

- Bartlett's significance test (normal distribution assumption) of the standard deviation ratios from the two samples had a P-Value of 0.027. If only two data sets are to be analyzed, an F test can also be performed. Bartlett's test can be used to compare the variances of multiple data sets.
- Levene's significance test for multiple group comparison of variances is less powerful that Bartlett's test. However, Levene's test is robust to the assumption of normality.
- You can add, remove or change chart elements such as title, labels, gridlines and data labels by clicking on the chart and selecting "+".

13.4 Example: IEE Demonstration of Process Improvement for a Continuous Response

Application: Showing and quantifying the benefits from an improvement project

- The Y response for a stable 30,000-foot-level report was unsatisfactory where data are from a period of process-output-response stability.
- A team implemented several changes within the process (Xs).
- A current 30,000-foot-level report's individuals chart has a staging that shows a Y response enhancement, presumed from the team's process improvement efforts.
- A SigmaXL hypothesis comparison test can statistically assess the equality of before-and after-change means and variance.

IEE Volume III Example and Dataset

- *IEE Volume III* Example 22.4: IEE Demonstration of Process Improvement for a Continuous Response
- Dataset (Smarter Solutions (2022): V3 C22, Exam 22-04, IEE Process Improve.xlsx

SigmaXL or EPRS Metric-App [Smarter Solutions (2020)] Input/Output

- Figure 13.5: EPRS Metric-App Input (Continuous Response, No Staging)
- Figure 13.6: EPRS Metric-App Input (Continuous Response, Staging)
- Figure 13.7: EPRS Metric-App Output (Continuous Response, Staging)
- Figure 13.8: SigmaXL Input (Hypothesis Test Comparison of Mean Before and After Change)
- Figure 13.9: SigmaXL Output (Hypothesis Test Comparison of Mean Before and After Change)

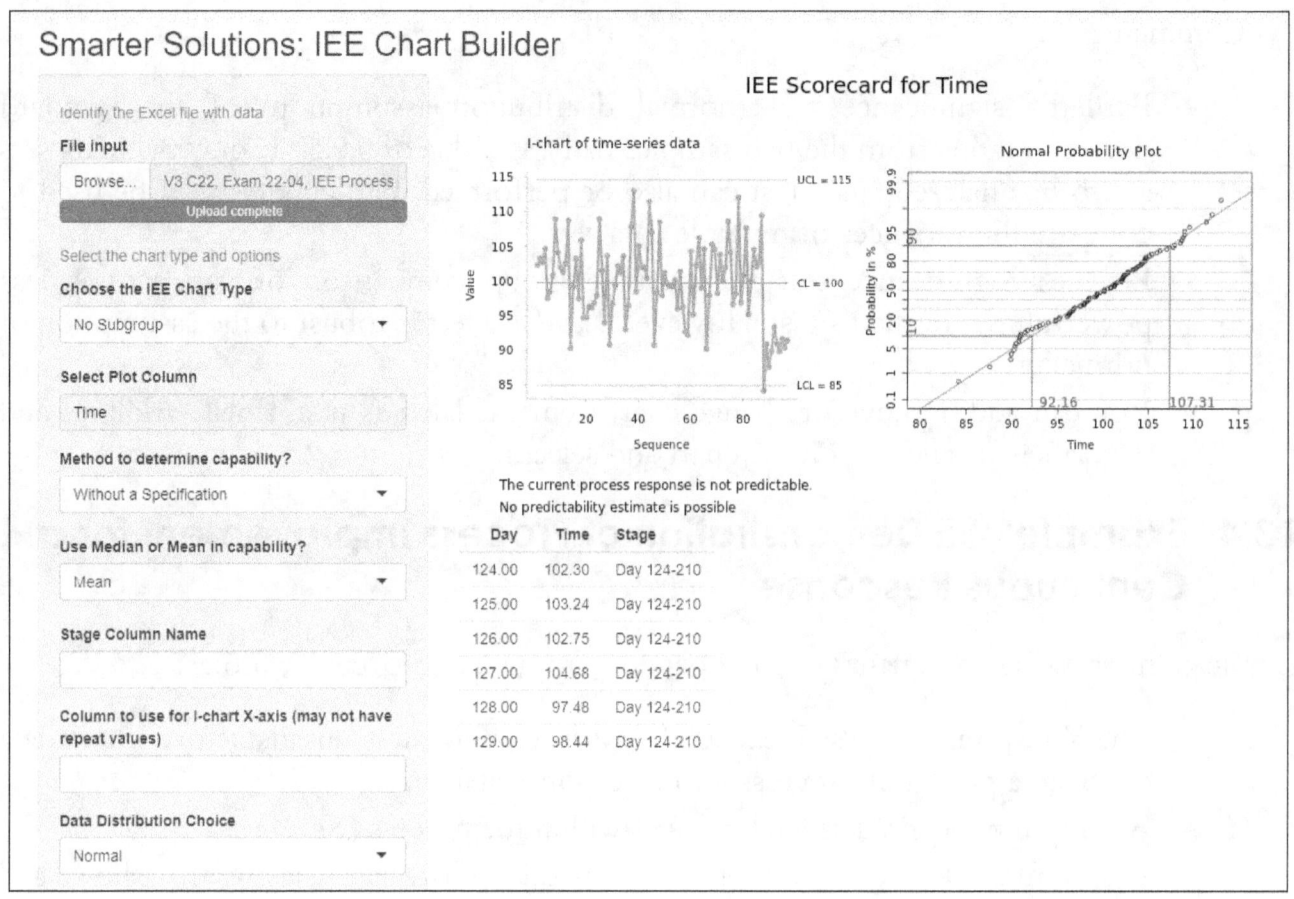

Figure 13.5: EPRS Metric-App Input (Continuous Response, No Staging)

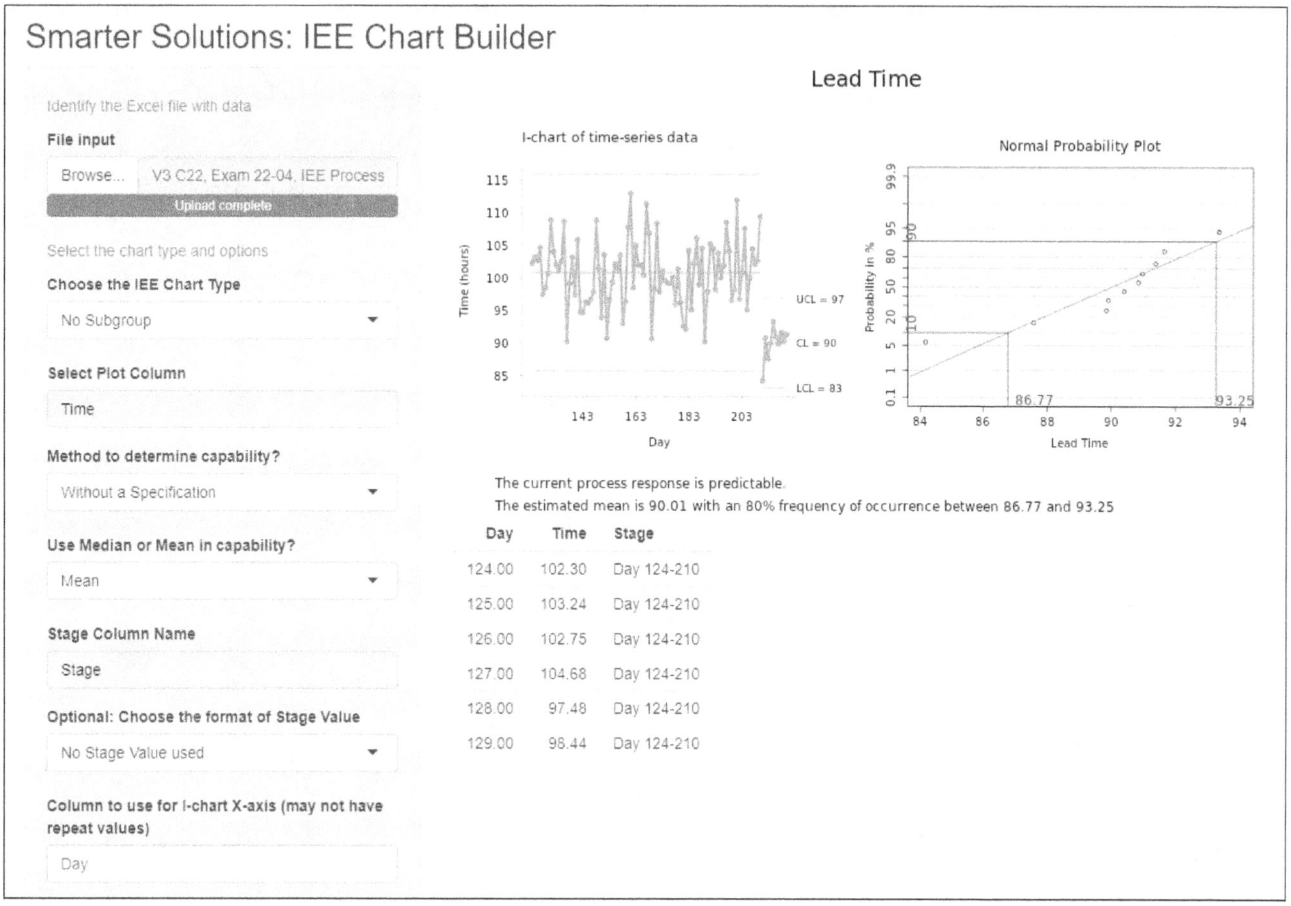

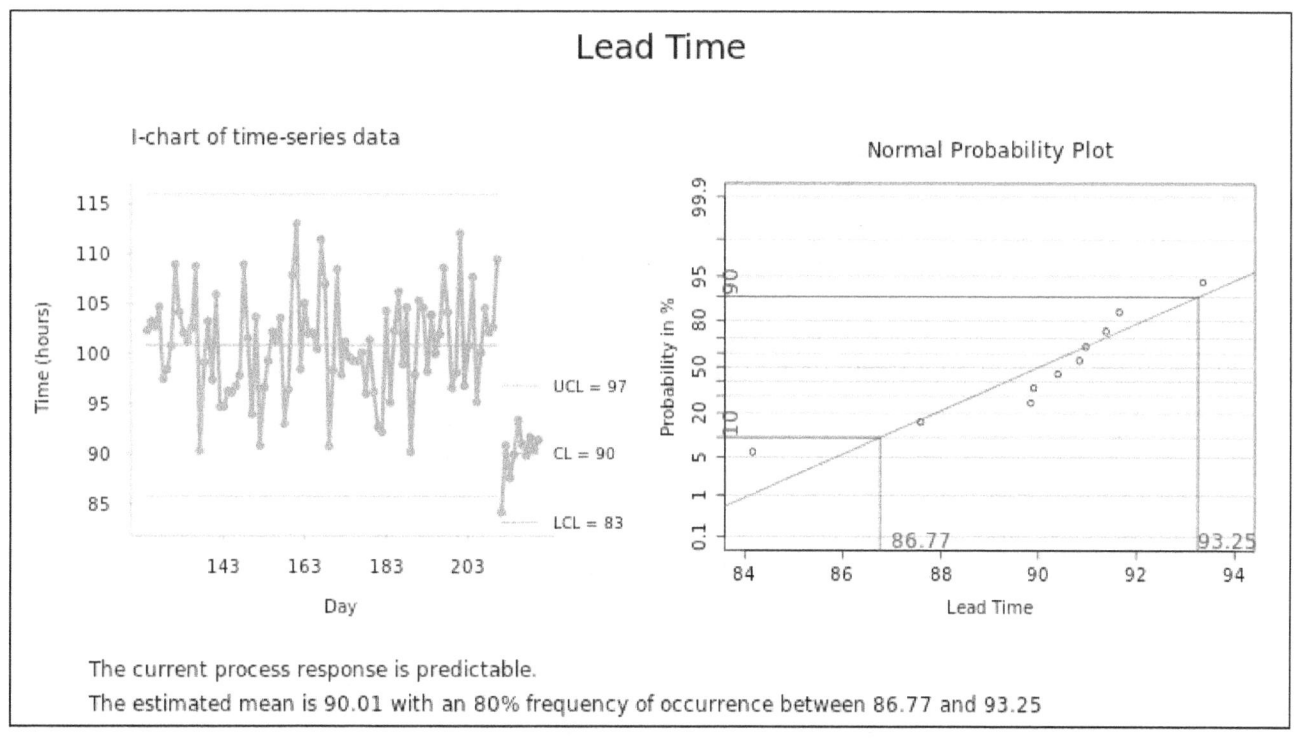

Smarter Solutions: IEE Chart Builder

Identify the Excel file with data

File input

Browse...   V3 C22, Exam 22-04, IEE Process

Upload complete

Select the chart type and options

Choose the IEE Chart Type

No Subgroup ▼

Select Plot Column

Time

Method to determine capability?

Without a Specification ▼

Use Median or Mean in capability?

Mean ▼

Stage Column Name

Stage

Optional: Choose the format of Stage Value

No Stage Value used ▼

Column to use for I-chart X-axis (may not have repeat values)

Day

Lead Time

I-chart of time-series data

Normal Probability Plot

UCL = 97
CL = 90
LCL = 83

86.77   93.25

The current process response is predictable.
The estimated mean is 90.01 with an 80% frequency of occurrence between 86.77 and 93.25

Day	Time	Stage
124.00	102.30	Day 124-210
125.00	103.24	Day 124-210
126.00	102.75	Day 124-210
127.00	104.68	Day 124-210
128.00	97.48	Day 124-210
129.00	96.44	Day 124-210

Figure 13.6: EPRS Metric-App Input (Continuous Response, Staging)

Lead Time

I-chart of time-series data

Normal Probability Plot

UCL = 97
CL = 90
LCL = 83

86.77   93.25

The current process response is predictable.
The estimated mean is 90.01 with an 80% frequency of occurrence between 86.77 and 93.25

Figure 13.7: EPRS Metric-App Output (Continuous Response, Staging)

Comment

- The Figure 13.7 the 30,000-foot-level report's individuals chart has a staging that indicates process improvement efforts reduced cycle time
- A statistical test and quantification of the magnitude of this process response change is shown in the next figures

SigmaXL Chart Function: Statistical Tools>2-Sample t-Test

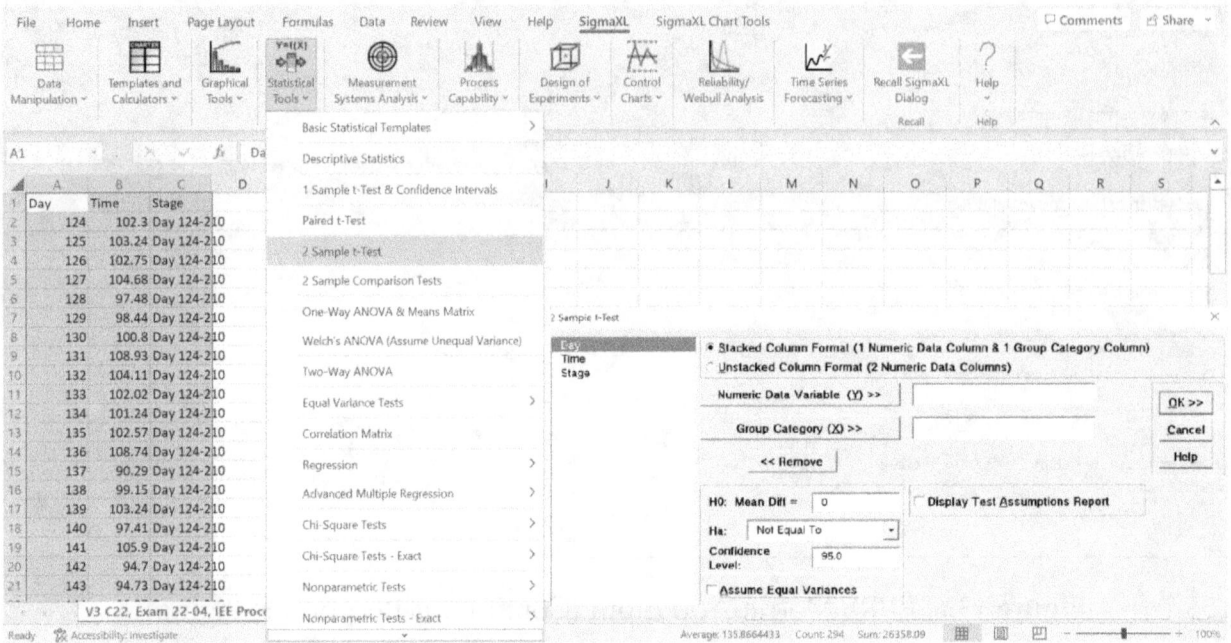

Figure 13.8: SigmaXL Input (Hypothesis Test Comparison of Mean Before and After Change)

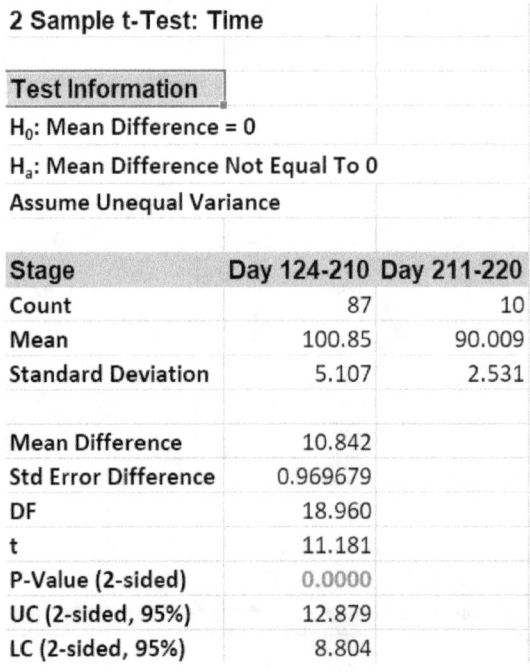

2 Sample t-Test: Time

Test Information

H_0: Mean Difference = 0

H_a: Mean Difference Not Equal To 0

Assume Unequal Variance

Stage	Day 124-210	Day 211-220
Count	87	10
Mean	100.85	90.009
Standard Deviation	5.107	2.531
Mean Difference	10.842	
Std Error Difference	0.969679	
DF	18.960	
t	11.181	
P-Value (2-sided)	0.0000	
UC (2-sided, 95%)	12.879	
LC (2-sided, 95%)	8.804	

Figure 13.9: SigmaXL Output (Hypothesis Test Comparison of Mean Before and After Change)

Comments

- The null hypothesis of the difference in the mean before and after the change equating to zero was rejected with a P-Value of 0.000
- The 95% confidence interval for the difference in means is 8.804 to 12.879
- You can add, remove or change chart elements such as title, labels, gridlines and data labels by clicking on the chart and selecting "+".

13.5 Example: Paired Comparison Testing

IEE Volume III Example and Dataset

- *IEE Volume III* Example 22.6: Paired Comparison Testing for Improved Gas Mileage
- Dataset (Smarter Solutions (2022): V3 C22, Exer 22-06, Compare A and B mach.xlsx

SigmaXL or EPRS Metric-App [Smarter Solutions (2020)] Input/Output

- Figure 13.10: SigmaXL Input (Paired Comparison Test)
- Figure 13.11: SigmaXL Output (Paired Comparison Test)

The paired t-Test performs a test for the mean difference between samples that are related or dependent.

SigmaXL Chart Function: Statistical Tools> Paired t-Test

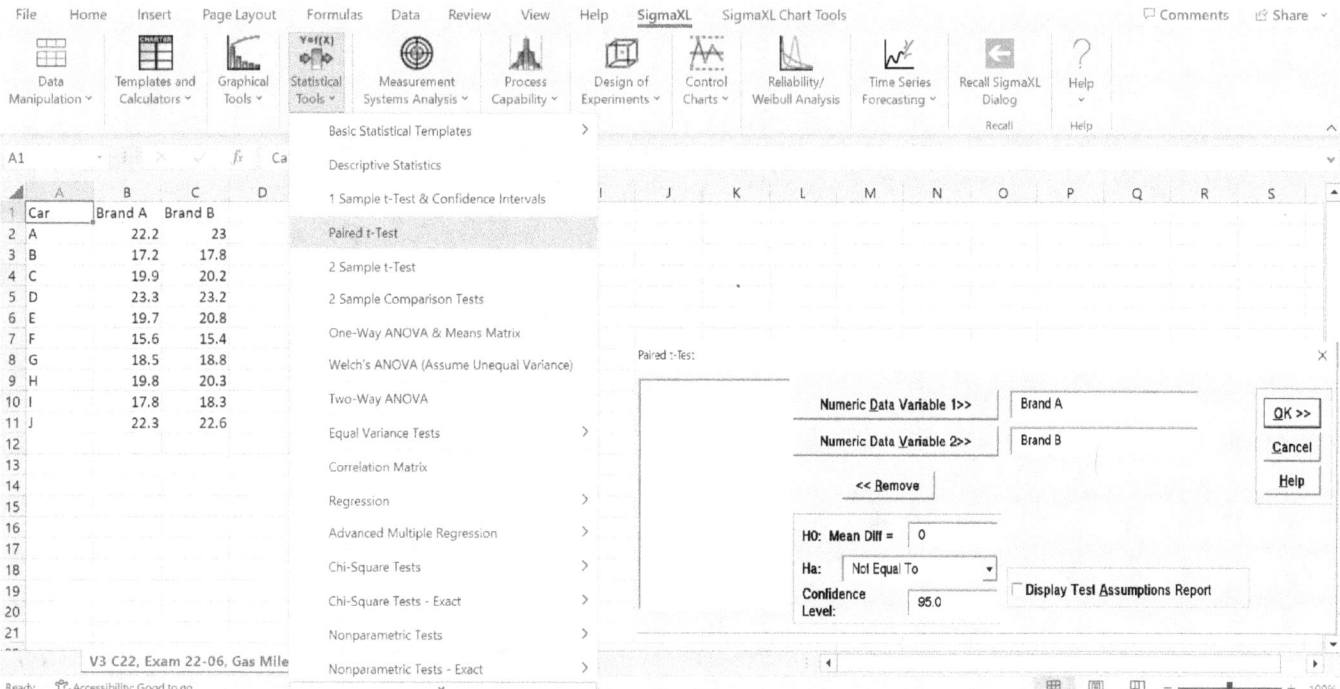

Figure 13.10: SigmaXL Input (Paired Comparison Test)

Paired t-Test

Test Information

H_0: Mean Difference = 0

H_a: Mean Difference Not Equal To 0

Results:	Brand A - Brand B
Count	10
Mean	-0.410000
StDev	0.387155
SE Mean	0.122429
t	-3.349
P-Value (2-sided)	0.0085
UC (2-sided, 95%)	-0.133046
LC (2-sided, 95%)	-0.686954

Figure 13.11: SigmaXL Output (Paired Comparison Test)

Comments

- The null hypothesis of the difference in means equating to zero is rejected with a P-Value of 0.009
- The 95% confidence interval for the mean difference is -0.687 to -0.133
- You can add, remove or change chart elements such as title, labels, gridlines and data labels by clicking on the chart and selecting "+".

14

IEE-DMAIC — Analyze Phase: Comparison Tests for Attribute Defective Rate Response

14.1 IEE-DMAIC Roadmap Component

Book 1 Reference: *IEE Volume III* – Chapter 23

Book 2 Reference: *Lean Six Sigma Project Execution Guide* – Section 7

Internet: www.smartersolutions.com/roadmap (clicking on highlighted area provides the flowchart below)

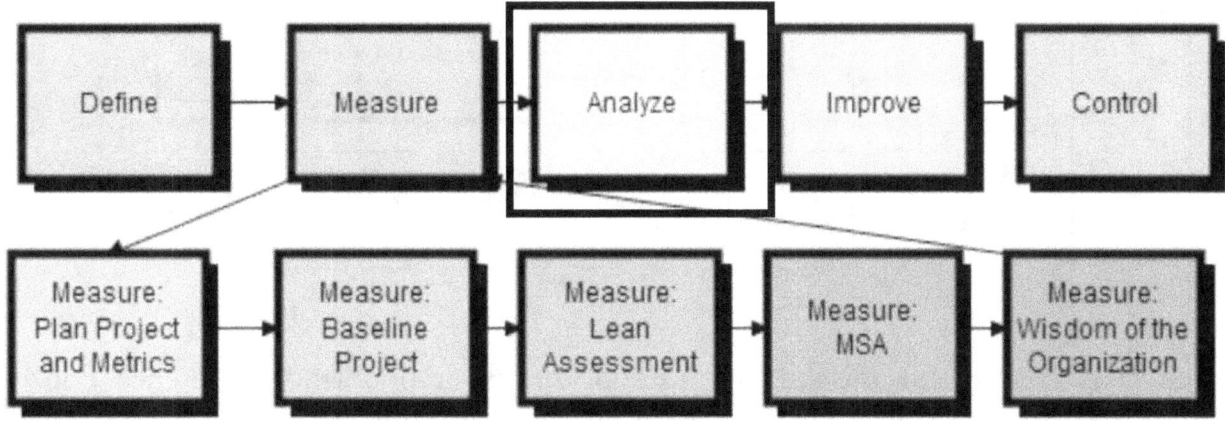

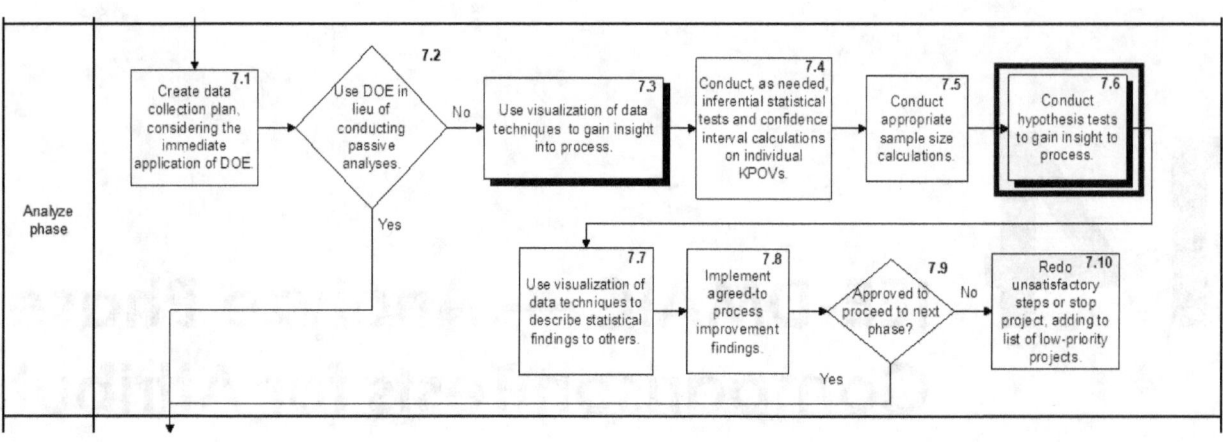

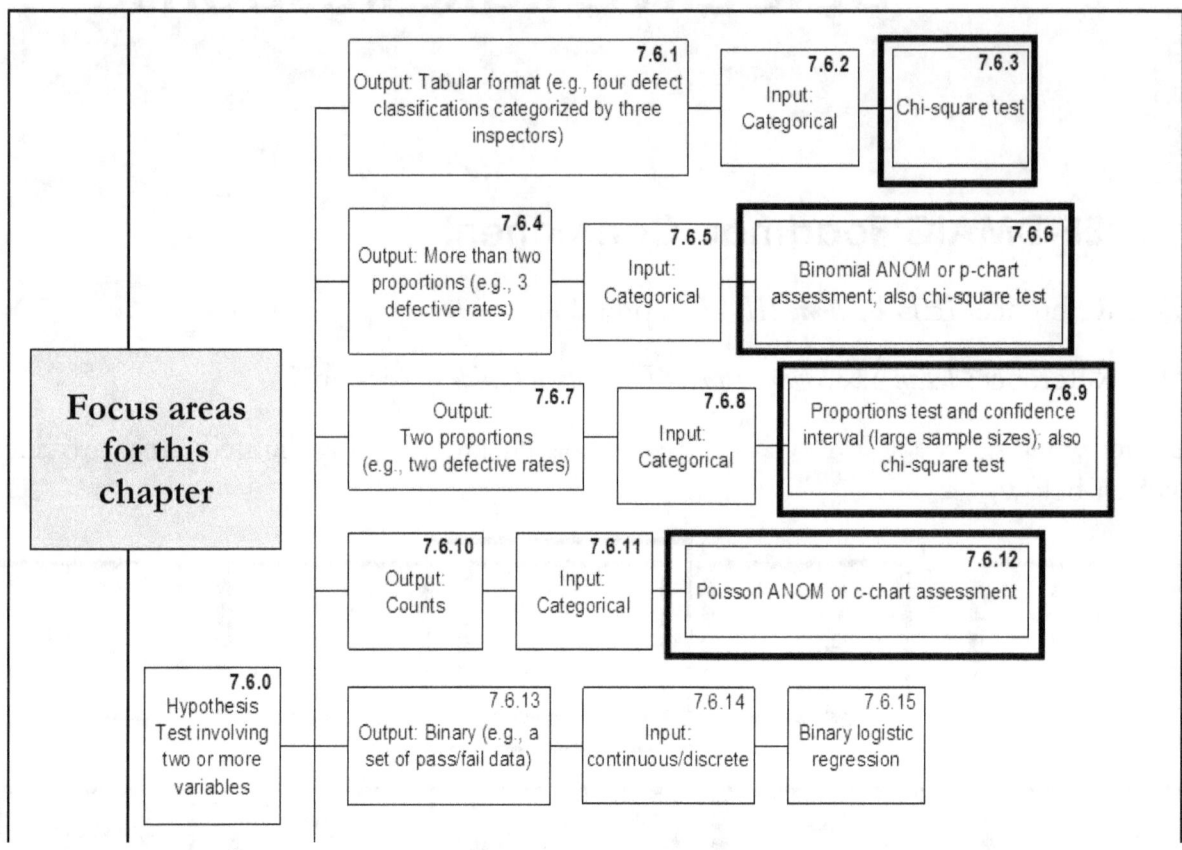

The last chapter and this chapter extend the single-population inference concepts described in Chapters 11 and 12 to compare more than one population. The previous chapter focused on continuous response situations, while this chapter addresses attribute defective rate response situations; e.g., does the failure frequencies of completing a purchase order differ between departments?

14.2 Example: Comparing Proportions

IEE Volume III Example and Dataset

- *IEE Volume III* Example 23.1: Comparing Proportions

- Dataset (Smarter Solutions (2022): V3 C23, Exam 23-01 comparing proportions.xlsx

SigmaXL or EPRS Metric-App [Smarter Solutions (2020)] Input/Output

- Figure 14.1: SigmaXL Input (Comparing Proportions)
- Figure 14.2: SigmaXL Output (Comparing Proportions)

The Chi-Square Test for Association is hypothesis test of independence, used to determine if there is any association between variables.

SigmaXL Chart Function: Statistical Tools>Tables>Chi-Square Tests> Chi-Square Test for Association – Two-Way Table Data

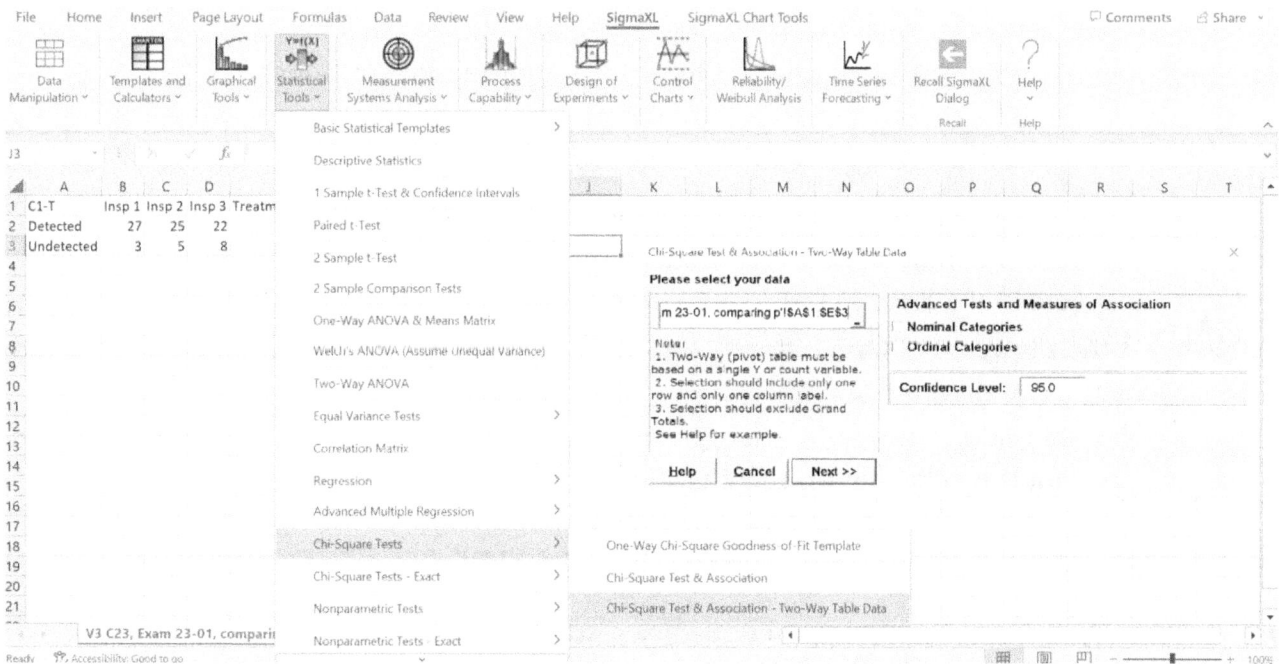

Figure 14.1: SigmaXL Input (Comparing Proportions)

Chi-Square Two-Way Table Statistics

Observed Counts	Insp 1	Insp 2	Insp 3
Detected	27	25	22
Undetected	3	5	8

Expected Counts	Insp 1	Insp 2	Insp 3
Detected	24.667	24.667	24.667
Undetected	5.333	5.333	5.333

Std. Residuals	Insp 1	Insp 2	Insp 3
Detected	0.469809	0.067115606	-0.536925
Undetected	-1.010362971	-0.144338	1.155

Chi-Square	2.889
DF	2
P-Value	0.2359

Figure 14.2: SigmaXL Output (Comparing Proportions)

Comment

- Since the P-Value in Figure 14.2 is more than 0.05, one could not reject at a level of 0.05 the null hypothesis that there is equality of detection rates between inspectors at a level of 0.05.
- If the sample size were larger, a significant detection rate between inspectors might have been detected.
- You can add, remove or change chart elements such as title, labels, gridlines and data labels by clicking on the chart and selecting "+".

14.3 Example: Comparing Nonconformance Rate Proportions

IEE Volume III Example and Dataset

- *IEE Volume III* Example 23.2: Comparing Non-conformance Proportions
- Dataset (Smarter Solutions (2022): V3 C23, Exam 23-01 comparing proportions.xlsx

SigmaXL or EPRS Metric-App [Smarter Solutions (2020)] Input/Output

- Figure 14.3: SigmaXL Input (Comparing Nonconformance Rate Proportions)
- Figure 14.4: SigmaXL Output (Comparing Nonconformance Rate Proportions)

The ANOM binomial proportion tests the hypothesis that all the proportions come from the same binomial distribution.

SigmaXL Chart Function: Graphical Tools>ANOM Binomial Proportions One-Way

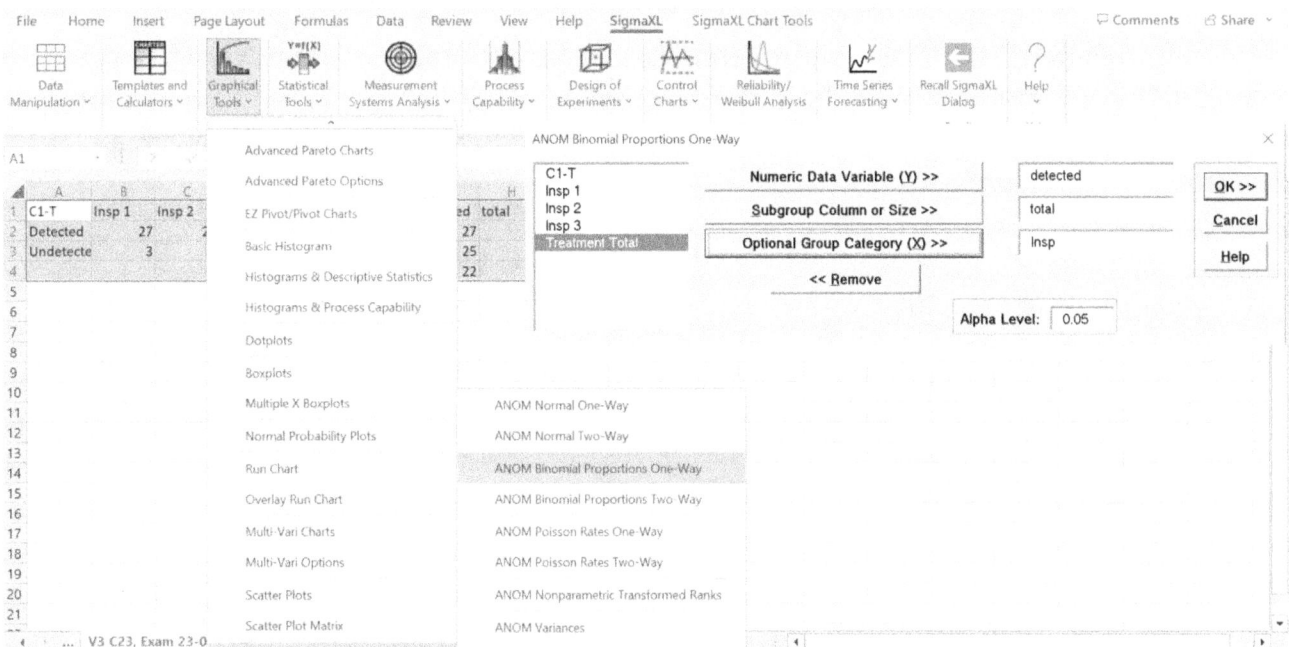

Figure 14.3: SigmaXL Input (Comparing Nonconformance Rate Proportions)

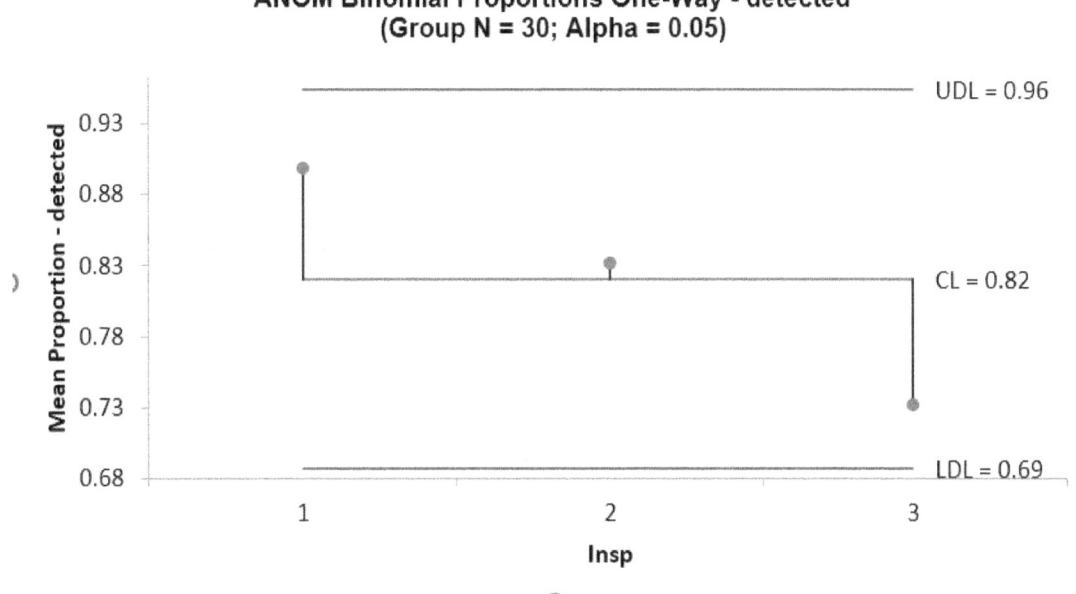

Figure 14.4: SigmaXL Output (Comparing Nonconformance Rate Proportions)

Comment

- From Figure 14.4, we fail to reject the null hypothesis that each inspector detection rate equals the overall detection rate of all inspectors.

- You can add, remove or change chart elements such as title, labels, gridlines and data labels by clicking on the chart and selecting "+".

14.4 Example: Hypothesis Test of Difference in Two Proportions

A team believed they made improvements to a process output failure rate. They needed to test the null hypothesis that the difference between before and after change failure rate equals zero, i.e., no change. They also wanted to determine the 95% confidence interval for the difference in failure rates.

- Before the process was changed: 6290 defects out of 620000
- After the procedure was altered: 4661 defects out of 490000

IEE Volume III Example and Dataset

- *IEE Volume III* Example 23.4: Difference in Two Proportions
- Dataset (Smarter Solutions (2022): None

SigmaXL or EPRS Metric-App [Smarter Solutions (2020)] Input/Output

- Figure 14.5: SigmaXL Input (Difference in Two Proportions)
- Figure 14.6: SigmaXL Output (Difference in Two Proportions)

The 2 proportions test performs a hypothesis test between the two proportions and displays a confidence interval.

SigmaXL Chart Function: Statistical Tools>Basic Statistical Templates>2 Proportions Test and Confidence Interval

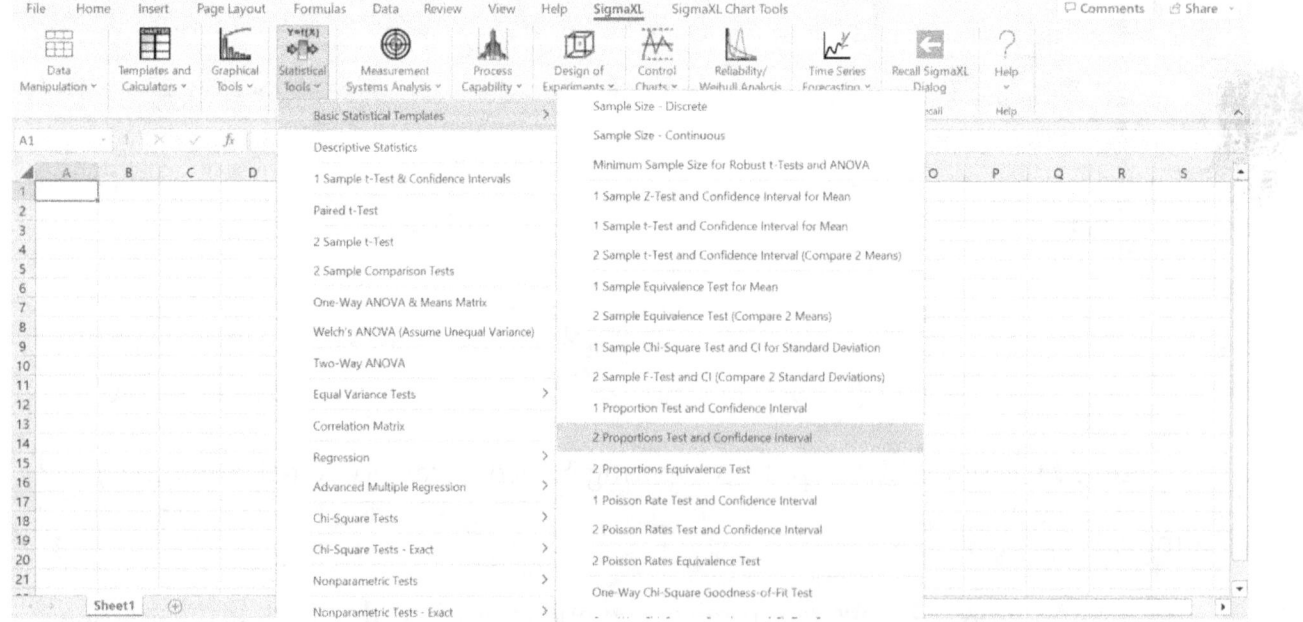

Figure 14.5: SigmaXL Input (Difference in Two Proportions)

Sigma XL	2 Proportions Test and Confidence Interval			
Sample Data (user inputs):			**Sample 1**	**Sample 2**
Number of Events	x		6,290	4,661
Sample Size	n		620,000	490,000
Null Hypothesis (hypothesized difference)	$H_0: P_1 - P_2 =$		0	
Alternative Hypothesis	$H_a: P_1 - P_2$		Not Equal To	
Confidence Level (enter .95 for 95%)	$100*(1-\alpha)\%$		95.0%	
Hypothesis Test Method			Fisher's Exact	
Confidence Interval Method			Newcombe-Wilson Score	
Results:				
Sample proportion (x/n)			0.0101	0.0095
Sample proportion difference			0.0006	
alpha			0.0500	
Minimum expected value (should be >= 5 for normal approximation)			4,834.2252	
Fisher's Exact probability P-Value (2-sided)			0.0008	
Upper Confidence Limit (2-sided)			0.0010	
Lower Confidence Limit (2-sided)			0.0003	

Figure 14.6: SigmaXL Output (Difference in Two Proportions)

Comments

- The null hypothesis that the difference in failure rates equals zero is rejected at a P-Value of 0.001
- The 95% confidence interval for the difference is 0.0003 – 0.0010
- You can add, remove or change chart elements such as title, labels, gridlines and data labels by clicking on the chart and selecting "+".

14.5 Example: IEE Demonstration of Process Improvement for an Attribute Defective Rate Response

Application: 30,000-foot-level report (Y) and Y=f(X) relationship

- The Y response in a 30,000-foot-level report was unsatisfactory.
- A team worked to change the process's Xs to improve the Y response.
- A 30,000-foot-level report (Y) of before and after the process-change data indicates that the process output response improved.

IEE Volume III Example and Dataset

- *IEE Volume III* Example 23.5: IEE Demonstration of Process Improvement for an Attribute Defective Rate Response
- Dataset (Smarter Solutions (2022): V3 C23, Exam 23-05, IEE Demonstrate Attrib Improve.xlsx

SigmaXL or EPRS Metric-App [Smarter Solutions (2020)] Input/Output

- Figure 14.7: EPRS Metric-App Input (Improved Failure Rate Response)
- Figure 14.8: EPRS Metric-App Output (Improved Failure Rate Response)
- Figure 14.9: SigmaXL Input (Hypothesis Test for Improved Failure Rate Response)
- Figure 14.10: SigmaXL Output (Hypothesis Test for Improved Failure Rate Response)

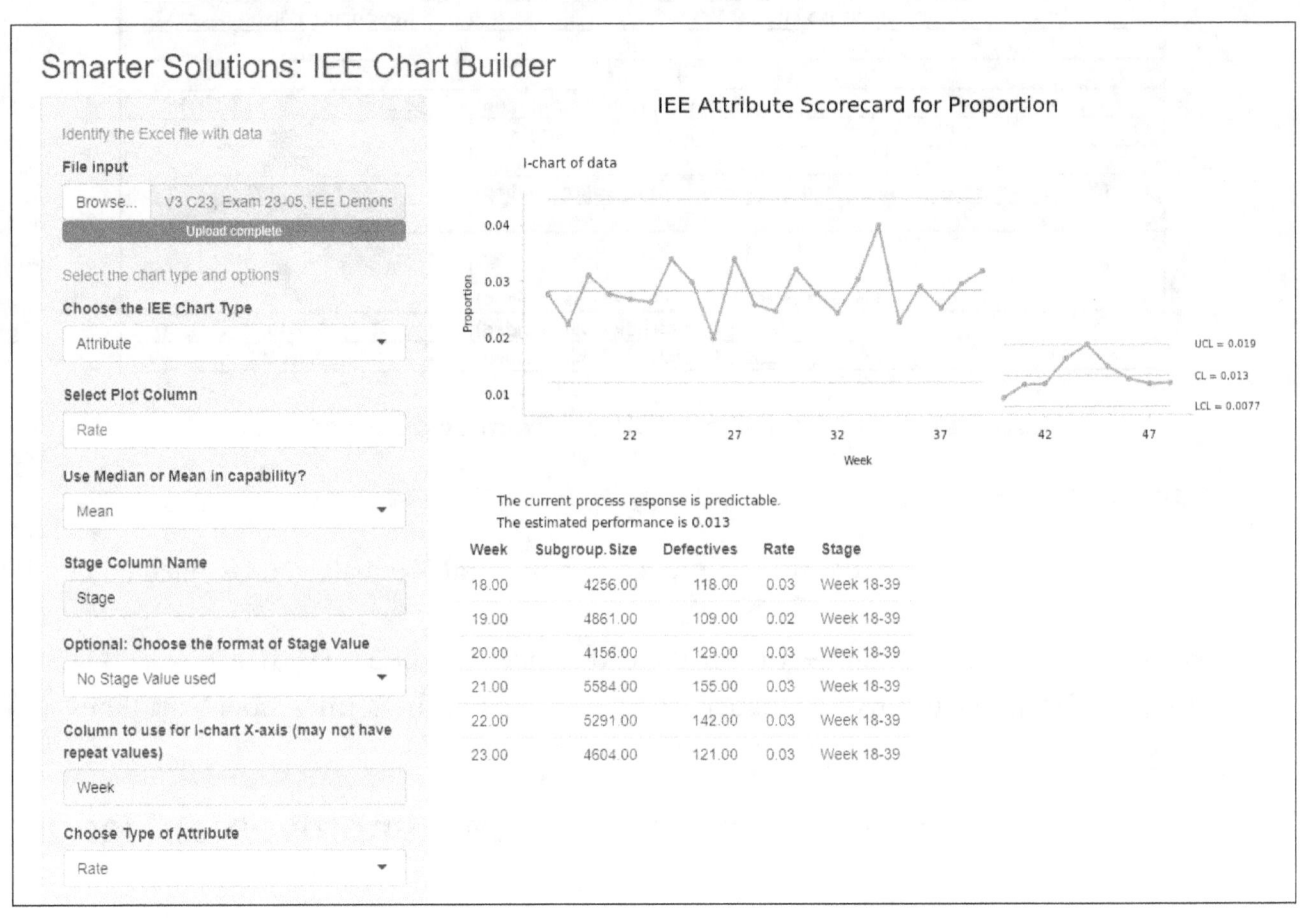

Figure 14.7: EPRS Metric-App Input (Improved Failure Rate Response)

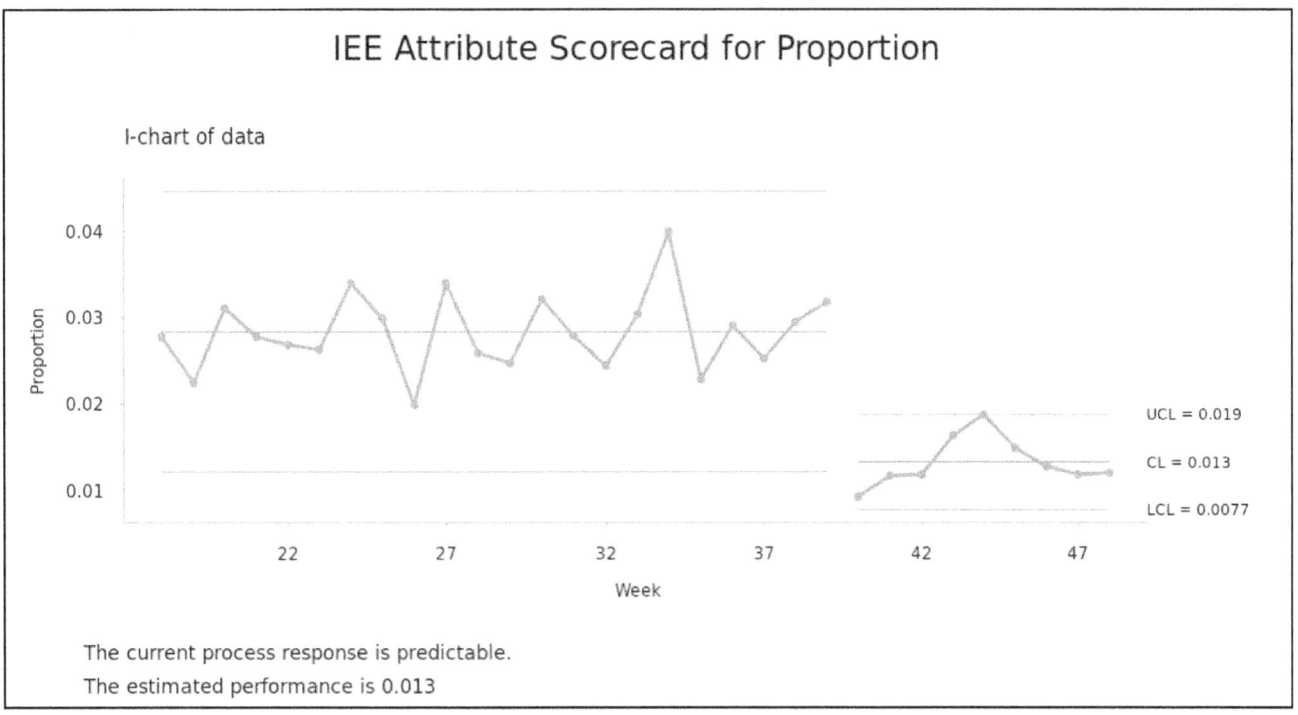

Figure 14.8: EPRS Metric-App Output (Improved Failure Rate Response)

Comment

- The 30,000-foot-level report's individuals chart in Figure 14.8 indicates that on week 40, there was a reduction in the proportion failure rate.
- The next figures will describe a hypothesis test of this difference and the determination of a confidence interval

SigmaXL Chart Function: Statistical Tools>Basic Statistical Templates>2 Proportions Test and Confidence Interval

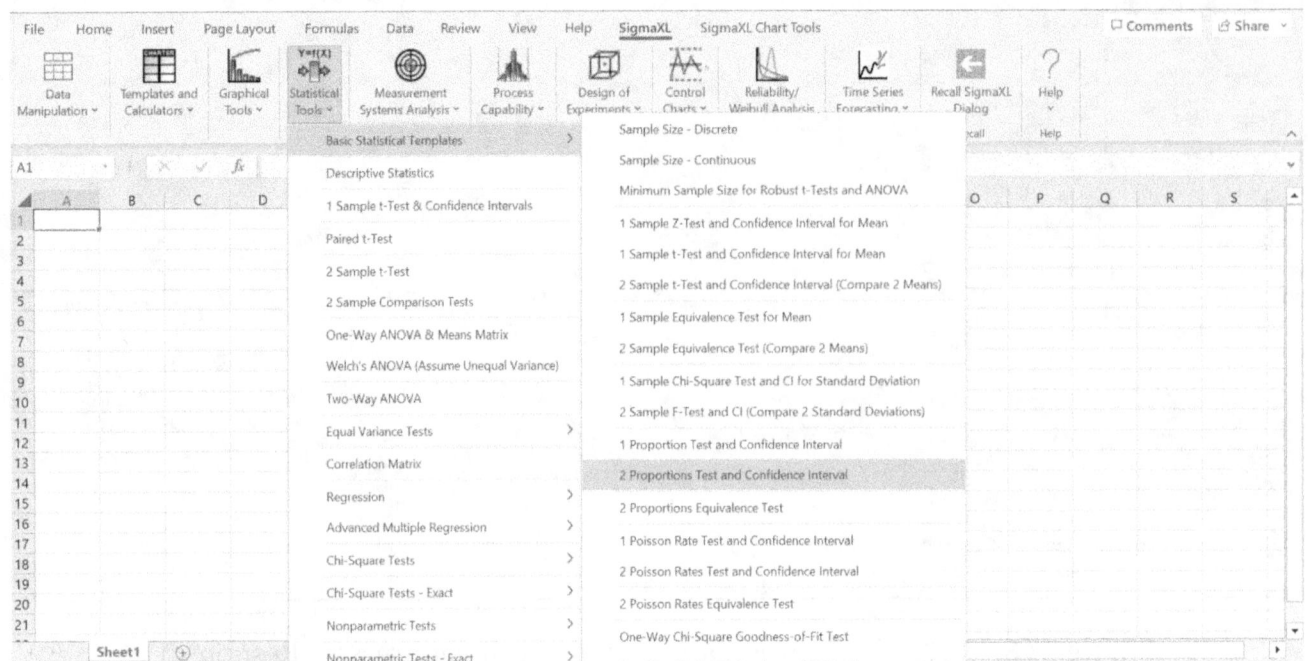

Figure 14.9: SigmaXL Input (Hypothesis Test for Improved Failure Rate Response)

2 Proportions Test and Confidence Interval			
Sample Data (user inputs):		**Sample 1**	**Sample 2**
Number of Events	x	3,072	573
Sample Size	n	108,795	43,808
Null Hypothesis (hypothesized difference)	H_0: P_1 - P_2 =	0	
Alternative Hypothesis	H_a: P_1 - P_2	Not Equal To	
Confidence Level (enter .95 for 95%)	100*(1-α)%	95.0%	
Hypothesis Test Method		Fisher's Exact	
Confidence Interval Method		Newcombe-Wilson Score	
Results:			
Sample proportion (x/n)		0.0282	0.0131
Sample proportion difference		0.0152	
alpha		0.0500	
Minimum expected value (should be >= 5 for normal approximation)		1,046.3763	
Fisher's Exact probability P-Value (2-sided)		0.0000	
Upper Confidence Limit (2-sided)		0.0166	
Lower Confidence Limit (2-sided)		0.0137	

Figure 14.10: SigmaXL Output (Hypothesis Test for Improved Failure Rate Response)

Comments

- A hypothesis test of the equality of the failure rate before and after the change is rejected at a P-Value of 0.000
- A 95% confidence interval for the project's failure rate reduction is 0.0137 – 0.0166
- You can add, remove or change chart elements such as title, labels, gridlines and data labels by clicking on the chart and selecting "+".

15

IEE-DMAIC — Analyze Phase: Variance Components

15.1 IEE-DMAIC Roadmap Component

Book 1 Reference: *IEE Volume III* – Chapter 24

Book 2 Reference: *Lean Six Sigma Project Execution Guide* – Section 7

Internet: www.smartersolutions.com/roadmap (clicking on highlighted area provides the flowchart below)

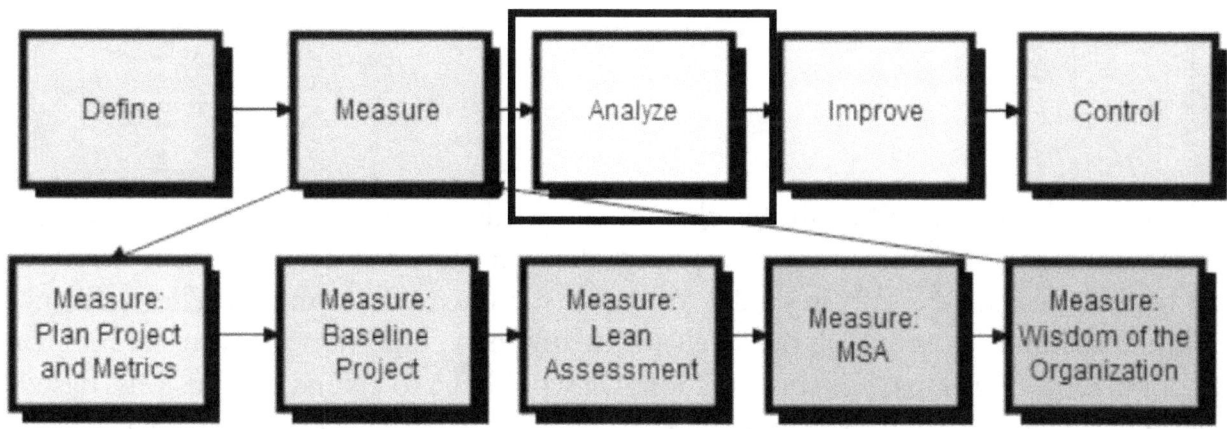

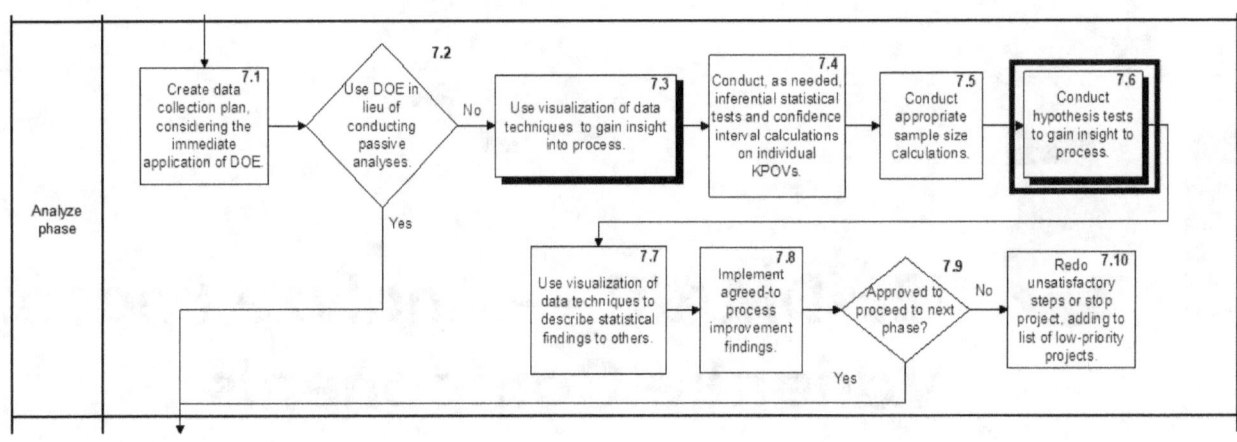

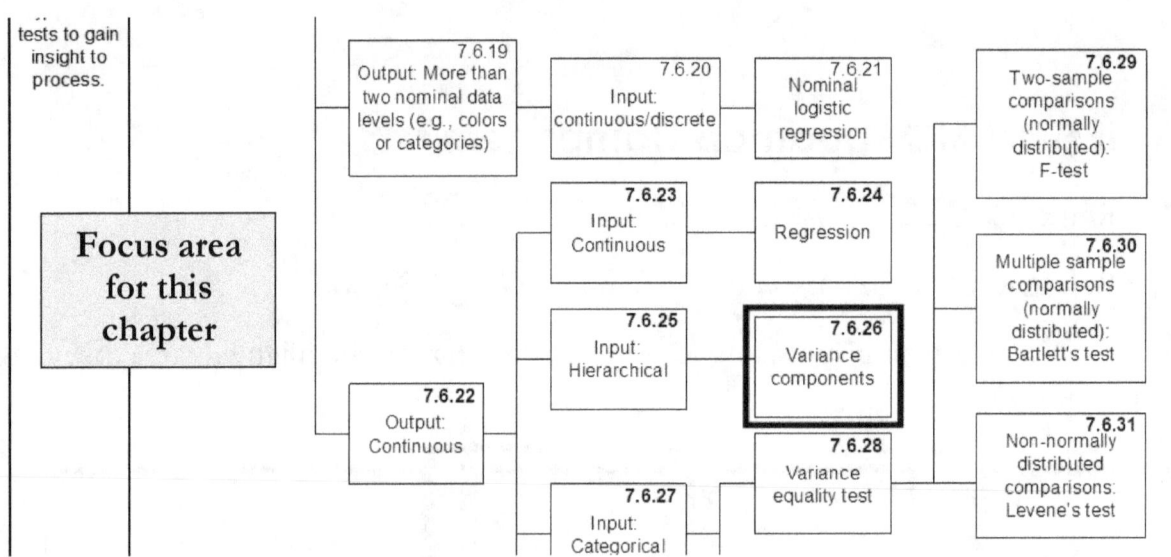

The methodology described in this chapter is a random effects model or components of variance model, as opposed to a fixed-effects model. The statistical model for this hierarchical model or fully nested ANOVA is similar to that of the fixed effects model. The difference is that in the random effects model, the levels (or treatments) could be a random sample from a larger population of groups. For this situation, we would like to extend conclusions, based on the sampling of levels, to all population levels, whether explicitly considered or not. In this situation, the test attempts to quantify the variability from factor levels.

15.2   Example: Variance Components of Pigment Paste

Application

- Fabric is woven on a large number of looms. It is suspected that variation can occur both within samples from fabric from the same loom and between different looms.
- To investigate this, four looms were randomly selected and four strength determinations were made on the fabric that was produced.

IEE Volume III Example and Dataset

- *IEE Volume III* Example 24.10: Variance Components
- Dataset (Smarter Solutions (2022): V3 C24, Exam 24-01 & 10, variance comp

SigmaXL or EPRS Metric-App [Smarter Solutions (2020)] Input/Output

- Figure 15.1: SigmaXL Input (Variance Components)
- Figure 15.2: SigmaXL Output (Variance Components)

ANOVA evaluates the importance of one or more factors by comparing the response variable means at the different factor levels. The null hypothesis states that all factor level means are equal, while the alternative hypothesis states that at least one of them is different.

SigmaXL Chart Function: Statistical Tools>One-Way ANOVA & Means Matrix

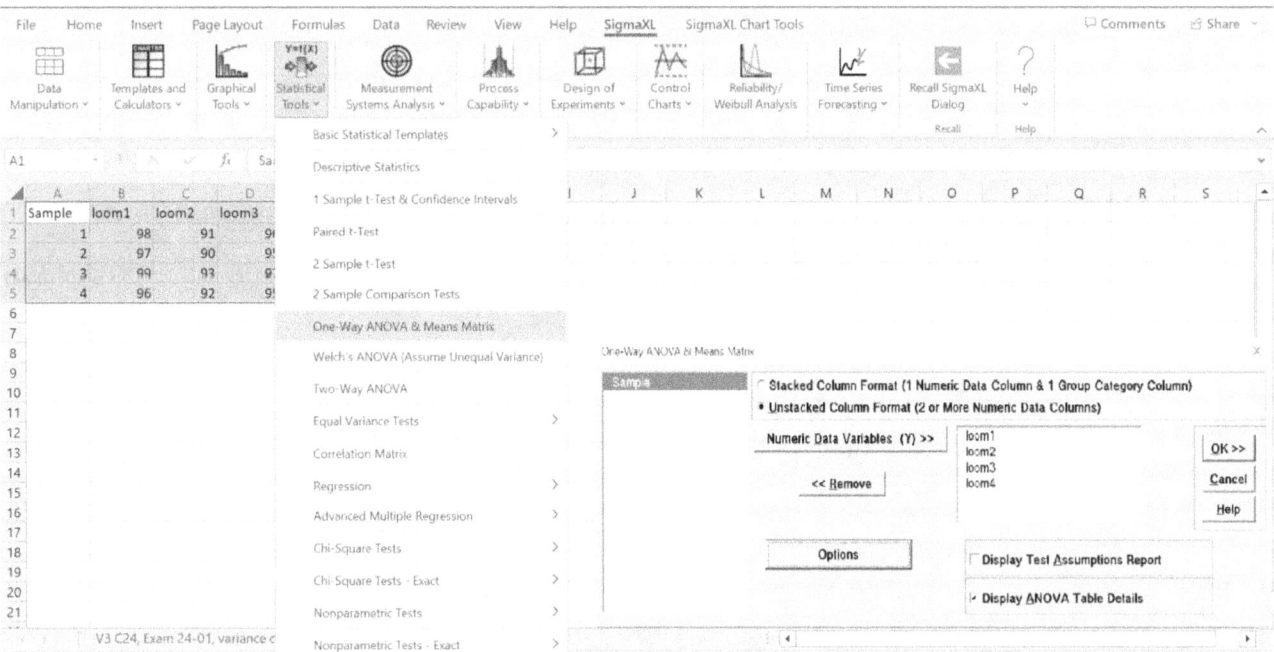

Figure 15.1: SigmaXL Input (Variance Components)

One-Way ANOVA & Means Matrix: Y

H_0: Mean 1 = Mean 2 = ... = Mean k

H_a: At least one pair Mean i ≠ Mean j

	loom1	loom2	loom3	loom4
Count	4	4	4	4
Mean	97.500	91.500	95.750	97
Standard Deviation	1.291	1.291	0.957427	1.826
UC (2-sided, 95.0%, pooled)	99.000	93.000	97.250	98.500
LC (2-sided, 95.0%, pooled)	96.000	90.000	94.250	95.500

ANOVA Table

Source	SS	DF	MS	F	P-Value
Between	89.1875	3.0000	29.7292	15.681	0.0002
Within	22.7500	12.0000	1.8958		
Total	111.9375	15.0000			

Figure 15.2: SigmaXL Output (Variance Components)

Comments

- A hypothesis test of the equality of means is rejected at a P-Value of 0.000
- These results indicate that there is a significant difference for the mean fabric strength between looms
- Investigators, given this information, discovered and addressed the problem
- You can add, remove or change chart elements such as title, labels, gridlines and data labels by clicking on the chart and selecting "+".

16 IEE-DMAIC — Analyze Phase: Correlation and Simple Linear Regression

16.1 IEE-DMAIC Roadmap Component

Book 1 Reference: *IEE Volume III – Chapter 25*

Book 2 Reference: *Lean Six Sigma Project Execution Guide – Section 7*

Internet: www.smartersolutions.com/roadmap (clicking on highlighted area provides the flowchart below)

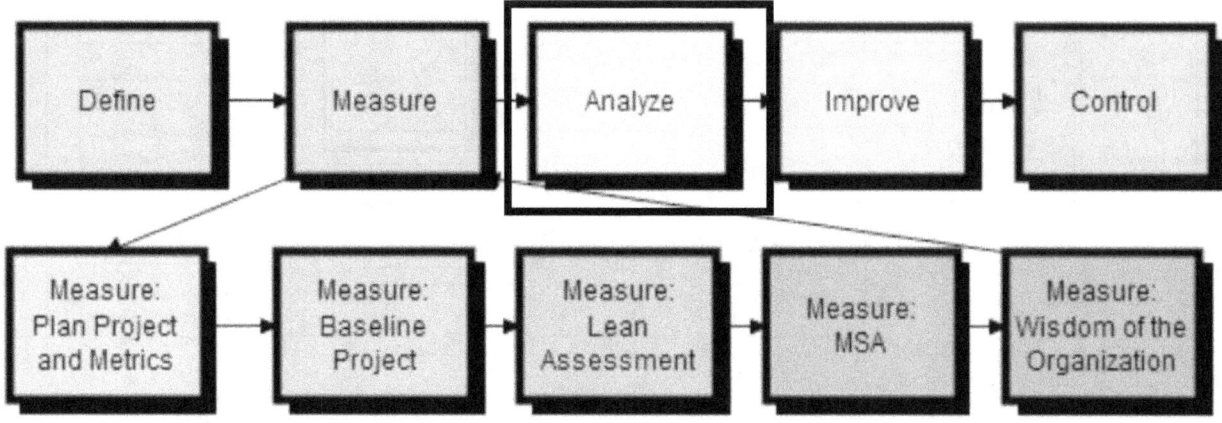

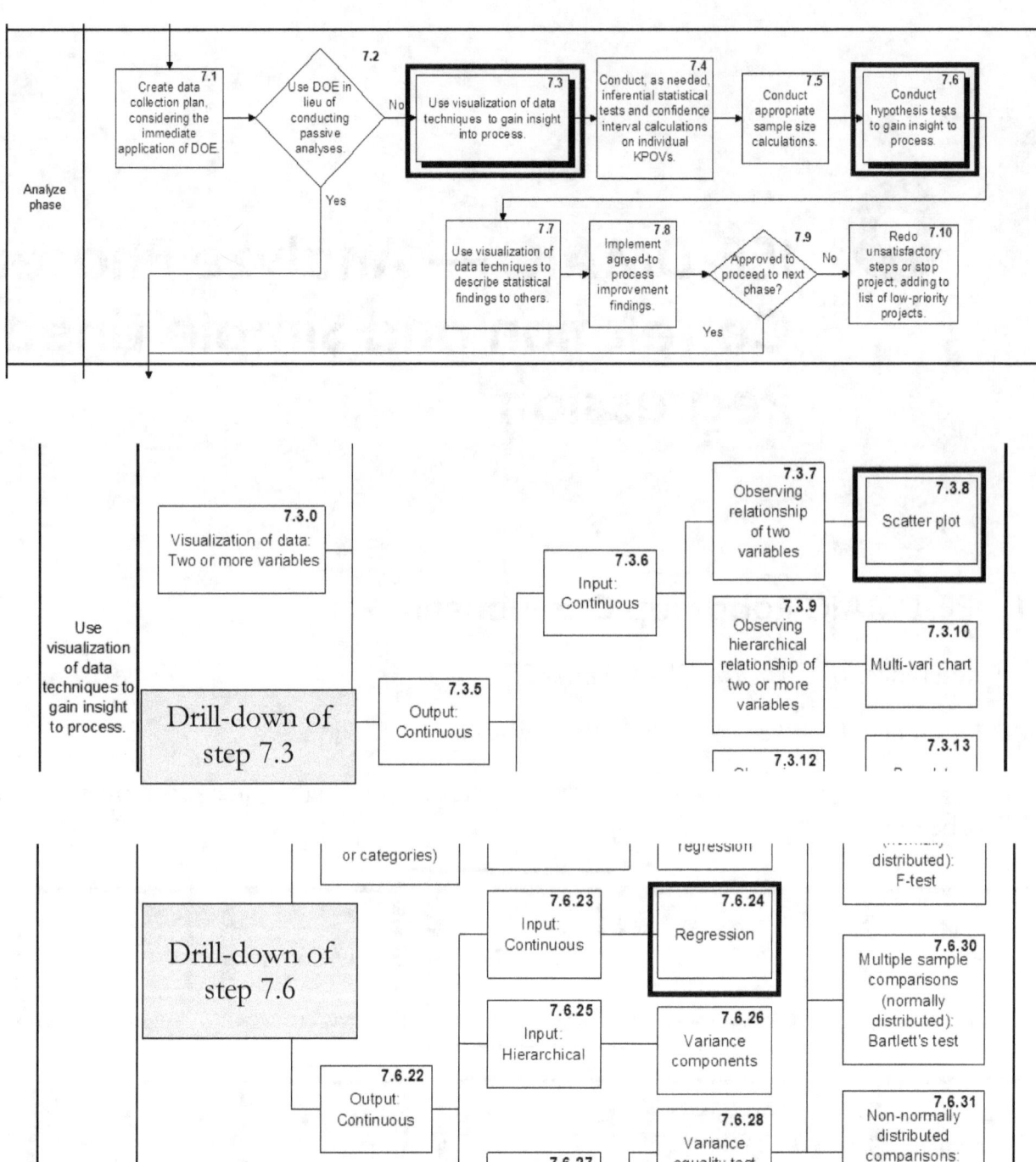

This chapter will describe the regression of two continuous variables; e.g., temperature versus a product dimension or invoice size versus Days Sales Outstanding (DSO) days beyond due date.

16.2 Background – Scatter Plot (Dispersion Graph)

A scatter plot or dispersion graph shows the relationship between two variables pictorially. It gives a simple illustration of how one variable can influence the other. One must exercise care when interpreting dispersion graphs. A plot that shows a relationship does not prove a genuine cause-and-effect relationship; i.e., it does not prove causation. Happenstance data can cause the appearance of a relationship. For example, the phase of the moon could appear to affect a process with a monthly business cycle.

16.3 Background – Correlation

A statistic that represents the strength of a linear relationship between two variables is the sample correlation coefficient (r). A correlation coefficient can take values between -1 and +1. A -1 indicates a perfect negative correlation, a +1 indicates a perfect positive correlation, and zero means no correlation.

16.4 Background – Simple Linear Regression

A correlation statistic only measures association, while regression model methods serve to develop quantitative variable relationships that are useful for estimation and prediction. In regression equations, the independent variable is X, while the dependent variable is Y. This section focuses on regression models that contain linear variables; however, regression models can also include quadratic and cubic terms; i.e., the model comprises of non-linear parameters.

16.5 Background – Analysis of Residuals

A statistical analysis model assumes errors are independent and follow a normal distribution with mean zero and a constant but unknown variance.

An essential method for testing the assumption of an experiment is residual analysis, where a residual is a difference between the observed value and the corresponding fitted value. Residual studies are essential in investigating the fitted model's adequacy and detecting departure from the model.

16.6 Example: Correlation and Scatter Plot

Application

- The magnitude of an organization's 30,000-foot-level delivery-time report is undesirable and needs reduction.
- One item from a team brainstorming session of Xs that could impact soft drink delivery time was the number of cases in a delivery.
- Over the recent stability region for this metric's 30,000-foot-level report, there was a monitoring of the times for 25 soft-drink deliveries (Y) as a function of delivery volume (X).
- Understanding any Y=f(X) relationship can provide insight into where Y improvement efforts should focus.

IEE Volume III Example and Dataset

- *IEE Volume III* Example 25.1: Correlation
- Dataset (Smarter Solutions (2022): V3 C25, Exam 25-01, Soft Drink Delivery.xlsx

SigmaXL or EPRS Metric-App [Smarter Solutions (2020)] Input/Output

- Figure 16.1: SigmaXL Input (Scatter Plot)
- Figure 16.2: SigmaXL Output (Scatter Plot)
- Figure 16.3: SigmaXL Input (Correlation)
- Figure 16.4: SigmaXL Output (Correlation)

SigmaXL Chart Function: Graphical Tools>Scatter Plots

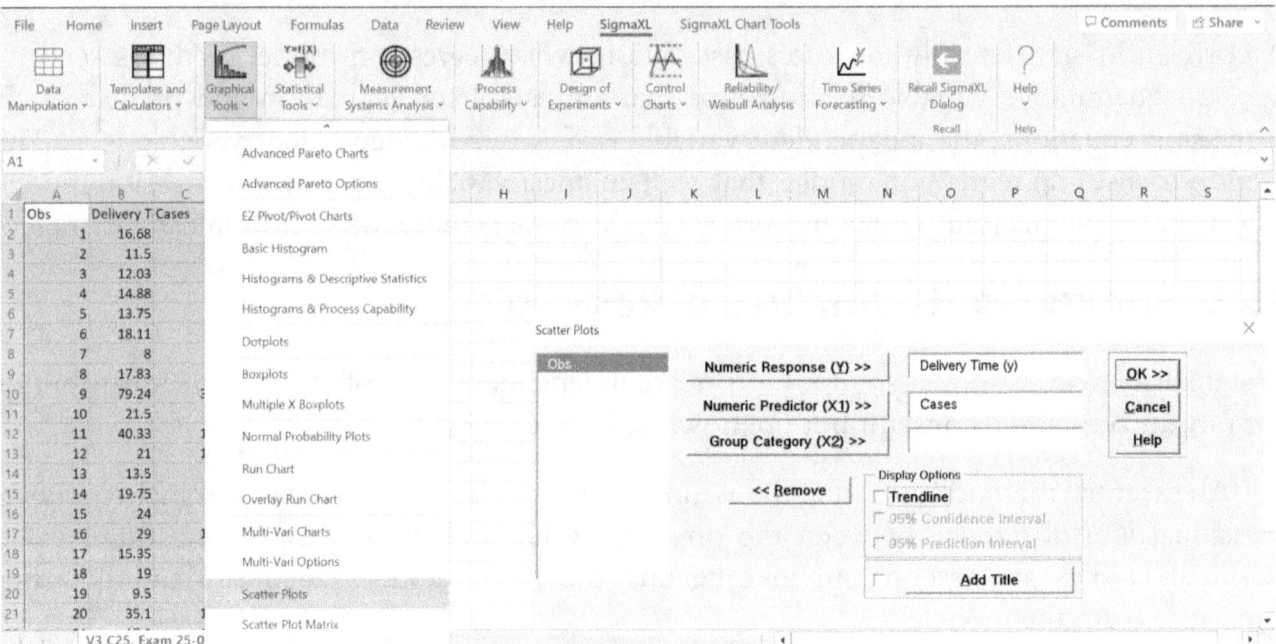

Figure 16.1: SigmaXL Input (Scatterplot)

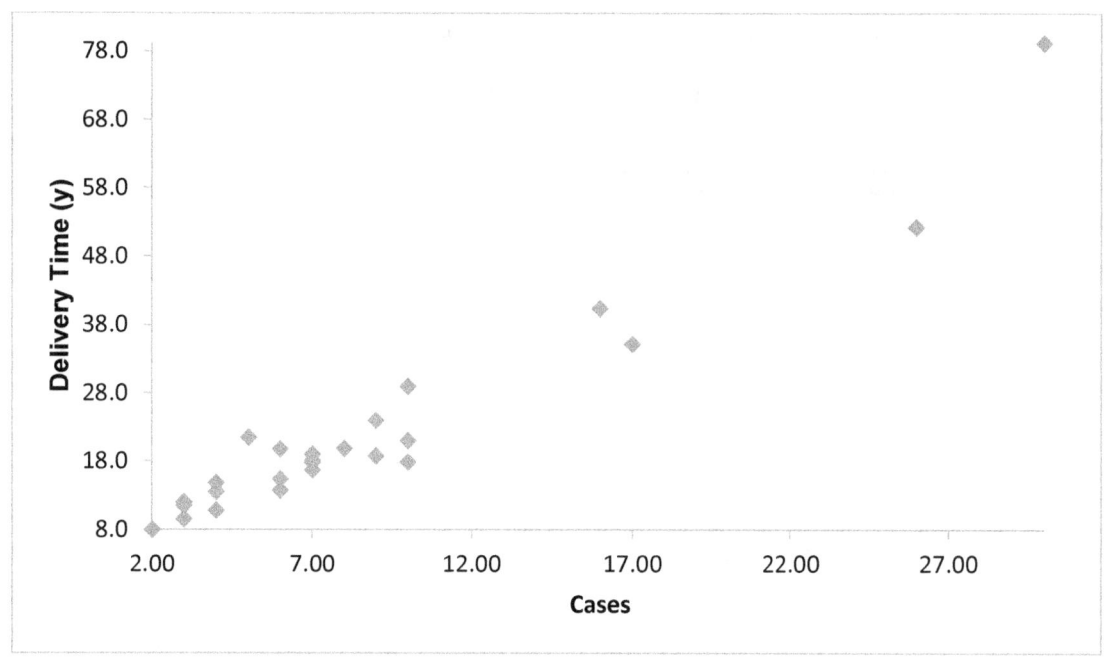

Figure 16.2: SigmaXL Output (Scatterplot)

SigmaXL Chart Function: Statistical Tools>Correlation Matrix

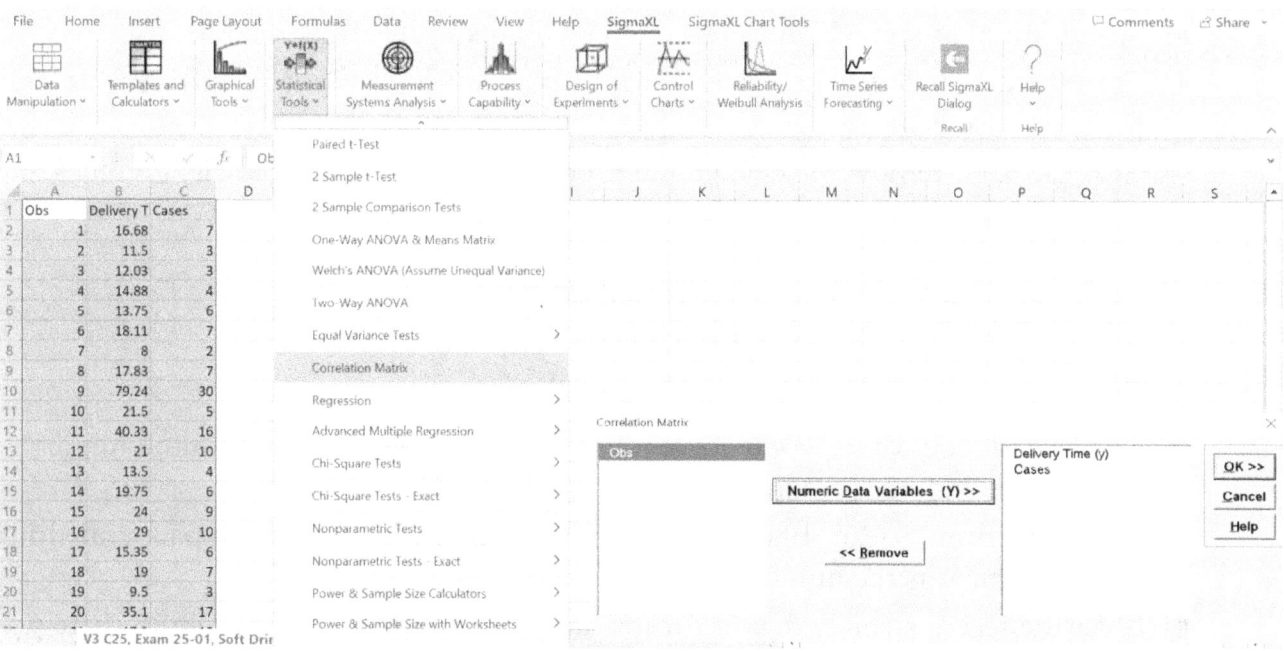

Figure 16.1: SigmaXL Input (Correlation)

Pearson Correlations	Delivery Time (y)	Cases
Delivery Time (y)	1	0.9646
Cases		1

Pearson Probabilities	Delivery Time (y)	Cases
Delivery Time (y)		0.0000
Cases		

Spearman Rank Correlations	Delivery Time (y)	Cases
Delivery Time (y)	1	0.8850
Cases		1

Spearman Rank Probabilities	Delivery Time (y)	Cases
Delivery Time (y)		0.0000
Cases		

Figure 16.2: SigmaXL Output (Correlation)

Comments

- There is a high Pearson correlation coefficient of 0.965
- Scatter plot has some high values that can dramatically affect the report-out
- To reduce overall delivery time, a team may want to look into a different process for large-case deliveries.
- You can add, remove or change chart elements such as title, labels, gridlines and data labels by clicking on the chart and selecting "+".

16.7 Example: Simple Linear Regression

Application

- The magnitude of an organization's 30,000-foot-level delivery-time report is undesirable and needs reduction.
- One item from a team brainstorming session of Xs that could impact soft drink delivery time was the number of cases in a delivery.
- Over the recent stability region for this metric's 30,000-foot-level report, there was a monitoring of the times for 25 soft-drink deliveries (Y) as a function of delivery volume (X).
- Understanding any Y=f(X) relationship can provide insight into where Y improvement efforts should focus.

IEE Volume III Example and Dataset

- *IEE Volume III* Example 25.2: Simple Linear Regression
- Dataset (Smarter Solutions (2022): V3 C25, Exam 25-01, Soft Drink Delivery.xlsx

SigmaXL or EPRS Metric-App [Smarter Solutions (2020)] Input/Output

- Figure 16.3: SigmaXL Input (Scatterplot with Trendline)
- Figure 16.4: SigmaXL Output (Scatterplot with Trendline)
- Figure 16.5: SigmaXL Input (Regression)
- Figure 16.6: SigmaXL Output (Regression)

SigmaXL Chart Function: Graphical Tools>Scatter Plots

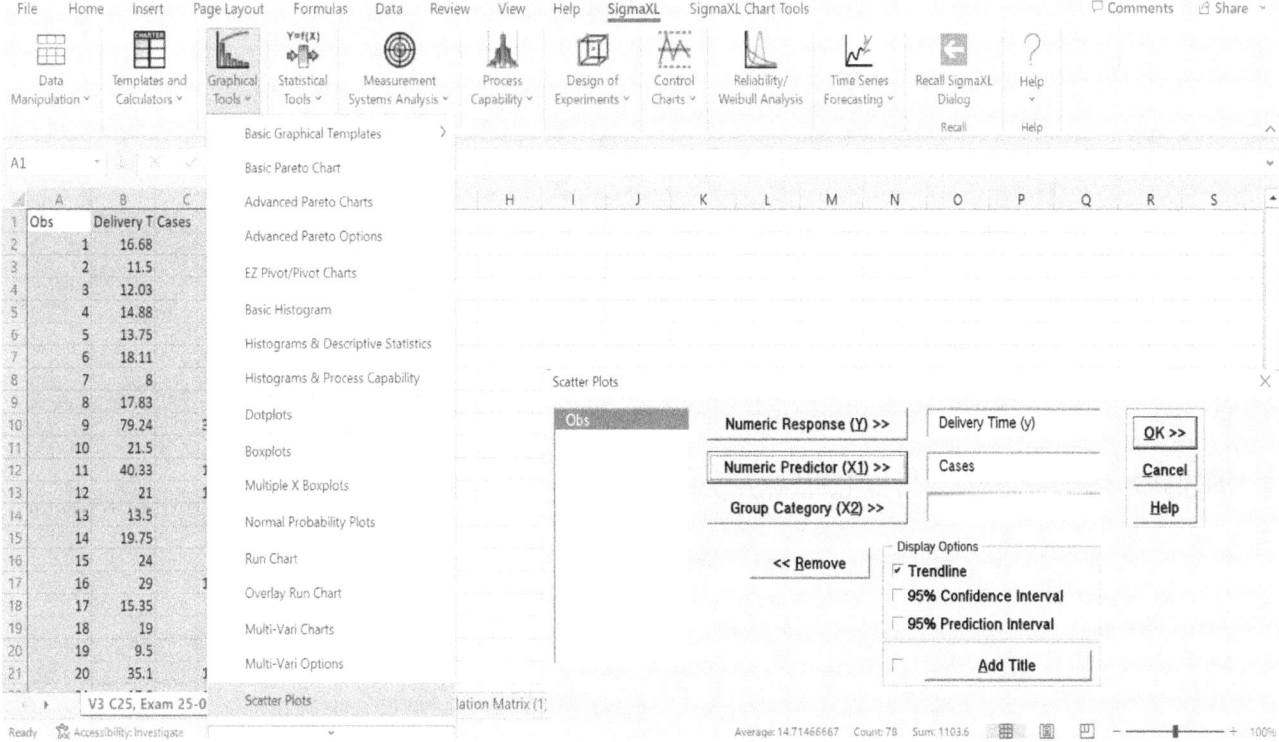

Figure 16.3: SigmaXL Input (Scatterplot with Trendline)

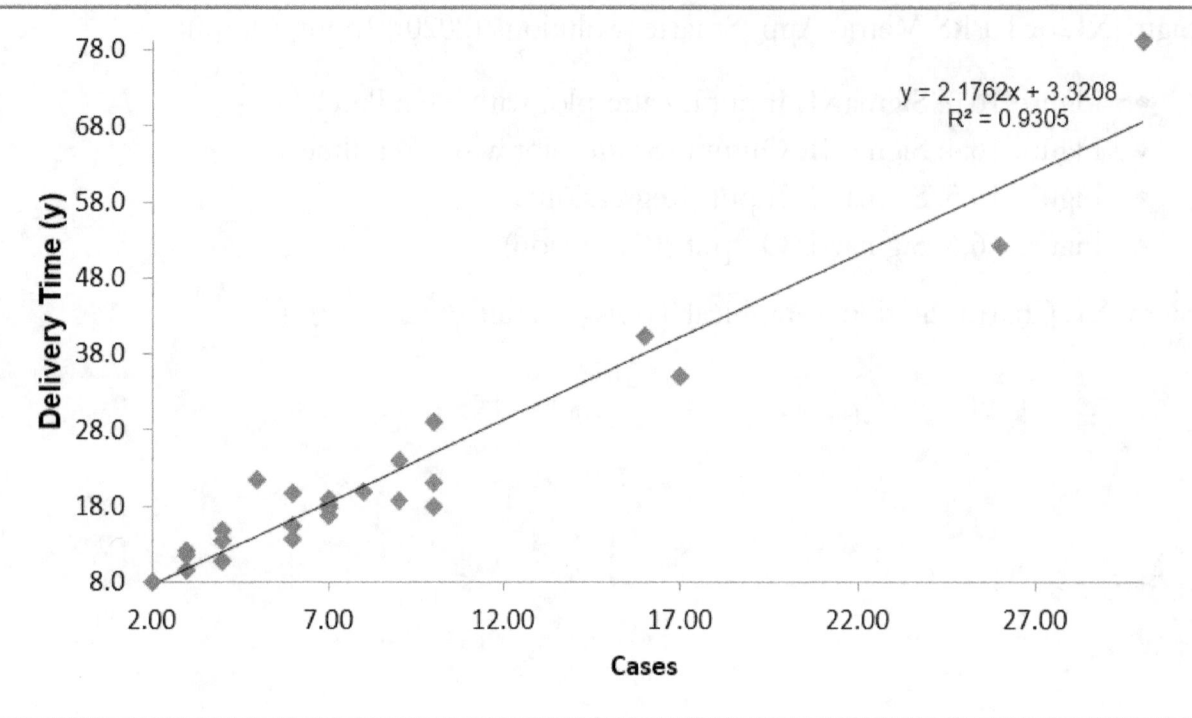

Figure 16.4: SigmaXL Output (Scatterplot with Trendline)

SigmaXL Chart Function: Regression>Multiple Regression

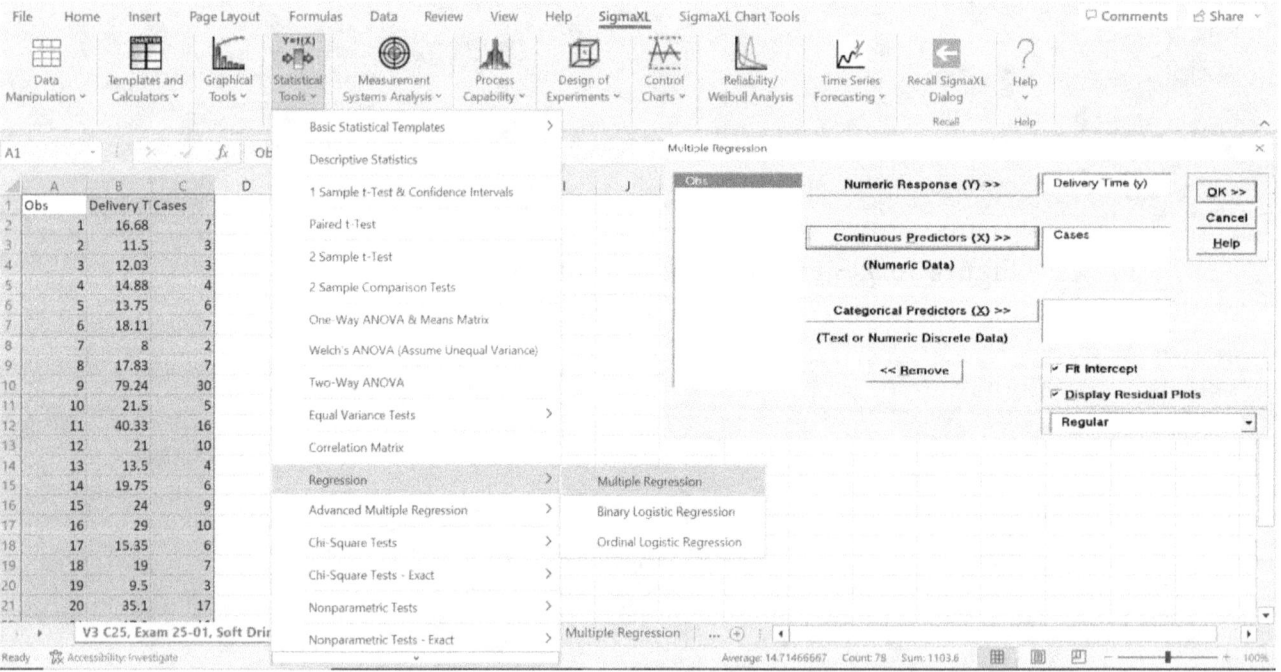

Figure 16.5: SigmaXL Input (Regression)

Multiple Regression Model: Delivery Time (y) = (3.321) + (2.176) * Cases

Model Summary:

R-Square	93.05%
R-Square Adjusted	92.75%
S (Root Mean Square Error)	4.181

Parameter Estimates:

Predictor Term	Coefficient	SE Coefficient	T	P	VIF	Tolerance
Constant	3.321	1.371	2.422	0.0237		
Cases	2.176	0.124030	17.546	0.0000	1	1.00000

Predicted Response Calculator:

Predictors	Enter Settings:	Predi...
Cases		

Analysis of Variance for Model:

Source	DF	SS	MS	F	P
Model	1	5382.4	5382.4	307.85	0.0000
Error	23	402.13	17.484		
Lack of Fit	11	288.29	26.208	2.763	0.0474
Pure Error	12	113.84	9.487		
Total (Model + Error)	24	5784.5	241.02		

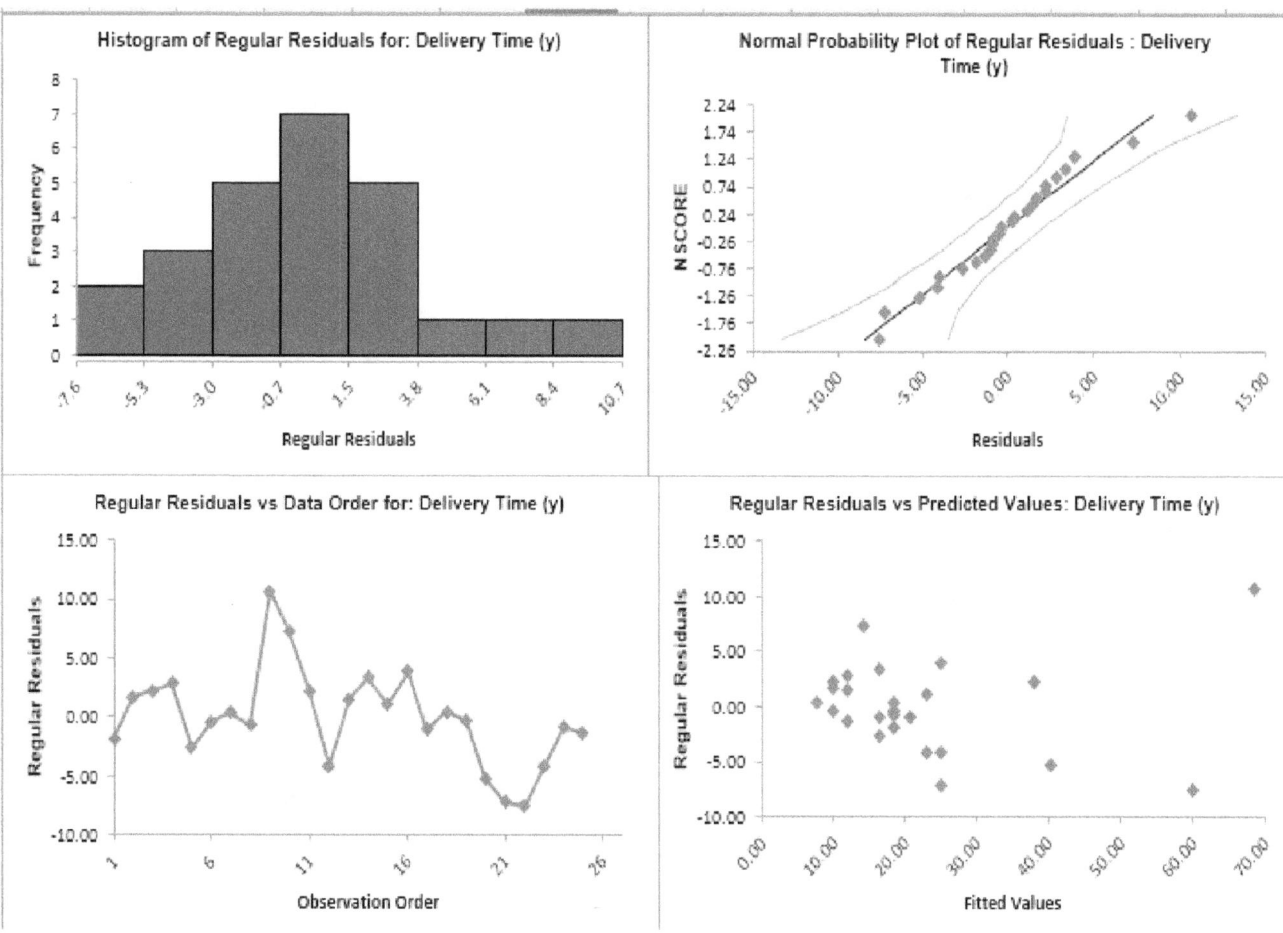

Figure 16.6: SigmaXL Output (Regression)

Comments

- The residuals appear well-behaved.
- The regression equation relationship is statistically significant in the Analysis of Variance (ANOVA) report since the P-Value is 0.000, much less than the team's alpha significance test criterion of 0.05.
- The best-estimate regression equation is Delivery Time (y) = 3.321 + 2.176 Cases.

- R-sq (adj) is 92.75%. This high value indicates that X variation explains a large percentage of the variability in Y.
- You can add, remove or change chart elements such as title, labels, gridlines and data labels by clicking on the chart and selecting "+".

17

IEE-DMAIC — Analyze Phase: Single-factor (One-way) Analysis of Variance (ANOVA) and Analysis of Means (ANOM)

17.1 IEE-DMAIC Roadmap Component

Book 1 Reference: *IEE Volume III* – Chapter 26

Book 2 Reference: *Lean Six Sigma Project Execution Guide* – Section 7

Internet: www.smartersolutions.com/roadmap (clicking on highlighted area provides the flowchart below)

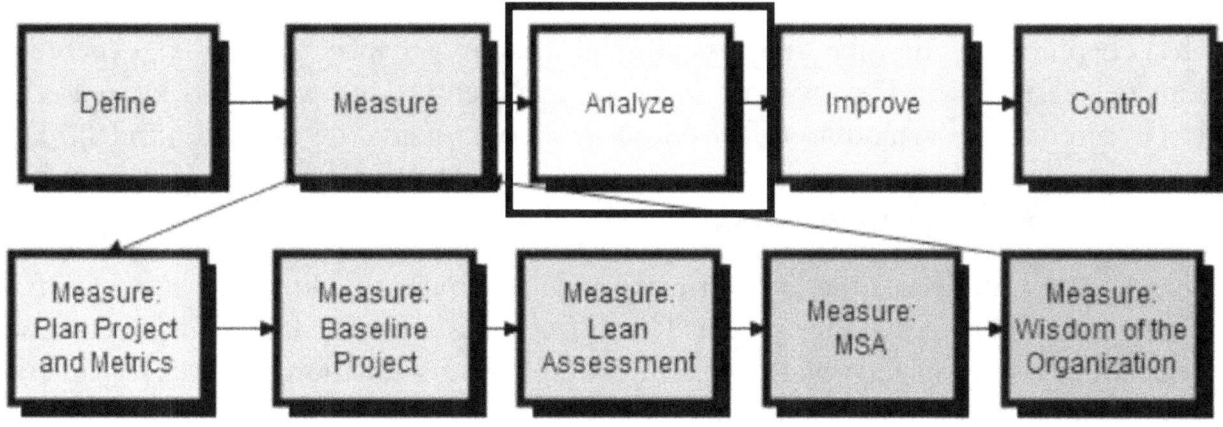

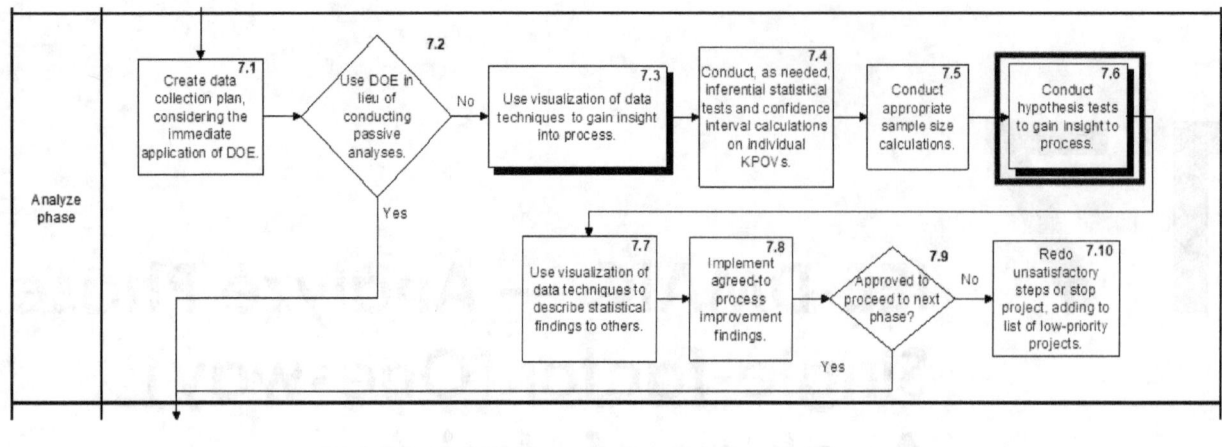

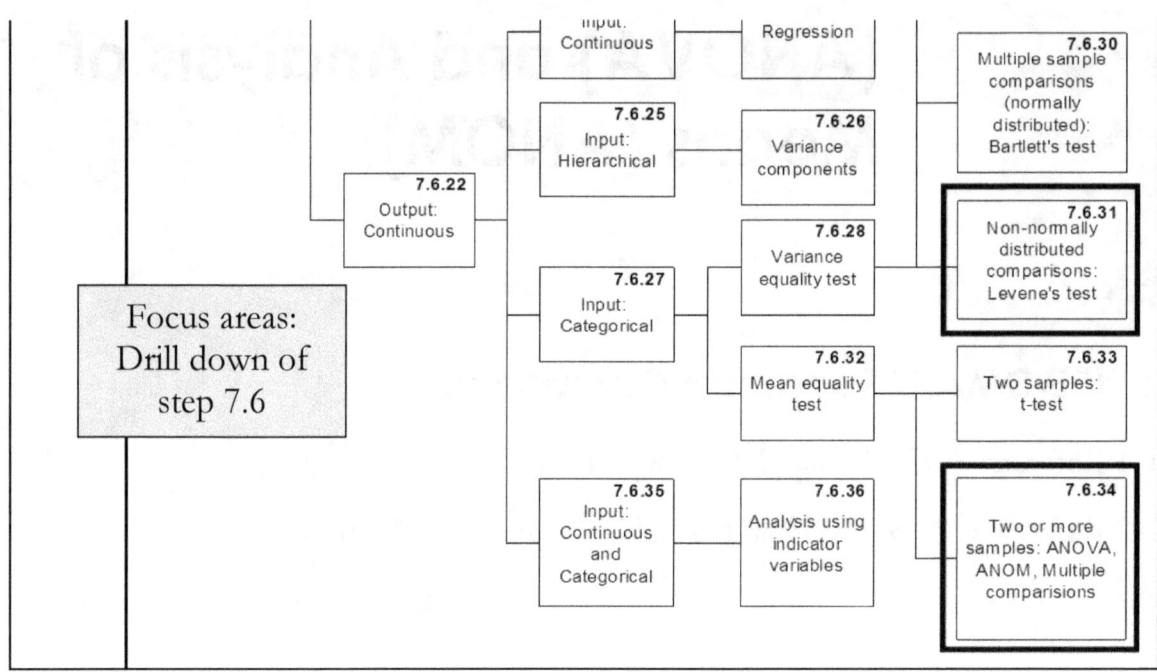

This chapter describes the single-factor analysis of variance (ANOVA) experiments (randomized design) with two or more levels or treatments. This method is a fixed-effects model (as opposed to a random-effects model or components-of-variance model). These techniques are applicable not only in the "improve" phase of the IEE DMAIC roadmap but also for analyses at the enterprise level.

The statistical model for the fixed-effects model is similar to that of the random-effects model or components-of-variance model. The difference is that with the fixed-effects model, the levels are chosen explicitly by the experimenter. For this situation, the test hypothesis is about the mean response effects due to factor levels, and conclusions apply only to the "factor levels" considered in the analysis.

17.2 Example: Single-factor Analysis of Variance

Application

- The magnitude of a manufactured product's 30,000-foot-level bursting strength report is undesirable and needs enhancement.
- Diaphragm type is a categorical-input (not continuous) item from a team brainstorming session of Xs that could impact bursting strength.
- Over a recent stability region for this metric's 30,000-foot-level report, there was a monitoring of burst strengths for seven different diaphragms.
- Analysis of Variance (ANOVA) techniques can determine if there is a statistically significant difference between diaphragm types, e.g., at a statistical significance level of 0.05.

IEE Volume III Example and Dataset

- *IEE Volume III* Example 26.1: Single-factor Analysis of Variance
- *Dataset (Smarter Solutions (2022): V3 C26, Exam 26-01, Single Factor Anova*

SigmaXL or EPRS Metric-App [Smarter Solutions (2020)] Input/Output

- Figure 17.1: SigmaXL Input (Single Factor ANOVA)
- Figure 17.2 A: SigmaXL Output (Single Factor ANOVA) Part 1 of 3
- Figure 17.2 B: SigmaXL Output (Single Factor ANOVA) Part 2 of 3
- Figure 17.2 C: SigmaXL Output (Single Factor ANOVA) Part 3 of 3

SigmaXL Chart Function: Statistical Tools>One-Way ANOVA & Means Matrix

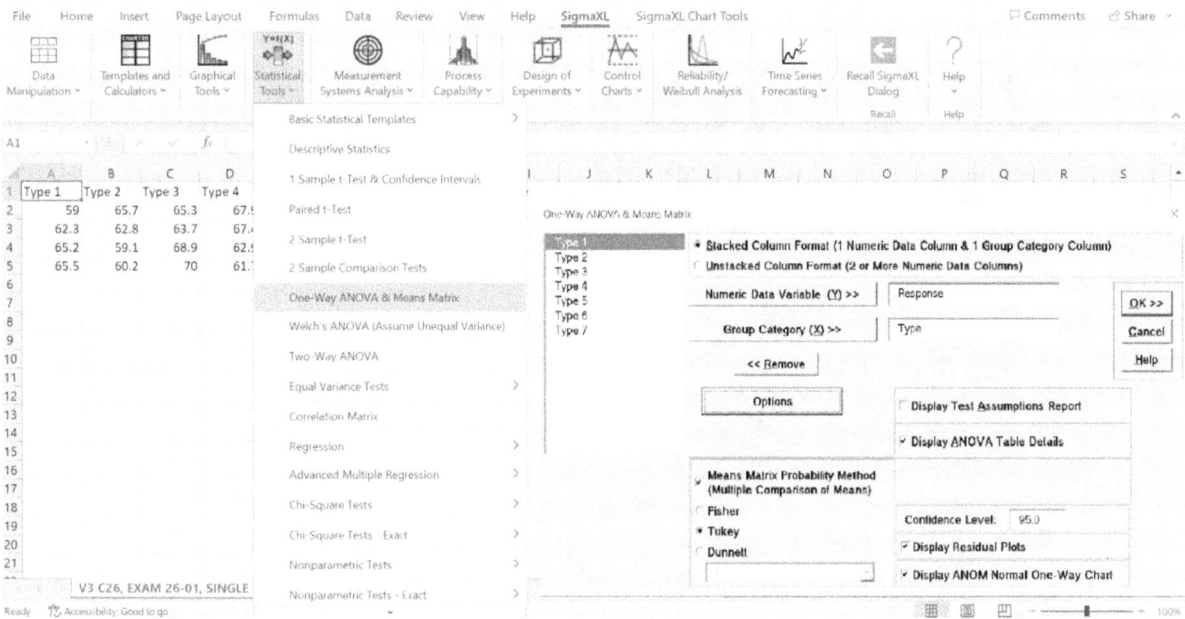

Figure 17.1: SigmaXL Input (Single Factor ANOVA)

Forrest W. Breyfogle III and Liviu Ibanescu

One-Way ANOVA & Means Matrix: Response

H_o: Mean 1 = Mean 2 = ... = Mean k
H_a: At least one pair Mean i ≠ Mean j

Type		1	2	3	4	5	6	7
Count		4	4	4	4	4	4	4
Mean		63	61.950	66.975	64.975	64.950	70.050	60
Standard Deviation		3.032	2.942	2.966	3.134	3.193	2.876	2.823
UC (2-sided, 95.0%, pooled)		66.117	65.067	70.092	68.092	68.067	73.167	63.117
LC (2-sided, 95.0%, pooled)		59.883	58.833	63.858	61.858	61.833	66.933	56.883

ANOVA Table					
Source	SS	DF	MS	F	P-Value
Between	265.3436	6.0000	44.2239	4.921	0.0028
Within	188.7050	21.0000	8.9860		
Total	454.0486	27.0000			

Pooled Standard Deviation =	2.3977		R-Sq =	58.44%
			R-Sq adj. =	46.57%

Figure 17.2 A: SigmaXL Output (Single Factor ANOVA) Part 1 of 3

Pairwise Mean Difference (row - column)	1	2	3	4	5	6	7
1	0	1.05	-3.975	-1.975	-1.950	-7.050	3
2		0	-5.025	-3.025	-3	-8.100	1.950
3			0	2.000	2.025	-3.075	6.975
4				0	0.025	-5.075	4.975
5					0	-5.100	4.950
6						0	10.05
7							0

Tukey Probabilities	1	2	3	4	5	6	7
1		0.9987	0.5165	0.9629	0.9650	0.0427	0.7879
2			0.2589	0.7817	0.7879	0.0146	0.9650
3				0.9606	0.9582	0.7690	0.0460
4					1.0000	0.2492	0.2688
5						0.2445	0.2738
6							0.0018
7							

Figure 17.2 B: SigmaXL Output (Single Factor ANOVA) Part 2 of 3

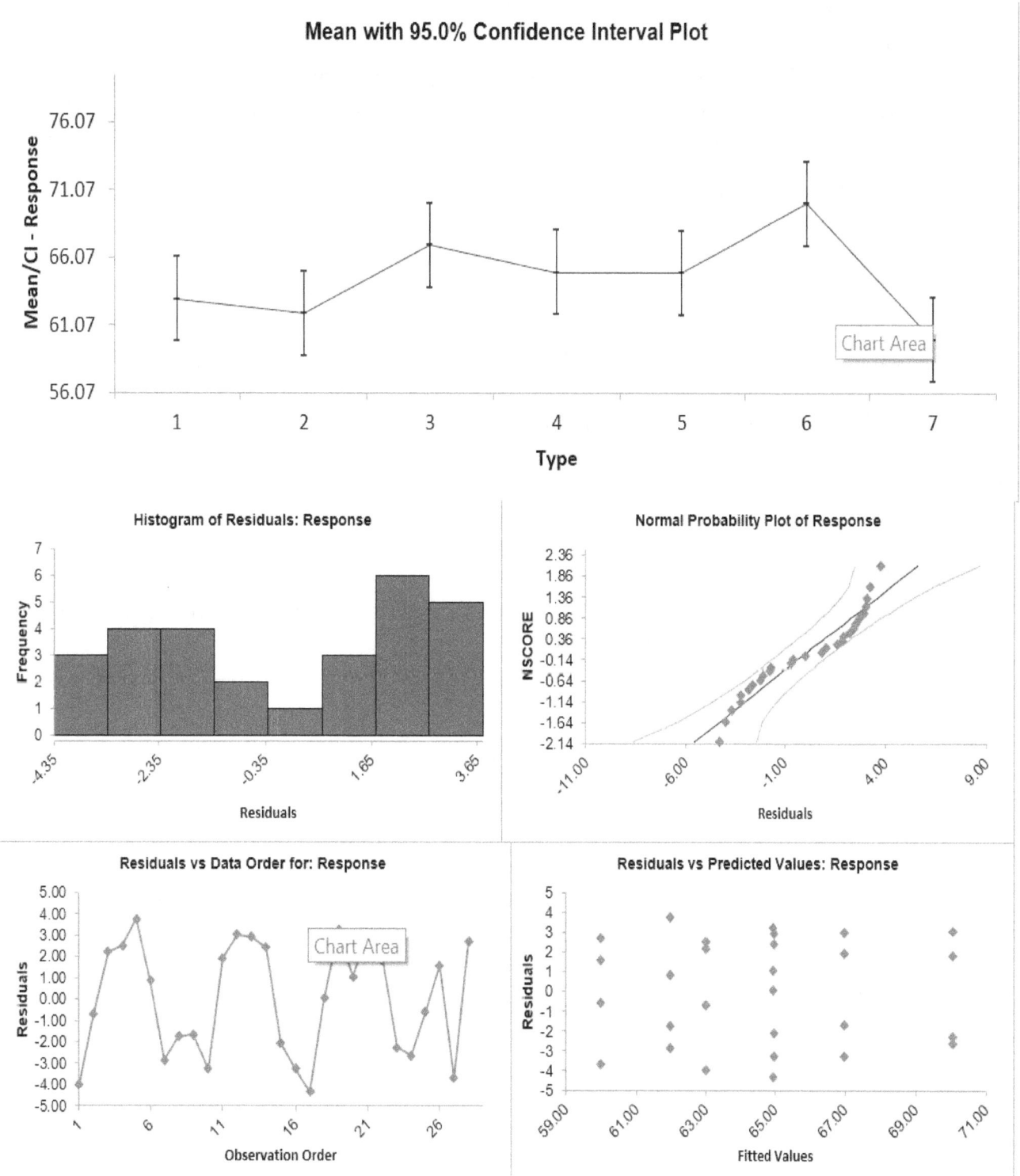

Figure 17.2 C: SigmaXL Output (Single Factor ANOVA) Part 3 of 3

Comments

- The ANOVA output in Figure 17.2 A indicates that rejection of the null hypothesis is appropriate because the P-Value is lower than a team's predetermined 0.05

criterion; however, this ANOVA assessment does not quantify how material types differ.

- With the Tukey multiple comparison models (Figure 17.2 B), one examines each comparison p-value. For example, we conclude that there is a significant difference between type 6 and type 7.
- The residuals shown in Figure 17.2 C are not as well-behaved as desired. A causal investigation of the residual patterns may provide helpful insight into what to do to improve the process's output response.
- The following example will apply ANOM techniques for the analysis of this dataset.
- You can add, remove or change chart elements such as title, labels, gridlines and data labels by clicking on the chart and selecting "+".

17.3 Example: Analysis of Means ANOM

Application

- The previous ANOVA example indicated a statistically significant difference in the bursting strengths of seven different types of rubber diaphragms (k = 7).
- The SigmaXL ANOM function can statistically test which diaphragms differ from the grand mean of all diaphragms.

IEE Volume III Example and Dataset

- *IEE Volume III* Example 26.2: Analysis of Means (ANOM)
- Dataset (Smarter Solutions (2022): V3 C26, Exam 26-01, Single Factor ANOVA

SigmaXL or EPRS Metric-App [Smarter Solutions (2020)] Input/Output

- Figure 17.3: SigmaXL Input (ANOM)
- Figure 17.4: SigmaXL Output (ANOM)

SigmaXL Chart Function: Graphical Tools>Analysis of Means>ANOM Normal One-Way

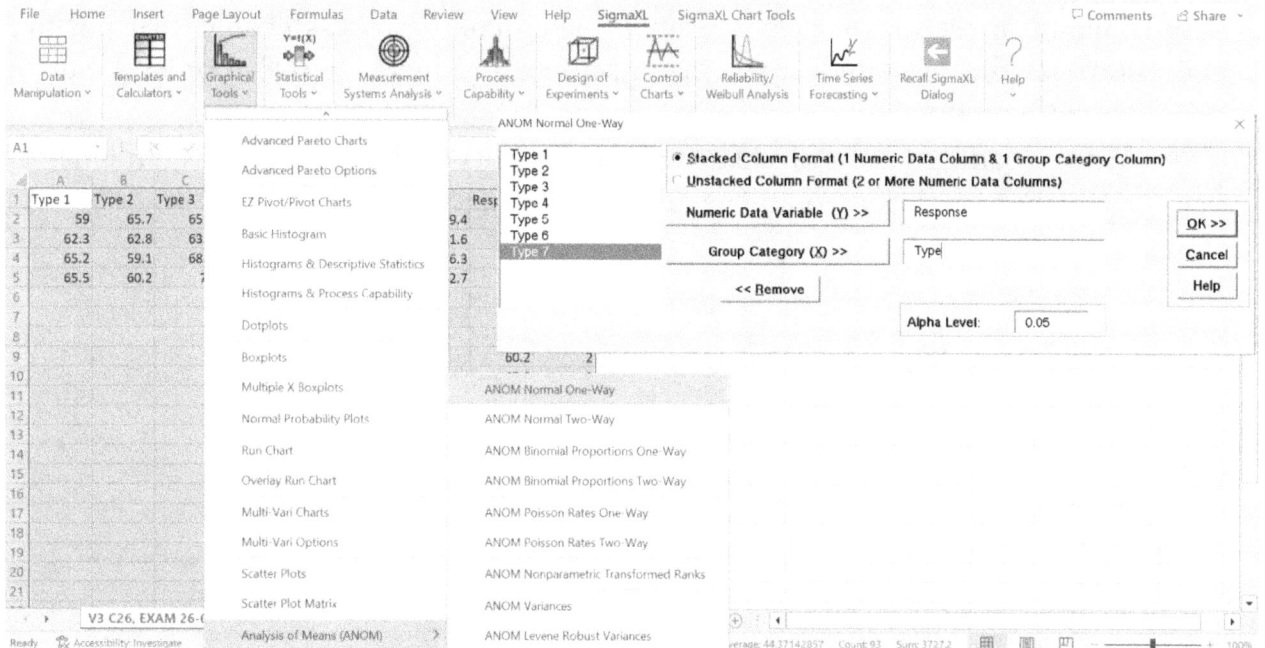

Figure 17.3: SigmaXL Input (ANOM)

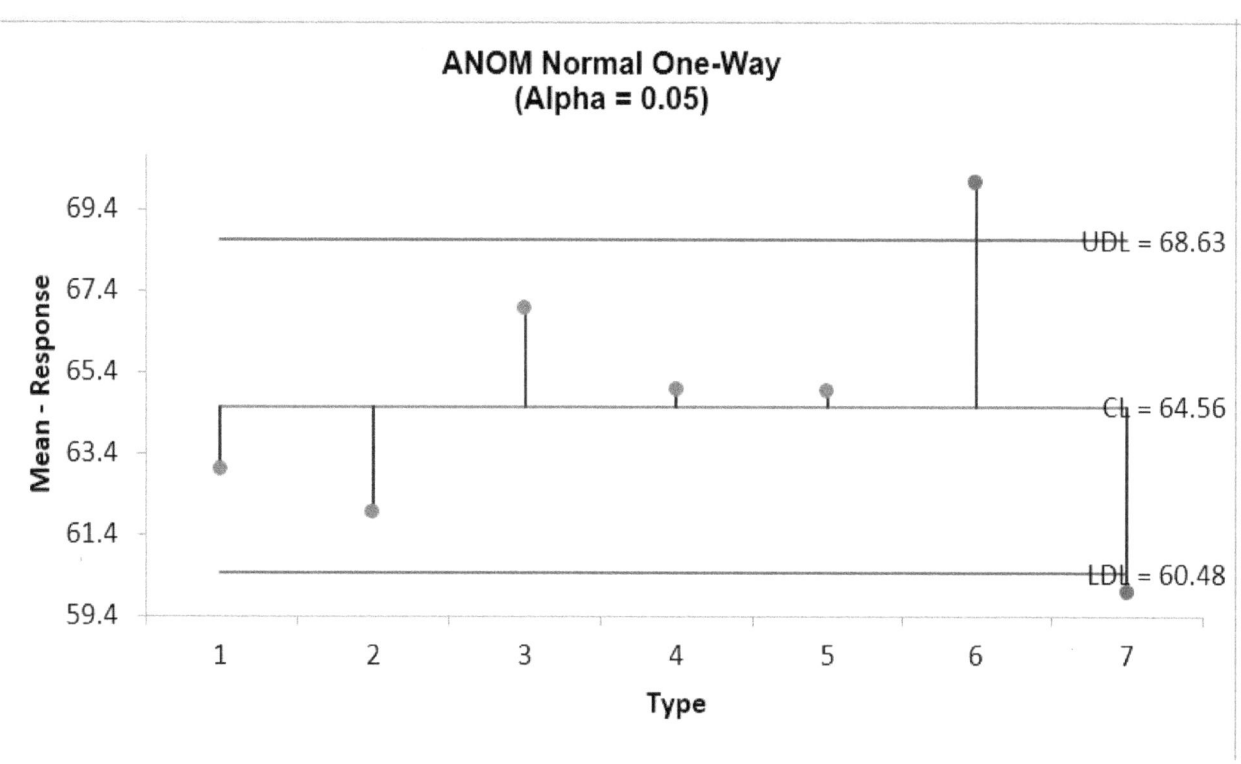

Figure 17.4: SigmaXL Output (ANOM)

Comments

- Figure 17.4 graphically illustrates that μ_6 and μ_7 are statistically different from the grand mean at a significance level of 0.05.

- This information can help a team to determine a process change that positively impacts the magnitude of a manufactured product's 30,000-foot-level bursting strength report.
- You can add, remove or change chart elements such as title, labels, gridlines and data labels by clicking on the chart and selecting "+".

18

IEE-DMAIC — Analyze Phase: Two-factor (Two-way) Analysis of Variance

18.1 IEE-DMAIC Roadmap Component

Book 1 Reference: *IEE Volume III* – Chapter 27

Book 2 Reference: *Lean Six Sigma Project Execution Guide* – Section 7

Internet: www.smartersolutions.com/roadmap (clicking on highlighted area provides the flowchart below)

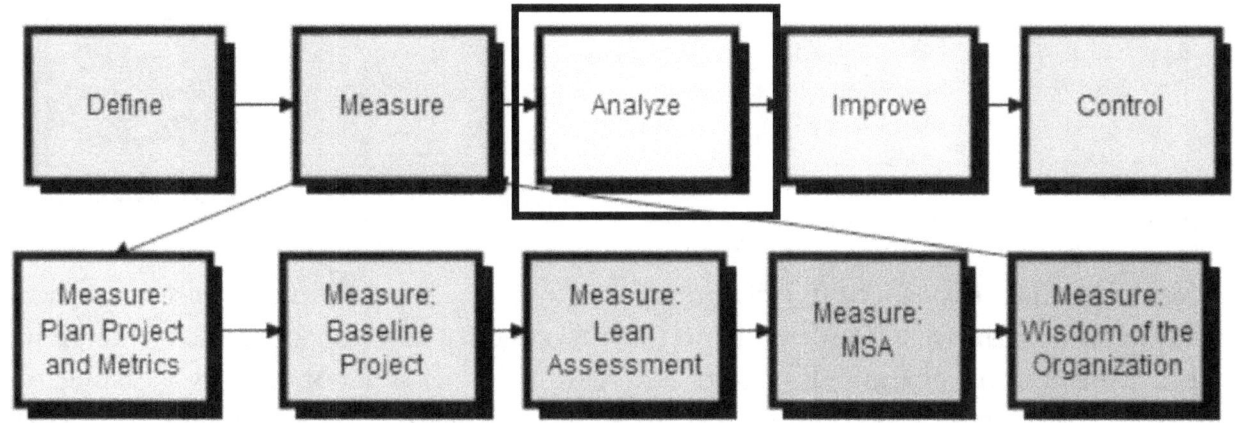

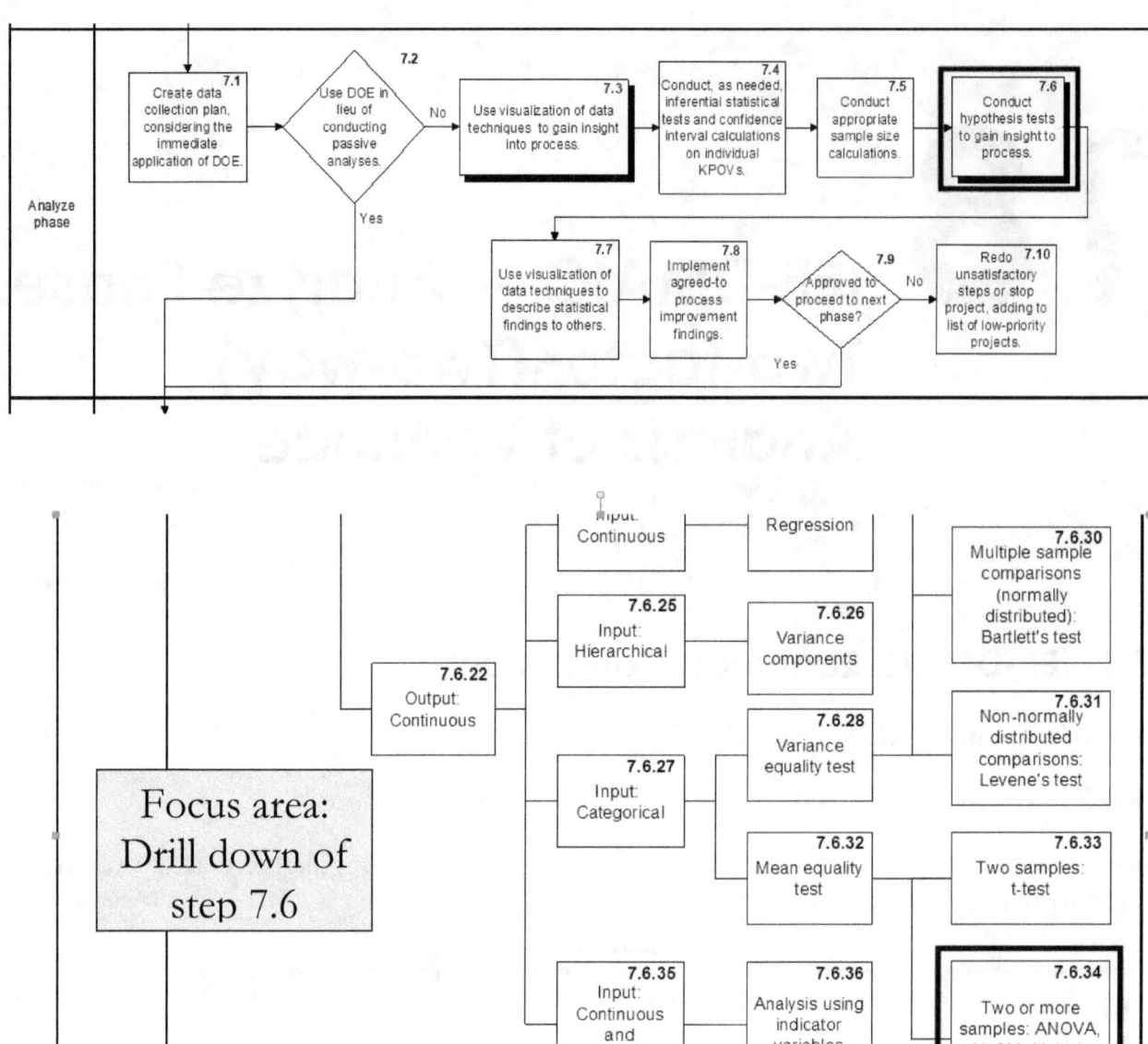

This chapter is the fourth of five chapters for assessing a population response as a function of multiple input situations. The first chapter of this series of chapters described a hierarchical structure. The second chapter described the regression of two continuous variables, e.g., methods for comparing two conditions or treatments. The last chapter described ANOVA and ANOM techniques.

Experiments often involve the study of more than one factor. Factorial designs are most efficient for the situation in which there is an investigation of combinations of levels of factors. These designs evaluate the change in response caused by different factor levels and the interaction of factors.

This chapter focuses on two-factor ANOVA or two-way ANOVA of fixed effects.

The following chapters describe factorial experiments with more than two factors.

18.2 Example: Two-factor Full Factorial Design

Application

- A device's battery is subject to extreme temperature variations.
- An engineer can select one of only three plate material types during development.
- After product shipment, the engineer has no control over temperature; however, she believes that temperature could degrade the practical life of the battery.
- The engineer would like to determine if one of the material types is robust to temperature variations.

IEE Volume III Example and Dataset

- *IEE Volume III* Example 27.1: Two-factor Factorial Design
- *Dataset (Smarter Solutions (2022): V3 C27, Exer 27-01, two factor, mach and oper.xlsx*

SigmaXL or EPRS Metric-App [Smarter Solutions (2020)] Input/Output

- Figure 18.1: SigmaXL Input (Two-Way ANOVA)
- Figure 18.2: SigmaXL Output (Two-Way ANOVA)
- Figure 18.3: SigmaXL Output (Two-Factor Interaction Plot)

SigmaXL Chart Function: Statistical Tools>Two-Way ANOVA

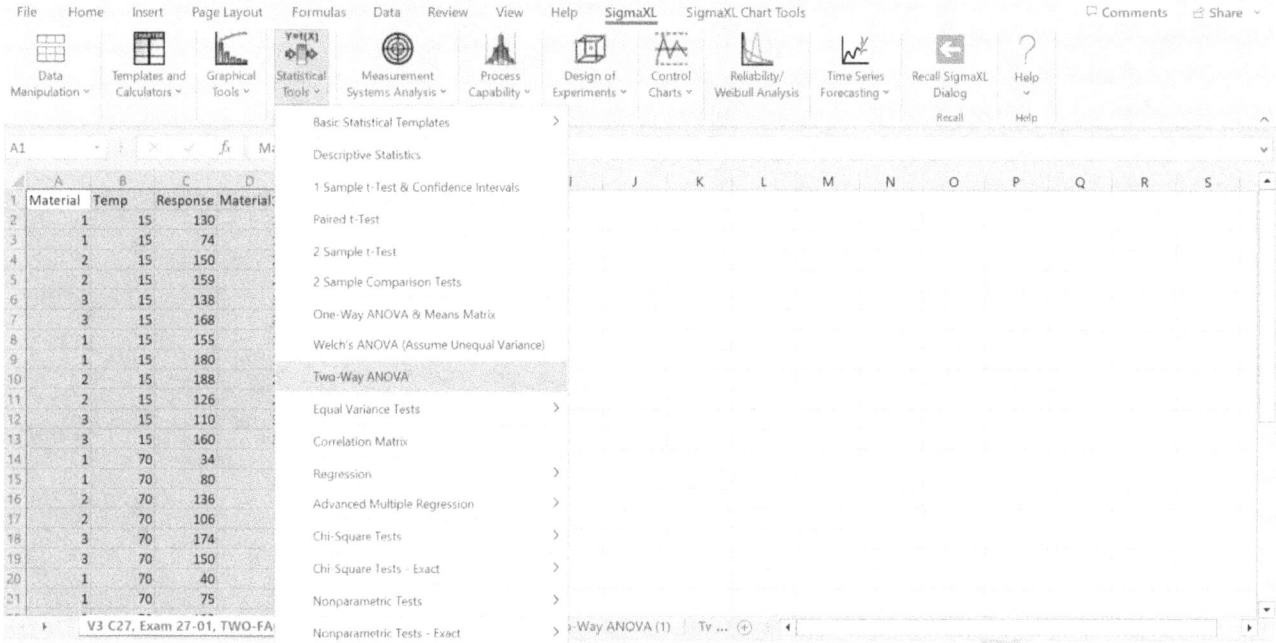

Figure 18.1: SigmaXL Input (Two-Way ANOVA)

Factor and Model Summary:

Number of Levels - Material	3
Number of Levels - Temp	3
Number of Replicates	4
Design Type:	Balanced
Confidence Level	95
R-Square	76.52%
R-Square Adjusted	69.56%
S (Pooled Standard Deviation)	25.985

Analysis of Variance:

Source	DF	SS	MS	F	P
Material	2	10684	5341.9	7.911	0.0020
Temp	2	39119	19559	28.968	0.0000
Interaction	4	9613.8	2403.4	3.560	0.0186
Error	27	18231	675.21		
Total	35	77647	2218.5		

Figure 18.2 A: SigmaXL Output (Two-Way ANOVA) Part 1 of 3

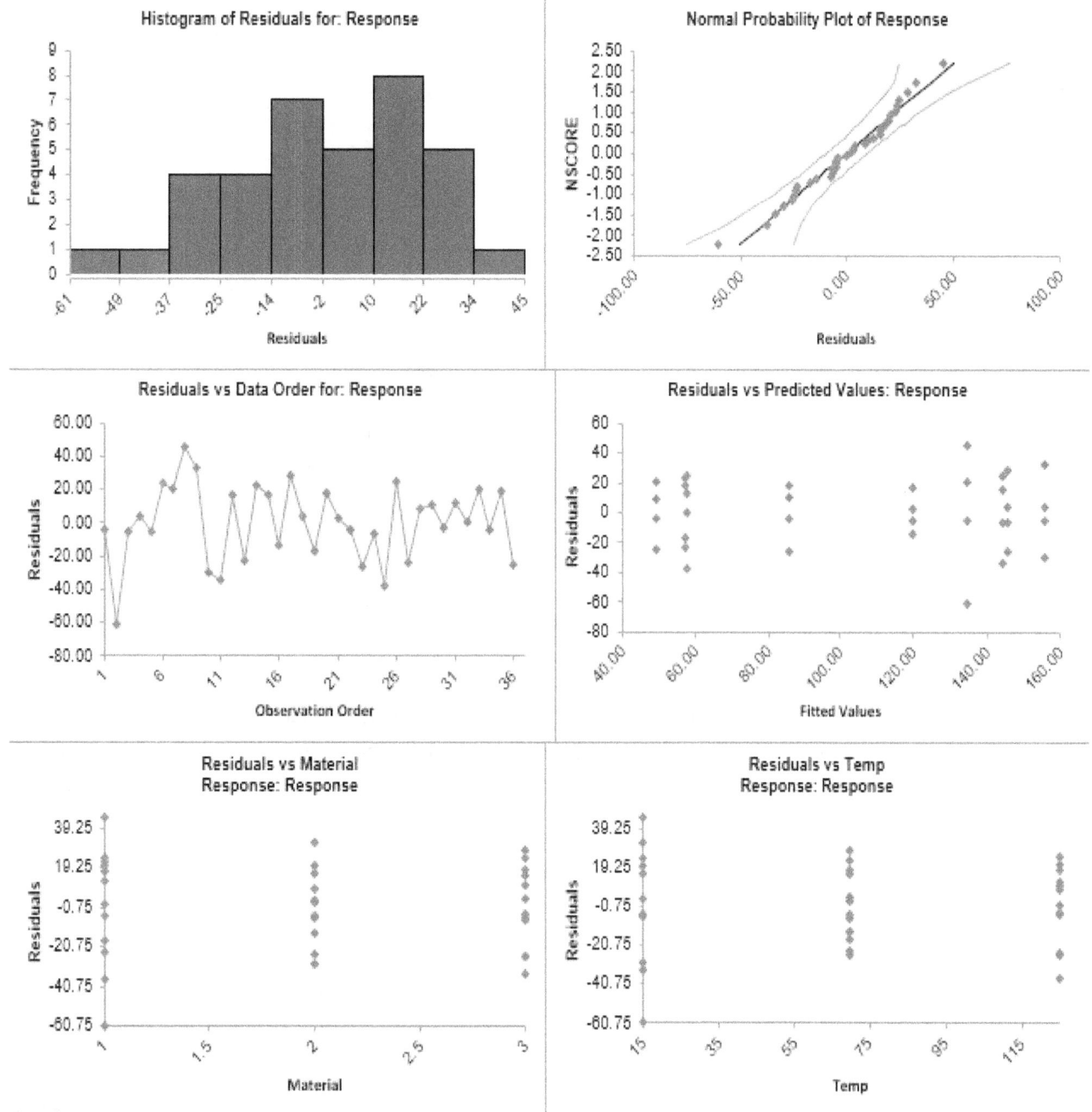

Figure 18.2 B: SigmaXL Output (Two-Way ANOVA) Part 2 of 3

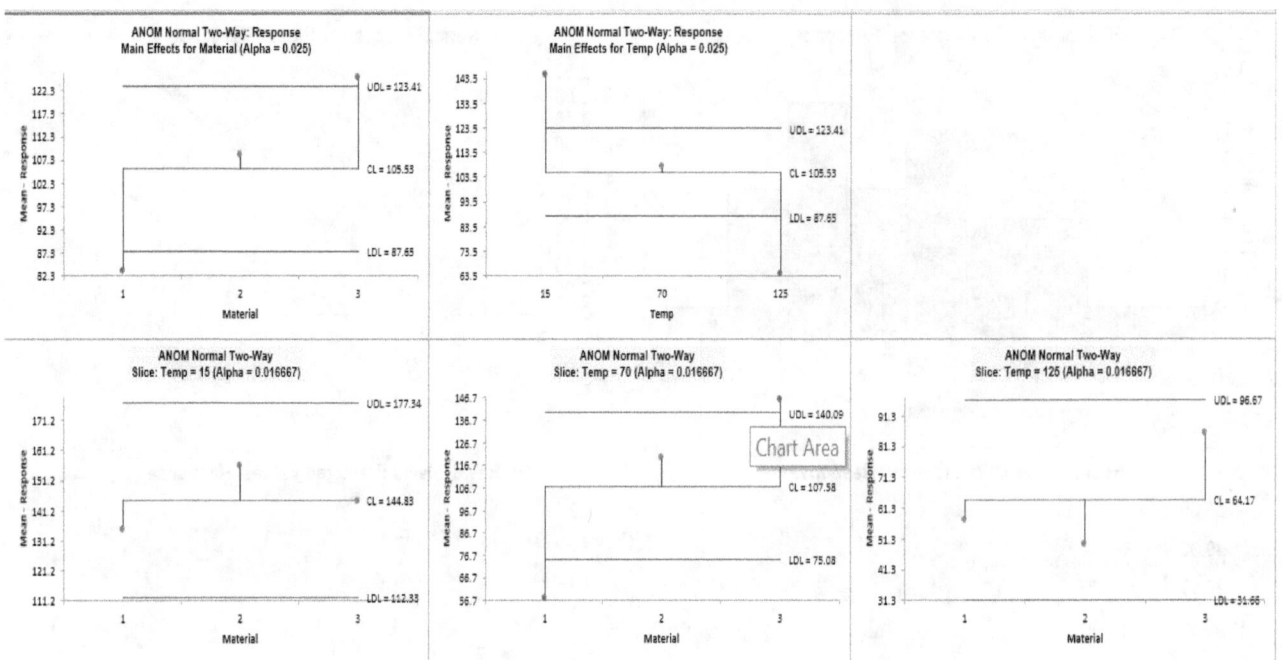

Figure 18.2 C: SigmaXL Output (Two-Factor Factorial Design) Part 3 of 3

Comments

- Using an $\alpha = 0.05$ criterion to the outputs shown in Figure 18.2 A, one concludes that there is a statistically-significant interaction between material types and temperature because the interaction probability value is less than 0.05.
- The residuals are well-behaved.

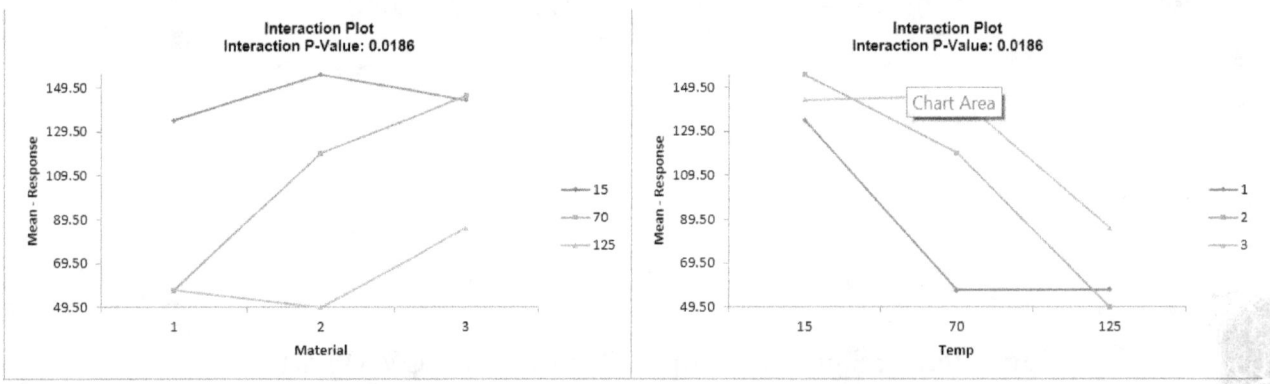

Figure 18.4: SigmaXL Output (Two-Factor Interaction Plot)

Comments

- The significance of the interaction term in Figure 18.2 statistically quantifies the lack of parallelism of the lines in Figure 18.3.
- This interaction plot shows a degradation in life with an increase in temperature regardless of material type.

- If this battery should experience less loss of life at elevated temperatures, type 3 material seems to be the best choice.
- You can add, remove or change chart elements such as title, labels, gridlines and data labels by clicking on the chart and selecting "+".

19

IEE-DMAIC — Analyze Phase: Multiple Regression, Logistic Regression

19.1 IEE-DMAIC Roadmap Component

Book 1 Reference: *IEE Volume III* – Chapter 28

Book 2 Reference: *Lean Six Sigma Project Execution Guide* – Section 7

Internet: www.smartersolutions.com/roadmap (clicking on highlighted area provides the flowchart below)

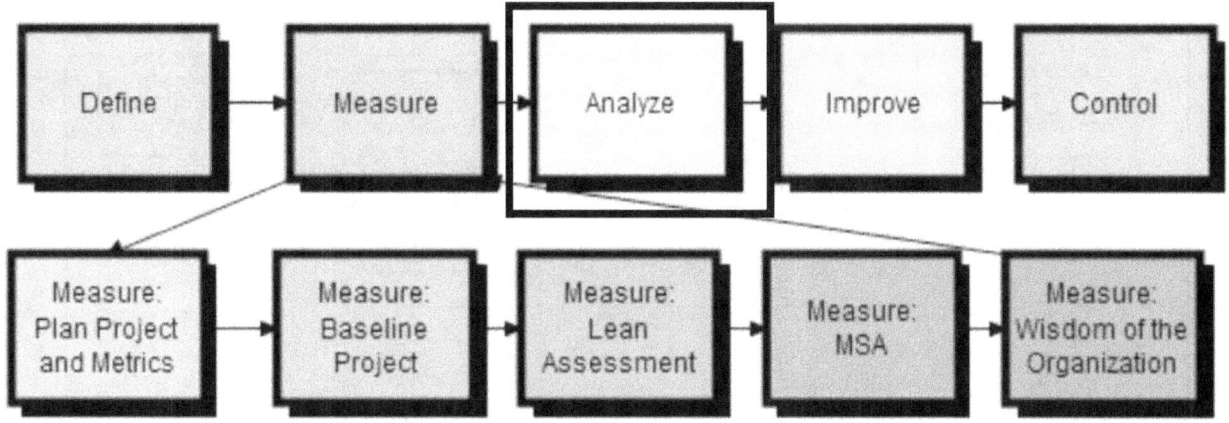

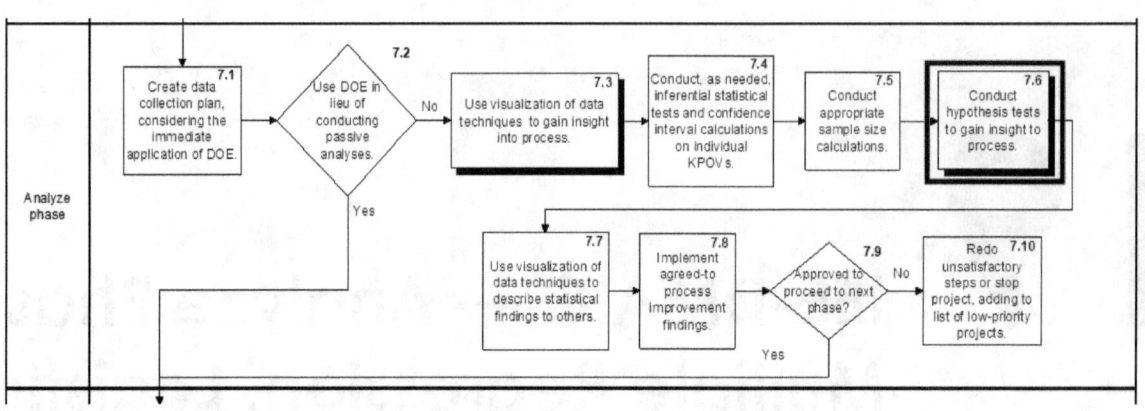

Analyze phase

7.1 Create data collection plan, considering the immediate application of DOE.

7.2 Use DOE in lieu of conducting passive analyses. — No — Yes

7.3 Use visualization of data techniques to gain insight into process.

7.4 Conduct, as needed, inferential statistical tests and confidence interval calculations on individual KPOVs.

7.5 Conduct appropriate sample size calculations.

7.6 Conduct hypothesis tests to gain insight to process.

7.7 Use visualization of data techniques to describe statistical findings to others.

7.8 Implement agreed-to process improvement findings.

7.9 Approved to proceed to next phase? — No — Yes

7.10 Redo unsatisfactory steps or stop project, adding to list of low-priority projects.

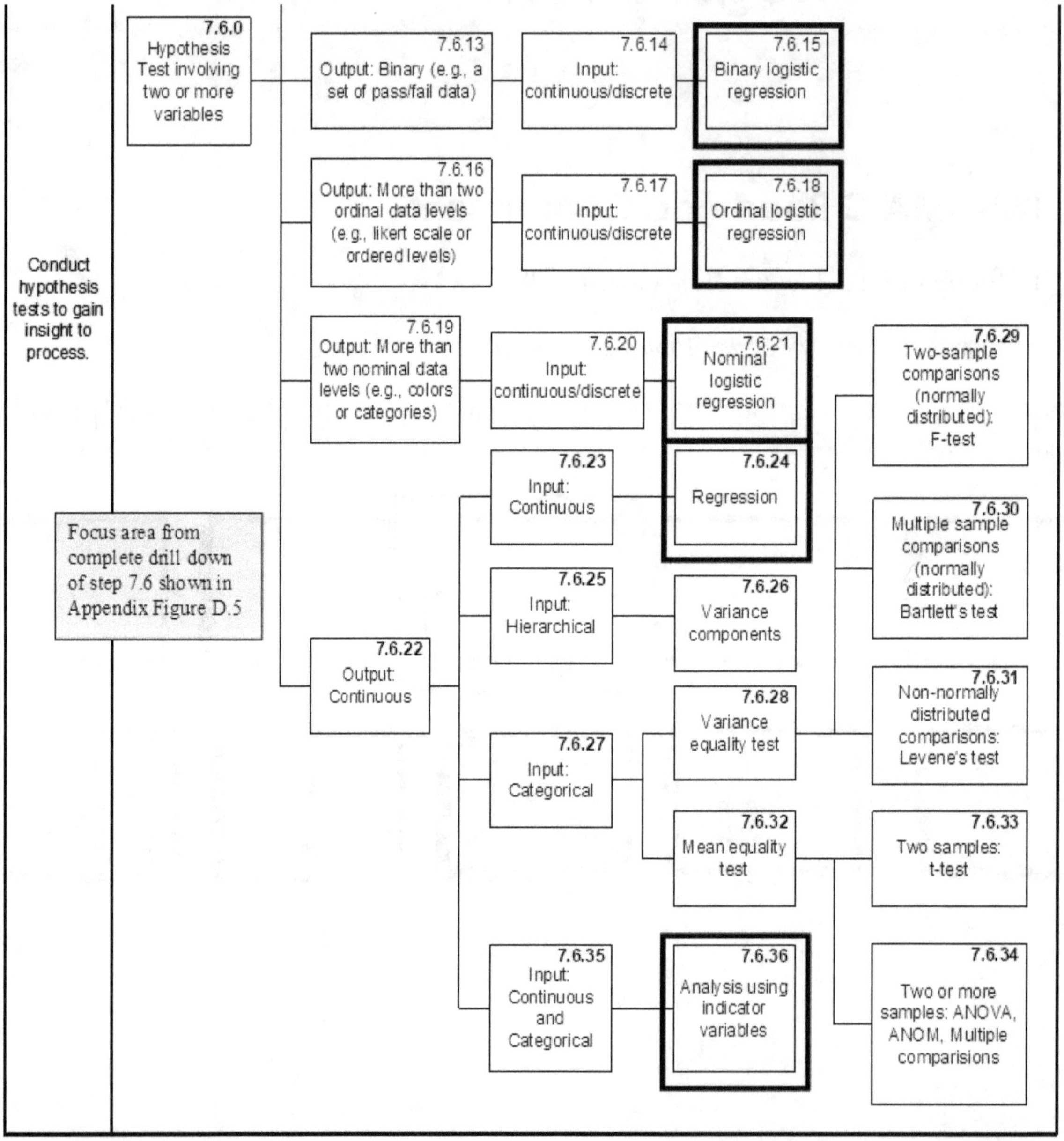

Conduct hypothesis tests to gain insight to process.

7.6.0 Hypothesis Test involving two or more variables

7.6.13 Output: Binary (e.g., a set of pass/fail data)

7.6.14 Input: continuous/discrete

7.6.15 Binary logistic regression

7.6.16 Output: More than two ordinal data levels (e.g., likert scale or ordered levels)

7.6.17 Input: continuous/discrete

7.6.18 Ordinal logistic regression

7.6.19 Output: More than two nominal data levels (e.g., colors or categories)

7.6.20 Input: continuous/discrete

7.6.21 Nominal logistic regression

Focus area from complete drill down of step 7.6 shown in Appendix Figure D.5

7.6.22 Output: Continuous

7.6.23 Input: Continuous

7.6.24 Regression

7.6.25 Input: Hierarchical

7.6.26 Variance components

7.6.27 Input: Categorical

7.6.28 Variance equality test

7.6.32 Mean equality test

7.6.35 Input: Continuous and Categorical

7.6.36 Analysis using indicator variables

7.6.29 Two-sample comparisons (normally distributed): F-test

7.6.30 Multiple sample comparisons (normally distributed): Bartlett's test

7.6.31 Non-normally distributed comparisons: Levene's test

7.6.33 Two samples: t-test

7.6.34 Two or more samples: ANOVA, ANOM, Multiple comparisions

19.2 Example: Multiple Regression

Application

- The 30,000-foot-level Y response report for product strength is unsatisfactory.
- Two X inputs that a team thought could impact the Y response were hydraulic pressure during a forming process and acid concentration.
- The following multiple regression analysis assesses whether these Xs significantly impact the Y response.

IEE Volume III Example and Dataset

- *IEE Volume III* Example 28.1: Multiple Regression
- *Dataset (Smarter Solutions (2022): V3 C28, Exam 28-01, Product Strength.xlsx*

SigmaXL or EPRS Metric-App [Smarter Solutions (2020)] Input/Output

- Figure 19.1: SigmaXL Input (Multiple Regression)
- Figure 19.2A: SigmaXL Output (Multiple Regression) – Part 1 of 2
- Figure 19.2B: SigmaXL Output (Multiple Regression) – Part 2 of 2

SigmaXL Chart Function: Statistical Tools>Regression>Multiple Regression

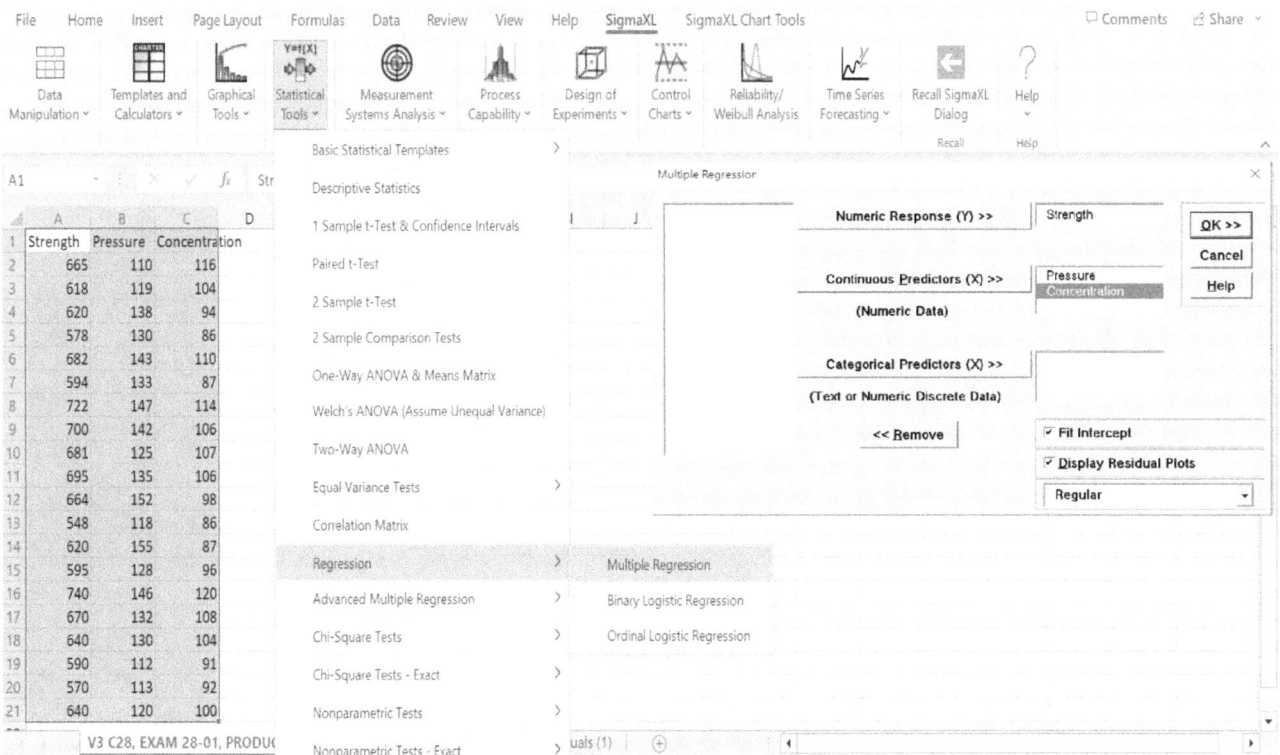

Figure 19.1: SigmaXL Input (Multiple Regression)

Multiple Regression Model: Strength = (16.277) + (1.572) * Pressure + (4.163) * Concentration

Model Summary:	
R-Square	92.82%
R-Square Adjusted	91.97%
S (Root Mean Square Error)	15.100

Parameter Estimates:

Predictor Term	Coefficient	SE Coefficient	T	P	VIF	Tolerance
Constant	16.277	44.300	0.367417	0.7178		
Pressure	1.572	0.260603	6.031	0.0000	1.0237	0.976833
Concentration	4.163	0.333958	12.465	0.0000	1.023716115	0.976833

Analysis of Variance for Model:

Source	DF	SS	MS	F	P
Model	2	50101	25050	109.87	0.0000
Error	17	3876.0	228.00		
Total (Model + Error)	19	53977	2840.9		

Durbin-Watson Test for Autocorrelation in Residuals:

DW Statistic	1.442
P-Value Positive Autocorrelation	0.0743
P-Value Negative Autocorrelation	0.8936

Figure 19.2A: SigmaXL Output (Multiple Regression) – Part 1 of 2

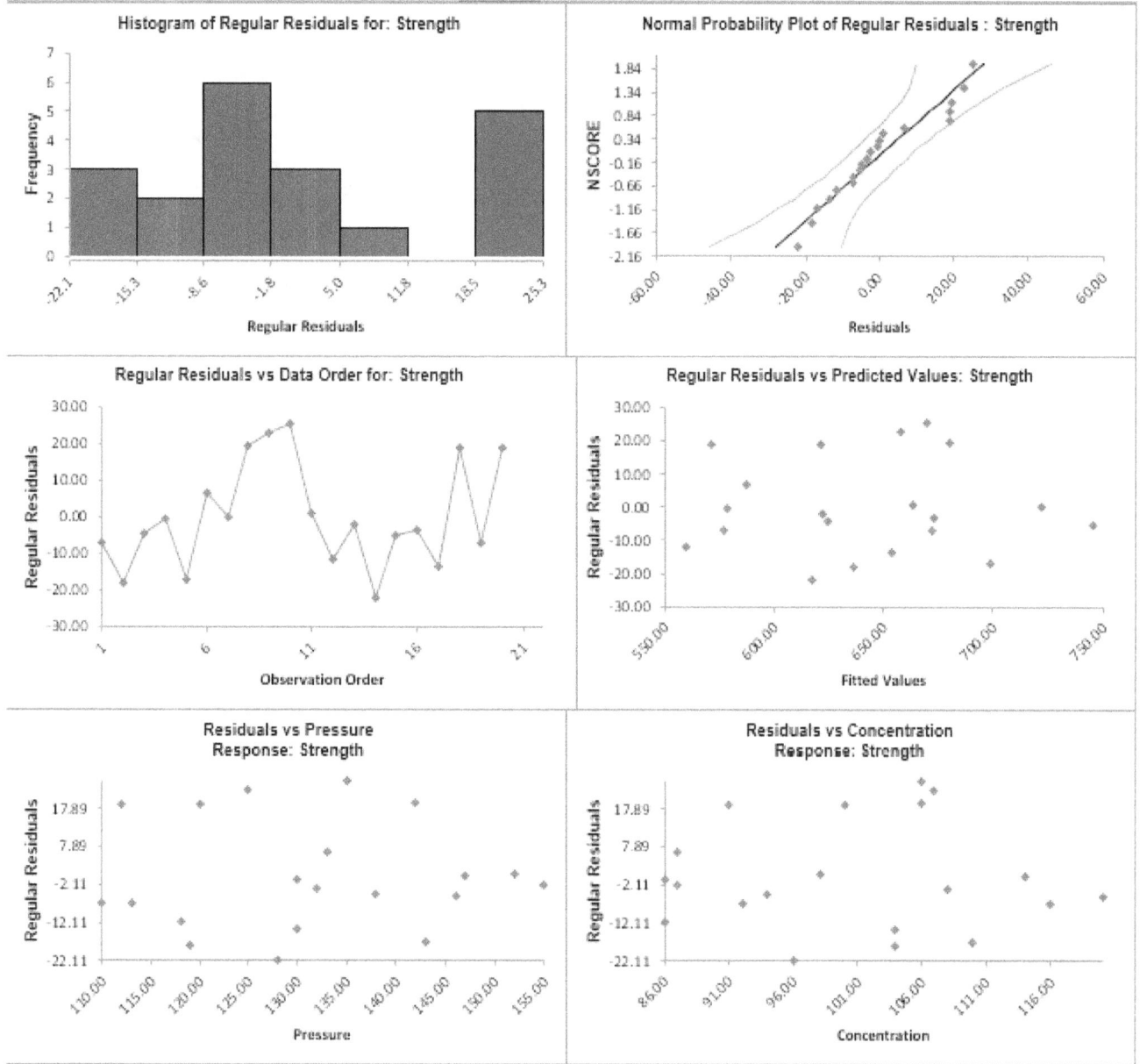

Comments

- Both pressure and concentration are significant; each has a P-Value of 0.000
- The residuals are well behaved
- You can add, remove or change chart elements such as title, labels, gridlines and data labels by clicking on the chart and selecting "+".

19.3 Example: Multiple Regression Best Subset Analysis

Application

- The 30,000-foot-level Y response report for a product is unsatisfactory.
- Four continuous-response X inputs that a team thought could impact the Y response were designated A, B, C, and D.

- The following multiple regression best subset analysis assesses which of these Xs significantly impacted the Y response.

IEE Volume III Example and Dataset

- *IEE Volume III* Example 28.2: Multiple Regression Best Subset Analysis
- *Dataset (Smarter Solutions (2022): V3 C28, Exam 28-02, Four Factor Throughput.xlsx*

SigmaXL or EPRS Metric-App [Smarter Solutions (2020)] Input/Output

- Figure 19.3: SigmaXL Input (Multiple Regression Best Subset Analysis)
- Figure 19.4A: SigmaXL Output (Multiple Regression Best Subset Analysis) – Part 1 of 3
- Figure 19.4B: SigmaXL Output (Multiple Regression Best Subset Analysis) – Part 2 of 3
- Figure 19.4C: SigmaXL Output (Multiple Regression Best Subset Analysis) – Part 3 of 3

SigmaXL Chart Function: Statistical Tools>Advanced Multiple Regression>Fit Multiple Regression Model

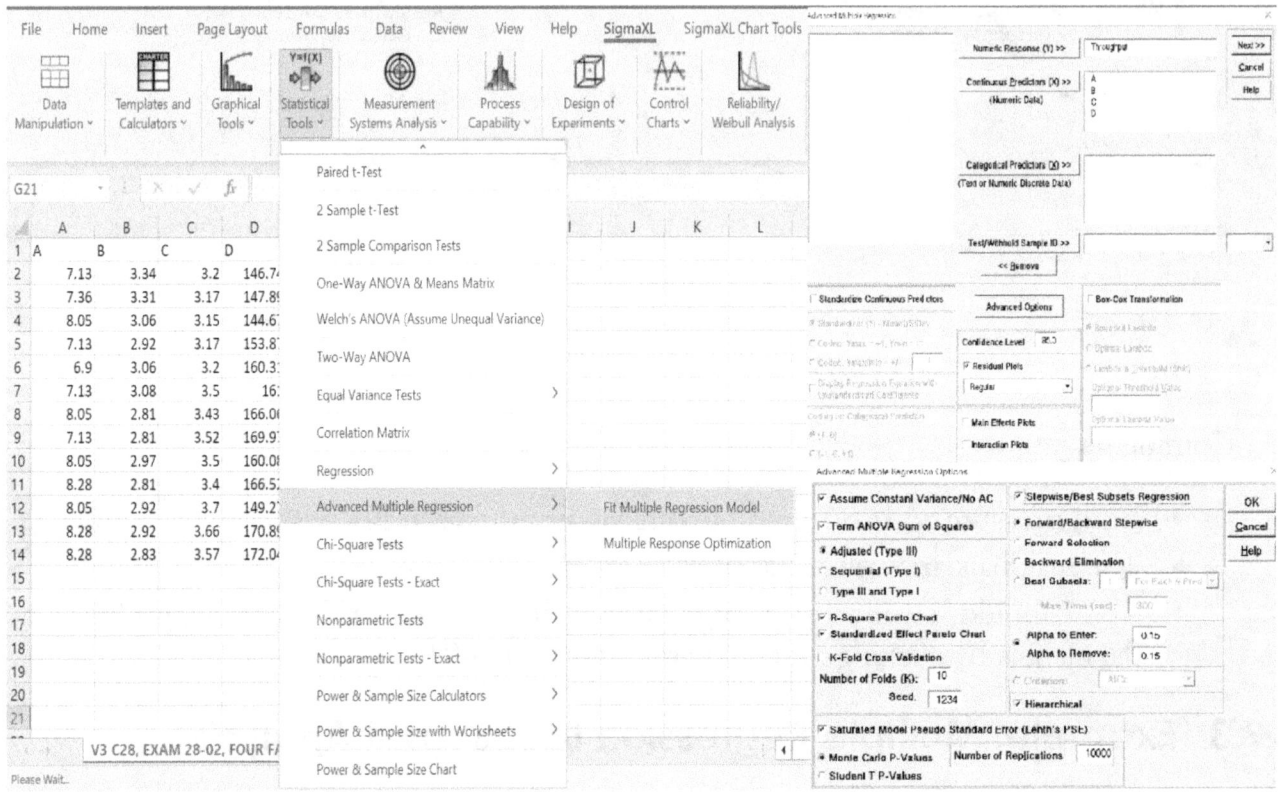

Figure 19.3: SigmaXL Input (Multiple Regression Best Subset Analysis)

Multiple Regression Model: Throughput = (3.87023) + (0.393328)*A + (3.19347)*C + (0.0161887)*D

Model Summary	
R-Square	98.47%
R-Square Adjusted	97.96%
R-Square Predicted	94.78%
S (Root Mean Square Error)	0.1245

Model Information	
Continuous Predictor Standardization/Coding	N/A
Categorical Predictor Coding	N/A
Box-Cox Transformation Lambda/Threshold	N/A
Stepwise Method: Fwd/Back - Hierarchical	Alpha (0.15, 0.15)

Parameter Estimates						
Predictor Term	Coefficient	SE Coefficient	T	P	VIF	Tolerance
Constant	3.870226949	0.712725711	5.4302	0.0004		
A	0.393327864	0.077343789	5.0854	0.0007	1.3685	0.7307
C	3.193472273	0.252330522	12.6559	0.0000	1.9294	0.5183
D	0.016188677	0.004569838	3.5425	0.0063	1.5412	0.6488

Analysis of Variance for Model					
Source	DF	SS	MS	F	P
Model	3	8.981432968	2.993810989	193.0138	0.0000
Error	9	0.139597801	0.015510867		
Total (Model + Error)	12	9.121030769	0.760085897		

Figure 19.4A: SigmaXL Output (Multiple Regression Best Subset Analysis) – Part 1 of 3

Comments

- Best model for throughput (Y) has A, C, and D terms (Xs), provides a reasonable model estimate with the fewest number of terms
- The regression equation for a 3-parameter model is: Throughput = 3.87 + 0.393 A + 3.19 C + 0.0162 D
- Variance inflation factor (VIF) measures the amount of multicollinearity in multiple regression variables. A VIF of three or below is not a cause for concern, and the regression results are less reliable as the VIF increases.

Analysis of Variance for Predictors (Adjusted Type III)							
Predictor Term	DF	SS	MS	F	P	R-Square	Std. Effect (T)
A	1	0.401138742	0.401138742	25.8618	0.0007	4.40%	5.0854
C	1	2.484407297	2.484407297	160.1720	0.0000	27.24%	12.6559
D	1	0.194651219	0.194651219	12.5493	0.0063	2.13%	3.5425

Durbin-Watson Test for Autocorrelation in Residuals	
DW Statistic	2.4680
P-Value Positive Autocorrelation	0.7358
P-Value Negative Autocorrelation	0.1100

Breusch-Pagan Test for Constant Variance (Normal)			
H0: Variance is constant; Ha: Variance is not constant.			
Predictor Term	Chi-Square	DF	P-Value
All Terms	2.93037	3	0.4025
A	2.2501	1	0.1336
C	1.9211	1	0.1657
D	1.29962	1	0.2543

Figure 19.4B: SigmaXL Input (Multiple Regression from Best Subset Analysis) – Part 2 of 3

Comments

- Analysis of Variance for predictors show that all 3 terms are statistically significant

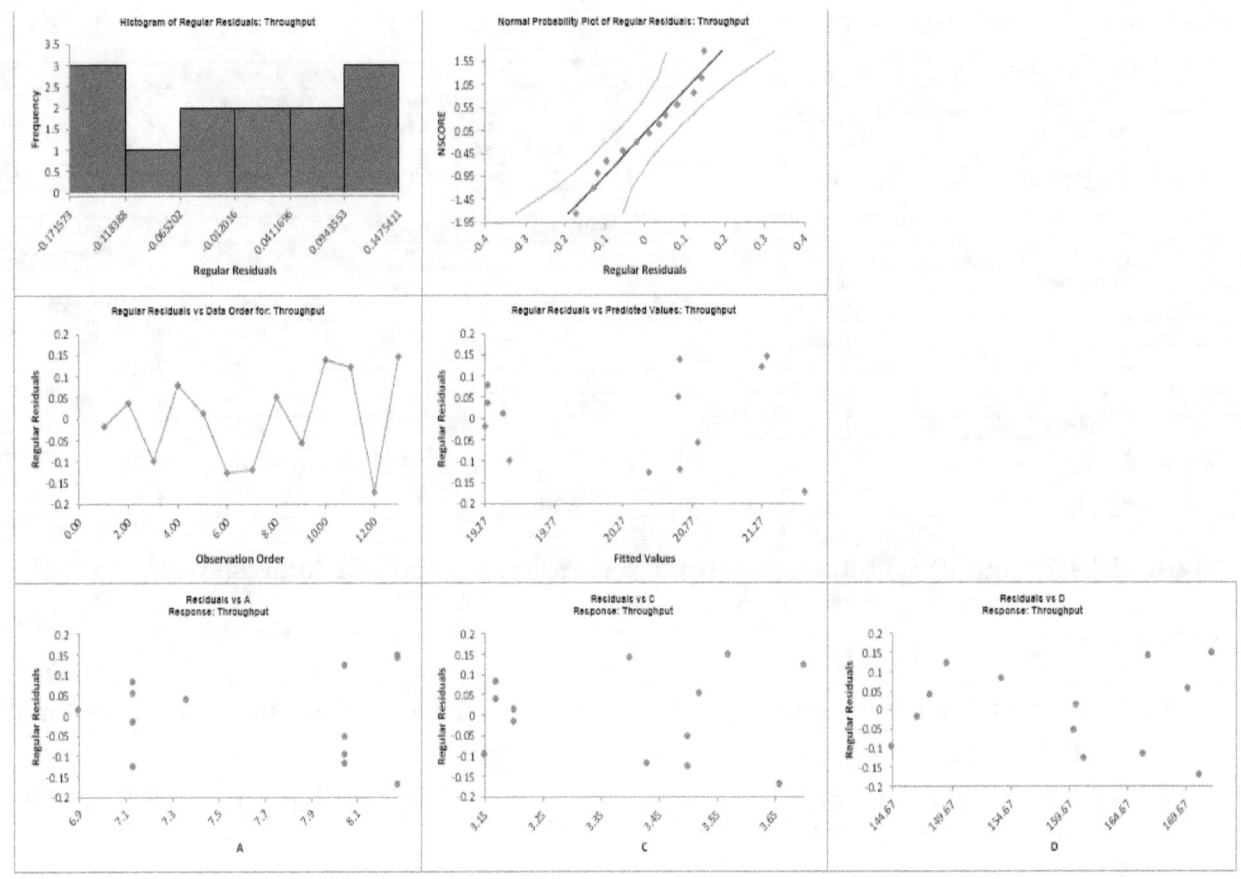

Figure 19.4C: SigmaXL Output (Multiple Regression from Best Subset Analysis) – Part 3 of 3

Comments

- There were no observed problems with the residual analysis.

19.4   Example: Fit Multiple Regression Model

Application

- The 30,000-foot-level Y response metric for a product is unsatisfactory.
- A team identified two discrete factors and a continuous-response X input that they thought could impact the Y response.
- The following analysis assesses which Xs may significantly affect the Y response.

IEE Volume III Example and Dataset

- *IEE Volume III* Example 28.4: GLM with Factors and Covariates
- *Dataset (Smarter Solutions (2022): V3 C28, Exam 28-04, indicator variables with covariate.xlsx*

SigmaXL or EPRS Metric-App [Smarter Solutions (2020)] Input/Output

- Figure 19.7 A: SigmaXL Input (Multiple Regression Model) Part 1 of 2
- Figure 19.7 B: SigmaXL Input (Multiple Regression Model) Part 2 of 2
- Figure 19.8 A: SigmaXL Output (Multiple Regression Model) Part 1 of 2
- Figure 19.8 B: SigmaXL Output (Multiple Regression Model) Part 2 of 2

SigmaXL Chart Function: Statistical Tools>Advanced Multiple Regression> Fit Multiple Regression Model

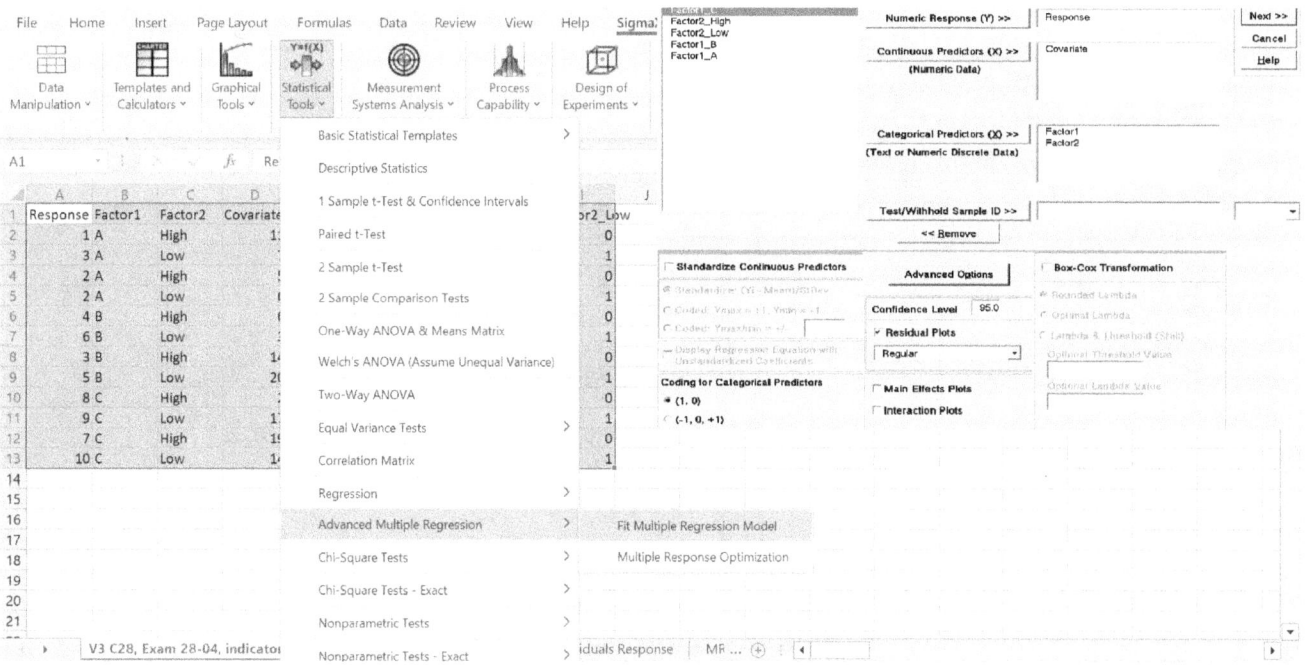

Figure 19.7A: SigmaXL Input (Multiple Regression Model) Part 1 of 2

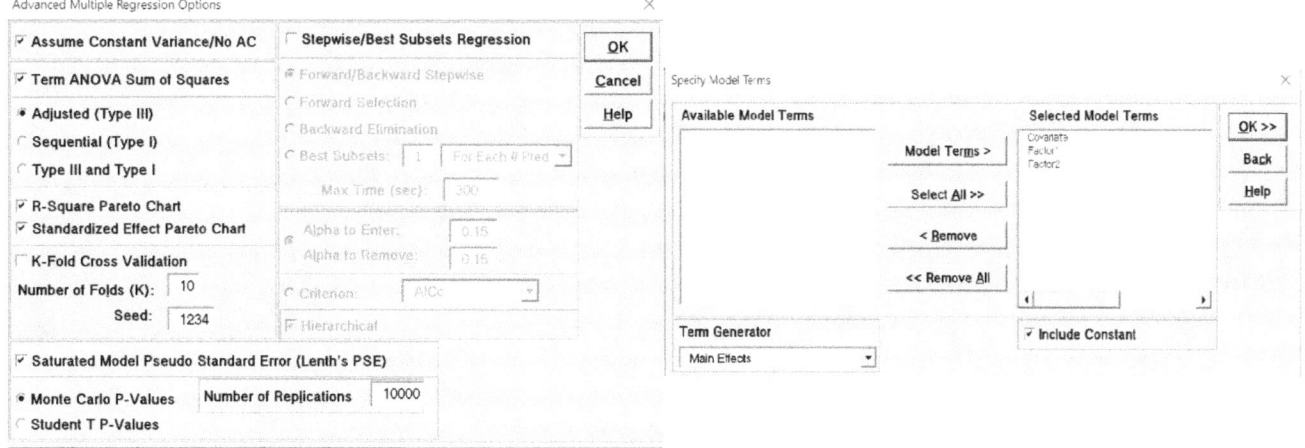

Figure 19.7B: SigmaXL Input (Multiple Regression Model) Part 2 of 2

Multiple Regression Model: Response = (1.55032) + (-0.0597901)*Covariate + (2.70927)*(IF(Factor1="B",1,0)) + (6.84379)*(IF(Factor1="C",1,0)) + (1.76632)*(IF(Factor2="Low",1,0))

Model Summary	
R-Square	97.59%
R-Square Adjusted	96.21%
R-Square Predicted	93.85%
S (Root Mean Square Error)	0.5808

Model Information	
Continuous Predictor Standardization/Coding	N/A
Categorical Predictor Coding	(1,0)
Box-Cox Transformation Lambda/Threshold	N/A
Stepwise Method	N/A

Information Criteria and Validation	
AICc	43.3459
BIC	29.4554
R-Square 10-Fold	N/A
S 10-Fold	N/A

Parameter Estimates						
Predictor Term	Coefficient	SE Coefficient	T	P	VIF	Tolerance
Constant	1.55031949	0.387910417	3.9966	0.0052		
Covariate	-0.0597901	0.030393202	-1.9672	0.0899	1.2068	0.8287
Factor1_B	2.70926518	0.424238552	6.3862	0.0004	1.4228	0.7028
Factor1_C	6.84379279	0.446320659	15.3338	0.0000	1.5748	0.6350
Factor2_Low	1.76631675	0.339126033	5.2084	0.0012	1.0228	0.9777

Predictors	Enter Settings:	Predicted Response
Covariate	10.33333333	0.93248897
Factor1	A	
Factor2	High	

Goal:	Target
Target:	

Analysis of Variance for Model					
Source	DF	SS	MS	F	P
Model	4	95.63874943	23.90968736	70.8810	0.0000
Error	7	2.361250571	0.33732151		
Total (Model + Error)	11	98	8.909090909		

Analysis of Variance for Predictors (Adjusted Type III)							
Predictor Term	DF	SS	MS	F	P	R-Square	Std. Effect (T)
Covariate	1	1.305416096	1.305416096	3.8699	0.0899	1.33%	1.9672
Factor1	2	81.13091083	40.56545541	120.2575	0.0000	82.79%	12.9517
Factor2	1	9.150797622	9.150797622	27.1278	0.0012	9.34%	5.2084

Figure 19.8 A: Output (Multiple Regression Model) Part 1 of 2

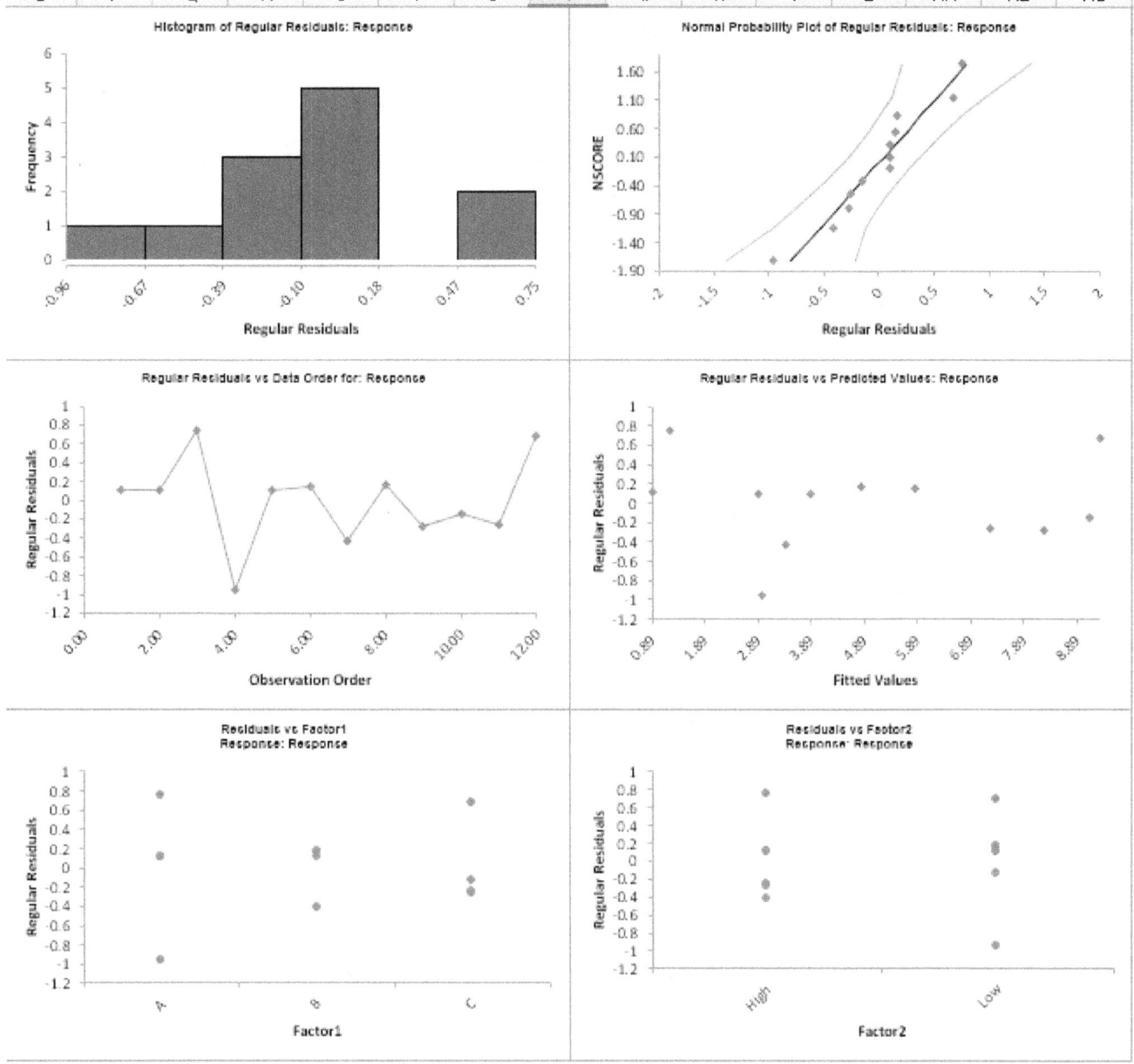

Figure 19.8 B: Output (Multiple Regression Model) Part 2 of 2

Comments

- This analysis indicates the significance of the model's factors and covariate X inputs.
- A team could use this information to determine the best X settings to improve the 30,000-foot-level report response (Y) from the regression equation.

19.5 Example: Binary Logistic Regression

Application

- The 30,000-foot-level Y failure rate reporting response for ingots is unsatisfactory.
- A team identified heat and soak as two X inputs that they thought could impact the Y response.
- The following Binary Logistic Regression analysis assesses which Xs may significantly affect the Y pass/fail response.
- Any X input significance can influence a team's direction for improving the Y-response enhancement process.

IEE Volume III Example and Dataset

- *IEE Volume III* Example 28.5: Binary Logistic Regression for Ingot Preparation
- Dataset (Smarter Solutions (2022): V3 C28, Exam 28-05, Ingot logistic regression.xlsx

SigmaXL or EPRS Metric-App [Smarter Solutions (2020)] Input/Output

- Figure 19.9: SigmaXL Input (Binary Logistic Regression)
- Figure 19.10 A: SigmaXL Output (Binary Logistic Regression) Part 1 of 2
- Figure 19.10 B: SigmaXL Output (Binary Logistic Regression) Part 2 of 2

SigmaXL Chart Function: Statistical Tools>Regression>Binary Logistic Regression

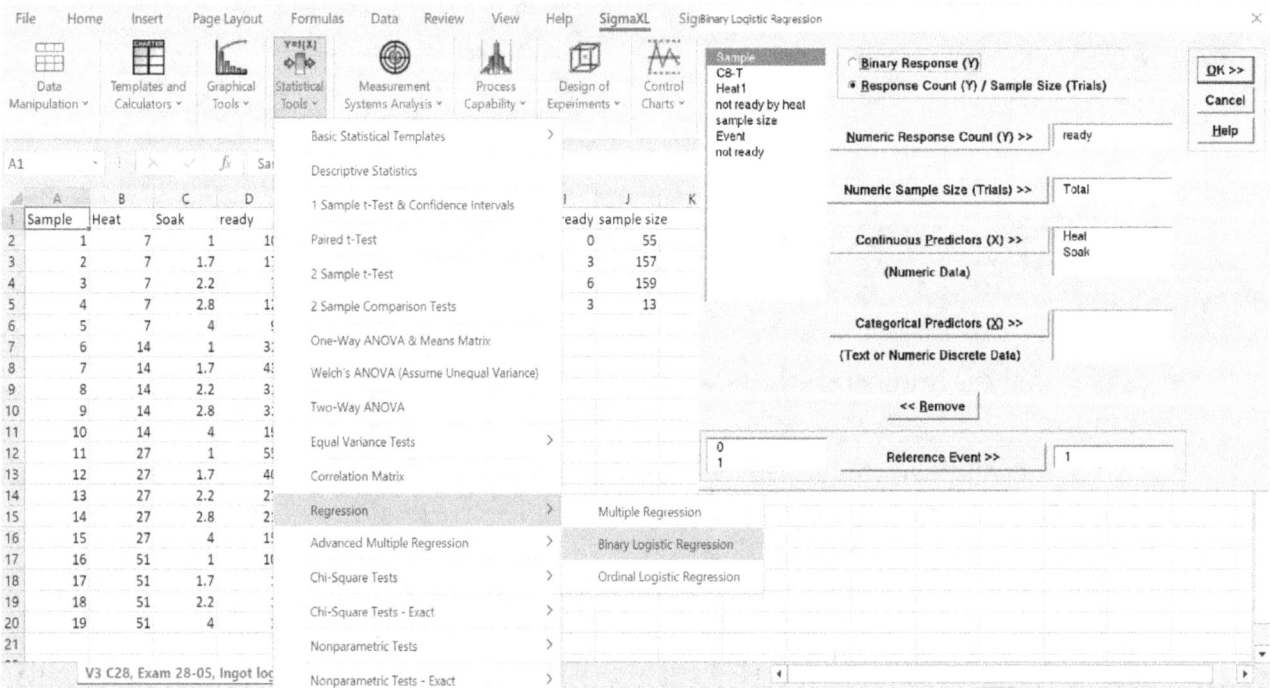

Figure 19.9: SigmaXL Input (Binary Logistic Regression)

Binary Logistic Regression Model: ln(Py/(1-Py)) = (5.559) + (-0.082030802) * Heat + (-0.056771312) * Soak
Logit Link

Response Summary: ready

Value		Count	Proportion	Reference Event
	0	12	0.031007752	
	1	375	0.968992248	x
Total		387		

Parameter Estimates:

Term	Coefficient	SE Coefficient	Z	P	Odds Ratio	Lower 95% Odds Ratio	Upper 95% Odds Ratio
Constant	5.559	1.120	4.965	0.0000			
Heat	-0.082030802	0.023734471	-3.456	0.0005	0.921244	0.879369	0.965112
Soak	-0.056771312	0.331213	-0.171404	0.8639	0.944810	0.493640	1.808

Figure 19.10 A: SigmaXL Output (Binary Logistic Regression) Part 1 of 2

Model Summary and Goodness-of-Fit Statistics:

Log-Likelihood	-47.673
Test that all slope coefficients are equal to zero:	
Likelihood Ratio Chi-Square (G)	11.643
DF	2
P-Value	0.0030
McFadden's Pseudo R-Square	10.88%
Goodness-of-Fit Tests (P-Value < .05 indicates Lack-of-Fit):	
Pearson Residuals Chi-Square	13.543
DF	16
P-Value	0.6327
Deviance Residuals Chi-Square	13.753
DF	16
P-Value	0.6171
Hosmer-Lemeshow Chi-Square	4.070
DF	5
P-Value	0.5394
Measures of Association	
Concordant	3201
Discordant	724
Ties	575
Total	4500
Concordant Percent	71.13
Discordant Percent	16.09
Ties Percent	12.78
Goodman-Kruskal Gamma	0.631083
Somers' D	0.550444
Kendall's Tau-a	0.0332

Observed and Predicted Outcomes:

Observed Outcome	Predicted Outcome		Row Total
	$\hat{Y} = 0$	$\hat{Y} = 1$	
Y = 0	0	12	12
Y = 1	0	375	375
Column Total	0	387	387
Percent Correctly Predicted:	96.90%		

Figure 19.10 B: SigmaXL Output (Binary Logistic Regression) Part 2 of 2

Comments

- The Heat variable is found significant at a P-Value of 0.0005
- The Soak variable is not found significant
- The residual analysis indicates that there should be a causal investigation of some datum points
- A team could use this information to determine what changes to make in the process to reduce the 30,000-foot-level reported failure rate

20

IEE-DMAIC — Improve Phase: Design of Experiments (DOE)

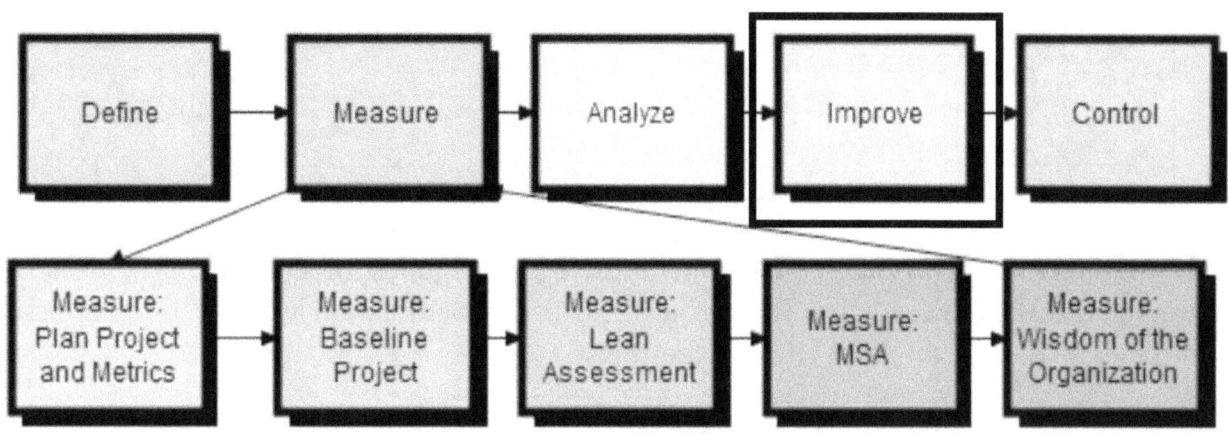

20.1 IEE-DMAIC Roadmap Component

Book 1 Reference: *IEE Volume III* – Chapters 29 – 34

Book 2 Reference: *Lean Six Sigma Project Execution Guide* – Section 8

Internet: www.smartersolutions.com/roadmap (clicking on highlighted area provides the flowchart below)

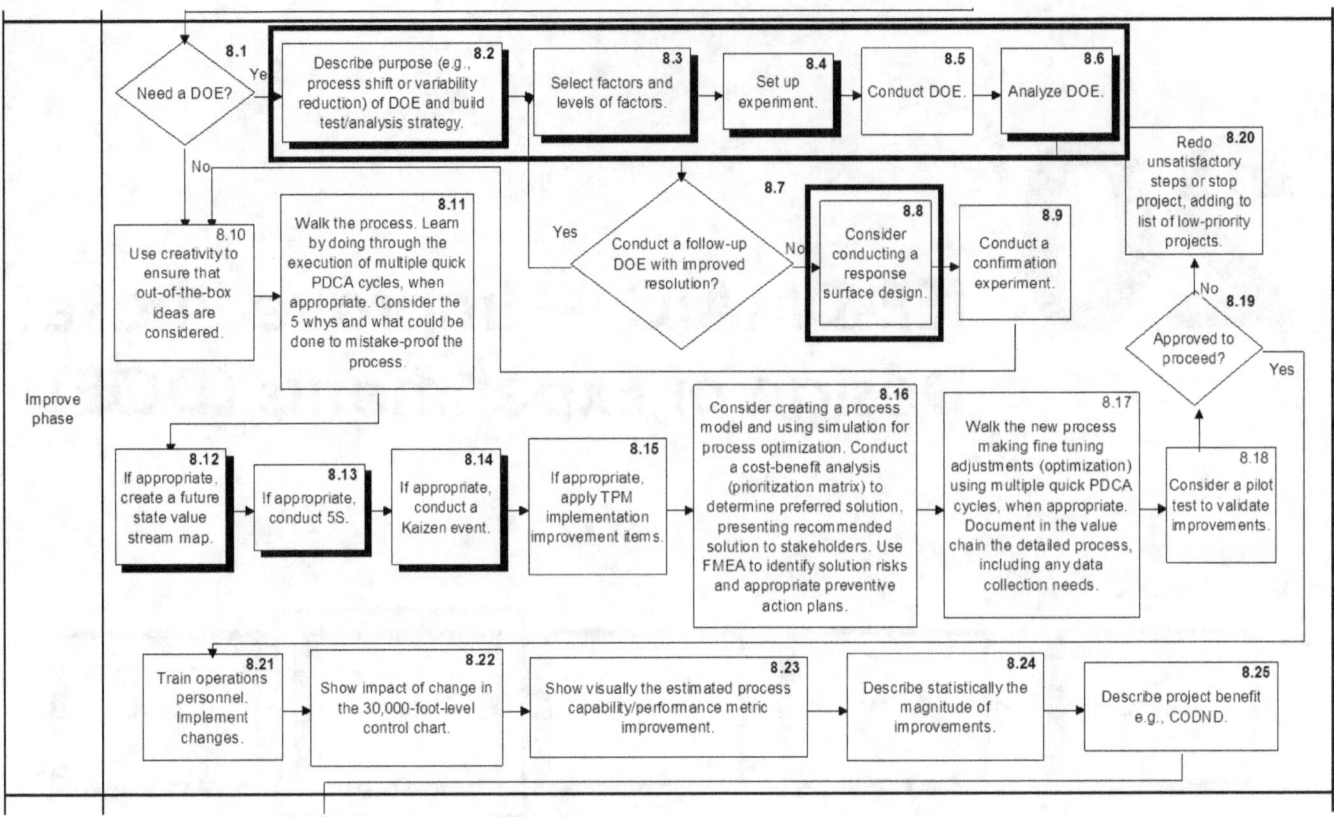

This IEE DMAIC improve-phase includes the mechanics of conducting a design of experiments (DOE); however, the IEE project execution roadmap includes DOE as a possible tool in the early part of the DMAIC analyze-phase.

20.2 Example: Resolution V DOE

Application

- The 30,000-foot-level Y response report for the settle-out time of a stepper motor is unsatisfactory.
- A team identified five X factors for inclusion in a DOE to determine what factor levels might reduce the settle-out time of the stepper motor.
- The following DOE assesses which Xs might significantly impact the Y response.
- Any identified factor-level significance can influence a team's direction for improving the Y-response process.
- The DOE trials in the dataset below were created outside of SigmaXL. Because of this, one needs to use SigmaXL's function to create a custom design, as shown in Figure 20.3.

IEE Volume III Example and Dataset

- *IEE Volume III* Example 32.1: A Resolutions V DOE
- Dataset (Smarter Solutions (2022): V3 C32, Exam 32-01, Stepper motor DOE.xlsx

SigmaXL or EPRS Metric-App [Smarter Solutions (2020)] Input/Output

- Figure 20.1: SigmaXL Input (Creating a Resolution V DOE)
- Figure 20.2: SigmaXL Output (Creating a Resolution V DOE)
- Figure 20.3: SigmaXL Input (Analyze a Design Resolution V DOE)
- Figure 20.4: SigmaXL Output (Analyze **a** Design Resolution V DOE)
- Figure 20.5: SigmaXL Output (Analyze **a** Design Resolution V DOE)
- Figure 20.6: SigmaXL Output (Analyze a Design Resolution V DOE – Pareto Chart of Coefficients)
- Figure 20.7: SigmaXL Input (Analysis of a Resolution V DOE –factors only)
- Figure 20.8 A: SigmaXL Output (Analysis of a Resolution V DOE –factors only) Part 1 of 2
- Figure 20.8 B: SigmaXL Output (Analysis of a Resolution V DOE –factors only) Part 2 of 2

SigmaXL Chart Function: Design of Experiments>2-Level Factorial/Screening>2 -Level Factorial/Screening Design

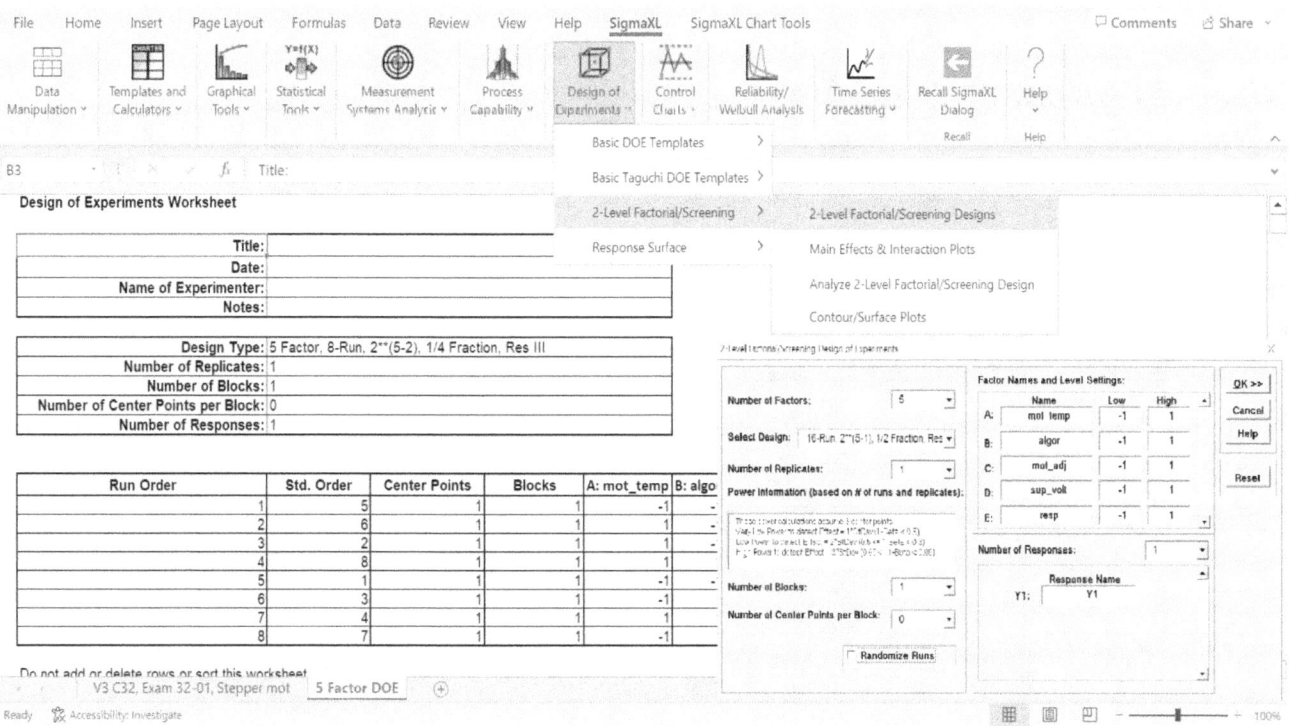

Figure 20.1: SigmaXL Input (Creating a Resolution V DOE)

Run Order	Std. Order	Center Points	Blocks	A: mot_temp	B: algor	C: mot_adj	D: sup_volt	E: algor_mtr	resp
1	7	1	1	1	-1	-1	-1	1	5.6
2	6	1	1	1	1	-1	-1	-1	2.1
3	11	1	1	1	1	1	-1	1	4.9
4	16	1	1	1	1	1	1	-1	4.9
5	14	1	1	-1	1	1	1	1	4.1
6	5	1	1	1	-1	1	1	1	5.6
7	9	1	1	-1	1	-1	1	-1	1.9
8	2	1	1	1	-1	1	-1	-1	7.2
9	13	1	1	1	1	-1	1	1	2.4
10	10	1	1	-1	1	1	-1	-1	5.1
11	8	1	1	-1	-1	1	1	-1	7.9
12	15	1	1	1	-1	-1	1	-1	5.3
13	12	1	1	-1	1	-1	-1	1	2.1
14	1	1	1	-1	-1	1	-1	1	7.6
15	3	1	1	-1	-1	-1	1	1	5.5
16	4	1	1	-1	-1	-1	-1	-1	5.3

Figure 20.2: SigmaXL Output (Creating a Resolution V DOE)

Comments

- This is a SigmaXL standard design for a 5-factor, 16-trial experiment
- For this design, one would enter trial responses in a column to the right of the design for analysis
- SigmaXL Chart Function: Design of Experiments>2-Level Factorial/Screening>Analyze 2-Level Factorial /Screening Design

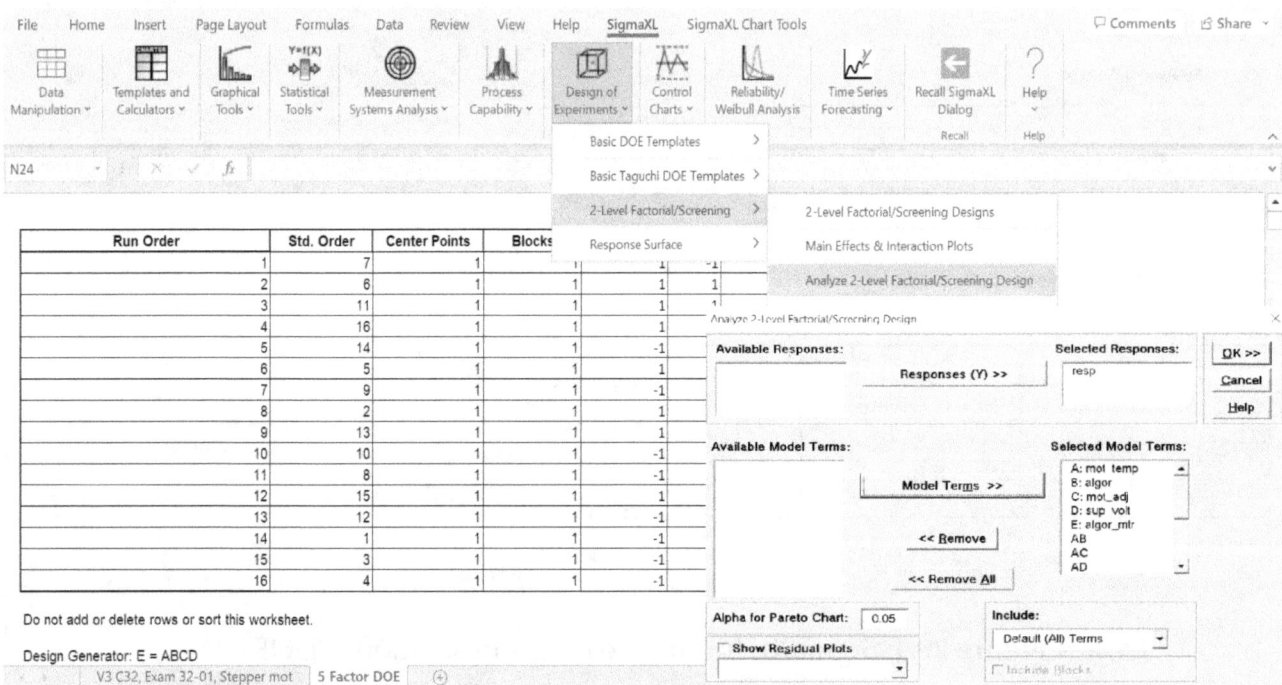

Figure 20.3: SigmaXL Input (Analyze a Design Resolution V DOE)

SigmaXL® and Lean Six Sigma

File　Home　Insert　Page Layout　Formulas　Data　Review　View　Help　**SigmaXL**　SigmaXL Chart Tools

| Data Manipulation ⌄ | Templates and Calculators ⌄ | Graphical Tools ⌄ | Statistical Tools ⌄ | Measurement Systems Analysis ⌄ | Process Capability ⌄ | Design of Experiments ⌄ | Control Charts ⌄ | Reliability/ Weibull Analysis |

J50　▾　⋮　✕　✓　*fx*

Design of Experiments Analysis

DOE Multiple Regression Model: resp = (4.84375) + (-0.09375) ˚ A: mot_temp + (-1.40625) ˚ B: algor + (1.06875) ˚ C: mot_adj + (-0.14375) ˚ D: sup_volt + (-0.11875) ˚ E: algor_m

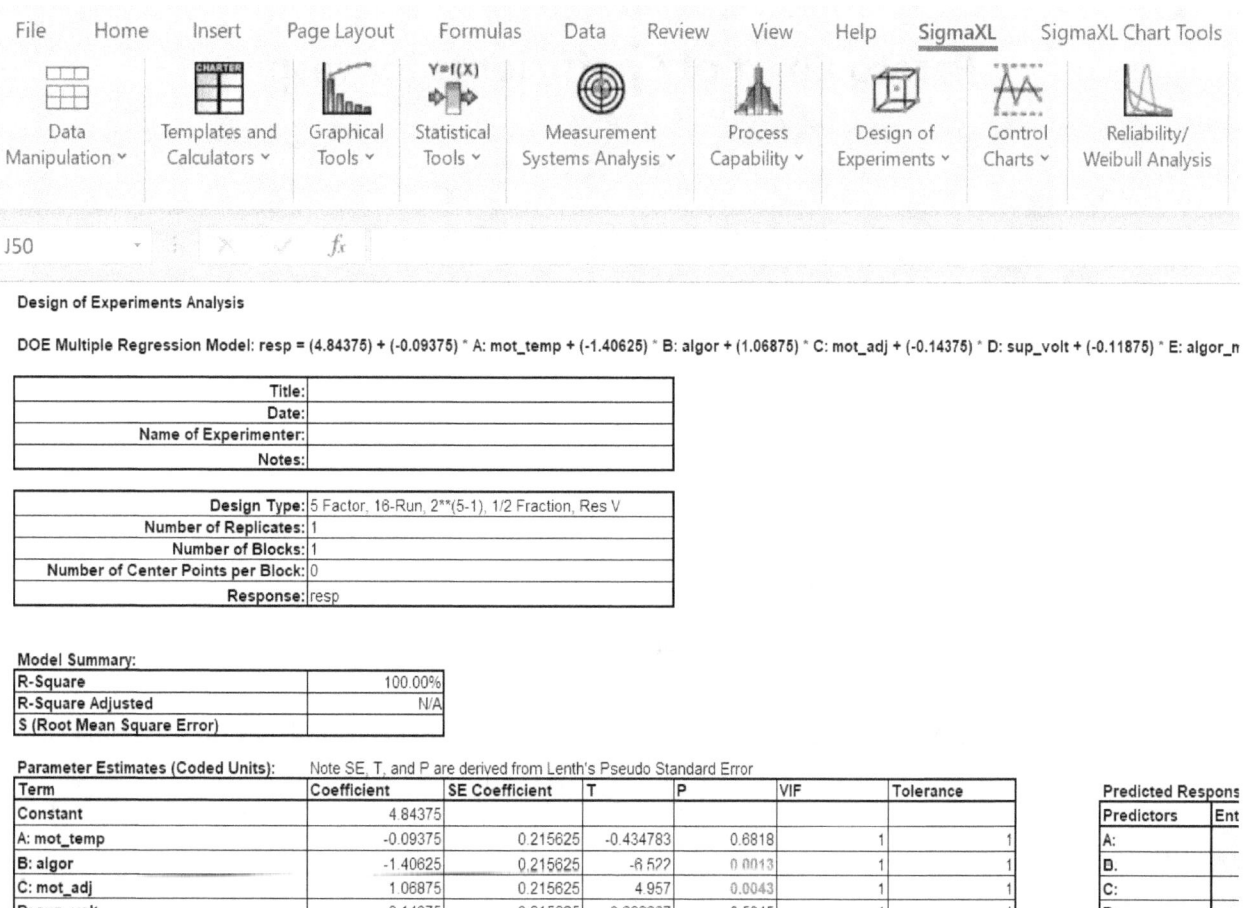

Title:	
Date:	
Name of Experimenter:	
Notes:	

Design Type:	5 Factor, 16-Run, 2**(5-1), 1/2 Fraction, Res V
Number of Replicates:	1
Number of Blocks:	1
Number of Center Points per Block:	0
Response:	resp

Model Summary:

R-Square	100.00%
R-Square Adjusted	N/A
S (Root Mean Square Error)	

Parameter Estimates (Coded Units):　Note SE, T, and P are derived from Lenth's Pseudo Standard Error

Term	Coefficient	SE Coefficient	T	P	VIF	Tolerance
Constant	4.84375					
A: mot_temp	-0.09375	0.215625	-0.434783	0.6818	1	1
B: algor	-1.40625	0.215625	-6.522	0.0013	1	1
C: mot_adj	1.06875	0.215625	4.957	0.0043	1	1
D: sup_volt	-0.14375	0.215625	-0.666667	0.5345	1	1
E: algor_mtr	-0.11875	0.215625	-0.550725	0.6055	1	1
AB	0.23125	0.215625	1.07246377	0.3325	1	1
AC	-0.16875	0.215625	-0.782609	0.4693	1	1

Predicted Respons

Predictors	Ent
A:	
B:	
C:	
D:	
E:	

Figure 20.4: SigmaXL Output (Analyze a Design Resolution V DOE)

Parameter Estimates (Coded Units):　Note SE, T, and P are derived from Lenth's Pseudo Standard Error

Term	Coefficient	SE Coefficient	T	P	VIF	Tolerance
Constant	4.84375					
A: mot_temp	-0.09375	0.215625	-0.434783	0.6818	1	1
B: algor	-1.40625	0.215625	-6.522	0.0013	1	1
C: mot_adj	1.06875	0.215625	4.957	0.0043	1	1
D: sup_volt	-0.14375	0.215625	-0.666667	0.5345	1	1
E: algor_mtr	-0.11875	0.215625	-0.550725	0.6055	1	1
AB	0.23125	0.215625	1.07246377	0.3325	1	1
AC	-0.16875	0.215625	-0.782609	0.4693	1	1
AD	-0.05625	0.215625	-0.260870	0.8046	1	1
AE	-0.00625	0.215625	-0.0289855	0.9780	1	1
BC	0.24375	0.215625	1.130	0.3096	1	1
BD	0.03125	0.215625	0.144928	0.8904	1	1
BE	0.05625	0.215625	0.260870	0.8046	1	1
CD	-0.14375	0.215625	-0.666667	0.5345	1	1
CE	-0.24375	0.215625	-1.130	0.3096	1	1
DE	-0.18125	0.215625	-0.840580	0.4389	1	1

Figure 20.5: SigmaXL Output (Analyze a Design Resolution V DOE)

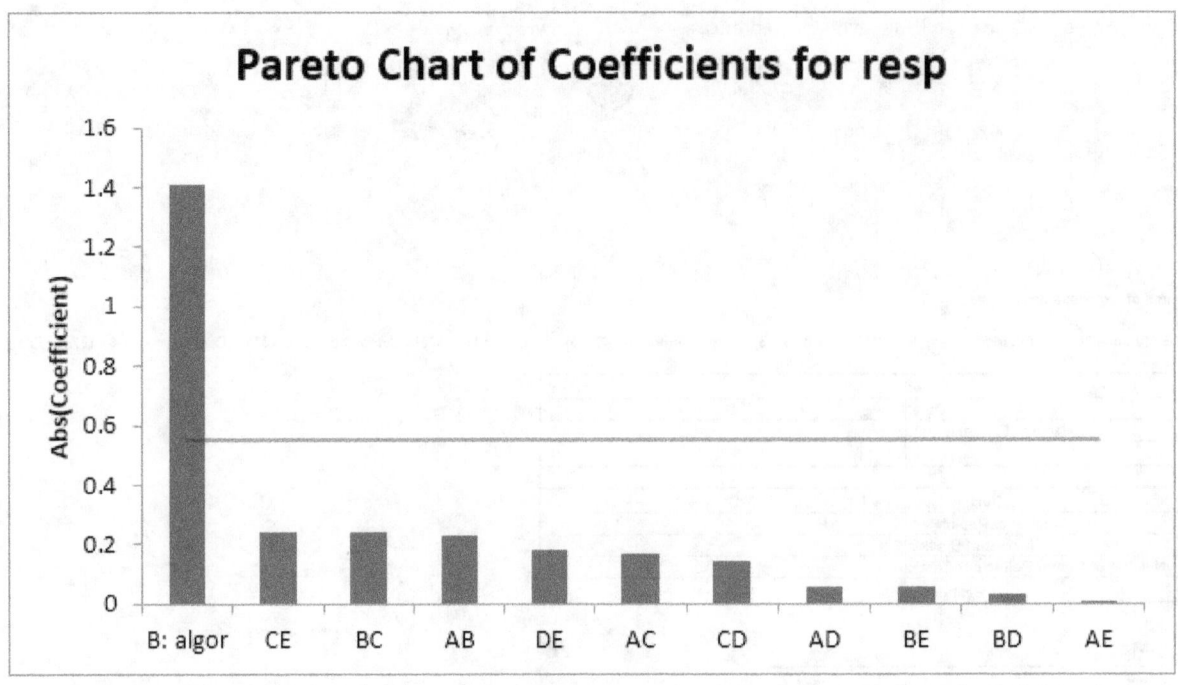

Figure 20.6: SigmaXL Output (Analyze a Design Resolution V DOE – Pareto Chart of Coefficients)

Comments

- Factors B (Algor) and C (Mot_adj) are the only factors that appear significant
- The analysis did not identify any two-factor interaction as an X input that would impact the Y settle-out time response
- A model of only the main effects for X inputs is shown in the following figures

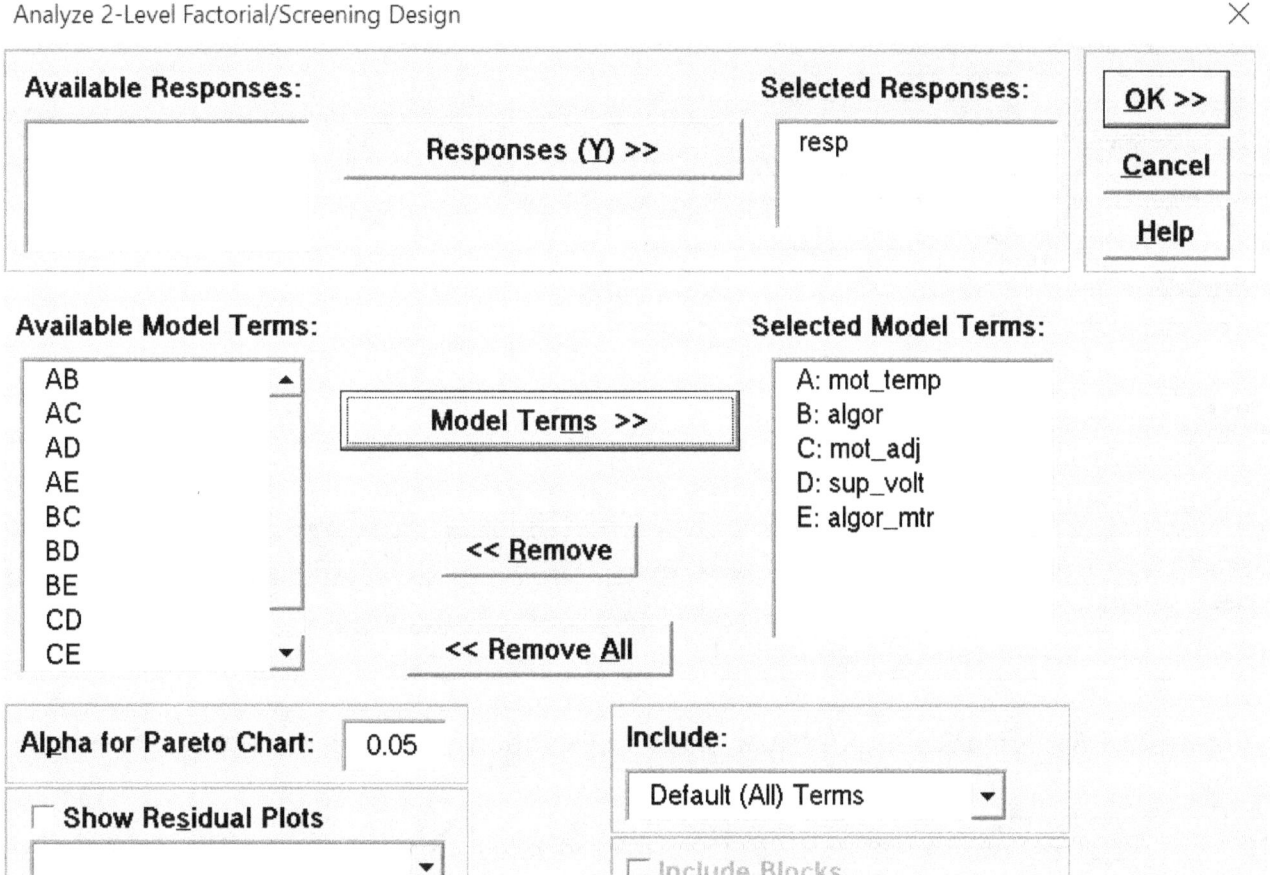

Figure 20.7: SigmaXL Input (Analysis of a Resolution V DOE –factors only)

Comment

- The model input shown in Figure 20.7 included all the main effects
- However, one could have entered into the model only factors B and C from the previous Figure 20.5

Design of Experiments Analysis

DOE Multiple Regression Model: resp = (4.84375) + (-0.09375) * A: mot_temp + (-1.40625) * B: algor + (1.06875) * C: mot_adj + (-0.14375) * D: sup_volt + (-0.11875) * E: algor_mtr

Title:	
Date:	
Name of Experimenter:	
Notes:	

Design Type:	5 Factor, 16-Run, 2**(5-1), 1/2 Fraction, Res V
Number of Replicates:	1
Number of Blocks:	1
Number of Center Points per Block:	0
Response:	resp

Model Summary:

R-Square	92.36%
R-Square Adjusted	88.54%
S (Root Mean Square Error)	0.647012

Parameter Estimates (Coded Units):

Term	Coefficient	SE Coefficient	T	P	VIF	Tolerance		Predicted Response Calc
Constant	4.84375	0.161753091	29.945	0.0000				Predictors	Enter Act
A: mot_temp	-0.09375	0.161753091	-0.579587	0.5750	1	1	A:	
B: algor	-1.40625	0.161753091	-8.694	0.0000	1	1	B:	
C: mot_adj	1.06875	0.161753091	6.607	0.0001	1	1	C:	
D: sup_volt	-0.14375	0.161753091	-0.888700	0.3950	1	1	D:	
E: algor_mtr	-0.11875	0.161753091	-0.734144	0.4797	1	1	E:	

Figure 20.8 A: SigmaXL Output (Analysis of a Resolution V DOE –factors only) Part 1 of 2

Model Summary:

R-Square	92.36%
R-Square Adjusted	88.54%
S (Root Mean Square Error)	0.647012

Parameter Estimates (Coded Units):

Term	Coefficient	SE Coefficient	T	P	VIF	Tolerance
Constant	4.84375	0.161753091	29.945	0.0000		
A: mot_temp	-0.09375	0.161753091	-0.579587	0.5750	1	1
B: algor	-1.40625	0.161753091	-8.694	0.0000	1	1
C: mot_adj	1.06875	0.161753091	6.607	0.0001	1	1
D: sup_volt	-0.14375	0.161753091	-0.888700	0.3950	1	1
E: algor_mtr	-0.11875	0.161753091	-0.734144	0.4797	1	1

Analysis of Variance for Model:

Source	DF	SS	MS	F	P
Model	5	50.613	10.123	24.181	0.0000
Error	10	4.186	0.418625		
Total (Model + Error)	15	54.799	3.653		

Durbin-Watson Test for Autocorrelation in Residuals:

DW Statistic	1.479
P-Value Positive Autocorrelation	0.1530
P-Value Negative Autocorrelation	0.8476

Figure 20.8 B: SigmaXL Output (Analysis of a Resolution V DOE –factors only) Part 2 of 2

Comments

- This SigmaXL analysis indicates the significance of the factors algor and mot_adj.
- This analysis also identified an outlier datum point. *IEE Volume III* describes removing this outlier and refining the regression equation.

20.3 Example: Response Surface Methodology (RSM)

Application

- The magnitude of the 30,000-foot-level Y response reporting for product yield was unsatisfactorily low.
- An earlier two-level factorial experiment of many X-factor considerations indicated that reaction time and temperature were significant Xs to increase the Y response.
- Previous experimentation also revealed that there could be a non-linear Y=f(X) relationship; hence, the team needed to design and conduct a Response Surface Methodology (RSM) experiment.
- The process-improvement team chose a central composite design to investigate further a potential non-linear Y=f(X) relationship for improving the production process.
- For this situation, the second-degree model can be fit using the natural levels of the variables (e.g., time = 80) or the "coded levels" (e.g., time = - 1).
- A statistical analysis of yield in terms of the coded variables follows.
- Like the previous DOE example, this dataset RSM design was created outside SigmaXL; hence, the design dataset needed "customization."

IEE Volume III Example and Dataset

- *IEE Volume III* Example 34.1: Response Surface Design
- Dataset (Smarter Solutions (2022): V3 C34, Exam 34-01, response surface design.xlsx

SigmaXL or EPRS Metric-App [Smarter Solutions (2020)] Input/Output

- Figure 20.9: SigmaXL Input (RSM Design Creation)
- Figure 20.10: SigmaXL Output (RSM Design Creation)
- Figure 20.11: SigmaXL Input (Analyze RSM)
- Figure 20.12: SigmaXL Output (Analyze RSM)
- Figure 20.13: SigmaXL Output (Analyze RSM)
- Figure 20.14 A: SigmaXL Output (Analyze RSM)
- Figure 20.14 B: SigmaXL Output (RSM Design Analysis) Part 2 of 2
- Figure 20.15: SigmaXL Input (RSM Surface Plot Creation)
- Figure 20.16: SigmaXL Output (RSM Surface Plot)

SigmaXL Chart Function: Design of Experiments>Response Surface>Response Surface Design

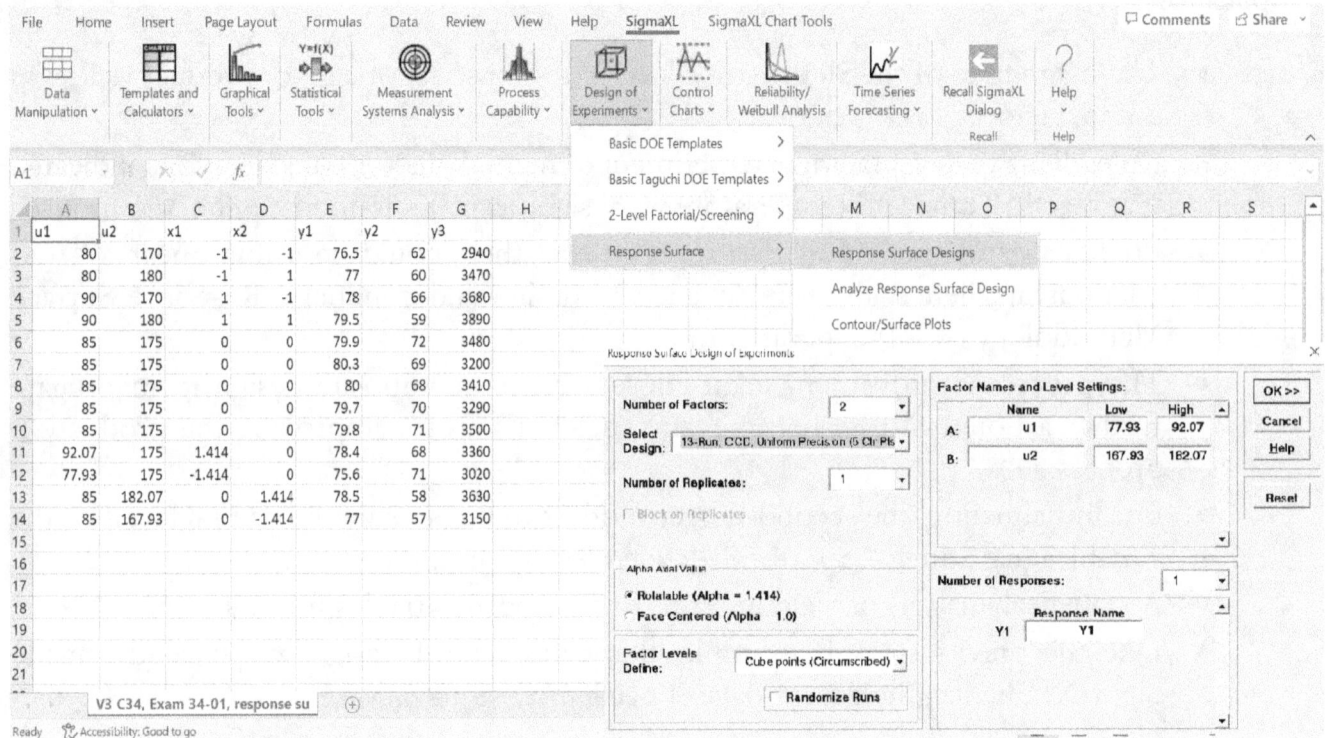

Figure 20.9: SigmaXL Input (RSM Design Creation)

Design Type:	2 Factor, 13-Run, CCD, Uniform Precision (5 Ctr Pts)
Alpha Axial Value:	Rotatable (Alpha = 1.414)
Factor Levels Define:	Cube points (Circumscribed)
Number of Replicates:	1
Block on Replicates:	N/A
Number of Responses:	1

Run Order	Std. Order	Center Points	Blocks	A: u1	B: u2	Y1
1	1	1	1	80	170	76.5
2	2	1	1	80	180	77
3	3	1	1	90	170	78
4	4	1	1	90	180	79.5
5	5	1	1	85	175	79.9
6	6	1	1	85	175	80.3
7	7	1	1	85	175	80
8	8	1	1	85	175	79.7
9	9	0	1	85	175	79.8
10	10	0	1	92.07	175	78.4
11	11	0	1	77.93	175	75.6
12	12	0	1	85	182.07	78.5
13	13	0	1	85	167.93	77

Figure 20.10: SigmaXL Output (RSM Design Creation)

Comment

- Figure 20.10 shows the SigmaXL output for a standard SigmaXL RSM design

SigmaXL Chart Function: Design of Experiments>Response Surface>Analyze Response Surface Design

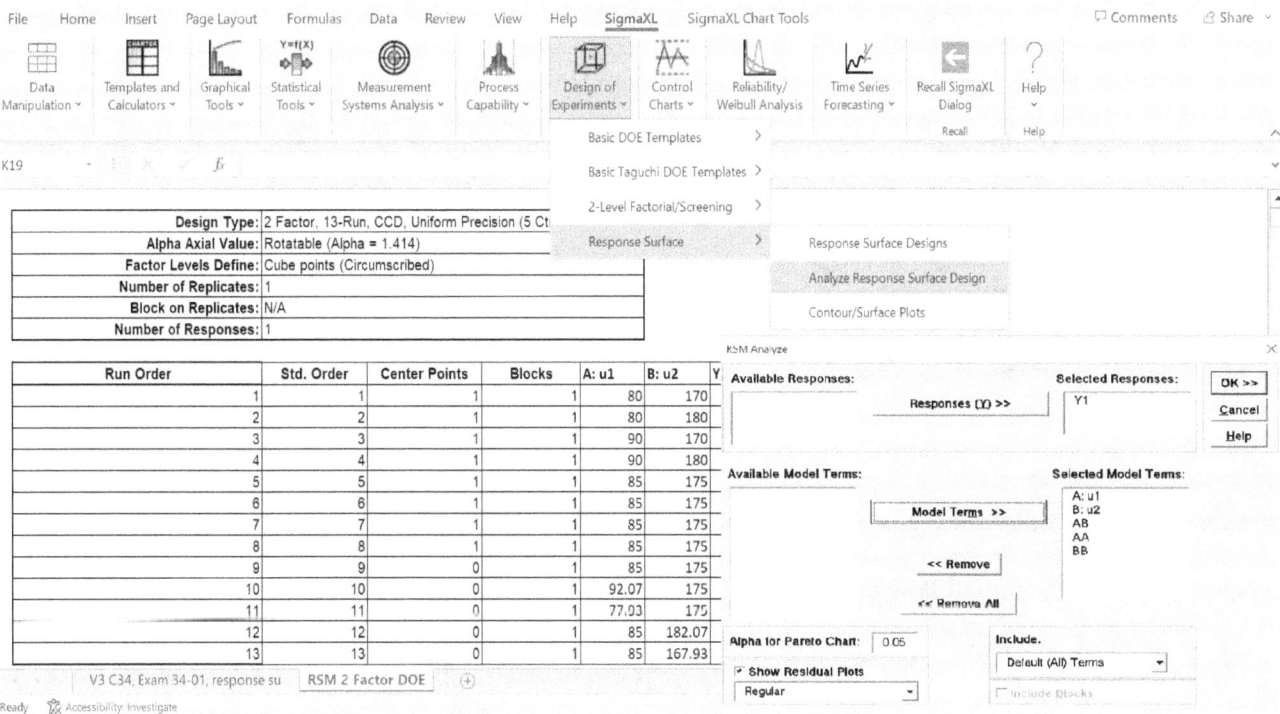

Figure 20.11: SigmaXL Input (Analyze RSM)

Response Surface Methods Analysis

RSM Regression Model: Y1 = (79.93995461) + (1.407001057) * A: u1 + (0.728496753) * B: u2 + (0.499849) * AB + (-2.75206719) * AA + (-2.00206719) * BB

Title:	
Date:	
Name of Experimenter:	
Notes:	

Design Type:	2 Factor, 13-Run, CCD, Uniform Precision (5 Ctr Pts)
Alpha Axial Value:	Rotatable (Alpha = 1.414)
Factor Levels Define:	Cube points (Circumscribed)
Number of Replicates:	1 - Center Points are excluded from the model
Block on Replicates:	N/A
Response	Y1

Model Summary:

R-Square	98.27%
R-Square Adjusted	97.04%
S (Root Mean Square Error)	0.266290

Parameter Estimates (Coded Units):

Term	Coefficient	SE Coefficient	T	P	VIF	Tolerance
Constant	79.93995461	0.11908862	671.26	0.0000		
A: u1	1.407001057	0.133135072	10.568	0.0000	1	1
B: u2	0.728496753	0.133135072	5.472	0.0009	1	1
AB	0.499849	0.266209834	1.878	0.1025	1	1
AA	-2.75206719	0.201907343	-13.630	0.0000	1.017267626	0.983025484
BB	-2.00206719	0.201907343	-9.916	0.0000	1.017267626	0.983025484

Figure 20.12: SigmaXL Output (Analyze RSM)

Analysis of Variance for Model:

Source	DF	SS	MS	F	P
Model	5	28.247	5.649	79.669	0.0000
Error	7	0.496373	0.0709105		
Lack of Fit	3	0.284373	0.09479116	1.789	0.2886
Pure Error	4	0.212000	0.053		
Total (Model + Error)	12	28.743	2.395		

Durbin-Watson Test for Autocorrelation in Residuals:

DW Statistic	0.818068
P-Value Positive Autocorrelation	0.0159
P-Value Negative Autocorrelation	0.9796

Figure 20.13: SigmaXL Output (Analyze RSM)

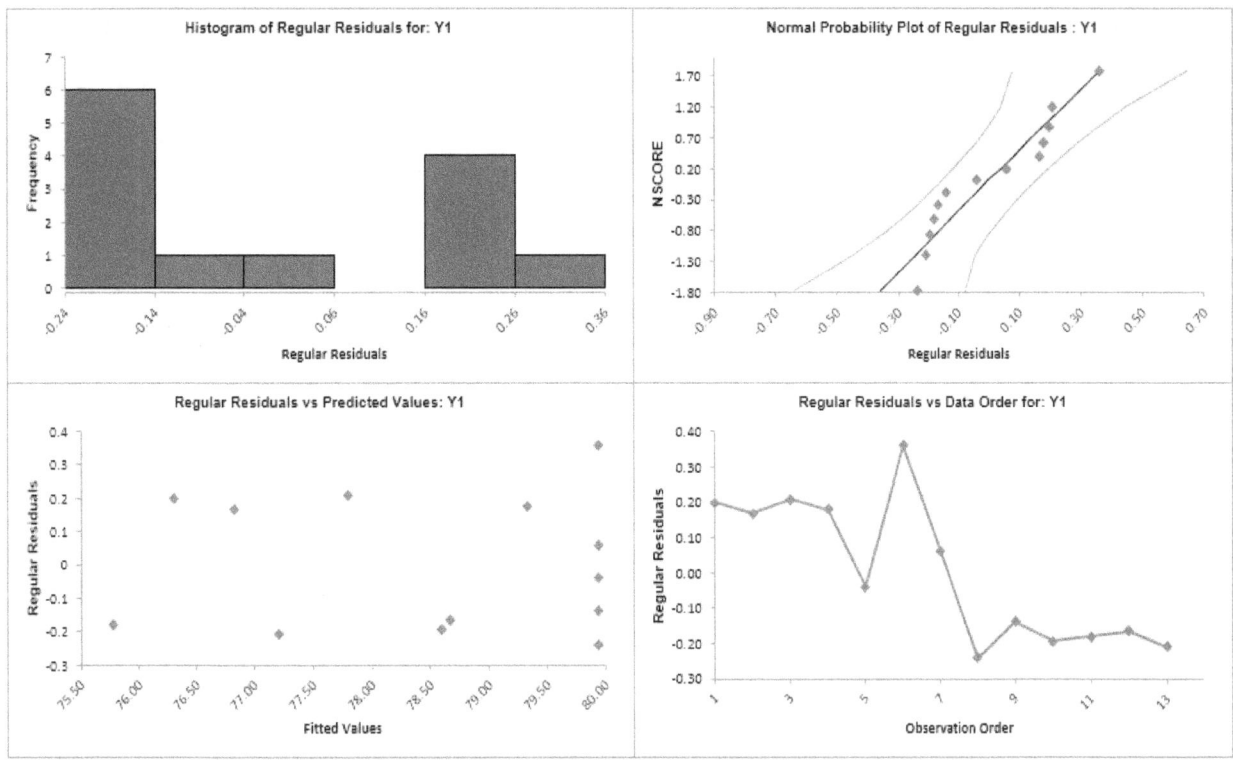

Figure 20.14: SigmaXL Output (Analyze RSM)

Comments

- All terms in the model were significant at a level of 0.05, except for the AB interaction term, which had a P-Value of 0.103.

- The interaction term was left in the model; however, one could remove the interaction term and redo this analysis.

- From the Observation Order graph (residual analysis), an investigation into why the magnitude of residuals decreased from observation eight onward would be appropriate.

- Figures 20.15 and 20.16 provide a contour plot of the created model

SigmaXL Chart Function: Design of Experiments>Response Surface>Contour/Surface Plot

Figure 20.15: SigmaXL Input (RSM Surface Plot Creation)

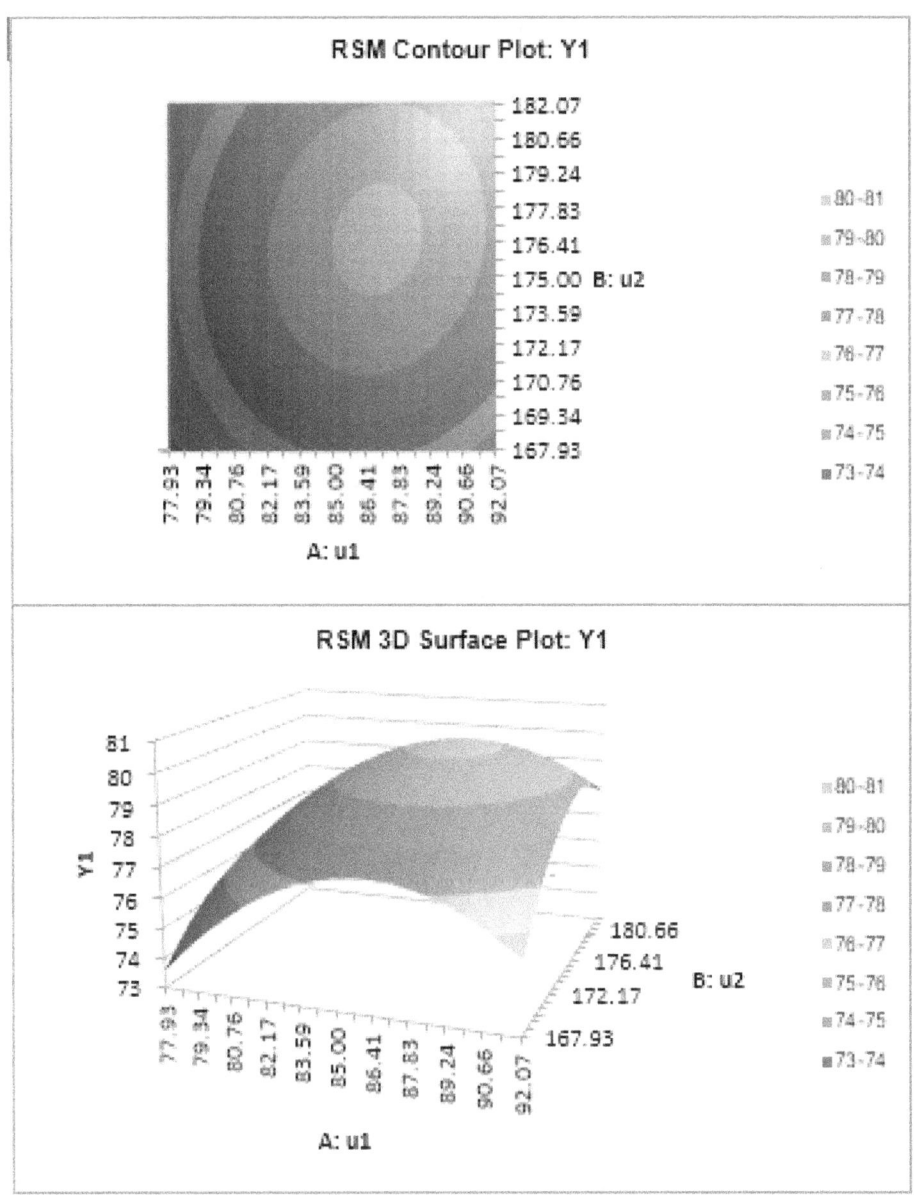

Figure 20.16: SigmaXL Output (RSM Surface Plot)

Comment

- Figure 20.16 indicates a maximization of y1 (yield) when u1 (time) is about 87 and u2 (temperature) is 176
- A team could use this information to improve a process so that this project's 30,000-foot-level reported metric improves

21

IEE-DMAIC — Improve Phase: Selecting, Implementing, and Demonstrating Improvements

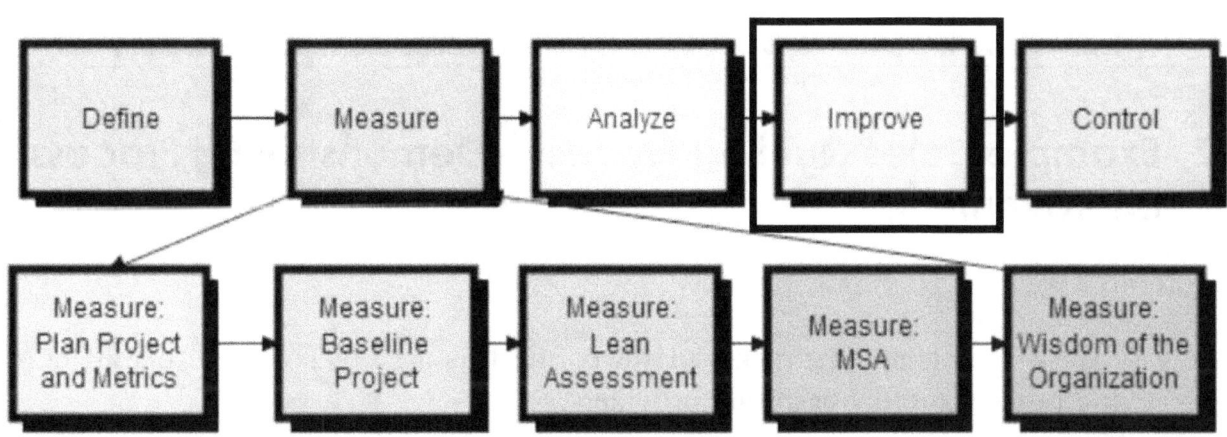

21.1 IEE-DMAIC Roadmap Component

Book 1 Reference: *IEE Volume III – Chapter 37*

Book 2 Reference: *Lean Six Sigma Project Execution Guide – Section 8*

Internet: www.smartersolutions.com/roadmap (clicking on highlighted area provides the flowchart below)

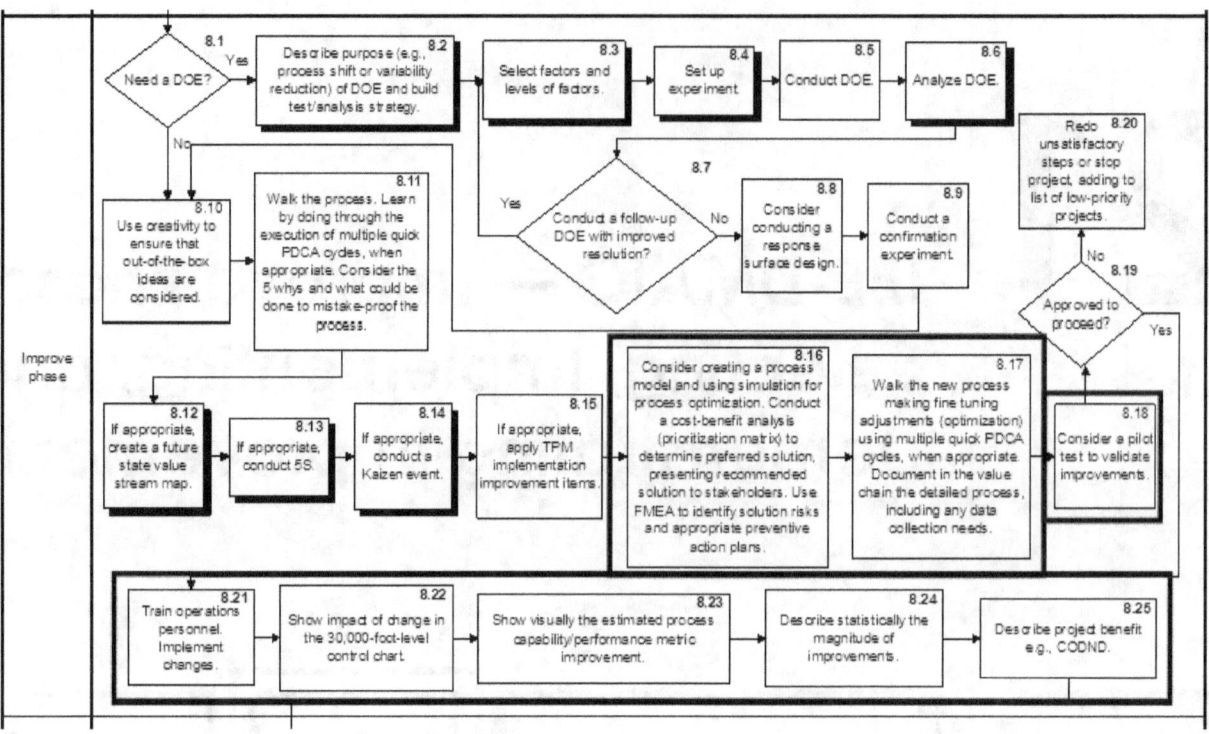

21.2 Example: Sales Quoting Process – Demonstrating Process Improvement

Application

- ABC is a company that makes plastic connectors used by computer manufacturers and hi-tech Internet hardware providers.

- The company's 30,000-foot-level report for sales of one product line had been floundering for several months and is not satisfactory.

- The company has been facing a weak market for the past six months, with sales at 50% of the forecast.

- The manager responsible for this product line met with a Lean Six Sigma Black Belt to determine what to do to improve their situation within the current market and prepare for the future.

- At first, the discussion focused on product quality and delivery time, which were poor due to a recent change in manufacturing sites.

- To ensure they were considering the entire value stream, the team initially studied a supply chain flowchart from a high-level viewpoint. The team then incorporated improvements to the process from what they learned from this flowchart and discussions with operational personnel.

- Described next is the 30,000-foot-level report of sales before and after this process change.

IEE Volume III Example and Dataset

- *IEE Volume III* Example 37.1: Sales Quote Process
- Dataset (Smarter Solutions (2022): V3 C37, Exam 37-02 Cable Quote Process.xlsx

SigmaXL or EPRS Metric-App [Smarter Solutions (2020)] Input/Output

- Figure 21.1: EPRS Metric-App Input (Demonstrating Process Improvement)
- Figure 21.2: EPRS Metric-App Output (Demonstrating Process Improvement)
- Figure 21.3: SigmaXL Input (Demonstrating Process Improvement)
- Figure 21.4: SigmaXL Output (Demonstrating Process Improvement)

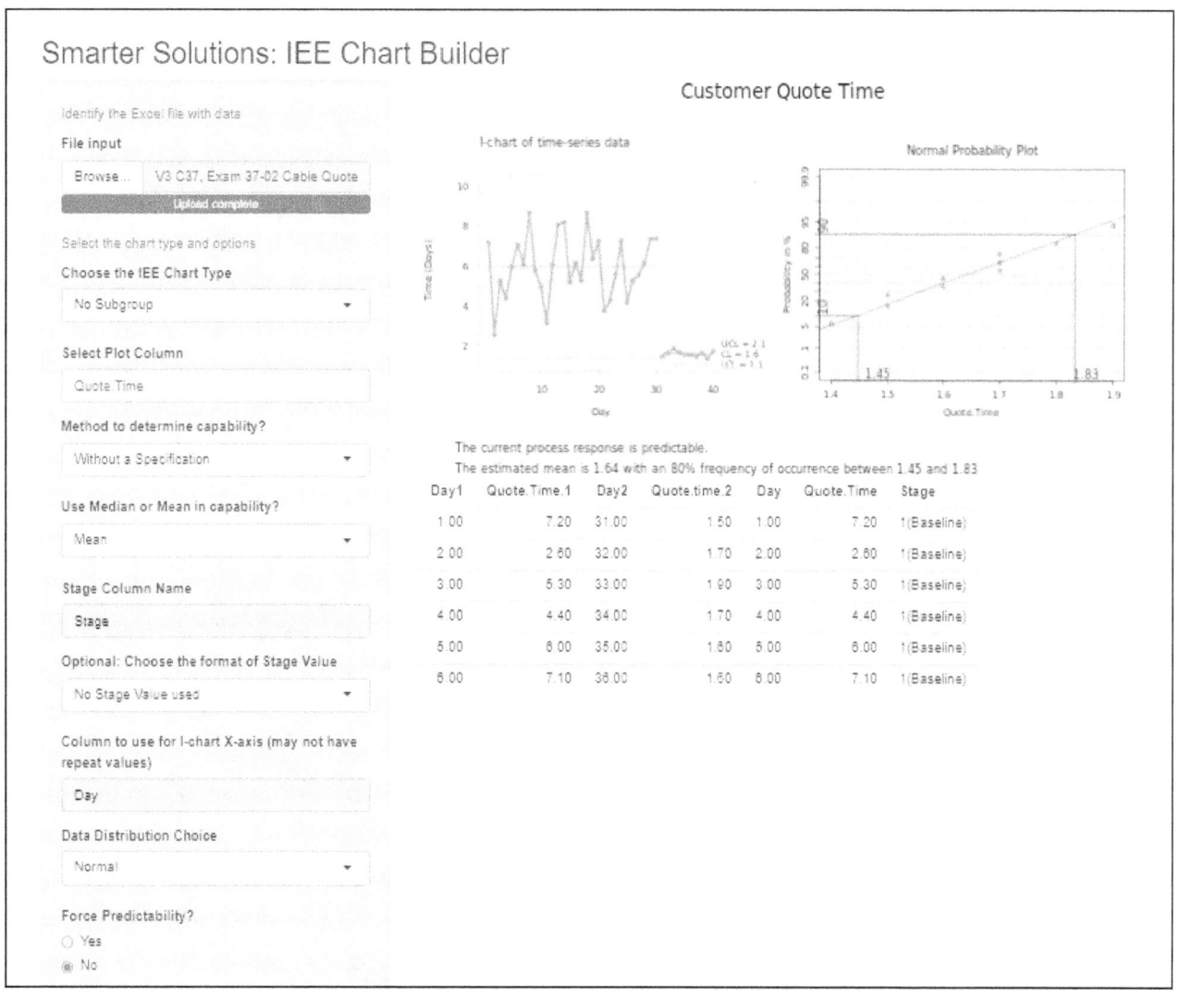

Figure 21.1: EPRS Metric-App Input (Demonstrating Process Improvement)

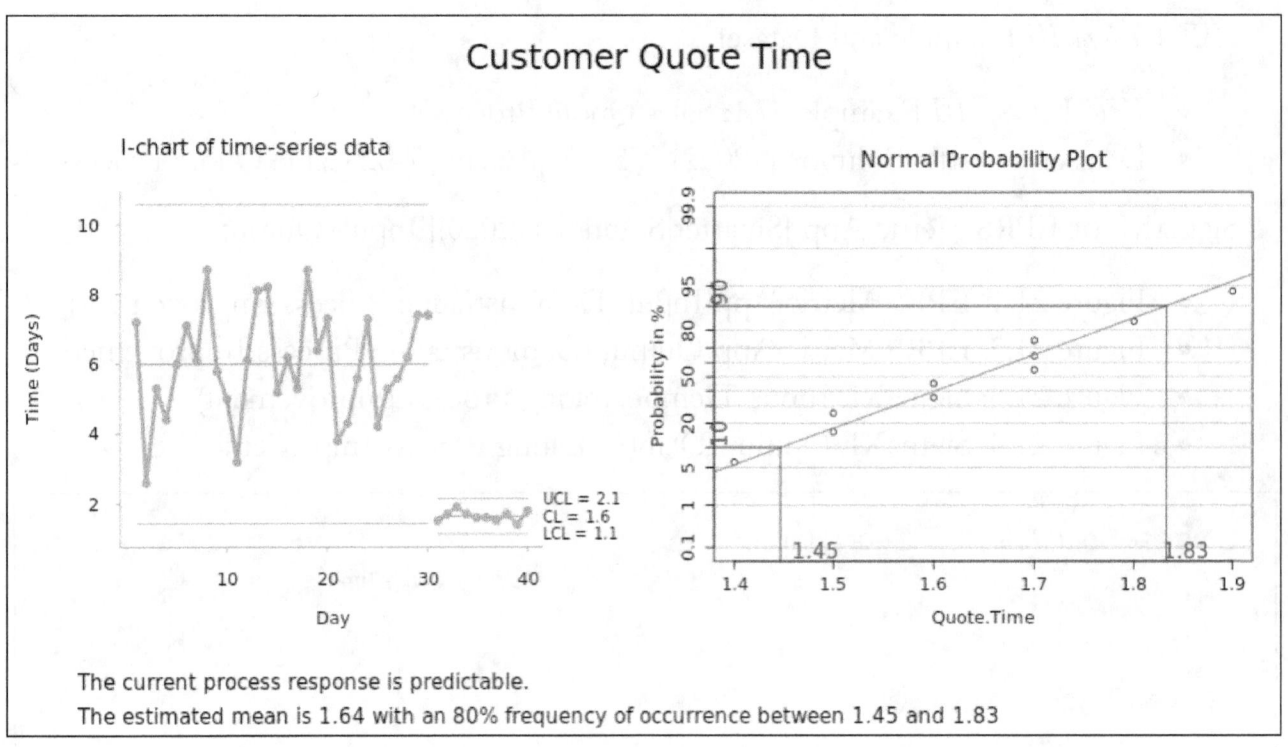

Figure 21.2: EPRS Metric-App Output (Demonstrating Process Improvement)

Comments

- If this new estimated mean and 80% frequency of occurrence rate (after a team's process improvement work) is still unacceptable, there is a need for further process improvement.

SigmaXL Chart Function: Graphical Tools>Dotplots

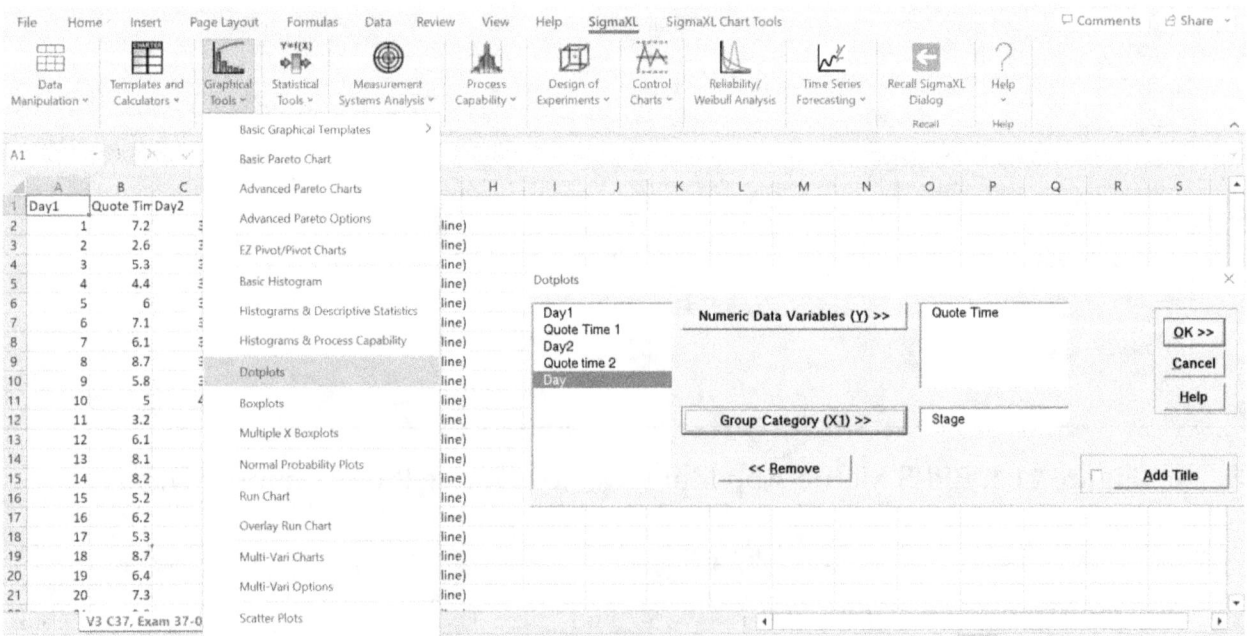

Figure 21.3: SigmaXL Input (Demonstrating Process Improvement)

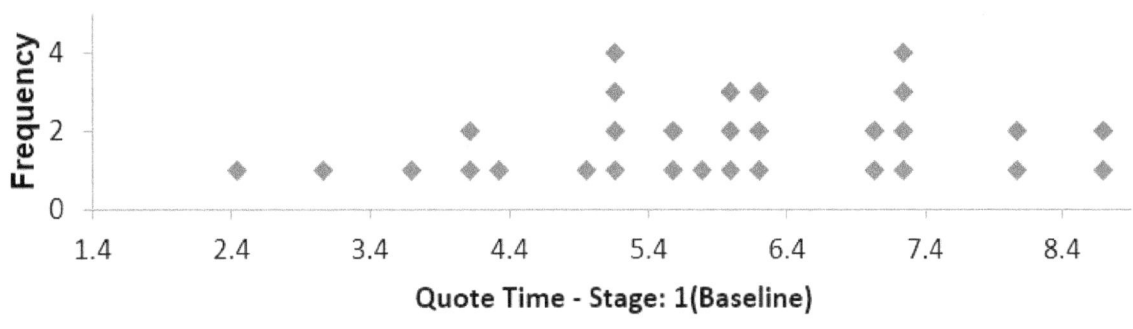

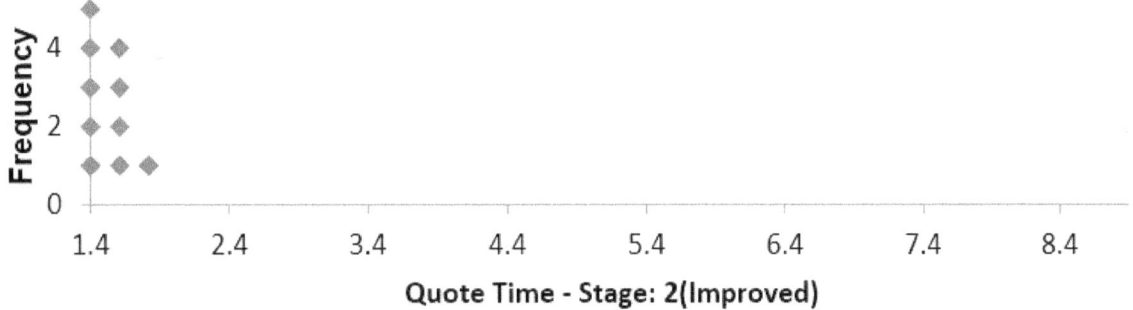

Figure 21.4: SigmaXL Output (Demonstrating Process Improvement)

Comments

- The 30,000-foot-level report (Figure 21.2) showed a new level of process performance around a mean of 1.6 days.
- The dot plot (Figure 21.4) is a simple way to convey the capability of the new quoting process relative to the old quoting system.
- A probability plot could estimate the expectation for the percentage of time that quotes will be within two days; i.e., the best estimate is that this will occur 99% of the time.
- While there might be some work still to do in this process, the Lean Six Sigma Black Belt and the team had essentially achieved their objective of reducing the quoting time to less than two days.
- The process owners (marketing and sales) agreed to monitor the execution of the process so that the completion of all quotes will be in less than two days.

22 IEE-DMAIC — Control Phase

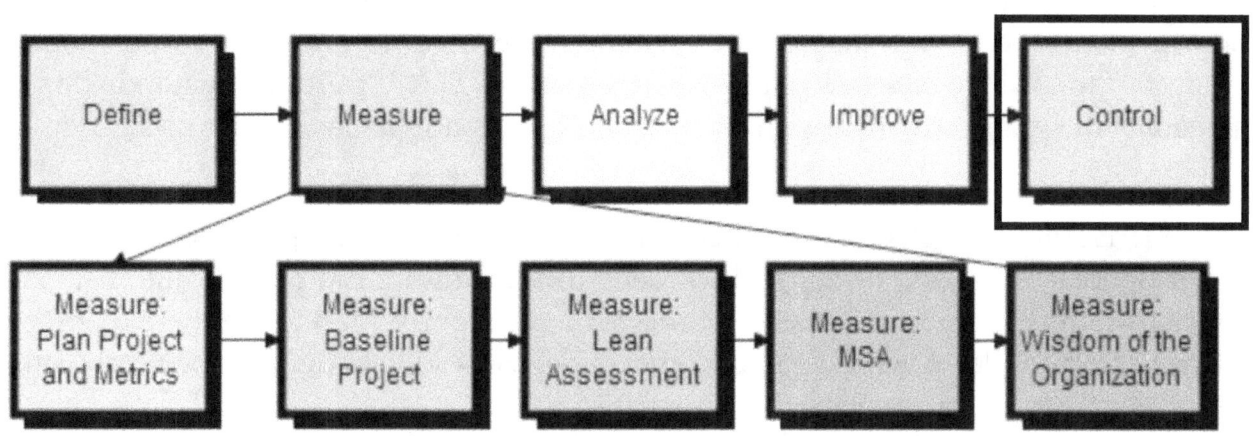

22.1 IEE-DMAIC Roadmap Component

Book 1 Reference: *IEE Volume III* – Chapters 38 and 39

Book 2 Reference: *Lean Six Sigma Project Execution Guide* – Section 9

Internet: www.smartersolutions.com/roadmap (clicking on highlighted area provides the flowchart below)

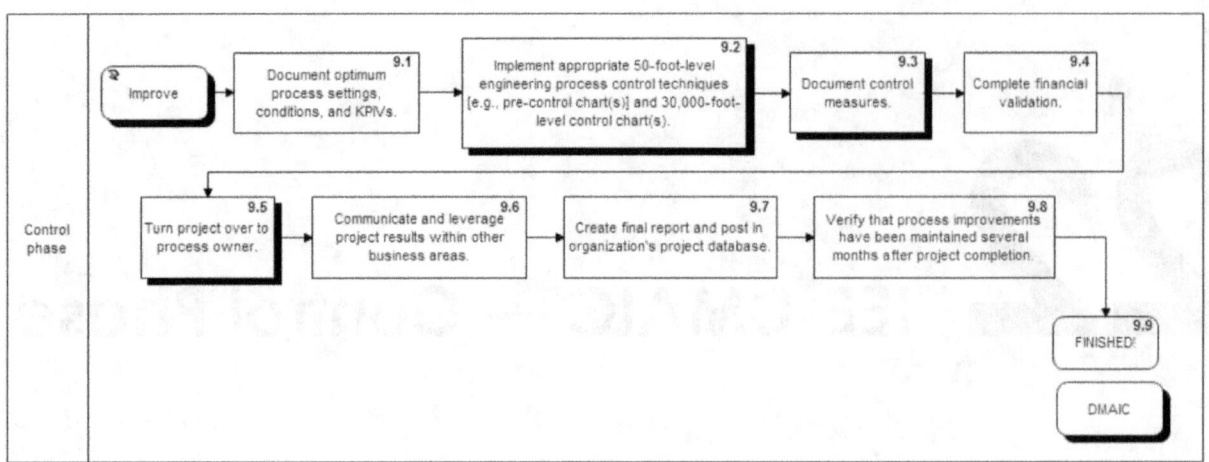

Lean Six Sigma project report-outs often state for the "Control" phase of the DMAIC roadmap that someone will periodically examine the process to ensure that operations are continually following the new process procedures. This "control" methodology for maintaining the gain from process improvement efforts is not practical and typically does not get done.

The IEE Enterprise Performance Reporting System (EPRS) enterprise software provides a better option. Among other things, EPRS enterprise software can provide automatic daily updates to completed projects' 30,000-foot-level metric reports. Monitoring these reports can provide a means to detect when a project's metric degrades so that there can be timely actions to resolve any procedure-implementation issues.

More information about EPRS enterprise software is available in the article "Integrated Enterprise Excellence (IEE) Business Management System Software." (Smarter Solutions 2019)

PART 4:
Appendix

23 List of Acronyms and Symbols

Some symbols used locally in this volume are not shown.

AD	Anderson Darling (statistic)
AIAG	Automotive Industry Action Group
ANOM	Analysis of means
ANOVA	Analysis of variance
AQL	Accept quality level
ASQ	American Society for Quality (Previously ASQC, American Society for Quality Control)
BB	Black belt
CCD	Central Composite Design (Response surface design)
CI	Confidence interval
CL	Centerline in a control chart
Cp	Capability index (AIAG 1995b) – does not address process centering within specification limits
Cpk	Capability index (AIAG 1995b) – addresses process centering within specification limits
C&E	Cause-and-Effect (Diagram)
CODND	Cost of doing nothing differently
COPQ	Cost of poor quality
C/T	Cycle time
DCP	Data collection plan
df	Degrees of freedom

DMAIC	Define-measure-analyze-improve-control
DOE	Design of experiments
DPMO	Defects per million opportunities
DPU	Defects per unit
DSO	Days sales outstanding
EBIDA	Earnings before interest, depreciation, and amortization
EIP	Enterprise improvement plan
EPM	Enterprise process management
EPRS	Enterprise performance reporting system
EPRS Metric-App	Free app for creating 30,000-foot-level reports from Excel-formatted datasets (Smarter Solutions 2020)
$F_{\alpha, v1; v2}$	Value from the F distribution for α risk and v_1 and v_2 degrees of freedom (Table F in *IEE Volume III*)
FMEA	Failure mode and effects analysis
Gage R&R	Gage repeatability and reproducibility
GB	Green belt
GLM	General linear model
H_0	Null hypothesis
H_a	Alternative hypothesis
IEE	Integrated Enterprise (process) Excellence
in.	Inches
ImR chart	Individuals control chart and moving range chart (Same as XmR chart)
KPIV	Key process input variables
KPOV	Key process output variables
LCL	Lower control limit
LDL	Lower decision level (in ANOM)
L/T	Lead time
MBB	Master black belt
ML	Maximum likelihood
MR	Moving range
MSA	Measurement systems analysis

n	Sample size
NID $(0,\sigma^2)$	Modeling errors are often assumed to be normally and independently distributed with mean zero and a constant but unknown variance
p-chart	Control chart of fraction nonconforming
PDCA	Plan-do-check-act
ppm	Parts per million (defect rate)
P	Probability
P_p	Performance index (AIAG 1995b); calculated using long-term standard deviation
P_{pk}	Performance index (AIAG 1995b); calculated using long-term standard deviation
R	Range
RSM	Response surface methodology
r	Number of failures, correlation coefficient
R^2	Coefficient of determination
s	Standard deviation of a sample
SIPOC	Supplier-input-process-output-customer
SPC	Statistical process control
Spec	Specification (limit)
SS	Sum of squares
Std. dev.	Standard deviation
$t_{\alpha;v}$	Value from the t-distribution for α risk and v degrees of freedom
UCL	Upper control limit
UDL	Upper decision level (ANOM)
VIF	Variance inflation factor
VOP	Voice of the process
WIP	Work in process
WOTO	Wisdom of the organization
XmR (chart)	Control chart of individual and moving range measurements
$\bar{x}$	Mean of a variable x
$\bar{x}$ chart	Control chart of means; i.e., $\bar{x}$ chart

α	Alpha, risk of rejecting the null hypothesis erroneously
β	Beta, risk of not rejecting the null hypothesis erroneously
λ	Lambda, hazard rate; intensity term in the NHPP equation
μ	Mu, population true mean
$\hat{\mu}$	Estimate of population mean
ν	Nu, degrees of freedom
ρ	Rho, actual failure rate of population, correlation coefficient between two variables
ρ_a	A single failure rate test criterion
ρ_t	The highest failure rate that is to be exhibited by the samples in a time-terminated test before a "pass test" statement can be given
ρ_1	Higher failure rate (failures/unit time) involving β risk in Poisson sequential testing (typically assigned equality to failure rate criterion ρ_a)
ρ_0	Lower failure rate (failures/unit time involving α risk in Poisson sequential testing
ρ_α	Used when calculating sample size for a fixed length test; the failure rate at which α is to apply
ρ_β	Used when calculating sample size for a fixed length test; the failure rate at which β is to apply
Σ	Mathematical summation
σ	Sigma, population standard deviation
$\hat{\sigma}$	Estimate of population standard deviation

24 Glossary

Accept quality level (AQL): The maximum proportion of defective units in a sampling plan that can be considered satisfactory as the process average.

Accuracy: The closeness of agreement between an observed value and the accepted reference value (AIAG 2002).

Alias: *See* Confounded.

Alpha (α) risk: Risk of rejecting the null hypothesis erroneously. This risk is also called type I error or producer's risk.

Alternative hypothesis (H_a): *See* Hypothesis testing.

Analysis of means (ANOM): ANOM is a statistical procedure to compare individual groups' to the overall mean of all groups.

Analysis of variance (ANOVA): ANOVA is a statistical procedure for analyzing the differences in the means of two or more groups.

Anderson Darling (Statistic): Measures how well data follow a distribution. A smaller statistical value indicates a better distribution fit. This statistic is used to compare competing distribution fits.

Attribute data (Discrete data): The presence or absence of some characteristic in each device under test, e.g., proportion nonconforming in a pass/fail test.

Average: A location parameter; frequently the arithmetic mean.

Bar charts: Horizontal or vertical bars that graphically illustrate the magnitude of multiple situations.

Baseline: Beginning information from which a response change is assessed.

Beta (β) risk: Chance of not rejecting the false null hypothesis; also called type II error or consumer's risk.

Black belts (BBs): Process improvement Six Sigma and IEE practitioners received detailed, practical training in the methodology. It is most desirable that black belts are dedicated resources; however, many organizations utilize part-time resources. During training, black belt trainees lead the execution of a project with in-class report-outs and critiques. Between training sessions, black belt trainees should receive project coaching, which is very important for their success.

Bottom Line: The final profit or loss that a company experiences at the end of a given period of time.

Box-Cox transformation: A Box-Cox statistical transformation is a general approach for transforming data to a normal distribution, where there is a transformation of Y values to the power of λ, i.e., Y^λ.

Brainstorming: Consensus-building among experts about a problem or issue using group discussion.

Capability/performance metric: *See* Process capability/performance metric.

Capability, Process: See Process capability.

Categorical variables: Represent types of data that may be divided into groups. Category variables include race, gender, age group, and educational level. As an alternative, the latter two variables could be considered numerically by using exact values for age and highest grade completed. It is often more informative to categorize such variables into a relatively small number of groups.

Cause-and-effect diagram (C&E diagram): This technique, sometimes called an Ishikawa diagram or fishbone diagram, is useful in problem solving using brainstorming sessions. With this technique, possible causes from such sources as materials, equipment, methods, and personnel are typically identified as a starting point to begin discussion.

Central composite rotatable design: A type of response surface design (RSM) experiment design

Chi-square test: The proper statistical name is the chi-square test of independence. This statistical test methodology is different from the chi-square goodness of fit test, which has another purpose. The only similarity is that the chi-square statistic is used for estimating significance. This book uses the term chi-square test to describe a chi-square test of independence.

Coded levels: Regression analysis of factorial or response surface data has model levels that are the natural levels of the factors (e.g., 5.5 and 4.5 V) or the coded factor levels (e.g., −1 and +1).

Coefficient: *See* Regression analysis.

Coefficient of determination (R^2): The coefficient of determination is the square of the correlation coefficient. Values for R^2 describe the percentage of variability accounted for by the model. For example, $R^2 = 0.8$ indicates that the model accounts for 80% of the variability in the data.

Coefficient of variation: A measure of dispersion where standard deviation is divided by the mean and is expressed as a percentage.

Common cause: Common cause is the natural or random variation that is inherent in a process over time, affecting every outcome of the process. If a process output response is in control, it has only common cause variation and can be said to be predictable. When a process experiences common cause variability but does not meet customer needs, the process response is not capable. Process procedures or input variable change is needed to improve this situation, i.e., this metric creates a pull for project creation.

Confidence interval: Confidence interval is the region containing the limits or band of a parameter with an associated confidence level that the bounds are large enough to contain the actual parameter value. The bands can be single-sided to describe an upper/lower limit or double-sided to describe both upper and lower limits.

Confounded: Two factor effects that are represented by the same comparison are aliases of one another, i.e., different names for the same computed effect. Two effects that are aliases of one another are confounded, or confused, with one another. Although the word *confounded* is commonly used to describe aliases between factorial effects and block effects, it can more generally be used to describe any effects that are aliases of one another.

Consumer's risk: *See* Beta (β) risk.

Contingency tables: If each member of a sample is classified by one characteristic into S classes, and by a second characteristic into R classes, the data may be presented by a contingency table with S rows and R columns. Contingency tables can also determine the statistical independence of the statistical test inputs.

Continuous data (Variables data): Data that can assume a range of numerical responses on a continuous scale, as opposed to data that can take only discrete levels.

Continuous distribution: A distribution used in describing the probability of a response when the output is continuous (see Response).

Continuous data response: *See* Response.

Control chart: A procedure used to track a process with time for the purpose of determining if common or special causes exist.

Control: In control is used in process control charting to indicate when a control chart shows that there are no indicators that the process has any special-cause events.

Correlation coefficient (r): A statistic that describes the strength of a relationship between two variables is the sample correlation coefficient. A correlation coefficient can take values between -1 and +1. A -1 indicates perfect negative correlation, while a +1 indicates perfect positive correlation, and a zero indicates no correlation.

Cost of doing nothing differently (CODND): To keep IEE from appearing as a quality initiative, I prefer to reference the Six Sigma metric COPQ as the cost of doing nothing differently (CODND), which has even broader costing implications than COPQ. In this volume, I make reference to the CODND.

Cost of poor quality (COPQ): Traditionally, cost of quality issues have been given the broad categories of internal failure costs, external failure costs, appraisal costs, and prevention costs. See Glossary description for cost of doing nothing differently. Within Six Sigma, COPQ addresses the cost of not performing work correctly the first time or not meeting customer's expectations.

Covariate: Covariate is a quantitative variable that can be included within an ANOVA model. This may be a variable where the level is measured but not controlled as part of the design. For this situation, when the covariate is entered into the model, the error variance would be reduced. A covariate may also be a quantitative variable where its levels were controlled as part of the experiment. For both situations, the statistical model contains a coefficient for the covariate, which would be interpreted as a predictor in a regression model.

Customer: Someone for whom work or a service is performed. The end user of a product is a customer of the employees within a company that manufactures the product. There are also internal customers in a company. When an employee does work or performs a service for someone else in the company, the person who receives this work is a customer of this employee.

Cycle Time: Frequency that a part/product is completed by process. Also, time it takes for operator to go through work activities before repeating the actions. In addition, cycle time can be used to quantify customer order to delivery time.

Dashboard: See Scorecard.

Days Sales Outstanding (DSO): In general, the average number of days it takes to collect revenue after a sale has been made. In this volume, DSO is considered to be the number of days beyond the due date that a payment is to be received; i.e., for an invoice 3 indicates that payment was received three days late, while -2 indicates receipt was two days early.

Discrete data: Discrete data are based on counts. Only a finite number of values are possible, and the values cannot be subdivided meaningfully; e.g., the number of parts damaged in shipment.

Defect: A nonconformity or departure of a quality characteristic from its intended level or state.

Defective: A nonconforming item that contains at least one defect or having a combination of several imperfections, causing the unit not to satisfy intended requirements.

Deming, Dr. W, Edwards: As an American statistician, Dr. Deming is known for his top management teachings in Japan after World War II. Dr. Deming made a significant contribution to Japan becoming renown for its high-quality, innovative products.

Descriptive statistics: Descriptive statistics help pull valuable information from data, whereas probability provides a basis for inferential statistics and sampling plans.

Degrees of freedom (df or ν): DF quantifies the number of independently available measurements for estimating a population parameter. For a random sample from a population, the number of degrees of freedom is equal to the sample size minus one.

Design of experiments (DOE): A structured experiment where the response effects of several factors are studied at one time.

Discrete data (Attribute data): The presence or absence of some characteristic in each device under test; e.g., proportion nonconforming in a pass/fail test.

Discrimination (of a measurement system): Alias smallest readable unit, discrimination is the measurement resolution, scale limit, or smallest detectable unit of the measurement device and standard. It is an inherent property of gage design and reported as a unit of measurement or classification. The number of data categories is often referred to as the discrimination ratio (not to be confused with the discrimination ratio used in Poisson sequential testing) since it describes how many classifications can be reliably distinguished given the observed process variation (AIAG 2002).

Distinct data categories: The number of data classifications (ndc) or categories that can be reliably distinguished, determined by the effective resolution of the measurement system and part variation from the observed process for a given application. (AIAG 2002)

Distribution: A pattern that is followed from a random sample from a population. Described normal, Weibull, Poisson, binomial, and lognormal distributions are applicable to the modeling of various industrial situations.

DMAIC: Define-measure-analyze-improve-control Six Sigma process improvement roadmap.

Dot plot: A plot of symbols that represent individual observations from a batch of data.

Double-sided test: A statistical consideration whereby, for example, an alternative hypothesis is that the mean of a population is not equal to a criterion value. *See* single-sided test.

DPMO: When using the non-conformance rate calculation of defects per million opportunities (DPMO), one needs first to describe what the opportunities for defects are in the process; e.g., the number of components and solder joints when manufacturing printed circuit boards. Next, the number of defects is periodically divided by the number of opportunities to determine the DMPO rate.

Effect: The main effect of a factor in a two-level factorial experiment is the mean difference in responses between the two levels of the factor, which is averaged over all levels of the other factors.

Enterprise improvement plan (EIP): EIP is a project drill-down strategy that follows: goal—strategies—high potential area—projects.

Enterprise process management (EPM): Rather than having a governance model that addresses initiatives as separate entities, in IEE a value chain EPM function can orchestrates the overall system. The EPM function is responsible for integrating, overseeing, and improving the execution of organizational processes, utilizing the 9-step IEE roadmap.

EPRS Metric-App Free app for creating 30,000-foot-level reports from Excel-formatted datasets (Smarter Solutions 2020).

Error (experimental): Ambiguities during data analysis caused from such sources as measurement bias, random measurement error, and mistake.

Experimental error: Variations in the observed response under identical test conditions; also called residual error.

Factorial experiment: *See* Full factorial experiment and Fractional factorial experiment.

Factors: Variables that are studied at different levels in a designed experiment.

Failure: A device is said to fail when it no longer performs its intended function satisfactorily.

Failure mode and effects analysis (FMEA): Analytical approach directed toward problem prevention through the prioritization of potential problems and their resolution. Opposite of fault tree analysis.

Failure rate: Failures/unit time or failures/units of usage, i.e., 1/MTBF. Sample failure rates are: 0.002 failures/hour, 0.0003 failures/auto miles traveled, 0.01 failures/1000 parts manufactured. Failure rate criterion (ρ_a) is a failure rate value that is not to be exceeded in a product. Tests to determine if a failure rate criterion is met can be fixed or sequential in duration. With fixed-length test plans, the test design failure rate (ρ_t) is the sample failure rate that cannot be exceeded in order to certify the criterion (ρ_a) at the boundary of the desired confidence level. With sequential test plans, failure rates ρ_1 and ρ_0 are used to determine the test plans.

Firefighting: The practice of giving much focus to fixing the problems of the day/week. The usual corrective actions taken in fire-fighting, such as tweaking a stable/predictable process, do not create any long-term fixes and may actually cause process degradation.

Fixed-effects model: A factorial experiment where the levels of the factors are chosen explicitly by the experimenter, as opposed to a random effect or components-of-variance model.

Fractional factorial experiment: A fractional factorial experiment is a designed experiment strategy that simultaneously assesses several factors/variables in one test. For this experimentation, there is a testing of only a partial set of all possible combinations of factor levels to identify significant factors more efficiently. This type of test is much more efficient than a traditional one-at-a-time test strategy.

Full factorial experiment: Full factorial experimentation is when testing all combinations of factor levels.

Gage: Any device used to obtain measurements. The term is frequently used to refer specifically to shop floor devices, including go/no-go devices.

Gage repeatability and reproducibility (R&R) study: The evaluation of measuring instruments to determine capability to yield a precise response. Gage repeatability is the variation in measurements, considering one part and one operator. Gage reproducibility is the variation between operators measuring one part.

General linear model (GLM): GLM is a way of assessing several multiple linear regression models simultaneously.

Hard savings: Hard savings directly impact the bottom line.

Histogram: A frequency diagram in which bars proportionally in area to the class frequencies are erected on the horizontal axis. The width of each section corresponds to the class interval of the variate.

Hypothesis: A tentative statement with a possible explanation for some event or phenomenon. Hypotheses are not theoretical statements; instead, hypotheses have a testable statement, which might include a prediction.

Hypothesis testing: Consists of a null hypothesis (H_0) and alternative hypothesis (H_a) where, for example, a null hypothesis indicates equality between two process outputs and an alternative hypothesis statement that shows non-equality. Through a hypothesis test, there is a decision on whether to reject a null hypothesis or not reject a null hypothesis. When there is a rejection of a null hypothesis, there is a α risk of error. Most typically, there is no risk assignment when we fail to reject the null hypothesis. However, there could be an appropriate sample size determination so that there is a rejection of the null hypothesis with a β risk of error.

IEE: *See* Integrated enterprise excellence.

IEE scorecard/dashboard metric reporting process:

1. Assess process predictability.
2. When the process is considered predictable, formulate a prediction statement for the latest stability region. The usual reporting format for this statement is:

   a. When there is a specification requirement: the nonconformance percentage
   b. When there are no specification requirements: median or mean response and 80% frequency of occurrence rate

IEE-DMAIC (Roadmap): An IEE enterprise define-measure-analyze-improve-control roadmap, which contains among other things a value chain measurement and analysis system where metric improvement needs can pull for project creation.

Individuals chart: A control chart of individual values where between-subgroup variability affects the calculated upper and lower control limits, i.e., the width between the upper and lower control limits increases when there is more between subgroup variability. When a plotted individuals chart data from a high-level, 30,000-foot-level, perspective is within the upper and lower control limits and there are no patterns, the process is said to be stable/predictable. In IEE, this common cause state is referenced as a predictable process. Upper and lower control limit lines (UCL and LCL) are independent of specification limits or targets.

In control: The description of a process where variation is consistent over time; i.e., only common causes exist. The process is predictable.

Inferential statistics: From analyzing samples, we can make statements about the population using inferential statistics.

Infrequent subgrouping/sampling: Traditionally, rational subgrouping issues involve the selection of samples that yield relatively homogeneous conditions within the subgroup for a small region of time or space, perhaps five in a row. For an $\bar{x}$ and R chart, the within-subgroup variation defines the limits of the control chart on how much variation should exist between the subgroups. For a given situation, a differing subgrouping/sampling methodology can dramatically affect the measured variation within subgroups, which in turn affects the width of the control limits. For the high-level metrics of IEE, we want infrequent subgrouping/sampling so that short-term variations caused by KPIV perturbations are viewed as common cause variability; i.e., typical process variability is to occur between subgroups in an individuals control chart. This type of control chart can reduce the amount of firefighting in an organization. However, this does not mean that a problem does not exist within the process. When process capability/performance metric improvements are needed for these metrics, we can initiate an IEE project; i.e., IEE projects are pulled into the system as the metrics require them.

Integrated Enterprise (process) Excellence (IEE, I double E): A roadmap for the creation of an enterprise process system in which organizations can significantly improve both customer satisfaction and their bottom line. IEE is a structured approach that guides organizations through the tracking and attainment of organizational goals. IEE goes well beyond traditional Lean Six Sigma and the balanced scorecard methods. IEE integrates enterprise process measures and improvement methodologies with tools such as Lean and Theory of constraints (TOC) in a never-ending pursuit of excellence. IEE becomes an enabling framework, which integrates, improves, and aligns with other initiatives such as Total Quality Management (TQM), ISO 9000, Malcolm Baldrige Assessments, and the Shingo Prize. IEE is the organizational orchestration that moves toward the achievement goal of the three Rs of Business; i.e., everyone is doing the Right things and doing them Right at the Right time.

Interaction: Two or more variables interact to affect another variable in a non-additive manner

KPIV (Key Process Input Variable): Factors within a process correlated to an output characteristic(s) essential to the internal or external customer. Optimizing and controlling these is vital to the improvement of the KPOV.

KPOV (Key Process Output Variable): Characteristic(s) of the output of a process that are important to the customer. Understanding what is important to the internal and external customer is essential to identifying KPOVs.

Least squares: A method used in regression to estimate the equation coefficients and constant so that the sum of squares of the differences between the individual responses and the fitted model is a minimized.

Levels: The settings of factors in a factorial experiment (e.g., high and low levels of temperature).

Logit (transformation): A type of data transformation sometimes advantageous in factorial analysis when data

have an upper and lower bound restriction (e.g., 0 - 1 proportion defective).

Main effect: An estimate of the effect of a factor measured independently of other factors.

Mallows Cp Statistic: A value used to determine the smallest number of parameters that should be used when building a model. The number of parameters corresponding to the minimum of this statistic is the minimum number of parameters to include during the model-building process.

Master black belts (MBBs): Black belts who have undertaken advanced Lean Six Sigma training and have a proven track record delivering results through various projects and project teams. MBBs should be dedicated resources to the deployment. Their responsibilities include coaching black belts, monitoring team progress, and assisting teams when needed.

Maximum likelihood estimator (MLE): Maximum likelihood estimates are calculated through maximizing the likelihood function. For each set of distribution parameters, the likelihood function describes the chance that the actual distribution has the parameters based on the sample.

Mean: The mean of a sample ($\bar{x}$) is the sum of all the responses divided by the sample size. The population mean (μ) is the sum of all measurements divided by the population size. From a random sample of a population, a calculated mean ($\bar{x}$) is an estimate for the population mean (μ).

Mean square: Sum of squares divided by degrees of freedom.

Measurement systems: The complete process of obtaining measurements. This includes the collection of equipment, operations, procedures, software, and personnel that affects the assignment of a number to a measurement characteristic.

Measurement systems analysis: *See* Gage repeatability and reproducibility (R&R).

Measurement system error: The combined variation due to gage bias, repeatability, reproducibility, stability and linearity (AIAG 2000)

Median: For a sample, the number that is in the middle when all observations are ranked in magnitude. For a population, the value at which the cumulative distribution function is 0.5.

Metric: a measurement that quantifies a particular characteristic

Multicollinearity: Multicollinearity is prevalent in a statistical model when there is near-linear dependencies between regressors in a statistical model (*See* Variance inflation factor [VIF]).

Multi-vari chart: A multi-vari chart displays the variation within units, between units, between samples, and between lots.

Nested data: A nested experiment design occurs when the trials are not fully randomized sets. Unlike complete randomization, test trials are structured so that some factor considerations are randomized within other factors.

Nonconformance: A nonconformance is a failure to meet specification requirements.

Normal distribution: A normal distribution is a bell-shaped distribution that is often useful to describe various physical, mechanical, electrical, and chemical properties.

Null hypothesis (H_0): *See* Hypothesis testing.

One-way analysis of variance: *See* single-factor analysis of variance.

Ordinal: Possesses natural ordering.

Orthogonal: An experimental design is call orthogonal if observed variates or linear combinations of them are independent.

Outlier: A data point that does not fit a model because of an erroneous reading or some other abnormal situation.

Out of control: Control chart that exhibits special-cause conditions.

Pareto chart: A graphical technique used to quantify problems so that effort can be expended in fixing the "vital few" causes, as opposed to the "trivial many." Named after Vilfredo Pareto (born 1848), an Italian economist.

Pareto principle: The Pareto principle is that eighty percent of the trouble comes from 20% of the problems, i.e., the vital few issues.

Part variation (PV): Related to measurement systems analysis, PV represents the expected part-to-part and time-to-time variation for a stable process (AIAG 2002).

Passive analysis: In IEE and a traditional DMAIC, most Six Sigma tools are applied in the same phase. However, the term passive analysis is often used in IEE to describe the analyze phase, where process data are observed passively, i.e., with no process adjustments, in an attempt to find a causal relationship between input and output variables. It should be noted that improvements can be made in any of the phases. If there is "low-hanging fruit" identified during a brainstorming session in the measure phase, this improvement can be made immediately, yielding a dramatic improvement to the 30,000-foot-level reported output metric.

Percent (%) R&R: The percentage of process variation related to the measurement system for repeatability and reproducibility.

Performance, Process: *See* Process performance.

Plan-do-check-act (PDCA) or Plan-do-study-act (PDSA): PDCA is frequently referred to as the Deming cycle or Shewhart cycle. The check step can be replaced by a study step; i.e., PDSA. PDCA has the following components: Plan – Recognize a need for change, then establish objectives and process for delivering desired results; Do – Implement change that is to be assessed; Check – study results and identify lessons learned; Act – Use lessons learned to take appropriate action if the change was not satisfactory repeat the process.

Point estimate: An estimate calculated from sample data without a confidence interval.

Population: Statistically a population is a group of data from a single distribution. In a practical sense, a statistical population could also be considered a segment or a group of data from a single source or category. In the process of explaining tools and techniques, multiple populations may be discussed as originating from different sources, locations, or machines.

Precision: The net effect of discrimination, sensitivity, and repeatability over the operating range (size, range, and time) of the measurement system. In some organizations, precision is used interchangeably with repeatability. In fact, precision is most often used to describe the expected variation of repeated measurements over the range of measurement; that range may be size or time. The use of the more descriptive component terms is generally preferred over the term *precision* (AIAG 2002).

Predictable: The UCL and LCL lines in a 30,000-foot-level individuals chart are calculated from the data. Specifications do not affect an individuals chart's UCL and LCL lines. An individuals chart is a statement of the voice of the process (VOP) relative to whether the process is considered stable or not.

Predictable process: A stable, controlled process where variation in outputs reported in a 30,000-foot-level metric is only caused by natural or random variation of the process inputs or the process procedures itself.

Prediction Interval: Describes a likely range for a single new observation at a specified predictor setting.

Preventive action: A preventive action is taken to eliminate a potential nonconformity cause or other undesirable situation.

Proactive Testing: In IEE and a traditional DMAIC, most Six Sigma tools are applied in the same phase. The descriptive term proactive testing is often used within IEE to describe the improve phase. The reason for this is that within the improve DMAIC phase design of experiments (DOE), tools are typically used. In DOE you can make many adjustments to a process in a structured fashion, observing/analyzing the results collectively; i.e., proactively testing to make a judgment. It should be noted that improvements can be made in any of the phases. If there is low- hanging fruit identified during a brainstorming session in the measure phase, this improvement can be made immediately, yielding a dramatic improvement to the 30,000-foot-level reported output metric.

Probability (P): Probability is a numerical expression for the likelihood of an occurrence.

Probability plot: Data are plotted on a selected probability plot coordinate system to determine if a particular distribution is appropriate (i.e., the data plot as a straight line) and to make statements about percentiles of the population. A probability plot can provide predictions about stable/predictable processes reported at the 30,000-foot-level.

Process: A method to make or do something that involves a number of steps.

Process capability indices (Cp and Cpk): Cp is a measurement of the allowable tolerance spread divided by the actual 6σ data spread. Cpk has a similar ratio to that of Cp, except that this ratio considers the shift of the mean relative to the central specification target.

Process capability: AIAG (2005) definition for the variables data case is 6σ range of a process's inherent variation; for statistically stable process output responses, where σ is usually estimated by (R-bar/d_2). For the attribute data case, it is generally defined as the average proportion or rate of defects or defectives; e.g., center of an attribute control chart.

Process capability/performance metric: IEE uses the term process capability/performance metric to describe a process's predictive output in terms that everyone can understand. The process to determine this metric is: 1. An infrequent subgrouping/sampling plan is chosen so that the typical variability from process input factors occurs between subgroups, e.g., subgroup by day, week, or month. 2. The process is analyzed for predictability using one or two individuals charts. 3. For the region of predictability, the non-compliant proportion is estimated and reported. If there are no specifications, the estimated median or mean response and 80% frequency of occurrence are reported.

Process cycle efficiency: The amount of value-added process time divided by total lead time.

Process performance: The AIAG (2005) definition is the 6σ range of a process's total variation, where σ is usually estimated by *s*, the sample standard deviation.

Process flow diagram (chart): Path of steps of work used to produce or do something.

Producer's risk: *See* Alpha (α) risk.

Pull for project creation: This term is derived from the Lean term, pull. An IEE deployment objective is that performance metric ownership is assigned through the business value chain, where metric tracking is at the 30,000-foot-level. In the E-DMAIC process, the enterprise is analyzed as a whole to determine what performance metrics need improvement and by how much so that whole-organizational goals can be met. These metric improvement needs would then create a pull for project creation. *See* push for project creation.

Pure error: *See* residual error

P-value or P: P-value is the significance level for a term in a model.

Qualitative factor: A qualitative factor in a statistical model has categorical levels, e.g., product origination where the factor levels are supplier A, supplier B, and supplier C.

Quantitative factor: A quantitative factor in a statistical model is continuous, e.g., a product can be manufactured with a process temperature factor between 50°C and 80°C.

Randomizing: A statistical procedure used to avoid bias possibilities as the result of influence of systematic disturbances, which are either known or unknown.

Random: Having no specific pattern.

Random effects (or components of variance) model: A factorial experiment where factor variance is investigated, as opposed to a fixed effects model.

Range: For a set of numbers, the absolute difference between the largest and smallest value.

Regression analysis: Data collected from an experiment are used to quantify empirically through a mathematical model the relationship that exists between the response variable and influencing factors. In a simple linear regression model, $y = b_0 + b_1x + \varepsilon$, x is the regressor, y is the expected response, b_0 and b_1 are coefficients, and ε is random error.

Regressor: *See* Regression analysis.

Repeatability: The variability resulting from successive trials under defined conditions of measurement. Often referred to as equipment variation (EV), however, this can be misleading. The best term for repeatability is within-system variation when the measurement conditions are fixed and defined, i.e., fixed part, instrument, standard, method, operator, environment, and assumptions. In addition to within-equipment variation, repeatability will include all within variation from the conditions in the measurement error model. (AAIG 2002)

Replication: Statistical test replication trials occur when there is an occurrence of experimental trials under identical conditions.

Reproducibility: The variation in the average of measurements caused by a normal change condition(s) in the measurement process. Typically, reproducibility is the consideration of variation in average measurements of the same part between different appraisers (operators) using the same measurement instrument and method in a stable environment. This assessment is often valid for manual tools influenced by the operator's skill. It is not valid, however, for measurement processes, i.e., automated systems, where the operator is not a significant source of variation. For this reason, reproducibility is the average variation *between* systems or measurement conditions. (AIAG 2002)

Residuals: In an experiment, the differences between experimental responses and predicted values that are determined from a model.

Residual error: Also call experimental error. An ANOVA output can list residual error as having a pure error and lack-of-fit component. Pure error is represented by replicates since the differences between observed responses are caused by random variation. During model term reduction when a resulting lack-of-fit P-value is less than the selected α level, the term that was removed from the model should be retained.

Resolution III: A DOE where main effects and two-factor interaction effects are confounded.

Resolution IV: A DOE where the main effects and two-factor interaction effects are not confounded; however, two-factor interaction effects are confounded with each other.

Resolution V: A DOE where all main effects and two-factor interaction effects are not confounded with other main effects or two-factor interaction effects.

Resolution V+: Full factorial designed experiment.

Response: Three described outputs are continuous (variables), attribute failure rate (discrete), and logic pass/fail. A measurement response is considered continuous if any value can be taken between limits (e.g., 2, 2.0001, and 3.00005). A measurement response is said to be attribute if the evaluation takes on a pass/fail proportion output; e.g., 999 out of 1000 sheets of paper, on average, can be fed through a copier without a jam. In this series of volumes, a response is considered to be logic pass/fail if combinational considerations are involved that are said always to cause an event either to pass or fail; e.g., a computer display design will not work in combination with a particular keyboard design and software package.

Response surface methodology (RSM): RSM is the empirical study of relationships between one or more responses and input variable factors. RSM can determine the *best* input variables to optimize a response or better understand the overall system response.

Risk priority number (RPN): Product of severity, occurrence, and detection rankings within an FMEA. RSM is the ranking of RPN prioritizes design concerns; however, issues with a low RPN still deserve special attention if the severity ranking is high.

Robust DOE: A DOE strategy where focus is given within the design to the reduction of variability.

Run chart: A time series plot permits the study of observed data for trends or patterns over time, where the x-axis is time and the y axis is the measured variable.

Sample: A selection of items from a population.

Sampling distribution: A sampling distribution is obtained from a parent distribution by random sampling.

Sample size: The number of observations made or the number of items taken from a population.

Satellite-level: In IEE, satellite-level describes a high-level IEE business metric that has infrequent subgrouping/sampling so that short-term variations, which are caused by typical variation from key process input variables, will result in individuals charts that view these as common-cause variability. This metric has no calendar boundaries, and the latest region of stability can be used to provide a predictive statement for the future.

Scatter plot: A plot to assess the relationship between two variables. A scatter plot is sometimes called a scatterplot or a scatter diagram.

Scorecard: A scorecard helps manage an organization's performance through the optimization and alignment of organizational units, business processes, and individuals. A scorecard can also provide goals and targets, which is to help individuals understand their corporate contribution. Scorecards span the operational, tactical and strategic business aspects and decisions. A dashboard displays information so that an enterprise can be run effectively. A dashboard organizes and presents information in a format that is easy to read and to interpret. In the IEE series of book, IEE performance measurement is referred to as either a scorecard or scorecard/dashboard.

Sensitivity: Smallest input signal that results in a detectable (discernible) output signal for a measurement device. An instrument should be at least as sensitive as its unit of discrimination. Sensitivity is determined by inherent gage design and quality, in-service maintenance, and operating conditions. Sensitivity is reported in units of measurement (AIAG 2002).

Shewhart control chart: Dr. Shewhart is credited with developing the standard control chart test based on 3σ limits to separate the steady component of variation from assignable causes.

Sigma: The Greek letter (σ) that is often used to describe the standard deviation of a population.

Significance: A statistical statement indicating that the level of a factor causes a difference in a response with a certain degree of risk of being in error.

Single-factor analysis of variance ANOVA: ANOVA is one-way analysis of variance with two levels (or treatments) that is to determine if there is a statistically significant difference between level effects.

Single-sided test: A statistical consideration where, for example, an alternative hypothesis is that the mean of a population is less than a criterion value. *See* double-sided test.

SIPOC (supplier-input-process-output-customer): A tool that describes the events from trigger to delivery at the targeted process. Provides a snapshot of workflows, where the process aspect of the diagram consists of only 4-7 blocks.

Six Sigma: A term coined by Motorola that emphasizes the improvement of processes for the purpose of reducing variability and making general improvements. GE in the mid-1990s expanded the scope of Six Sigma so that it became a project-based selection and execution system with a support infrastructure, where projects were to have organizational benefits.

SMART goals: Not everyone uses the same letter descriptors for SMART. My preferred descriptors are italicized in the following list: S - *specific*, significant, stretching; M - *measurable*, meaningful, motivational; A - agreed upon, attainable, achievable, acceptable, action-oriented, *actionable*; R - realistic, *relevant*, reasonable, rewarding, results-oriented; T - *time-based*, timely, tangible, trackable.

Special cause: Variation in a process from a reason that is not an inherent part of that process. That is, it's not a common cause.

Specification: A criterion that is to be met by a part or product.

Stability: References statistically demonstrated stability of a measurement process output response over time reported at the 30,000-foot-level or satellite-level. Statistical stability implies a prediction statement can be made for the process, which includes the process' operating output measurement noise variation.

Standard deviation (σ, s): Standard deviation is a mathematical quantity that describes response variability. Standard deviation equals the square root of variance. The standard deviation of a sample (s) is used to estimate the standard deviation of a population (σ).

Standard error: The square root of the variance of the sampling distribution of a statistic.

Statistical process control (SPC): SPC is applying statistical techniques to control processes. SPC is often considered a subset of SQC, where the emphasis in SPC is on the tools associated with the process but not on product acceptance techniques.

Stories: An explanation for the up-and-down from the previous quarter or yearly scorecard/dashboard metrics. This is not dissimilar to a nightly stock market report of the last day's activity, where the television or radio reporter gives a specific reason for even small market movements. This form of reporting provides little, if any, value when it comes to making business decisions for a data-driven company.

Subgrouping: Traditionally, rational subgrouping issues involve the selection of samples that yield relatively homogeneous conditions within the subgroup for a small region of time or space, perhaps five in a row. Hence, the within-subgroup variation defines the limits of the control chart on how much variation should exist between the subgroups. For a given situation, differing subgrouping/sampling methodologies can dramatically affect the measured variation within subgroups, affecting the width of the control limits. For the high-level metrics of IEE, we want infrequent subgrouping/sampling so that typical short-term KPIV perturbations are viewed as common-cause variability. A 30,000-foot-level individuals chart, which is created with infrequent subgrouping/sampling, can reduce the amount of firefighting in an organization. However, this does not mean that a problem does not exist within the process. IEE describes approaches to view the process capability/performance metric, or how well the process meets customer specifications or overall business needs. When improvements are needed to a process capability/performance metric, we can create an IEE project that focuses on this need; i.e., IEE projects are pulled for creation when metric improvements are needed.

Sum of squares (_SS_): The summation of the squared deviations relative to zero, to level means, or the grand mean of an experiment.

Test: Assessment of whether an item meets specified requirements by subjecting the item to a set of physical, environmental, chemical, or operating actions/conditions.

The balanced scorecard: See Balanced scorecard (the).

Theory of constraints (TOC): Constraints in TOC can originate from an internal resource, market, or policy. The outputs of a system are a function of the whole system, not just individual processes. System performance is a function of how well constraints are identified and managed. When we view our system as a whole, we realize that the output is a function of the weakest link. The weakest link of the system is the constraint. If care is not exercised, an organization can focus on a subsystem that, even though improved, does not impact the overall system output. Organizations need to focus on the orchestration of efforts so that there is an optimization of the comprehensive system, not individual pieces. Unfortunately, organization charts lead to the workflow by function, which can result in competing forces within the organization. With TOC, systems are viewed as a whole and work activities are directed so that the whole system performance measures are improved.

Three Rs of business: Everyone doing the Right things and doing them Right at the Right time.

30,000-foot-level: A Y variable response that is used in IEE to describe a high-level project or operation metric that has infrequent subgrouping/sampling so that short-term variations, which might be caused by typical KPIV swings, will result in charts that view these perturbations as common cause variability. It is not the intent of the 30,000-foot-level individuals chart to provide timely feedback for process intervention and correction, as traditional control charts do. For example, 30,000-foot-level metrics are lead time, inventory, defective rates, and a critical manufactured part's dimension. There can be a drill down to a 20,000-foot-level metric if there is an alignment, e.g., the most significant product defect type. A 30,000-foot-level individuals control chart can reduce the amount of firefighting in an organization when used to report operational metrics. As a business metric, 30,000-foot-level reporting can lead to more efficient resource utilization and fewer playing games with the numbers.

TOC: *See* Theory of constraints.

Trend chart: Shows data trends over time. A trend chart is sometimes called a run chart.

Trial: One of the factor combinations in an experiment.

t test: A statistical test that utilizes tabular values from the *t* distribution to assess, for example, whether two population means are different.

Two-sided test: *See* Double-sided test.

Uncertainty (δ): An amount of change from a criterion considered acceptable. This parameter is used when considering β risk in sample size calculation.

Value chain (IEE): Describes in flowchart fashion primary and support organizational activities and their accompanying 30,000-foot-level or satellite-level metrics reports. For example, the primary activity flow is to develop a product—market a product—sell a product—produce a product—invoice/collect payments—report satellite-level metrics. Example support activities include IT, finance, HR, labor relations, safety & environment, and legal.

Variables data (Continuous data): Data that can assume a range of numerical responses on a continuous scale, as opposed to data that can take only discrete levels.

Variables: Factors within a designed experiment.

Variance (Statistical) [σ^2, s^2]: A measure of the dispersion of observations based upon the mean of the squared deviations from the arithmetic mean

Variance inflation factor (VIF): VIF is a calculated quantity for each term in a regression model that measures the combined effect of the dependencies among the regressors on the variance of that term. One or more large VIFs can indicate multicollinearity.

Validation is proof after the implementation of an action over time, where the act does what is intended. *See* verification.

Voice of the process (VOP): VOP quantifies what the process delivers. A voice-of-the-process to voice-of-the-customer needs assessment can identify process improvement focus areas, e.g., a 30,000-foot-level reporting assessment indicates an 11% delivery-time non-conformance rate.

25 References

AIAG (2008), *Advanced Product Quality Planning (APQP) and Control Plan Reference Manual*, Chrysler Corporation, Ford Motor Company, General Motors Corporation

AIAG (2005), *Statistical Process Control (SPC) Reference Manual*, Third edition, Chrysler Corporation, Ford Motor Company, General Motors Corporation

AIAG (2008), *Potential Failure Mode and Effects Analysis (FMEA) Reference Manual*, Chrysler Corporation, Ford Motor Company, General Motors Corporation

AIAG (2010), *Measurement Systems Analysis (MSA) Reference Manual*, Automotive Industry Action Group, Chrysler Corporation, Ford Motor Company, General Motors Corporation

Breyfogle, F. W. (2021), "An App Alternative: New Process Capability Reporting App and How-to Business Management Enrichments," Quality Progress, October 2021 https://www.smartersolutions.com/orl/Free_App_for_Process_Capability_Study_2-0.pdf

Breyfogle, F. W. (2020a), *Management 2.0: Discovery of Integrated Enterprise Excellence*, Citius Publishing, Austin TX https://www.amazon.com/dp/B08FL2L2Y6/

Breyfogle, F. W. (2020b), *Leadership System 2.0: Implementing Integrated Enterprise Excellence*, Citius Publishing, Austin TX https://www.amazon.com/dp/B08HFKPSCQ/

Breyfogle, F. W. (2018), "The Improvement of Scorecard Management: Comparing Deming's red bead experiment to red-yellow-green scorecards," *Quality Progress*, October 2018 https://smartersolutions.com/pdfs/articles/Deming-red-bead-experiment-and-red-yellow-green-scorecards.pdf

Breyfogle. F. W. (2014), "30,000-foot-level Performance Metric Reporting, *Six Sigma Forum Magazine*, February 2014 https://www.smartersolutions.com/pdfs/articles/30000-ft-level-performance-metric-reporting_6sigmaforum.pdf

Breyfogle, F. W. (2010), *Lean Six Sigma Project Execution Guide: The Integrated Enterprise Excellence (IEE) Process Improvement Project Roadmap*, Citius Publishing, Austin, TX https://www.amazon.com/dp/061534948X/

Breyfogle, F. W. (2008a), *Integrated Enterprise Excellence Volume I - The Basics: Four Golfing Buddies Going Beyond Lean Six Sigma and the Balanced Scorecard*, Bridgeway Books, Austin, TX https://www.amazon.com/dp/1934454125/

Breyfogle, F. W. (2008b), *Integrated Enterprise Excellence Volume II - Business Deployment: A Leaders' Guide for Going Beyond Lean Six Sigma and the Balanced Scorecard*, Bridgeway Books, Austin, TX https://www.amazon.com/dp/193445415X

Breyfogle, F. W. (2008c), *Integrated Enterprise Excellence Volume III - Improvement Project Execution: A Management and Black Belt Guide for Going Beyond Lean Six Sigma and the Balanced Scorecard*, Bridgeway Books, Austin, TX https://www.amazon.com/dp/1934454168/

Breyfogle, F. W. (2008d), *The Integrated Enterprise Excellence System: An Enhanced Approach to Balanced Scorecards, Strategic Planning and Business Improvement*, Bridgeway Books, Austin, TX https://www.amazon.com/dp/1934454117/

Breyfogle, F. W. (2003), *Implementing Six Sigma: Smarter Solutions® Using Statistical Methods, 2nd Edition*, John Wiley & Sons, Inc, Hoboken, NJ

Collins, Jim (2001), *Good to Great: Why Some Companies Make the Leap... and Others Don't*, HarperCollins Publishers Inc., New York, NY

Deming, W. E. (1986), *Out of the Crisis,* Massachusetts Institute of Technology, Cambridge, MA

Smarter Solutions (2023), *SigmaXL and Lean Six Sigma* book datasets. To receive a copy of the datasets referenced in this book, send your datasets request to info@smartersolutions.com

Smarter Solutions (2020), A free app for creating 30,000-foot-level reports from Excel-formatted datasets is available at https://smartersolutions.com/free-business-process-management-software/

Smarter Solutions (2019) "Integrated Enterprise Excellence (IEE) Business Management System Software." https://smartersolutions.com/integrated-enterprise-excellence-iee-business-management-system-software/

Smarter Solutions (2015a), "Forrest Favorites" webpage (Describes issues with many commonplace business practices and what to do to resolve the problems) https://smartersolutions.com/resources/forrest-favorites/.

Smarter Solutions (2015b) "Issues and Resolution to p-chart Control Limits Formula False Signals" https://smartersolutions.com/resources/p-chart-issues-and-resolution/

Smarter Solutions (2015c) "Issues and Resolution to xbar and R chart Formula Problems" https://smartersolutions.com/resources/x-bar-and-r-control-chart-issues-and-resolution/

Smarter Solutions (2015d) "Issues and Resolution to C-chart Formula Problems" https://smartersolutions.com/resources/c-chart-issues-and-resolution/

26 Acknowledgements

Forrest's wife, Becki, has supported him in his IEE passion over the years with its enhanced methodology for business process improvements so the big-picture benefits.

Rick Haynes has done excellent work creating the free r-coded software EPRS Metric-App (Smarter Solutions (2020)

Rick Haynes, Doug Wheeler, Chinh Tran, and Tri Pham have done a great job developing the Enterprise Performance Reporting System (EPRS) software that supports IEE metric reporting and its organizational implementation. (Smarter Solutions 2019)

Liviu's wife, Magda, has been a constant supporter from the start of his continuous improvement journey, leading organizational teams across virtually all functions in their pursuit of operational excellence and financial results

Diane Tilley and her stats team for offering clarification, as well as updates on the next SigmaXL version and for offering our students, partners, colleges and universities a cost-effective, powerful, and easy to use tool, enabling users to measure, analyze, improve and control their processes across all fields and disciplines

To Forrest Breyfogle, my co-author, for his unwavering commitment and unabated enthusiasm for continuous improvement opportunities, wherever they may be found

www.ingramcontent.com/pod-product-compliance
Lightning Source LLC
Chambersburg PA
CBHW082144120626

46553CB00010B/2752